Gender and Citizenship in the Global Age

Genre et citoyenneté à l'ère de la mondialisation

This book is a product of the CODESRIA Gender Symposium

Ce livre est une compilation des articles issus du Symposium sur le genre du CODESRIA

Gender and Citizenship in the Global Age

Genre et citoyenneté à l'ère de la mondialisation

Edited by / Sous la direction
Laroussi Amri
Ramola Ramtohul

CODESRIA

Council for the Development of Social Science Research in Africa
DAKAR

© CODESRIA 2014

Council for the Development of Social Science Research in Africa
Avenue Cheikh Anta Diop, Angle Canal IV
BP 3304 Dakar, CP 18524, Senegal
Website: www.codesria.org

ISBN: 978-2-86978-589-2

Typesetting: Alpha Ousmane Dia
Cover Design: Ibrahima Fofana

Distributed in Africa by CODESRIA
Distributed elsewhere by African Books Collective, Oxford, UK
Website: www.africanbookscollective.com

The Council for the Development of Social Science Research in Africa (CODESRIA)
is an independent organisation whose principal objectives are to facilitate research,
promote research-based publishing and create multiple forums geared towards the
exchange of views and information among African researchers. All these are aimed
at reducing the fragmentation of research in the continent through the creation of
thematic research networks that cut across linguistic and regional boundaries.

CODESRIA publishes *Africa Development*, the longest standing Africa based social
science journal; *Afrika Zamani*, a journal of history; the *African Sociological Review*;
the *African Journal of International Affairs*; *Africa Review of Books* and the *Journal of
Higher Education in Africa*. The Council also co-publishes the *Africa Media Review*;
Identity, Culture and Politics: An Afro-Asian Dialogue; *The African Anthropologist*
and the *Afro-Arab Selections for Social Sciences*. The results of its research and other
activities are also disseminated through its Working Paper Series, Green Book Series,
Monograph Series, Book Series, Policy Briefs and the CODESRIA Bulletin. Select
CODESRIA publications are also accessible online at www.codesria.org.

CODESRIA would like to express its gratitude to the Swedish International
Development Cooperation Agency (SIDA/SAREC), the International Development
Research Centre (IDRC), the Ford Foundation, the MacArthur Foundation, the
Carnegie Corporation, the Norwegian Agency for Development Cooperation
(NORAD), the Danish Agency for International Development (DANIDA), the French
Ministry of Cooperation, the United Nations Development Programme (UNDP), the
Netherlands Ministry of Foreign Affairs, the Rockefeller Foundation, FINIDA, the
Canadian International Development Agency (CIDA), the Open Society Foundations
(OSFs), TrustAfrica, UN/UNICEF, the African Capacity Building Foundation
(ACBF) and the Government of Senegal for supporting its research, training and
publication programmes.

Contents/Sommaire

Contributors/Contributeurs

Laroussi Amri est Professeur de Sociologie, Chercheur Senior, Directeur de l'Unité de Recherches « Développement Local-Approches Comparées », Université de Tunis el Manar. Il a publié notamment : *Les femmes soufies ou la passion de Dieu,* (en collaboration avec Nelly Amri), (Labege : Dangles, 1992) ; *La femme rurale dans l'exploitation familiale : Nord-Ouest de la Tunisie – Pour une sociologie des ruptures,* (Paris : L'Harmattan, 2003) et *Association et genre en Tunisie* (à paraître en 2014).

Mfon Umoren Ekpootu is a lecturer in the Department of History and Diplomatic Studies at the University of Port Harcourt, Nigeria. Her doctoral dissertation was on prostitution and child labour in the Cross River region of Nigeria. Her research is focused primarily on women, working children and sexuality. Her publications include: 'Contestations of Identity: Colonial Policing of Female Sexuality in Nigeria' in the *African Journal of Political Science*, and 'Interrogating Policies on Human Trafficking in Nigeria' [forthcoming]. Her recent paper, 'Getting them Young: Child Labour in Ikot Ekpene from a Historical Perspective', is a chapter in the recently published CODESRIA book, *Children and the Labour Process in Africa*. She is a SEPHIS Research Fellow and a SEPHIS-CODESRIA Young Historian. She is currently working on women, sexuality and the occult in Nigeria.

Prudentia Tamonkeng Fonkwe is from Cameroon. She is a trained Secondary school teacher. She also has a BA in English from the University of Yaoundé and a Masters degree in Women and Gender Studies from the University of Buea. She has taught in secondary and high schools in Cameroon but she currently works for the Ministry of Women Empowerment and the Family in Yaoundé.

Sharon Groenmeyer is an independent consultant and external collaborator of the International Labour Organisation in South Africa. She has a PhD from the Norwegian Univeristy of Science and Technology, Trondheim, Norway. She has published in the South African feminist journal *AGENDA* and the Women's Peacebuilders Network.

Felix Kiruthu is a lecturer in the Department of History. Since 1997, he has taught at the Department of History, Archaeology, and Political Studies, Kenyatta University, Nairobi, Kenya. Besides his research interest in gender studies, he also researched the urban history of Africa, with a special focus on informal enterprises. His other research interests include pedagogical methods in the study of history, as well as peace and conflict studies.

Jacques Tshibwabwa Kuditshini est Docteur en Sciences Politiques et Administratives. Membre de plusieurs associations savantes, il est actuellement Fellow à l'Institut d'Etudes Avancées de Nantes en France. Il enseigne les sciences politiques à l'Université de Kinshasa depuis 1997. Il participe aux programmes de recherche initiés par le CODESRIA, le Musée royal de l'Afrique centrale (Tervuren/Belgique), l'Institut Français d'Afrique du Sud, l'Université de Witwatersrand et l'Agence Universitaire de la Francophonie. Il a publié dans des revues à comité de lecture et participé à plusieurs colloques internationaux.

Ivan Marowa is a Junior Fellow with Bayreuth International Graduate School of African Studies (BIGSAS), Universität Bayreuth, Germany. He comes from Zimbabwe and holds a Masters degree in African History from the University of Zimbabwe. His research is based on Zimbabwe and focuses on oral narratives, the environment, social memories and gender issues from a historical perspective. He is currently conducting research for his doctoral studies on 'Environment and Social Memory', which focuses on two groups of people that were forcibly relocated in 1958. He has written articles dealing with memory and on engendering the African public sphere. He has participated in CODESRIA workshops and conferences and has published in the CODESRIA Journal - *Identity, Culture and Politics: An Afro-Asian Dialogue.*

Samwel Ong'wen Okuro holds a PhD in History and is currently a Senior Lecturer at Bondo University, Kenya. An economic historian, his research interests include human rights, gender and agrarian processes in Africa. His recent publications include 'Daniel arap Moi and the Politics of HIV/AIDS in Kenya, 1983-2002' in *African Journal of AIDS Research*, Vol. 8, 275-283, 2009; 'Our Women must Return Home: Institutional Patriarchy in Colonial Central Nyanza District, 1945-1963' in *Journal of Asian and African Studies*, Vol. 45 (5), 2010; and 'Struggling with In-laws and Corruption – The Impact of HIV/AIDS on Widow's and Orphan's Land Rights in Kombewa Division, Kenya' in Birgit Englert and Elizabeth Daley (eds), 2008, *Falling Between Two Stools – Women's Land Rights in Eastern Africa*, London: James Currey.

Hezron Ndunde Otieno is an independent researcher. His interests span issues of gender, women, youth and children, the environment and information and communications technologies. He was previously a Tutorial Fellow at the Institute of Development Studies in Nakuru, Kenya, and an Adjunct Lecturer at the Highlands College of Technology, Kericho, where he tutored in community development studies. He also conducted research in the Research and Extension Department of Egerton University, Kenya.

Ramola Ramtohul is postdoctoral research fellow at the Institute for Women and Gender Studies in the Department of Jurisprudence at the University of Pretoria, South Africa; she was previously a lecturer in Sociology and Gender Studies at the University of Mauritius. She has a PhD in gender studies from the University of Cape Town, South Africa. Her research interests include intersectionality and women's political activism in plural societies, as well as women's rights, citizenship and democracy in postcolonial contexts. She has published in the South African feminist journal AGENDA, and with CODESRIA.

Sabastiano Rwengabo holds a Master's degree in Public Administration and Management and a BA in Political Science and Sociology from Makerere University, Uganda. He also has a Postgraduate Certificate in Research Methodology from the Centre for Basic Research (CBR), Uganda. He attended CODESRIA's 2008 and 2009 Governance Institutes. He has published on electoral democracy in Uganda and he is currently investigating 'Religion and Democratisation Processes in Africa' (under TrustAfrica's 'Meeting the

Challenge of Pluralism and Democracy in Africa' project); and on governing urban security in the age of privatisation (under the Global Consortium for Security Transformation (GCST) investigation on privatisation of Security). His research interests include: regionalism/international organisations; international migration; security; governance and democratisation; and pluralism and governance.

Mustapha Ziky est Docteur d'Etat en sciences économiques et Professeur de l'Enseignement Supérieur (PES) à l'Université Cadi Ayyad de Marrakech au Maroc. Il est membre fondateur et actuellement directeur adjoint du Groupe de Recherche et d'Etude en Management et Ingénierie de Développement (GREMID). Abondamment investi dans l'enseignement et la recherche en macroéconométrie, en finance et en économies sociale et politique, il a publié plusieurs ouvrages et articles.

Introduction

Gender and Citizenship in the Global Age

Laroussi Amri and Ramola Ramtohul

Introduction

African scholarship on gender and citizenship in this globalised era is still in the infancy stage, which makes this volume a timely publication. The volume seeks to fill a void in the scholarly writings and theorisation on this important topic.

The papers collected in the volume were first presented at the 2008 CODESRIA Symposium held in Cairo on Gender and Citizenship in the Global Age. The book further demonstrates CODESRIA's sustained commitment to encouraging research in gender and contributing to the production of gender scholarship in Africa. The volume presents case studies of different African contexts, illustrating the gendered aspects of citizenship as experienced by African men and women. Citizenship carries manifold gendered aspects and given the distinct gender roles and responsibilities attributed to men and women, globalisation affects the citizenship of African men and women in different ways. The papers illustrate some of the different ways in which the citizenship of African men and women has been affected. Sometimes these are positive and sometimes they are negative. In some cases, new forms of citizenship emerge, especially in the current era that is dominated by a neoliberal focus. This volume is not exclusive in terms of theorisation, rather focuses on African contexts, emphasises local culture and practices and their implications for citizenship, and makes a good base for further scholarly work on gender and citizenship in Africa.

General Framework of Analysis

It is pertinent to ask what the *African experience and identity* contribute to the debate on citizenship and their connection to the public and private spaces in a globalised era, particularly from a gendered perspective. The papers in this collection address this central issue, some explicitly, while others do so in a more implicit manner.

Stages of African Identity Building

By *African identity*, we refer to common characteristics of African ethnic groups. Several qualities and experiences, such as negritude and the establishment of community, describe this identity. These reveal the relics of domination of white men when analysed at historical and anthropological levels. While we do not claim to offer an exhaustive definition of the African identity, we focus on those aspects that are relevant to the research theme.

The book examines two major aspects of the African identity. First was colonialism, which lasted for a long time. It was a historical experience that varied from one country to another. Secondly, the nature of domination that African endured during the colonial period was not only military, political or economic. Above all, it was fundamentally cultural. Unfortunately, this cultural domination has survived the colonial period and now operates as a kind of the democratic ideal inspired by European 'models' and political systems, the adoption of colonial languages and lifestyles, civic and scientific training, as well as the conception of the world and society among other things. The main facet of this cultural domination lies in the fact that it targets the reversal of the African *ethnos* (Balandier 2000). This concept refers to the state of distress and has a foundation whose indigenous social formation is essentially based on an African community model. These two historical experiences define the African identity in terms of an argument by denial. A more positive definition privileges the struggle aspect and rejects the negative aspects. It thus takes strong willpower to move from the *ethnos* to the *socius* (Balandier ibid), which is a new situation that gives a different value to social life.

The plundering of Africa was the third crucial stage that the African identity experienced. Here, there was an awareness of the *economic foundations of social relations*, in terms of an internal expression of domination as well as in the form of neocolonial external relations, which eventually vanished in the 1980s.[1] Anthropologists and Marxists indeed highlighted a crucial aspect of the African persona. Next came the stage of 'Afro pessimism', which prompted

Jean Pierre Dorzon (2002) to observe that Africanism had lost the meaning it had acquired since the 1950s, namely, that of a discipline made up of history, geography, ethnology and sociology. As a result of this, a climate of 'Afro-pessimism' (the cause of which becomes evident in civil wars, the decline of certain states and the AIDS pandemic) as well as neocolonialism finally became dominant. Today, Africans are confronting more general phenomena and movements that circulate between Africa, Europe, North and South America.

Afro-pessimism did not flourish extensively. Flashes of free thought and citizenship practice characterised the second half of the 20th century when the gains in gendered terms were highly visible. *Stiwanism* (from STIWA – Social Transformation Including Women of Africa), as advocated by Omolara Ogundipe-Leslie, is one of these expressions that is still in its infancy. Even if little has been written on *Stiwanism*, it remains a project to formulate and conceive – one that will be authentically African. *Stiwanism* evolves in a global framework marked by the demand for better economic conditions for women, with a fair share of the nation's wealth, but also for more global recognition of women's rights in patriarchal societies.

Africa: Birthplace of Citizenship

Political and civic experiences of citizenship date back to ancient times in Africa. The term citizenship appeared in Alexandria, which became a large city reserved for the elite coming from Macedonia and was later opened to the rest of the inhabitants. During these ancient times, custom, including that observed in Pharaonic Africa (Egypt) considered citizenship as a sign of belonging to the city. With the advent of modern periods, citizenship took on the meaning of belonging to a state (there is no citizen without a state). In this semantic transformation probably lies the anthropological assertion of the usurpation of the city by the state, a basic idea that was confirmed by the research of Pierre Clastres (1974).[2]

This facet of citizenship in Egypt can be considered as an extension of the Hellenistic civilisation. However, we focus on the practice of citizenship, which benefitted people from Macedonia who were able to live in Alexandria. This flexibility was not governed by a rigorous and strict principle of identity. It is this practical aspect, which drew our attention, to highlight it and underline the difference from the prevailing conception and practice in the typical Greek example of the *deme* (an administrative subdivision), which was stricter and lapsed into an identity-biased approach. Yet, the difference between Greco-

Latin citizenship and ancient Egyptian citizenship lies in the fact that, until now, the countries of the North have linked this concept to a semantic content based on the notion of identity. The good seeds should be preserved (citizens, natives of the country), at the expense of the bad ones (slaves, women and foreigners or immigrants). In Pharaonic Egypt, chauvinism was less obvious.

This introduction consists of three sections: the first deals with the concept of citizenship, the second addresses the questions of citizenship and gender as expressions of social movements while the third introduces the papers in this volume.

The Concept of Citizenship

Citizenship is a highly contested concept which carries immense political value. It is closely connected with political and social identity. Citizenship has been the locus of intense struggle in Western democracies as well as in postcolonial nations. The concept of citizenship has been historically associated with the development of political thought, where it was linked with the development of a moral being, identified with a community which was broader than one based on lineage (Halisi *et al.* 1998). According to Shklar (1991: 4), citizenship is 'the legal recognition, both domestic and international, that a person is a member, native-born or naturalized, of a state'. Max Weber (1968) distinguished three distinct meanings of citizenship in social history: classes that share a specific communal or economic interest; membership determined by rights within the state; and strata defined by standard of living or social prestige.[3] Debates about citizenship have, in fact, been largely assumed to be debates about the implications of being a member of a state (Squires 1999).

T.H. Marshall played a seminal role in expanding the conceptualisation and theorisation of citizenship in terms of rights granted to the individual by the state. According to Marshall (1965), citizenship entailed civil rights such as liberty of the person and freedom of thought or religion; political rights such as the right to participate in the exercise of political power; but also necessitated social rights such as the right to economic welfare and security, to work and to have a minimum standard of living. Marshall's definition of citizenship, therefore, took the focus beyond government, politics and the legal system, to consider interactions of people with collective groupings at all levels of society (Sweetman 2003). Marshall's model of citizenship was very influential and still structures contemporary debate. It opened the way to discuss degrees of citizenship obtained by different social groups at different times (Walby 1997). It was, nonetheless, subject to extensive criticism and the social model of citizenship that he contributed to was expanded and deepened by approaches that emphasise the flexibility of social membership, the limitations of citizenship merely as rights, and by perspectives that emphasise identity and difference (Isin and Turner 2007). Indeed, Marshall's analysis was mainly focused on the white, male, working class segment of the British industrial society, which was a society without empire and devoid of internal inequalities apart from class (Fraser and Gordon 1994). It was also silent on gender and race and the rights of the people whose lands were colonised and taken and whose way of life was disrupted (Kabeer 2006).

More recent approaches indicate that citizenship goes beyond the legal and political relationship between individual and the state, to involve participation in civil society (Kymlicka 1995; Isin and Wood 1999). Charles Tilly, for instance, posits that citizenship can be interpreted from four angles, namely as a category, role, tie and identity. As a *category*, citizenship designates a set of actors, i.e. citizens, distinguished by their shared privileged position vis-à-vis a particular state. As a *role*, citizenship includes the totality of an actor's relations to others, which depend on his/her relations to a particular state. As a *tie*, citizenship identifies a mutual relation between an actor and state agents that can be enforced. Moreover, as an *identity*, citizenship refers to the experience and public representation of category, tie or role (Tilly 1996: 7-11). Tilly's conception of citizenship complements that of Marshall. The criteria for citizenship will, however, vary from country to country. In fact, as a social construct, citizenship includes political, socio-economic, cultural and psychological dimensions that develop in specific contexts and that change over space and time (Dobrowolsky and Tastsoglou 2006). According to Molyneux (2007: 65), the contextual nature of citizenship defines its meaning for women in three main ways: first, the rights and responsibilities that citizenship entails are specified within a particular legal tradition and guaranteed by a particular state form; secondly, citizenship signifies social and political membership of a nation-state and makes claims on loyalty and identity within a set of specific cultural understandings in which ideas of womanhood are often central; and thirdly, within political practice, struggles for citizenship rights are played out within different political discourses and opportunity contexts. The variability of each has implications for how gender issues are framed, and affects the degree to which women can participate as well as the manner in which they do so (Molyneux 2007: 65).

Citizenship and Postcolonial Contexts

Most of the theorisation and debate on citizenship has centred on the modern and recent experiences of Western societies. Few scholars have considered the relevance of this concept to non-Western societies and even fewer have focused on African contexts (Halisi *et al.* 1998). Problematic expectations of modernity in the developing world (Ferguson 1999; Moore 2005) have led to technocratic, disembedded and depoliticised approaches to 'development' where development has been conceived of as a unilinear process of standardised, calculable and predictable practices (Ferguson 1990). This has led to a much stronger focus on large-scale 'civic' citizenship at the expense of small-scale 'ethnic' citizenship, where the juridico-political basis of large-scale civic citizenship has been uncritically assumed to be more inclusive than the cultural basis of ethnic citizenship (Mamdani 1996; 2000). Nyamnjoh (2007) points out that the focus of analysis has centred almost exclusively on institutional and constitutional arrangements, thereby downplaying the hierarchies and relationships of inclusion and exclusion formed by race, ethnicity, class, gender and geography that determine accessibility to citizenship in real terms.

Colonialism had a distinct impact on citizenship in the colonies. While relationships between different imperial powers and their colonised subjects had obvious differences, yet they also shared remarkable similarities (Kabeer 2006). In this context, Mamdani (1996: 16) states that the colonial state was in every instance a historical formation and its structure came to share certain fundamental features because, everywhere, the organisation and reorganisation of the colonial state was a response to a central question, namely, how a tiny and foreign minority could rule over an indigenous majority. Ultimately, the colonisers chose indirect rule or association rather than assimilation, where they constructed the colonial edifice on pre-existing arrangements, institutions and identities, but in ways that promoted their goal of hegemony (Bose and Jalal 1998). Customary law and traditional authority were invoked to support the hierarchical ordering of society. However, these customs and traditions had been largely created or were re-interpretations and reifications which served the imperial project (Kabeer 2006). Such colonial strategies were implemented in India as well as on the African continent, and impacted heavily on the citizenship of people in these regions. These imperial tactics, in fact, created separate communities, each governed by its own customs and traditions, alongside a civil society, with a modicum of civil rights, in which selected representatives of the colonised groups interacted on unequal terms with the representatives of the colonial powers (Kabeer 2006: 93).

Ekeh (1978) pioneered the study of citizenship in sub-Saharan Africa in the 1970s. He examined citizenship as an ideology of legitimation in Africa, recognising the fact that colonial rule had bisected African attitudes towards rights and obligations (Ekeh 1978). Ekeh's work suggests that modern ethnic conflict, most often rooted in the colonial past, has encouraged a 'dual citizenship consciousness' among Africans, as liberal citizenship has been mainly influenced by the colonial origins of the state in their societies (Halisi et al. 1998). Mamdani's seminal work on 'Citizen and Subject' (1996) shows how colonialism created two categories of people in the African public sphere in the colonies: citizens and subjects or the native and the citizen (Mamdani 1996). The 'native' spoke the language of tradition and followed indigenous customs whereas the 'citizen' possessed the power of rights, duties and privileges. The colonisers controlled the domain of the central state which was largely urban based and governed by civil laws, whereas the natives or the colonised were governed by a local state or the native authorities which enforced customary laws. This bifurcation of identities carried over into the postcolonial state as it was not reorganised to attenuate difference, either institutionally, ethnically, in terms of identity or symbolically (Adejumobi 2005). Adejumobi (2005: 28) pertinently notes that while national citizenship was liberalised with civil laws applicable to all, the local state remained largely ethnicised. The state system reinforced local ethnic and political identities, fragmented the political process and undermined the concept of common citizenship for the people of the country.

In a number of African states, tension is rife over access to and control of resources between different ethnic groups. Hence, Halisi *et al.* (1998: 347) argue that citizenship theory in African contexts needs to move beyond the dichotomy of identities to accommodate a newer set of societal tensions largely induced by intense, subnational, identity articulation, the regional and global migration of select African populations, liberal economic reforms, and democratic transitions that have altered state-citizen relations in Africa. Yet, it is important to recognise that the bifurcation of citizenship in Africa also had gendered effects. Tension exists between customary law and civil rights, especially over gender issues and women's rights, e.g., bodily autonomy, female genital mutilation, polygamy, inheritance, etc. This tension has a direct impact on women's citizenship as they are often caught in between and their rights violated in the name of 'culture and tradition'. In the current global age, it thus becomes important to analyse the extent to which the gap between these two dimensions of citizenship in African postcolonial states has been bridged. This aspect is of major concern to African women especially since African societies are historically patriarchal and a number of customary laws are discriminatory towards women.

Citizenship in the Global Era

While the concept of citizenship has been based on the notion of a society within the bounds of a state, globalisation is a phenomenon with political, economic, socio-cultural and technological dimensions, and refers to integration and inter-connectedness across national boundaries along these dimensions (Gans 2005). Globalisation entails transformations in relations between politics and economics, capital and labour, states and markets, international and domestic politics,[4] and such transformations have been accelerated by developments in technology and communications which enable fast, borderless and virtual transactions and decision making. Globalisation is not a uniform and unilinear process as it impacts differentially on different regions, classes and people (Pettman 1999). A significant characteristic of globalisation is the growing disparities of wealth between states. Within states, globalisation has led to increased poverty, unemployment, flexible labour requirements, loss or reduction of social welfare. Many of the people who have been severely affected by these problems are women and migrants who do not have access to formal citizenship. Globalisation thus exists in an uneasy relationship with citizenship. In fact, it has been argued that the discourse on national citizenship which tends to lay emphasis on large-scale, assimilationist and bounded belongin is being increasingly challenged in the current global era characterised by an upsurge in claims for rights and recognition by small-scale communities (Nyamnjoh 2007). Similarly, Gans (2005) argues that two aspects of globalisation have pertinent implications for citizenship, first, the movement of people across national boundaries to live and work. This calls into question issues of national identity and belonging, of membership in a polity, and of the rights that accrue to that membership. Secondly, transnational corporations have the potential to transgress national sovereignty. Transnational corporations exist in parallel with the nation-state and both complicate and diffuse the rights and privileges that accrue to citizenship (Gans 2005).

Held (1995, 1999) explored the implications of globalisation for citizenship, both at the domestic level and at the level of transnational or global institutions. According to him, globalisation is eroding the capacity for meaningful democratic citizenship at the domestic level, as nation-states lose some of their sovereignty. Globalisation at the political level has become more intense, especially with the hegemony of the neoliberal capitalist ideology. International codes of rights and privileges of individuals are being designed, institutionalised and gradually enforced by supra-national organisations

(Adejumobi 2005: 24). In this context, Lister (2003) introduces a multi-layered conceptualisation of citizenship whih enables citizenship to be defined over a spectrum that extends from the local to the global. In her view, the notion of global citizenship, which is reflected at the international level in terms of the rights and responsibilities associated with national citizenship, becomes a tool to challenge the exclusionary power of citizenship (Lister 2003). Here, the link between citizenship and human rights becomes more visible as the framework of global citizenship, especially through the United Nations and its associated bodies, encourages a focus on the responsibilities of affluent nations towards the citizens of poor nations, and also on a number of global issues, including environmental conservation and climate change. It also exerts pressure on states to respect the basic human rights of people, with the threat of economic sanctions and isolation. In terms of citizenship at the international level, one can also discern the steady growth of a global civil society through which social movements and non-governmental organisations have been pursuing their goals across national borders, often with the aim of enhancing the rights and citizenship of different populations and marginalised groups, including women. The rights of citizens are thus no longer the sole prerogative of states as legal norms and conventions, especially on issues governing civil rights, are evolving and nations are being encouraged and even coerced to acquiesce to them. Yet, Adejumobi (2005) cautions that the state remains a principal agent in global interactions and the institution of citizenship.

Some commentators argue that although globalisation involves a good degree of weakening of the power of the social, it entails a corresponding development of 'post-national' citizenship (Rose 1996), or in other words, globalisation is leading to the formation of new forms of citizenship. Soysal (1994) for instance, contends that national citizenship is losing ground to a more universal model of membership located within an increasingly de-territorialised notion of a person's universal rights. This newer form of citizenship in the global age is especially connected with the growth of guest-working in many societies, greater global interdependence, increased overlapping membership of different forms of citizenship and the emergence of universalistic rules and conceptions regarding human rights formalised by international codes and laws (Urry 1999). In the current global age, therefore, contemporary citizenship has become 'postmodern'. A wide variety of citizenships emerging in the contemporary global age have been identified. These include: cultural citizenship, minority citizenship, ecological citizenship, consumer citizenship and mobility citizenship. Hence, on the one hand, globalisation blurs the boundaries of citizenship, but on the other hand, it has created new forms of citizenship in the world today. The impact will nevertheless vary, depending on a range of socio-economic conditions in countries, including levels of development, gender, literacy and income, as well as the political system in place. At this level, it becomes interesting to explore new forms of citizenship emerging in African contexts and their gender dimensions.

Gender, Globalisation and Citizenship

The historical conceptualisation of citizenship dating from ancient Greece and which has been subject to widespread feminist critique, was highly exclusionary in the sense that only men of noble and royal family and upper class backgrounds were members of the state or full-fledged citizens; they were the only ones entitled to perform their civic duties. Women and slaves were denied citizenship long after the franchise had been extended to men of colour in most Western democracies. In most postcolonial countries, however, women were granted full-fledged citizenship concurrently with men at the time of independence. Feminist theorists have argued that despite the universal rhetoric on which they were based, civil, political and social citizenship were granted to different social groups within a given territory at different rates and times (Walby 1997:171). In certain Western democracies such as Britain, and in postcolonial democracies including Mauritius, civil citizenship for women came after political citizenship. Indeed, political citizenship often formed the power base from which women were able to win civil citizenship (Walby 1997). Movement towards the acquisition of social citizenship came later, with the development of the welfare state in certain countries, but this is under threat in the globalised era dominated by neoliberalism and the pressure to reduce government spending on social services. In fact, Sweetman (2003:4) notes that in global terms, women are the biggest group of people who are denied full citizenship rights. Gender inequalities, unequal power relations, especially women's exclusion from full citizenship and enjoyment of entitlements and rights, have myriad of impacts on women's citizenship in the current global age. In order to analyse specific impacts, it becomes important to deconstruct the term 'woman' and to be aware that women's multiple and different identities as women will lead to different experiences based on a number of social factors, including class, nationality, education, age, ethnicity, religion and sexual orientation.

Underpinning women's historical exclusion from citizenship in Western democracies has been the public-private divide, which entailed a rigid gendered separation of public and private spheres. Yet, the public-private divide also impacts on women's citizenship in postcolonial developing nations. While the 'public' represents universalism, justice and independence, the 'private' represents particularity, care and dependence on the other (Lister 2003). With the public-private divide, women experienced citizenship differently from men as full citizenship was largely determined by an individual's participation in the public sphere, principally characterised by full-time employment and political participation. Women were mainly confined to a private, domestic, care-taking role whereas men were presumed to be able to move freely between the private and the public spheres. Thus, according to Gouws (2010), if the state does not enforce rights in the domain of the private sphere where women's citizenship is often characterised by subordination and violence and thereby deemed inferior, women cannot be equal citizens with men. In African contexts, the domain of customary law that condones traditional practices such as polygamous marriage, female genital mutilation and paying bride price directly impact upon the citizenship of African women, denying them equality as citizens. There is also the issue of bodily integrity, namely reproductive rights including contraception, abortion and reproductive health, which have been largely treated as 'private', thereby denying women autonomy, equality and democratic participation. The reconfiguration of the relationship between the public and private domains, therefore, becomes essential for justice and equal citizenship in gender terms (Gouws 2010).

While in some countries women's citizenship is still largely restricted, in others the Constitution grants women full and equal citizenship. Yet laws, especially those dealing with issues of family and inheritance, often contradict national and international commitments to equality (Sweetman 2003; Gouws 2005). In this context, Gouws (2005:3) contends that citizenship is not simply determined by the inclusion in the nation-state through rights that confer upon people the status of citizens, it is also a practice that enables people to participate in the affairs of the nation-state. Applying a gender lens to the debate around citizenship in Africa exposes inequalities embedded in the nature of citizenship which are linked to the inability to claim rights as agents of citizenship (Gouws 2010). Nyamu-Musembi (2007) also stresses the importance of differentiating between formal citizenship and substantive citizenship. While formal citizenship is mainly concerned with rights and obligations between the state and citizens, substantive citizenship goes beyond the confines of formal politics and law to encompass the economic, social and political relationship between social groups and structures of power that mediate the standing of citizens.[5] Constraints imposed by lack of action on the part of state institutions or those imposed by norms, culture, relationships and institutions all have an impact on a person's substantive citizenship, often with strongly gendered characteristics.

Globalisation, while creating new opportunities on the one hand and eliminating a number of social services and entitlements, on the other, directly affects men and women's citizenship. The specific impact will be determined by a number of factors including gender, class, ethnicity, sexuality, culture and country of birth and citizenship. Lenz *et al.* (2007) mention the development of new patterns of gender orders in the global context as globalisation and economic transition lead to the unbinding of national orders. Indeed, with its neo-liberal market philosophy, globalisation has been pushing towards more 'flexible' work, growing gender competition at work and to the image of a 'flexible person' who constantly adapts to the challenges of globalisation.

Women have become the preferred candidates for 'flexible' jobs where tasks include light assembly work in export-processing zones or free-trade zones and subcontracted sweatshop/homework labour, as well as clerical and domestic work and sex tourism (Enloe 1989; Peterson and Runyan 1999; Pettman 1996). While providing women with a certain degree of economic autonomy, such advantages are largely short term, whereas the risks of exploitation in these jobs are high. With sex work, there is a major threat to women's bodily integrity and safety, especially where girls and women are trafficked as sex slaves. Feminist critiques of the global capitalist market have focused on gendered divisions of labour in which men's work has been privileged over women's work in terms of status, pay and working conditions. In developing countries, such inequalities were (re)produced through early colonisation practices and more recently through economic policies such as Structural Adjustment Programmes (SAP), imposed on the Southern nations by the North. Reductions in social welfare spending have had negative consequences on women who, in their domestic and reproductive roles, have had to compensate for state retreat or state failure to provide social infrastructure and support (Pettman 1999). Work carried out mainly by women in the 'private' domestic arena is, however, still not accounted for and reproductive work remains largely invisible or devalued. The withdrawal of food subsidies and focus on production for export rather than subsistence has also generated a massive crisis in reproduction as conditions necessary for sustaining daily living were no longer available (Afshar and Dennis 1992). Although the adverse effects of economic restructuring and SAP on women in developing countries have been well documented (Elson 1991; Afshar and Dennis 1992), the impact on the identities and citizenship of men in these countries is an area to be explored in greater depth.

Globalisation has led to an unprecedented rise in international migration of both men and women, to earn income and provide foreign exchange for their families and countries. Migration affects the citizenship of migrant men and women in various ways in both host and home countries. Some women have found autonomy and freedom from patriarchal bondage and conservative religious laws in host countries, whereas others have been exploited and turned into 'slaves' performing forced labour, including being sexually exploited. Feminist scholars have documented the rise in the international 'maid trade'; global sex trafficking and tourism as well as other services migrant women provide to elites in the big cities of the world (Enloe 1989; Pettman 1996; Peterson and Runyan 1999). Indeed, migration can also lead to new dependencies and reinforce existing gender boundaries and hierarchies. Moreover, home states have often been reluctant to defend the rights of their citizens, especially when they are dependent on remittances from overseas work as well as foreign aid and investment from host countries (Pettman 1999). Men have also been affected as they are in a different position of power in host countries and masculine culture may differ. These issues raise a number of questions on the impact on men and women as citizens, although different social positioning and skills lead to different experiences for the migrants.

At the political level, globalisation has driven the setting of norms and laws for gender equality worldwide, largely spurred by the UN Decade for Women and international policies focusing on gender mainstreaming. In this context, Ferree (2006:11) contends that globalisation catalysed the setting up of three groups of strategies geared towards meeting feminist demands to empower women: developing a 'women's policy machinery' within state institutions; building an issue advocacy network outside of formal institutions; and developing women's movement practices that led to knowledge creation. This has led to the abolition of direct and legal discrimination against women in most regions, although indirect discriminatory mechanisms still prevail, hindering women's full citizenship. Globalisation has also enhanced many women's political and economic citizenship by integrating them into political and economic decision-making bodies through affirmative action and quotas in some regions, but parity has yet to be reached in most countries. In this globalised age, one also finds women's movements and those of other social justice groups propagating new egalitarian norms that have contributed significantly to discourses of equality and legal amendments which have uplifted women's citizenship in a number of countries. These movements have provided knowledge and norms for achieving greater autonomy and equality and have extended transnational communication in which universal equality and cultural differences are acknowledged (Lenz et al. 2007).

While this theoretical discussion on gender and citizenship in the globalised age has focused primarily on the experiences of women, who have been a marginalised group in many ways, the implications of the factors mentioned above on men's citizenship nonetheless constitute a crucial component of a gender analysis of citizenship in this age. Scholarship on men's experiences and masculinities is a more recent field of study and research has shown that different groups of men have specific gendered experiences. There exists a multiplicity of masculinities or multiple cultural constructions of masculinity and patterns of men's lives both between cultures and within a given culture or community (Connell 2007). As such, any dividends that accrue to men from patriarchal privilege remain unevenly distributed. Bob Connell's notion of 'hegemonic' and 'subordinate' masculinities usefully encapsulates men's differential access to the power associated with their gender (Connell 1987: 183-2). He posits the existence of a hierarchy of masculinities, in which gender intersects with other factors such as class, race and sexuality. Hegemonic patterns of masculinity operate at the level of the whole society, enforcing male power and advantage. Hegemonic masculinity is constitutive of and embodied in numerous institutional practices and individual men are compelled to negotiate their identities in relation to practices and relationships informed by hegemonic masculinity (Hooper 2000).

Yet, globalisation reconfigures and reshapes the arena in which masculinities are articulated and transforms the shape of domestic and public patriarchies (Kimmel 2001). Globalisation has led to the gradual impoverishment of local peasantries as market criteria replaced subsistence and survival. Moreover, local crafts producers, small farmers and independent peasants have traditionally based their notions of masculinity on ownership of land and economic autonomy in their work. However, Kimmel (2001:24) notes that with globalisation, ownership and autonomy have been increasingly transferred higher up in the class hierarchy and outwards to the transnational corporations. Globalisation and its associated proletarianness have also also led to massive labour migration of male workers from their homes to migrant enclaves, squatter camps and labour camps (Kimmel 2001). Globalisation has, therefore, affected the autonomy and decision-making power of men in many communities, thereby affecting masculinities and gendered relations.

At another level, it is important to note that, overall, globalisation is an intrinsically gendered process, bifurcated towards a masculine culture. Indeed, the institutional arrangements of global society such as the market place, multinational corporations, transnational geo-political institutions such as the

United Nations, the World Bank, the International Monetary Fund (IMF) and the ideological principles governing them – for example, economic rationality and liberal individualism – express a highly gendered logic (Kimmel 2001). In this context, Connell (1998:15) states that the growing, unregulated power of transnational corporations places strategic power in the hands of particular groups of men, while the language of globalisation remains gender neutral, such that the 'individual' of neoliberal theory possesses the attributes and interests of a male entrepreneur. Therefore, patterns of masculinity embedded within these gendered institutions are also rapidly becoming the dominant, global, hegemonic model of masculinity, against which all local, regional and national masculinities are played out and to which they increasingly refer (Kimmel 2001). Given the gendered bias in global institutions, the impact of global and political restructuring has been greater on women, although 'weaker' groups of men have been marginalised at the same time. Here, men from the lower income groups in postcolonial nations become particularly vulnerable.

Social Movements and Disparities at the Level of 'Citizenship and Gender'

A quick historical reading of the class components of social movements that established citizenship reveals that it was mainly the slaves and peasants of both sexes who were bearers of a message of citizenship (Gauthier 2011).[6] Citizenship, as borne in the example of the 1789 French Revolution which was a powerful social movement, is the fulfilment of the serf's will for freedom, of slaves from sugar planters in the colonies, and of women and peasants (the peasant revolt and the 'Great Fear' around July 1789). The foundation of this citizenship lies in its liberating vision. It is thus important to identify the social actors at the most local, grassroots and popular levels of society. Such initiative at the level of revolutionary social movements can be found in the feminine and feminist expressions, which have been assimilated and boosted within and by gendered approaches.

African Contribution to the Gendered Approach

A critique of Western feminism helps discern the existence of several brands of feminism. There is talk of *polyversal* feminism (Zyllah Eisenstein)[7] as a prerequisite for a debate within women's liberation movements, and as a condition for liberating societies. The African contribution consisted of emphasising this diversity based on a critique of Western feminism that could only lead to an emancipatory approach for men and women at the same time. The 1980s witnessed the formation of new approaches, the most notable of which is the gendered approach. This is based on the belief that all forms of oppressive relations emanate from social interactions, the most prominent being that of the sexes. This is the most full-fledged definition of the gendered approach. The inequality between the sexes is a matter of lived social interaction at the cultural level (mentalities and orthodoxy), at the level of economic relationships (exploitation), as well as at the political (exclusion, ostracism, xenophobia, racism) and symbolic levels. It is nonetheless diluted by the values and roles that are affected by capitalism and patriarchy and translates into different roles for men and women. The level of polarity at the level of sex roles however varies for those who find themselves midway between both poles, for example in the case of homosexuality.

Stiwanism, as derived from STIWA[8] can be considered as an African expression of theoretical and practical interest in the social interactions to be modified through the equality of the sexes for the liberation of society. The virtue of the African contribution consists of assimilating the assets and positive aspects of feminism and integrating them in order to propose a social theory according to which sexual foundation is essential and connected to racial foundation. The second African contribution will consider this transformation as an ordinary query and not simply a matter of revolution of a privileged historical moment following which a new structure is set up for a long period of time. The most outstanding features of the profound changes in the social interaction of the sexes and their implications lie in their being an interrupted and continuing issue. Patriarchy and relationships of oppression have lasted for a long period of time and will continue existing in diverse forms.

Nnaemaka (2009) focused on the forms of negotiations, while maintaining the emphasis on the objectives of social liberation. It is from 'nego-feminism', which is one of Morala Ogundipe-Leslie's proposals and focuses for *Stiwanism,* that we can further delve into the African gendered approach and its input. Our approach stresses the necessity of concentrating on the ongoing and interrupted nature of these movements, calling for change in everyday social life and, therefore, not defying the spirit of African feminist theses. Both the masses and the elites are involved as a new type of citizen, revolutionary by negotiation, compromise, denunciation and the demystification of any form of alienation (sex, race, religion, class, etc.) at all levels. It is the African position that makes possible this commitment to finding pathways for change in the social relationships of the sexes.

Citizenship and Social Actors in a Global Framework

Peasants and the Social Contract (First Core of Social Citizenship):

During the social revolutions in the North and the South, the slaves and peasants constituted a potent force, for example, the peasant revolt during the French Revolution offered a *social contract* to the landlords, thereby putting forward a model of citizenship based on equality. This offer did not totally dispossess the landlords. In fact, the landlord structure consisted of two parts: the landlord's manor and the landholding domain. The social contract offered by the peasantry to the landlords involved a sharing of resources and authority. This concrete act of sharing could only lead to the declaration of human and citizenship rights, the most substantive clauses of which could form the essence of a Universal Declaration of Human Rights. Here, it is important to note that the working class is a rather recent force of change, compared to slaves and peasants. Citizenship was a matter of concern to these two social classes before the advent of the working class which is the outcome of industrialisation, one of the fundamental factors of social change.

Slaves of the Colonies and the Vision of the Global Citizen

Slaves, such as those of Saint-Domingue, fully expressed the ideals embodied in the meetings of the French Revolution colonial assemblies in 1791-93 (Gauthier 2005). Their own revolt which integrated the slogans of liberty and equality, a refrain taken up by French peasants during the French Revolution, enriched the social movement of protest and initiative by their cosmopolitan nature. This plea was set up at two levels: the first was individual and lay in the appearance of cosmopolitan patriots. This was connected with the global-dimension citizenship because from Saint Domingue and the West Indies to metropolitan France, a wave of revolutionary ideas and actions spread through the movement of men and women driven by the will for change, for example, the movement set up by the Creole settlers in support of the slaves in the sugar plantations. This support was made on the basis of skin colour and community. It is, therefore, by common skin relation that the movement, heading towards the principles of citizenship, managed to mobilise at two levels: the Creole settlers[9] and the slaves of the sugar plantations.

The second level focuses on the appearance of a new model of citizenship. It concentrates on the global dimension of the social contract where neither the economic aspects nor the social ones or political and cultural are evaded. It is the precursory model of social citizenship at the global level that is at the core of the debates on democracy, the gender approach and the egalitarian and free society nowadays. The 'social contract' in the historical and sociological conditions of the period, was bound to transform society locally as well as globally. This led to a universal appeal of social movements that established the citizenship of the modern period and brought new dimensions to the form of citizenship conceived in ancient times. The most important ones were those that consisted of incorporating citizenship in the register of equality from an economic perspective (for example, the equality of pay and the equality of professional status respectively). Moreover, citizenship resembles an *essentially social citizenship* today,[10] including the 'social contract' and also the legal right, in addition to its legitimacy. This involves the right to wellbeing at all levels (right to work, health, lodging, transport, education, culture, leisure, etc.), as well as political rights (right to vote, to be elected, right to political, union, corporatist, associative organisation, etc.) which are a guarantee for securing these social rights, and not only the legal and civic rights (right for a fair trial, property, residence, etc.) (Twine 1994).[11]

Social citizenship was often associated with the function of the welfare state. However, the African experience of citizenship shows that in many African countries, society takes care of itself, alone and often against the state in order to establish a social citizenship between citizens who are vigilant with regard to their equality not only before the law (equal rights) but also in the face of adversity (equality inspired by the need for solidarity). They were men and women, driven by the principle of equality of the sexes and involved in associations, socio-professional committees, bodies constituted as a fabric of the civil society, at the level of magistracy, solicitors, engineers, doctors, teachers, etc. It is this fabric that constitutes a defence that can replace the state to a certain extent. This suggests fitting citizenship in the essential register of solidarity, involving men and women in a relationship based on equity in the willing absence of the state as the primary guardian of wellbeing and welfare.

Migrants

In addition to peasants and slaves in the colonies, the social conditions of the globalisation of the debate on citizenship can be linked to a third social actor – migrants. This is a category that has often been concealed behind the discredited designation – foreigners. Since the appearance of the *deme* in ancient Greece, foreigners were excluded from citizenship, hence the struggle led for centuries by immigrant patriots in order to claim equality and enjoy citizenship. Several social movements have affected the march of immigrants towards equality and liberty. Confined to a lexis proper to demography, the migrant is in fact the core of several forces: those of the itinerant job seeker (because the national bodies in charge of his/her employment as a citizen are failing); those of the job provider seeking labour, but also those of the state and the host country (for immigrant workers). Thus, from the slaves in the Americas to immigrant workers of Europe, the struggle for citizenship saw powerful moments involving both men and women. The gains of the French Revolution in terms of human rights and freedom of citizens owe much to the slaves and sugar planters in Saint Domingue (Gauthier 2005). At the end of the 20th century, the immigrants, including second-generation North Africans and also the elderly men and women who were employed in the French factories that needed labour because of the shortage of workers, claimed the right to citizenship and equal treatment.[12]

In Europe and America, both men and women participated directly or indirectly in the social movements formed on the basis of migration and arising from the appropriation and domestication of the labour force by dominant capital as well as maintaining a demographic balance in European societies affected by ageing populations. An example of direct participation is the 'Marche Pour l'Egalité et Contre le Racisme in France',[13] whereas indirect participation includes the movement initiated by people of mixed race[14] during the French Revolution which facilitated the reinforcement of the Montagne's positions within the Assembly (Gauthier 2005) in favour of free citizens. It is, therefore, the social movements initiated by the migrants, men and women, which paved the way for a debate about citizenship. At the same time, it must be noted that there has been a dual oppression of immigrant women,[15] as women first, and then as foreigners. Moreover, the conditions of women workers, especially black women suffering from exploitation because of their skin colour, leads to stigmatisation.

Conjunction Between Movements of Ideas and Social Movements

Despite women's participation, the French Revolution did not provide them with the status of a full citizen. It was only in 1946 that women were granted the right to vote in France. The issue of political rights seems to have been perceived as the core of citizenship participation from which women were excluded. It is evidently a global struggle which, today, thanks to 'gender' as a concept, as an approach and as a paradigm, seems to have brought to the forefront to press for equality between the sexes as the basis of a new citizenship. It is the global framework, which, today, helps one to reveal the input of Africanism as far as the gender issue is concerned. This paradigm is to be taken as a theoretical construct deriving from the production of ideas and theories in the social sciences, but also as a frame growing out of the world's social movements. The three social actors who contributed the most to the new form of citizenship, namely peasant(s), slave(s) and migrant(s), include both men and women.

The research papers in this reader

The papers collected in this volume from the Gender Symposium underline the global framework with reference to the local context of the specific countries. There are thirteen papers spread over twelve countries, some from the authors' country of origin. The themes and sub-themes proposed in the Symposium, and which were at the core of the call for papers, form the common denominator of all the papers. The areas explored and which cut across the papers focus on patriarchy, gender and citizenship in the global age. The analytical content of the studies presented include the following sub-themes: (i). The body; (ii). Laws, protocol texts, international treaties; (iii). The public sphere and the private sphere; (iv). Leadership and chiefdom; (v). Obstacles to women's advancement ; and (vi). Globalisation.

The body

The body can be a means employed by women to impose themselves socially but the body trade has also been considered as part of the socio-professional sphere. This argument is made by feminists who subscribe to the approach of the empowerment of women, as it can be considered a final obstacle to the achievement of a human being's dignity. In this case, the body trade is the worst kind of oppression inflicted on women. These issues are raised in Mfon Umoren Ekpootu's[16] study of sexual trade. In his paper, Ndunde Otieno[17] asserts that the situation created by video images and the investment made by women in the musical field largely contributed to a break with dominant patriarchal discourse according to which women are not allowed or expected to expose their bodies (for example, through dancing) in public.

Laws, Rights, Protocols, International Treaties and Declarations

The authors examine this theme particularly in relation to the Convention on the Elimination of All Forms of Discrimination Against Women (CEDAW), which was ratified by many African nations. The Southern African Development Community (SADC) protocol, the SADC Declaration on Gender and Development as well as the Beijing Declaration were also ratified by many countries, including South Africa. However, there was also resistance to the adoption of certain international treaties and protocols. While exploring the impact of globalisation on women's rights in Mauritius, Ramola Ramtohul cites an example of 'the manner in which women's movements used the United Nations instruments to press for changes in marriage laws in the 1970s' while Okuro (Kenya) focuses on the role of international treaties in the improvement of Kenyan women's citizenship experience and the limitations at the level of enforcement due to financial constraints.

Public Sphere, Private Sphere

For Sabastiano Rwengabo[18] (Uganda), 'the globalisation of democracy and women's emancipation were necessary forces which underlay the reconstitution of the public sphere'. His analysis places both world processes – democratisation and women's emancipation – in the perspective of citizenship. The author explains how these processes have further motivated Uganda's political leaders – the government of the National Resistance Movement (NRM) under President Yoweri Museveni – to establish constitutional and institutional mechanisms aimed at bringing more women into the political and administrative cadres since 1995. The paper shows how women were active as rebels, collaborators and rebel chiefs; hence they could not be excluded from the reconstruction of society.

For Sharon Groenmeyer[19] (South Africa), 'citizenship is a contested, contradictory and multi-layered concept, which reinforces the separation of the public and private spheres'. She thus calls for 'a rethinking of citizenship in the globalisation era to admit both the public and private spheres'. She also suggests that citizenship should be tested against private life and sexuality. In private life, intimacy plays a role and 'the concepts of intimate citizenship are found in heterosexual practices'. In the light of Sharon Groenmeyer's paper, we understand that interdependence and the link between public and private spheres are central to gender and gender analysis. We cannot tackle the inequalities of social structures without observing intimate social relationships. The ideologies based on political and economic norms are doomed to fail maybe because they are linked to intimacy.

Leadership and Chiefdom

For Fonkwe Tamonkeng Prudentia,[20] 'women chiefs and notables are well respected in society'. However, despite their high status, women continue to do household chores as mothers and housewives and remain submissive to their husbands. She states that the difficulty is to completely assert their authority and she identifies unequal power relations between the sexes and affirms that 'the status quo has not changed'.

Obstacles to Women's Advancement

Mustapha Ziky discusses 'the presence of diverse forms of exclusion of women in the: educational, environmental, political, social and cultural».[21]

The latter restrict women's citizenship in Morocco.

Globalisation

Almost all the papers concur on the obvious effects of globalisation: ratified protocols, international organisations,[22] etc. However, the authors analyse globalisation differently. Felix Macharia Kiruthu[23] analyses the negative effects of Structural Adjustment Policies (SAP) on a district in the Kenyan capital, Nairobi. SAP was largely the backbone of the integration of the countries of the South in the neoliberal policy framework advocated by international bodies such as the International Monetary Fund.

Globalisation can be approached in terms of a 'new world order' (Mfon Ekpotoo), with what it subsumes as pernicious significances which we are entitled to consider as an extension of the preceding historical period. This period fits the term in correlation with the concept of 'international division of labour' as a masterpiece of the system which is generally unfavourable to the countries of the South, including those in Africa. Globalisation has, in addition, probably been approached in positive and negative terms at the same time, as in the case of the studies by Ivan Marowa[24] or Ramola Ramtohul.[25] The latter, without underestimating the negative aspects, states that 'with the new international division of labour and the creation of an industrial free zone, globalisation opened up the gate for the economic autonomy of women belonging to the working classes with limited employment in Mauritius'.

Angles of approach, variations and measures

The angles from which these themes are explored are diverse. They vary at the level of privilege, and also in the modes of treatment of the issues being reviewed.

- The individual and personal mode, immersed in the intimacy of sexual life, as is the case with Sharon Groenmeyer's study.

- The instructive academic mode (Mustapha Ziky and Jacques Tshibwabwa) versus the activist and militant mode.
- Gender opposed constructions: masculinity and femininity (Jacques Tshibwabwa, Mfon Umoren Ekpootu[26] Ivan Marowa)[27]
- The long term, long duration are portrayed as an approach in Jacques Tshibwabwa's study, whereas Rwengabo Sabastiano's or Felix Macharia Kiruthu's studies are inspired by the medium term at a time when the immediate approaches of recent sociology and history are reflected in studies such as Susan Kilonzo's.[28]

Another methodological subdivision can be established: this would be the ethnic perspective adopted by J. Tshibwabwa, compared to the entirely different societal perspective proposed by Hezron Ndunde Otieno's study.

Ultimately, we leave it to the reader to engage with the rich and varied themes and findings of these studies from 12 African countries.

Notes

1. Cited in the proceedings of the one-day tribute to G. Balandier (13 October 2000), « L'anthropologie à l'épreuve du temps (2-2002) », *Recherches Sociologiques,* cf. Jean Pierre Dozon's work on « L'histoire de l'africanisme ».
2. Pierre Clastres, 1974, *La société contre l'Etat,* Paris : Editions de Minuit , Collection « Critique ».
3. Weber (1968) – cited in Halisi *et al.* (1998).
4. Scholte (1996), Tooze (1997) – cited in Pettman (1999).
5. McEwan (2001), cited in Nyamu-Musembi (2007).
6. Gauthier, Florence, 2005-2010, « Très brève histoire de la révolution française, révolution des droits de l'homme et du citoyen », (Synthèses), Université Paris VII, Denis Diderot. Published online 2 December 2005.
7. It is Zillah Eisenstein who posed the question: 'what are the other centres of feminism other than the Western ones ? Is there a *polyversal* centre – a universal idea with local expressions?', Obioma Nnameka's paper, op. cit.
8. Social Transformation Including Woman of Africa
9. According to Gauthier (2005); 'The second generation of planters was largely mixed as well as the following ones until competition starts between Creole settlers (born in the colonies) and the new settlers who came for the sake of fortune. The latter thought it would be possible to dispossess the coloured settlers so as to take their property'. Op. cit. That is the historical context of alliance between sugar-planting slaves and Creole settlers who championed their cause and defended it at the Paris

Assembly, thus foreshadowing the cosmopolitan. It was the Creole settlers who went to Paris in support of the Montagne's theses. In this, they played the role of cosmopolitan patriots prematurely.

10. Peter Dwyer, *Understanding Social Citizenship: Themes and Perspectives for Policy and Practice*, The Policy Press and the Social Policy Association, 2004, reprinted 2008, University of Bristol.

11. F. Twine, 1994, *Citizenship and social rights: The interdependence of self and society*, London: Sage Publications.

12. Mogniss, H. Abdallah, « La Marche pour l'Egalité », *Plein Droit*, n° 55, 2002 « Parcours, filières et trajectoires »

13. In 1983, one hundred thousand people, mainly youth of both sexes, either descendants of or current immigrants from countries formally colonised by France (including Algeria and Tunisia, Senegal, Côte d'Ivoire, etc.) marched from Marseille to Paris demanding the right of citizenship. By the scale and nature of its demands, the march is a reminder of the marches launched by Mahatma Ghandi and Martin Luther King.

14. These were the coloured masters (of mixed race) born of black women and white men, who offered a priceless support for the Montagne, in 1791-1793, during the French Revolution in order to impose the measures for citizenship in the Assembly (Constituante).

15. In M. Gaëlle's exposé, we read: In France, foreign women are subject to a dual marginalisation, first, as foreigners and then as women. Law provisions are still marked by social discrimination, the dispersion of statutes and the suspicion regarding foreigners. All this encourages the precariousness of all foreigners and the ongoing condition of oppression of immigrant women. M. de Gaëlle, for *Mix-Cité* (1998) (Parts 1/2 de 'La Double Oppression des Femmes Immigrées').

16. Ekpootu: 'The Body as a Tool: Female Youth in Nigeria Negotiating the New Global Order'.

17. Hezron Ndunde Otieno: '*Genge* videos? Struggle over gender and citizenship in Kenya'.

18. Sabastiano Rwengabo, 'Uganda's Gendered Politics since 1995: Reconstituting the Public Sphere to Enhance the Presence and Participation of Women (Politique de genre de l'Ouganda depuis 1995 : Reconstitution de la sphère publique pour améliorer la présence et la participation des femmes).

19. Sharon Groenmeyer: 'Rethinking citizenship in a global age: A South African approach towards gender equality in intimate relationships' (Repenser la citoyenneté à l'ère de la mondialisation : Approche sud-africaine de l'égalité des sexes dans les relations intimes).

20. Fonkwe Tamonkeng Prudentia : 'The Acquisition of New Citizenship in the Global Village through the Emerging Female Chiefship in Bangwa land, Cameroon

(L'acquisition d'une nouvelle citoyenneté dans le village planétaire à travers la chefferie féminine émergeante à Bangwa, au Cameroun)'.

21. Mustapha Ziky: 'Citoyenneté et Développement Humain au Maroc face aux différentes formes d'exclusion: une approche genre'.

22. Ong'wen Okuro: 'Globalization and the Gender Question: The Role of the CEDAW in Enhancing Women's' Experience of Citizenship in Kenya'.

23. Felix Kiruthu: 'Masculinities, Femininities and Citizen Identities in a Global Era: The case study of Kiambu District in Kenya, 1980-2007'.

24. Ivan Marowa: 'Masculinity, Citizen Mobility and Globalisation: Rethinking Gender in terms of Masculinity and Femininity in the 21st century with reference to Zimbabwe'.

25. Ramola Ramtohul: 'Globalisation and Gendered Citizenship: The Mauritian Scenario (Mondialisation et citoyenneté sexuée : le scénario de Maurice)'.

26. Mfon Ekpootu: 'The Body as a Tool: Female Youths in Nigeria Negotiating the New Global Order'.

27. Ivan Marowa : 'Masculinity, Citizen Mobility and Globalisation: Rethinking Gender in Terms of Masculinity and Femininity in the 21st century with Reference to Zimbabwe'.

28. 'The Plight of Women in Kisumu District after the December 2007 Kenyan General Elections: An Ethnic Perspective.'

References

Abdallah, Mogniss H., 2002, La Marche pour l'Egalité, *Plein Droit*, n° 55, «Parcours, filières et trajectoires».

Adejumobi, S., 2005, 'Identity, Citizenship and Conflict: The African Experience', in Fawole, Alade W. and Ukeje, C. eds, *The Crisis of the State and Regionalism in West Africa: Identity, Citizenship and Conflict*, Dakar: CODESRIA.

Afshar, H. and Dennis, C., eds, 1992, *Women and Structural Adjustment Policies in the Third World*, London: Macmillan.

Bose, S. and Jalal, A., 1998, *Modern South Asia: History, Culture, Political Economy*, London: Routledge.

Clastres, P., 1974, *La Société contre l'Etat*. Paris: Editions de Minuit, Collection «Critique».

Colloque, 2004, '*Citoyen et Citoyenneté sous la Révolution française*', organisé par le Musée de la Révolution française et la Société des études robespierristes, 24-25 septembre 2004, Vizille, Isère, France. L'annonce du colloque a été publiée dans un message électronique le 16 juin 2004 par Nathalie Petiteau.

Connell, R., 2007, 'Men, Masculinity Research and Gender Justice', in I. Lenz, C. Ullrich and B. Fersch eds., *Gender Orders Unbound? Globalisation, Restructuring and Reciprocity*, Leverkusen: Barbara Budrich Publishers.

Connell, R.W., 1987, *Gender and Power*, Cambridge: Polity Press.

de Gaëlle, M., 1998, *Pour Mix-Cité* (Partie 1/2 de 'La Double Oppression des Femmes Immigrées').

Dobrowolsky, A. and Tastsoglou, E., 2006, 'Crossing Boundaries and Making Connections', in E. Tastsoglou and A. Dobrowolsky (eds.) *Women, Migration and Citizenship: Making Local, National and Transnational Connections*, Farnham: Ashgate.

Dorzon, J.P., 2002, «L'histoire de l'africanisme », « L'anthropologie à l'épreuve du temps », *Recherches Sociologiques*, (2002, 2), « Actes de la journée d'hommage à G. Balandier » (13 octobre 2000), Paris.

Dwyer, P., 2004, *Understanding Social Citizenship: Themes and Perspectives for Policy and Practice*, Bristol: The Policy Press and the Social Policy Association.

Ekeh, P., 1978, 'Colonialism and the Development of Citizenship in Africa: A Study in Ideologies of Legitimation', in Odite, O., ed., *Themes in African Social and Political Thought*, Enugu: Fourth Dimension Publishers.

Elson, D., ed, *Male Bias in the Development Process*, Manchester: Manchester University Press.

Enloe, C., 1989, *Bananas, Beaches, and Bases: Making Feminist Sense of International Relations*, Berkeley: University of California Press.

Ferguson, J., 1990, *The Anti-Politics Machine: 'Development', Depoliticization and Bureaucratic Power in Lesotho*, Cambridge: Cambridge University Press.

Ferguson, J., 1999, *Expectations of Modernity: Myths and Meanings of Urban Life on the Zambian Copperbelt*, Berkeley: University of California Press.

Ferree, M. M., 2006, 'Globalization and Feminism: Opportunities and Obstacles for Activism in the Global Arena', in Ferree, M. M. and Trip, A. M., eds, *Global Feminism: Transnational Women's Activism, Organizing, and Human Rights*, New York and London: New York University Press.

Fraser, N. and Gordon, L., 1994, 'Civil Citizenship Against Social Citizenship?', in Van Steenbergen, B., ed, *The Condition of Citizenship*, Thousand Oaks and New Delhi: Sage.

Gans, J. Sage, 2005, Citizenship in the Context of Globalization, Immigration Policy Working Paper 1, Udall Center for Studies in Public Policy, University of Arizona, (http://udallcenter.arizona.edu/programs/immigration/publications/Citizenship%20and%Globalization.pdf).

Gauthier, F., 2005 «*Très brève histoire de la révolution française, révolution des droits de l'homme et du citoyen*», (Synthèses), Université Paris VII, Denis Diderot. Mis en ligne le 2 décembre 2005.

Gouws, A., ed, *(Un)Thinking Citizenship: Feminist Debates in Contemporary South Africa,* Farnham: Ashgate.

Gouws, A., 2010, *A Gender Perspective on Citizenship in Africa,* http://africanarguments. org/2010/02/a-gender-perspective-on-citizenship-in-afric/

Halisi, C.R.D., Kaiser, P. J. and Ndegwa, S.N., 1998, 'Guest Editors' Introduction: The Multiple Meanings of Citizenship – Rights, Identity, and Social Justice in Africa', *Africa Today,* 45: 337-350.

Held, D., 1995, *Democracy and the Global Order – From the Modern State to Cosmopolitan Governance,* London: Polity Press.

Held, D., 1999, 'The Transformation of Political Community: Rethinking Democracy in the Context of Globalization', in Shapiro, I. and Hacker-Cordon, C., eds, *Democracy's Edges,* Cambridge: Cambridge University Press.

Hooper, C., 2000, 'Masculinities in Transition: The Case of Globalization', in Marchand, M. H. and Runyan, A. S., eds, *Gender and Global Restructuring: Sightings, Sites and Resistances,* London and New York: Routledge.

Isin, E. F. and Wood, P., 1999, *Citizenship and Identity,* London: Sage Publications.

Isin, E. F. and Turner, B.S., 2007, 'Investigating Citizenship: An Agenda for Citizenship Studies', *Citizenship Studies* 11(1): 5-17.

Kabeer, N., 2006, 'Citizenship, Affiliation and Exclusion: Perspectives from the South', *IDS Bulletin,* Vol. 37, No. 4, pp. 91-101.

Kimmel, M.S., 2001, 'Global Masculinities: Restoration and Resistance', in Pease, B. and Pringle, K. eds, *A Man's World? Changing Men's Practices in a Globalized World,* London and New York: Zed Books.

Kymlicka, W., 1995, *Multicultural Citizenship: A Liberal Theory of Minority Rights,* Oxford: Oxford University Press.

Kymlicka, W., 2001, *Politics in the Vernacular: Nationalism, Multiculturalism and Citizenship,* Oxford: Oxford University Press.

Lenz, I., Ullrich, C. and Fersch, B., 2007, 'Gender Orders Unbound: Globalisation, Restructuring and Reciprocity -- Introduction', in Lenz, I., Ullrich, C. and Fersch, B., eds, *Gender Orders Unbound? Globalisation, Restructuring and Reciprocity,* Leverkusen: Barbara Budrich Publishers.

Lister, R., 2003, *Citizenship: Feminist Perspectives,* 2nd ed., New York: New York University Press.

Mamdani, M., 1996, *Citizen and Subject: Contemporary Africa and the Legacy of Late Colonialism,* Cape Town: David Philip.

Mamdani, M., ed., 2000, *Beyond Rights Talk and Culture Talk,* Cape Town: David Philip.

Manning, J. C., 2009, *The Last Pharaohs, Egypt Under the Ptolemies,* 305-50, B.C.

Marchand, M.H. and Runyan, A.S., 2000, 'Introduction. Feminist Sightings of Global Restructuring: Conceptualisations and Reconceptualisations', in Marchand, M.H. and Runyan, A. S., eds, *Gender and Global Restructuring: Sightings, Sites and Resistances,* London and New York: Routledge.

Molyneux, M., 2007, 'Refiguring Citizenship: Research Perspectives on Gender Justice in the Latin American and Caribbean Region', in Mukhopadhay, M. and Singh, N., eds, *Gender Justice, Citizenship and Development.* Ottawa: IDRC.

Moore, D.S., 2005, *Suffering for Territory: Race, Place and Power in Zimbabwe,* Durham: Duke University Press.

Nnaemeka, O., 2009, «Autres Féminismes: quand la femme africaine repousse les limites de la pensée et de l'action féministes», USA : Indiana University..

Nyamnjoh, F.B., 2007, 'From Bounded to Flexible Citizenship: Lessons from Africa', *Citizenship Studies* 11(1): 73-82.

Peterson, V.S. and Runyan, A.S., 1999, *Global Gender Issues.* 2nd ed. Boulder: Westview Press.

Pettman, J.J., 1996, *Worlding Women: A Feminist International Politics,* London: Routledge.

Pettman, J.J., 1999, 'Globalisation and the Gendered Politics of Citizenship', in Yuval-Davis, N. and Werbner, P., eds, *Women, Citizenship and Difference,* London and New York: Zed Books.

Rose, N., 1996, 'Refiguring the Territory of Government', *Economy and Society,* No. 25, pp. 327-356.

Shklar, J., 1991, 'The Liberalism of Fear', in N. Rosenblum ed., *Liberalism and Moral Life,* Cambridge: Harvard University Press.

Soysal, Y., 1994, *Limits of Citizenship*, Chicago: University of Chicago Press.

Squires, J., 1999, *Gender in Political Theory,* Cambridge: Polity Press.

Sweetman, C., 2003, 'Editorial', *Gender and Development,* vol. 11, No. 3, pp 2-7.

Tilly, C., 1996, 'Citizenship, Identity and Social History', in C. Tilly (ed.), 'Citizenship, Identity and Social History', *International Review of Social History,* Supplement 3, Cambridge: Cambridge University Press.

Twine, F., 1994, *Citizenship and Social Rights: The Interdependence of Self and Society,* London: Sage Publications.

Urry, J., 1999, 'Globalization and Citizenship', *Journal of World-Systems Research,* 5(2): 311-324.

Walby, S., 1997, *Gender Transformations,* London and New York: Routledge.

1

Citoyenneté, démocratie et genre : le principe féminin comme alternative d'ensemble à la société actuelle[1]

Laroussi Amri

Démocratie et citoyenneté, les deux modèles historiques

Nous faisons la différence entre les deux termes, démocratie et citoyenneté, même s'ils constituent l'un pour l'autre un vase communicant. Nous citerons le mot démocratie dans le sens de *système politique historiquement daté et localisé.*[2] Le système politique athénien, de l'époque antique, tout comme le système politique européen, de l'époque moderne, sont des produits historiques. Quant à la citoyenneté, elle consiste en l'exercice des droits civiques et politiques. La citoyenneté suppose l'égalité devant la loi. Elle suppose aussi, de la part de l'individu, un ensemble de devoirs et de responsabilités, en contrepartie des droits dont il jouit dans la cité. Nous focaliserons notre intérêt, dans cette communication, plutôt sur le concept de démocratie.

Les sens historiques de la démocratie

La démocratie comme exclusion des femmes et des étrangers

La démocratie athénienne supposait que tous les citoyens sont égaux devant la loi. Toutefois tous les membres de la société ne sont pas des citoyens. Ne sont citoyens que ceux qui sont inscrits sur les registres du Dème (genre de commune qui est en même temps l'association des citoyens). Sont exclues d'inscription sur le registre les femmes. Le traité de Maastricht (Dalloz 1995:102), instituant l'Union Européenne, accorde la qualité de citoyen à toute personne ayant la nationalité d'un Etat Membre dans l'Union. Cette nationalité n'est accordée que selon des critères qui mettent hors de citoyenneté les étrangers.

De ces deux modèles se dégagent deux principes qui définissent historiquement la citoyenneté : le premier principe consiste en l'établissement d'un territoire de souveraineté pour une catégorie de personnes, le second principe consiste en une opération d'exclusion d'une catégorie de personnes « indésirables », entre autres au nom de cette souveraineté. De la démocratie athénienne à la démocratie européenne deux catégories de personnes ont été considérées indésirables : les femmes et les étrangers. Première constatation.[3]

La démocratie instaure la citoyenneté dans le cadre de l'ère de l'individu

La deuxième constatation consiste à relever le caractère individuel des attributs octroyés par la citoyenneté, au moment où la démocratie est annoncée comme un système. Le tout est conçu pour que le système soit au service de l'individu. Ce dernier s'avère ainsi la pierre angulaire du système démocratique. Tout se passe comme si la démocratie est ce qui, sur le plan collectif (niveau holiste), correspond à ce qui devrait être fait pour satisfaire la catégorie « individu » (niveau individualiste et atomisé). De cela on peut conclure que la démocratie et la citoyenneté sont deux pièces d'un même ensemble et que l'un ne peut pas fonctionner sans l'autre. L'une sied à l'autre. Cet aspect d'emboîtement des deux concepts, ainsi que les aspects complémentaires qui régissent leurs relations, est important à relever. Notons en outre que c'est plutôt le système qui est au service de l'individu que l'inverse.

C'est par conséquent dans cet espace sémantique circonscrit que nous utiliserons tout au long de cet article le sens de citoyenneté et le sens de démocratie. Dès qu'on sort de cette aire sémantique circonscrite, on le mentionnera.

Citoyenneté, démocratie et positivisme

Si l'on peut considérer la démocratie et la citoyenneté athénienne et la démocratie et la citoyenneté européenne comme les deux stations historiques les plus visibles situées aux deux pôles historiques (Grèce Antique et Europe des Temps Modernes), on peut considérer que la trajectoire parcourue entre ces deux pôles est jalonnée des victoires du positivisme dans les domaines du droit, des lettres, des humanités et des sciences sociales.

Le début des Temps Modernes (XVIe siècle) a correspondu en Europe à une revivification des humanités de l'âge antique. Depuis, les aspects qui valorisent *l'argument*, relevant de la sphère réflexive et parfois spéculative, ont pris le dessus sur les aspects qui valorisent *l'introspection et la compréhension* des actions des hommes en société. L'argument est plus fort, le raisonnement plus rigoureux, la logique irréprochable, l'administration de la preuve implacable, dès que le discours quitte l'interprétation subjective. De cette sorte, on est sûr d'emporter la conviction et, s'il le faut, l'adhésion réfléchie. Car cette seule marche et démarche de l'esprit est considérée comme impartiale. C'est même le gage de l'objectivité, seule catégorie qualifiée de scientifique : elle se prémunit contre les passions et toute forme d'incursion des sentiments dans l'émission du jugement. L'objectivité est ainsi érigée en point focal du raisonnement sain et juste. L'objectivité ne peut être atteinte que par la considération de ce qui est peut-être prouvé, c'est-à-dire *reconnu comme* un phénomène à marche forcée, à avènement inéluctable, prouvé (c'est-à-dire se fondant sur des arguments) par l'observateur extérieur. Ce caractère d'extériorité garantit plus que tout autre les conditions de l'objectivité. C'est même une condition de la neutralité scientifique.[4] La vérité d'un phénomène ou d'une action, par conséquent, n'est atteinte qu'en l'abordant dans le caractère tangible et extérieur dans lequel il (ou elle) se manifeste. L'organe spécialiste de l'argumentation est, bien entendu, selon la connaissance en vigueur à ces époques et même aux époques modernes, la Raison.

Ce qu'on peut, en tout cas, retenir c'est que l'*extériorité* des phénomènes, y compris humains, a pris le dessus sur leur « intériorité ». Ce dernier terme est même impropre pour l'époque considérée et on peut reprocher à cette façon de voir une sorte d'anachronisme, tellement la mentalité scientifique était totalement consacrée à faire triompher l'âge de la raison et de l'objectivité (Renaissance et Temps Modernes) sur l'âge antérieur, celui des passions (en grande partie religieuses) et de la subjectivité (plusieurs textes du Moyen âge européen illustrent cela, on peut citer à titre indicatif l'exemple de textes comme « La dent d'or » de Fontenelle, les textes des encyclopédistes comme Diderot, pour ne citer que le plus connu. On peut se référer aux textes dont le contenu est focalisé sur les critiques à l'endroit des préjugés, en tant que phénomènes subjectifs, etc.).

Il n'est point possible, dans le cadre de cette communication, circonscrite, dans le temps et l'occasion, de faire l'exposé et le bilan de ces assertions sur la Renaissance européenne du XVIe siècle et son prolongement dans les siècles ultérieurs, passant par le siècle des Lumières, et son ancrage dans ce parcours scientifique, profondément inscrit dans le sillage de ce qui deviendra par la suite, en plus du paradigme de l'*enlightment*, le paradigme *positiviste*. C'est à ce dernier qu'on s'intéresse ici. Pour nous limiter à l'espace français, en tant qu'illustration rapide et succincte, on peut revenir à Descartes, dont le rationalisme tente de définir méthodiquement les techniques et les procédés à suivre pour asseoir la preuve. On peut revenir à Voltaire pour montrer les prolongements de l'exercice de la Raison pour faire reculer l'intolérance qui se fonde sur les passions religieuses. La tolérance consistant en un comportement à l'égard de l'autre à prouver dans le caractère patent des relations sociales de voisinage, de proximité et de traitement mutuel des questions communes dans l'espace de la cité. En consécration ultime de ce processus, Montesquieu a mis au point la séparation des pouvoirs comme une garantie qui préserve les droits des citoyens et assure au système la stabilité et la continuité.

Malgré ses aspects « progressistes » (dirait Marx), le positivisme peut être soumis à la technique de l'évaluation dont l'incarnation formalisée consiste en un bilan. Tout bilan comporte deux colonnes : une pour les choses positives, la deuxième pour les choses négatives (ou rentrées et sorties). On verra dans une première colonne les éléments qui favorisent une lecture progressiste du positivisme, dans l'autre colonne on s'apercevra qu'il y a des aspects moins lumineux. Dans ce bilan critique du positivisme, il ne s'agira pas d'ignorer les aspects émancipatoires de la Raison à l'époque décrite. Il faut reconnaître que ce mouvement de célébration intellectuelle des mérites de la Raison est « bénéfique », surtout quand on voit les atrocités des âges antérieurs (prédominance des mythes et des préjugés, domination de l'Eglise comme consécration institutionnelle et historique des paradigmes métaphysiques, de nature théologique, hagiologique, avec ce que cela suppose comme gouvernement de Dieu dont le roi est le représentant sur terre, régissant les régimes politiques; alors, on comprend, certes, le caractère profondément « progressiste » de l'avènement de l'âge de la Raison et de l'objectivité qui a fait reculer l'âge des mythes et des légendes, mais aussi l'âge des préjugés et de la subjectivité.

Les moments les plus forts du positivisme sont : la raison, les techniques de la preuve, le primat des caractères observables de l'extérieur de tout phénomène considéré, la prééminence de la reconnaissance sociale d'un phénomène indépendamment de ses gestations internes, le résultat étant le critère ultime du jugement et qu'on exprime aujourd'hui dans le monde des affaires, des compétitions, scolaires et sportives, des actions collectives orientées et dirigées, sous l'expression : l'obligation de résultat. C'est là l'avènement de l'ère de l'efficacité sous la houlette de la Raison, avec ses prolongements dans l'action sociale : le pragmatisme.

C'est dans ce cadre paradigmatique d'ensemble qualifié de profondément positiviste que la notion de citoyenneté et son corollaire, la démocratie, ont connu leurs gestations historiques, sur le plan heuristique.

Un bilan critique et exhaustif du positivisme, n'ignorant pas les aspects négatifs, prospecterait deux voies de « dérapages » incarnées dans ces deux dimensions du positivisme : celle de sa prégnance jusqu'à aujourd'hui dans la genèse et le développement du capitalisme, celle de son impact sur l'évolution des sciences humaines et sociales, outre les sciences dures. Nous n'allons pas nous étendre sur ces deux dimensions (épistémologiques et sociologiques) : ce sont des critiques qu'on pourrait lui adresser et que le lecteur avisé pourrait aisément entrevoir à travers ces lignes.[5] Cependant nous dirons un mot sur son effet sur les sciences sociales et humaines.

Impact du positivisme sur les sciences sociales et humaines

En effet, le positivisme a atteint le noyau dur des sciences sociales. Pour nos illustrations et nos exemples, restons dans la même aire : la France. L'avènement des thèses durkheimiennes sur la définition des faits sociaux que le sociologue, en tant qu'homme de science, doit adopter, insiste sur des caractères précis, tel que leur caractère contraignant, indépendant de la volonté des individus, outre le caractère tangible, mais aussi – trait important-et ce qui nous intéresse au plus haut point dans notre exposé : leur caractère d'*extériorité*.[6] On peut prolonger davantage l'exposé des principaux caractères du positivisme et leur insertion dans la dynamique conceptuelle des diverses disciplines des sciences sociales, telles que le droit social, la sociologie, les sciences politiques, et même en sciences humaines : la philosophie, l'histoire et la psychologie, notamment.

C'est dans ces spécificités de la connaissance qui a dominé l'époque des Temps Modernes, en prolongement de l'époque des Antiquités, que les termes de démocratie et de citoyenneté sont à considérer, c'est-à-dire dans leurs gestations localisées et datées, autrement dit relatives à des époques historiques bien déterminées.

La critique du positivisme a été faite. Nous n'allons pas nous étendre la dessus dans le cadre de cette communication. L'approfondissement de la critique du positivisme est à faire. Les indications de base qui nous permettent, à partir des acquis des sciences sociales aujourd'hui, d'approfondir le bilan du positivisme (aspects positifs et aspects négatifs, pour les pays du Sud, aire d'alternatives encore possibles à notre avis) sont à chercher en partie dans la phénoménologie, en tant que science humaine, dont l'origine est philosophique, depuis Edmund Husserl, mais aussi dans son prolongement en sciences sociales, (avec Weber, outre les tenants des approches intéractionnistes, A. Schultz, G.H. Mead, Peter Berger et Thomas Luckmann,[7] etc.). Elle est à chercher en outre et particulièrement dans les courants de pensée qui traversent aujourd'hui les recherches sociales (l'Ecole de Francfort et ce qu'elle représente dans son histoire, dette au marxisme et aux approches critiques qui l'ont conforté et accompagné, Samir Amin, Gunder Franck, Celso Furtado, Rodolfo Stavenhagen, Anouar Abdelmalek, etc., auxquels il faudra ajouter dans le même prolongement les théoriciens de l'autogestion de l'après Deuxième Guerre mondiale, ainsi que les approches du constructivisme, tel que Bourdieu les a initiées, etc., outre l'école française et francophone du Don et ses prolongements en sciences politiques, en sociologie, en anthropologie, notamment).

D'autres courants de pensée pourront être ajoutés en fonction des thèmes particuliers à traiter. Gardons-nous de considérer éclectique cette façon de regrouper les acquis des sciences humaines et sociales, arguant que l'on ne peut pas mettre ensemble les conceptions issues de l'approche compréhensive et les conceptions matérialistes dialectiques de l'histoire, ni les approches de la dépendance avec les approches du Don. Nous considérons que les acquis des sciences humaines et sociales transcendent les contradictions, si elles existent, qui peuvent opposer les différentes écoles de pensée à une époque donnée.

Genre et société, l'alternative

Pays du Sud, pays d'alternatives

Nous considérons que les pays du Sud, en prenant appui sur les acquis théoriques obtenus de la critique approfondie du positivisme,[8] peuvent initier une autre approche des phénomènes classés habituellement sous le vocable de « démocratie » ou de « citoyenneté ».

Ceci a une entrée. Celle-ci est constituée d'une approche « genre » apprivoisée dans ses caractères productifs d'alternatives. C'est la condition *sine qua non*. En effet, c'est à partir d'une lecture pertinente des rapports des femmes à la société qu'on peut élaborer une réflexion sur les voies offertes et possibles aux sociétés futures, dans le sens de l'émancipation.[9]

Femmes et alternatives

La proposition de « la femme comme réservoir d'alternatives », fondements théoriques et choix méthodologiques (cas pertinent d'illustration)

Ce binôme associant les femmes aux alternatives dans un lien organique est possible à maintenir. D'abord il y a un fondement théorique à cela auquel le marxisme a énormément contribué. Il consiste en cette recherche de la matrice (la femme) qui condense en son sein l'exploitation, la domination, (les deux principaux caractères s'opérant sur le terrain concret des rapports des hommes entre eux), la mystification. Ce sont là *les trois caractères distinctifs de l'aliénation* que l'on pourra dépoussiérer, à bon escient, dans la littérature marxiste, pour l'essentiel. Quel serait le terrain de prédilection pour tester toute cette armature conceptuelle acquise tout au long des deux derniers siècles ?

Nous croyons que le fondement théorique, sur lequel se pose cette armature conceptuelle, a sa terre d'élection dans les pays du Sud. Notamment mais non exclusivement. C'est dans les milieux où se déploie *le travail*, où s'achète et se vend la force de travail, qu'on pourrait, le mieux, tester les composants de cette armature conceptuelle. Le travail, en tant que catégorie, demeure encore le meilleur paramètre qui permet de jauger l'injustice sociale : que les deux pôles de la contradiction vécue dans le travail soient des individus (un homme et une femme), ou des collectivités (le groupe des travailleurs face au groupe des dominants : capitalistes, sous des appellations diverses soient –ils (patrons, superviseurs, gestionnaires, contrôleurs, propriétaires des supports stratégiques de la sécurité du travail) : c'est là un parti pris scientifique que nous assumons.

Le deuxième choix, cette fois-ci à portée essentiellement méthodologique, porte sur le lien entre deux échelles : micro et macro. La bonne posture de réflexion sur le genre, croyons-nous, est de lier les deux échelles dans une relation pertinente, en *connectant le micro*, (i.e. la famille, les communautés réduites, les groupes restreints) au *niveau macro* (c'est-à-dire le niveau global de la société). Le mérite de cette posture tient au fait qu'elle nous permet de mettre en exergue les questions du pouvoir et de la morale, tant au niveau de l'individu et du groupe restreint, tel que la famille (micro) qu'au niveau de la société globale (macro).

Le pouvoir est à appréhender tout à la fois dans sa dimension laudative, c'est-à-dire un lieu qui suppose un consensus social dont la finalité est l'organisation sociale, et dans sa dimension péjorative, comme exercice de la violence, comme intervention dans les rapports de force. La morale est à appréhender ici dans sa cristallisation sociale dans un contrat régi par les principes des droits et responsabilités de l'homme et de la femme.

Le pouvoir et la morale sont les deux questions que l'on est censé jauger au niveau micro (la famille ou groupe restreint) et macro (la société globale), comme deux niveaux connectés et guère séparés. Grâce à cette saisie à double échelle, on peut, de façon précise, départager les rôles à l'intérieur de la famille et, partant, au sein de la société entre, d'un côté, les hommes, se chargeant principalement des tâches productives, et, de l'autre, les femmes, se chargeant principalement des tâches reproductives (dans le sens étendu du mot). C'est là le mérite des exemples, des illustrations ou des cas situés à un niveau micro et qui sont révélateurs des traits qui se situent au niveau macro de la société.

Quel est cet exemple qui cristallise cette fonction de témoin révélateur pour un chercheur en sciences sociales ? Cet exemple est, à notre avis, l'exploitation agricole familiale, cadre désigné d'évolution des paysannes, couche sociale qui incarne le mieux, dans la stricte sphère de la production des richesses matérielles, foncièrement économiques et où la catégorie « travail » joue un rôle capital, la misère des femmes plus que toute autre couche sociale, en tout cas plus que les femmes citadines.[10] Dans les pays du Sud, le travail des femmes dans les exploitations agricoles familiales illustre de façon éclatante les profondeurs et les dimensions du rapport d'injustice sociale : la femme y est *exploitée, dominée* et *mystifiée*, trois ingrédients de l'aliénation. Ce rapport d'injustice sociale met en présence un rapport de travail entre les deux catégories de sexes, les femmes et les hommes.

C'est pourquoi les exploitations familiales sont aujourd'hui un cadre concret de réflexion sur les alternatives éventuelles (sous forme de tendances ou de modèles) qui peuvent s'offrir à nous dans nos recherches sur « l'utopie réalisable ».[11]

Où réside la pertinence des exploitations agricoles familiales ? Elle réside dans le fait que dans ces exploitations agricoles familiales, le rapport au patron est conjugué au rapport à l'époux (partenaire) ou au père (ascendant) et au frère (collatéral), tous mâles ; le tout se déroulant dans un cadre mystificateur, (car temporisateur des conflits), tout en étant un ferment de la socialité et de la socialisation : *la famille* dont on retiendra les fondements éminemment communautaires. Le patron est le *pater familias*, le chef de famille. Dans les recherches en sciences sociales, le patronat, en tant que catégorie conceptuelle, a souvent été appréhendé pour l'intérêt qu'il recèle dans l'identification éclatante et dans l'analyse des rapports d'exploitation. Le patriarcat, quant à lui, a été appréhendé dans les sciences sociales et humaines, pour l'intérêt qu'il recèle dans l'identification et l'analyse des rapports de domination.

On le voit, dans les exploitations familiales, le patronat (qui peut prendre des formes capitalistes déguisées), y compris au sein de la famille, est conjugué au *patriarcat*. Le concept « exploitation » a été abondamment analysé, dont on peut retenir, pour l'essentiel, l'approche marxiste (malgré certaines limites qu'il est inutile de relever ici). Le concept de patriarcat a été analysé depuis l'avènement de la société primitive. Radcliffe Brown, dans *Structure et fonction dans la société primitive,* définit la société patriarcale comme suit :

On peut appeler patriarcale une société dans laquelle la descendance est patrili-
néaire (les enfants appartiennent au groupe du père), où le mariage est patrilocal
(l'épouse vient habiter dans le groupe local du mari), où l'héritage des biens et la
succession dans le rang social se font selon la lignée masculine et où l'autorité sur
les membres de la famille est entre les mains du père ou de ses parents (Radcliffe
Brown 1924, 1968).

Le patriarcat, on ne perdra rien à l'expliciter davantage, continue d'occuper une
place de choix dans la compréhension des phénomènes récents liés aux problèmes
du genre (pour rester dans l'actualité de la recherche en sciences sociales). On
peut commencer à le définir à partir de ses éléments fondateurs.[12]

En effet, il est constitué des trois noyaux d'inégalité originels, et qui sont
tous, notons-le, des *rapports* : celui des mâles aux femelles, celui des ascendants
aux descendants, celui des plus âgés aux moins âgés. Nous avons là les trois
variables essentielles du patriarcat, présentées anthropologiquement, dont la
variable sexuelle est aujourd'hui, historiquement, grâce aux découvertes de
l'approche genre, la plus déterminante. Le patriarcat et le patronat sont les
deux piliers fondamentaux de l'exploitation croisée à la domination.

L'alternative

Est alternative toute démarche qui inscrit dans un nouvel aménagement, en vue
de le transformer, *le cadre des rapports* relevant au moins des deux principaux
thèmes de l'aliénation : l'exploitation et la domination. Aujourd'hui, relève de
l'alternative toute modification de fond, de type structurel et institutionnel,
sur le plan tout à la fois tangible (production économique, infrastructures,
techniques, organisation du travail, accès au mode de distribution de la
production et de la richesse, etc., mais aussi niveaux divers relevant de la
reproduction du groupe) et symbolique (production de sens lié à ces types
de production matérielle, pour la reproduction du groupe, à quelque échelle
qu'il se situe, international, national, régional, local), touchant les rapports au
patronat et au patriarcat.

Pour arriver à poser la problématique de cette façon, les intellectuels ont
besoin de se débarrasser de deux niveaux d'opacité mentale. L'implication du
patriarcat sous cette forme dans la problématique du changement montre la
place centrale qu'occupent les femmes dans la recherche des pistes alternatives
aux conditions aliénantes de la société actuelle.

Jusqu'à maintenant, les écrits portant sur l'utopie salutaire et sur les pistes
alternatives ont privilégié le volet patronat et son cadre, à savoir le capitalisme et
ses contradictions historiques connues, pour l'essentiel, d'après la périodisation

encore globalement admise, même si elle demande à être revisitée, depuis le XVIe siècle jusqu'à nos jours. C'est l'occultation des aspects déterminants des rapports de patriarcat qui a aliéné à son tour la recherche des voies passantes du changement social. C'est un premier niveau de l'opacité mentale des intellectuels.

En plus de l'occultation de cet aspect, relevons, comme deuxième niveau d'opacité mentale des intellectuels et des chercheurs d'alternatives, l'absence d'appréhension judicieuse du croisement, fort pertinent pour la compréhension, entre capitalisme et patriarcat, entre exploitation et domination, dont la variable sexuelle est fondamentale, comme étant la plus importante des variables classiques du patriarcat, la variable déterminante, probablement. En saisissant la place capitale de la variable sexuelle dans le croisement, aujourd'hui prégnant dans les activités de production et de reproduction (dans le cadre capitaliste et patriarcal mentionné), on comprend le trésor d'alternatives que recèle l'approche genre apprivoisée dans ce sens. C'est ce que nous avons tenté de relever dans nos travaux de recherche en sciences sociales qui comprennent un volet empirique[13] et un volet théorique, intimement liés et dont on expose ici, à traits rapides, les aspects et les caractéristiques les plus distinctives.

Femmes et économie: les différents rapports à la production

L'approche « femmes » des problèmes sociaux que nous privilégions trouve un terrain de prédilection dans les questions économiques, car elle les privilégie, en tant que point de départ de l'analyse. Le niveau économique contribue fortement à situer de façon concrète la base première des enjeux, sur laquelle sont construites les stratégies et les objectifs réciproques des acteurs, hommes et femmes. En tant qu'instance, malgré son ancrage dans le registre positiviste, l'économique reste essentiel comme entrée pertinente pour étudier les rapports d'exploitation et de domination.

Les questions économiques se positionnent au carrefour des besoins de *vie décente* des gens. L'économie, cela veut dire la subsistance du groupe auquel on appartient, le premier de ces groupes étant la famille, considérée d'ailleurs, sociologiquement, comme un groupe primaire. L'économie, comme toutes les autres disciplines nourries de positivisme, opère dans le tangible et l'extérieur des faits sociaux qui sont aussi, pour l'essentiel, concernant la subsistance, des faits économiques : alimentation du groupe, entretien de ses besoins physiologiques, échange de biens avec l'entourage, qu'il relève des parents, des voisins ou des étrangers (des passagers ou des marchands réguliers avec lesquels on a établi ou conclu un marché ou une tradition d'échanges). Pour connaître à fond l'approche « femmes » en croisement avec l'économie, l'exemple le plus éloquent est, à l'état actuel de nos sociétés du Sud, celui de l'*exploitation familiale*. Dans les exploitations agricoles, les femmes (les paysannes) établissent des rapports divers autour des denrées qu'elles produisent et qui sont échangés avec les divers partenaires.

L'économie réside dans les activités qui se font au sein de l'exploitation familiale et qui permettent de dégager une production assurant autant que possible un niveau de richesse et de ressources (on dit aussi « revenu » et « output »), le minimum nécessaire à la vie du groupe familial (on dit « un niveau », car on aura souvent besoin de compléter le niveau atteint, généralement insuffisant, par un autre apport assuré par les membres de la famille qui émigrent en dehors de l'exploitation). Dans les conditions de production et de gestion de l'exploitation familiale, aujourd'hui le revenu provenant de la production que génère l'exploitation ne suffit pas à lui seul à assurer la vie décente du groupe, l'apport qui vient de l'émigration d'un ou de plusieurs membres de la famille pour chercher des subsides à l'extérieur de l'exploitation est vital. L'exploitation familiale n'assure plus aujourd'hui l'autonomie du groupe familial dans les conditions actuelles de la production de la richesse et de sa circulation/distribution, outre les perceptions et représentations des besoins de subsistance du groupe.[14]

Au sein de l'exploitation, le rapport de travail est un rapport de réciprocité entre membres de la famille fonctionnant ici comme une « communauté », terme qui mérite qu'on lui accorde aujourd'hui dans les sciences sociales un regain d'attention scientifique, car il est porteur de significations profondes pour une démarche traquant les alternatives.[15]

En dehors de l'exploitation, ce sont des rapports d'échange avec les parents quand ce n'est pas la réciprocité qui prévaut avec les voisins autant que possible pour réduire le coût du transport et du déplacement des biens à échanger, mais aussi avec les étrangers.[16] Cela étant dit, de nos jours, pour l'ensemble des sociétés de la planète, ce n'est pas la réciprocité qui semble de rigueur. C'est plutôt le marché qui régit de plus en plus le rapport d'échange avec les étrangers.

On remarque que nous utilisons une terminologie anthropologique : nous préférons en effet parler de « parents », de « voisins » et « d'étrangers » comme trois sommets d'échanges. Cela nous permet de rejoindre le registre des débats anthropologiques sur ces questions. Nous renvoyons, pour l'ancrage de cette terminologie, aux travaux de Karl Polanyi (*La Grande Transformation*) dans sa théorie substantiviste. Ces catégories de désignation, en tant que terminologie, permettent de placer le registre de l'analyse à un niveau universel et général assurant par là l'abstraction et la généralisation, conditions nécessaires pour prétendre proposer une appréhension à portée théorique des phénomènes. Karl Polanyi demeure à ce jour parmi les inspirateurs les plus pertinents des approches théoriques impliquant économie et anthropologie.

Au lendemain de la Deuxième Guerre mondiale, l'économiste et anthropologue qui a le mieux représenté, en tant que prolongement scientifique, ce mariage heureux entre économie et anthropologie proposé par Polanyi est, sans conteste, à notre avis, Serge Christopher Kolm. Ce dernier, à plusieurs égards, peut être considéré comme un des continuateurs de la pensée de Polanyi. Il a même proposé des apports inestimables qu'on peut situer aux croisements entre économie, anthropologie, sciences politiques et économie politique. Dans ce qui suit, nous dépasserons la stricte sphère économique, celle de la production et de l'échange (distribution), pour saisir la dimension qui a trait aux systèmes économiques.

Femmes et systèmes économiques

Parler des systèmes économiques relève de l'économie politique. Trois types d'économie politique ont égrené la vie collective en société. Les systèmes économiques éprouvés par l'histoire, selon Serge-Christopher Kolm, sont, à ce jour, au nombre de trois : « le Marché, ensemble d'échanges, le Plan, ensemble de transferts forcés, la Réciprocité, ensemble de dons » (Kolm1984:70). Nous empruntons à S-Ch Kolm ces catégories conceptuelles pour structurer nos propositions.

La femme, à notre avis, dans l'état actuel de nos sociétés, donne des gages probants pour être élue à devenir une artisane du troisième système, dont elle pourrait être l'axe central (Amri 2004:321). Les sociétés dont on parle ici, qui permettent ces amorces de réflexion sur les alternatives, sont celles qui sont demeurées essentiellement agraires, comme le sont aujourd'hui les sociétés du Sud dont les expériences d'industrialisation sont pour l'essentiel greffées, c'est-à-dire produites sous l'effet d'un rapport à l'extérieur et ne témoignent pas d'un développement issu d'une dynamique interne, inscrite dans les évolutions sociales, fruit d'une gestation endogène. Dans ces sociétés agraires, la femme est l'artisan, actuellement inconscient, d'un système économique fondé sur la gratuité généralisée, dont elle est le pivot.

Ce système est tiré, sur le plan empirique, de l'organisation des tâches (on remarquera que nous n'avons pas dit l'organisation du travail) au sein de l'exploitation familiale. Celle-ci procède d'un partage des fonctions et des tâches entre les membres de la famille selon non pas un principe de rémunération, mais selon un principe de don généralisé, dont l'aboutissement peut s'inscrire dans la production, comprise dans ses deux valeurs : d'usage et d'échange, comme il peut s'inscrire dans un rapport de reproduction. Les deux termes capitaux sont « production » et « reproduction », et c'est leur lien qui inscrit le sujet dans le domaine de la science politique.

Nous définissons ici la *science politique*, pour les besoins de nos propositions, comme étant le cadre d'analyse des rapports de pouvoir et de sa distribution au sein de la société. Cette affirmation théorique a son répondant sur le plan historique dans les différents systèmes politiques, dont la typologie est déterminée par le type de pouvoir qui la caractérise et les modes de distribution de ce pouvoir entre les différents acteurs sociaux.

Les femmes : de l'économie politique à la science politique

Des systèmes sociaux aux systèmes politiques

Généralement, la meilleure façon de soulever les problématiques de la science politique consiste en un retour à l'amont[17] qui est, à notre avis, l'économie politique autrement dit l'économie vue sous l'angle des systèmes et des rapports de pouvoir qu'elle implique dans les relations entre les acteurs, qu'ils soient des belligérants ou des partenaires, côté aval. Pour cela, nous allons essayer de voir comment se greffent sur le terrain de la production (économique, essentiellement), des positions de pouvoir (de type foncièrement politique) que chaque membre essaie de briguer au détriment du partenaire dans la relation en question, une relation ou, si l'on veut, *un rapport social* par excellence. Celui qui a brigué ce pouvoir extra muros dans l'expérience de la gente humaine en sociétés est l'homme en tant que genre.

Le rapport de l'homme à la femme dans l'exploitation familiale est fondé sur des mécanismes de pouvoir : la femme s'occupe de la plupart des tâches de production et de reproduction du groupe. L'homme s'occupe des tâches qui lui permettent d'accéder au prestige social, à la visibilité et à l'efficience sociale : activités qui mènent directement vers la sphère politique. Cette sphère politique est perçue et vécue par les individus mâles en tant qu'acquisition de titres et de titulatures, de façon formelle, ou en tant qu'acquisition d'un positionnement social favorable, de façon informelle : devenir le représentant de fait du groupe, le dépositaire de sa souveraineté, l'acteur qui négocie à l'extérieur du groupe, qui se charge de sa défense, mais aussi des tâches de visibilité sociale et d'octroi des identités individuelles et collectives du moment que l'homme se charge aussi de son inscription dans les registres administratifs (bulletins de naissance, cartes d'identité, attestation de la part du représentant local de l'Etat).

Répartition des tâches entre hommes et femmes dans une unité de travail (EAF)[18]

Dans ce qui suit, nous essayerons d'expliciter dans le détail, à des fins heuristiques, les trois catégories de tâches : tâches de production, tâches de reproduction et tâches de type politique et ce, à partir de notre enquête et étude (Amri 2003) parue en 2003. Ces tâches sont au nombre de trente trois et se répartissent comme suit :

Types	Tâches de production	Tâches de reproduction	Tâches politiques
Tâches	Labours, semailles, moisson, taille des arbres, travaux de construction, améliorations foncières, cueillette des olives, travail dans les champs (betterave à sucre), piquage des plantes, désherbage-binage, petit élevage, élevage gros bétail, nettoyage des étables, traite des vaches, transformation du lait, mise bas des animaux, travaux d'artisanat	Préparation des repas, toilette des enfants, vaisselle, lessive, cuisson du pain, préparation du thé, entretien du jardin potager, préparation annuelle de la *oula* (provisions diverses), nourriture et soins aux enfants et aux adultes, corvée d'eau, corvée de bois, chauffage de la maison, approvisionnement en produits alimentaires, vente des produits de la parcelle au marché	Tâches extérieures de représentation (contact avec les autorités locales, les citoyens, les institutions et l'administration), défense du groupe contre les menaces extérieures [19]

Les tâches de production

Sur le plan quantitatif, l'enquête nous a permis de montrer que les femmes se chargent de la plupart des tâches de production (9 tâches sur 17). Sur le plan qualitatif, les tâches qui sont laissées aux femmes sont *routinières* et d'*exécution*. Les chiffres suivants le prouvent : La cueillette des olives (51,42% contre 30, 96).[20] Le travail dans les champs de betterave à sucre (49,07% contre 34,62), le petit élevage (77,09% contre 9,38), l'élevage du gros bétail et son entretien (65,57% contre 19,41 pour le mari, le restant étant à la charge des enfants), le nettoyage des étables (69,41% contre 15,50%), la traite des vaches et des chèvres (84,9% contre 6,41), la transformation du lait (75,82% contre 12,2), la mise bas des animaux (47,62 contre 40,07). Les travaux d'artisanat (85,71% contre 0,44).

Si la femme est dominante dans 9 tâches de production sur un total de 17, l'examen de la structure de production au regard des tâches assumées en dominance par l'homme nous permet de dégager 8 tâches. L'homme est dominant plutôt dans les tâches de production suivantes (remarquons que ce sont *des tâches de conception et d'investissement,* sinon des tâches d'extérieur : les labours (74,5% contre 13,96 pour la femme), les semailles (70,33% contre 19,66), la moisson (54,8% contre 31,32), la taille des arbres (67,12% contre12,5), les travaux de construction (76,39% contre 12,70), les améliorations foncières (70,30% contre 12,22), le piquage des plantes (53,06% contre 35,07), le désherbage, le binage, etc. (47,82% contre 42,81).

Les différences de rôles entre les deux sexes

La première des différences dans les rôles entre les deux sexes, au niveau de la structure de production, *la femme se situe au niveau qualitatif et non au niveau quantitatif.* A ce dernier niveau, en effet, il y a égalité ou presque (léger déséquilibre : la femme assurant 9 tâches, l'homme assurant 8 tâches, ce qui est négligeable comme différence). Au niveau qualitatif, il est capital de relever que la femme s'occupe des tâches de production, qui se situent à l'extérieur des murs de l'exploitation, travaillant souvent en tant que « salariée » chez des tierces personnes, alors que l'homme se charge des tâches qui se trouvent à l'intérieur de l'exploitation, confirmant ainsi *ses prétentions à propos du patrimoine, fondement, à notre avis, de l'exercice du patriarcat.*

Les tâches de production où le mari est dominant sont principalement des tâches liées à la terre à l'intérieur de l'exploitation. Malgré leur caractère « intra » exploitation, ce sont des *tâches à forte visibilité,* car ce sont des activités qui ont leur saison, leurs techniques (rendez-vous, visites, etc.) de contact en ville, pour la réparation de la charrue, pour l'achat des semences et des outils nécessaires, donc qui exigent une négociation avec les fournisseurs, avec les propriétaires de machines (moisson ou labours, et même parfois semailles).

Les tâches de production où la femme est dominante sont principalement les tâches d'intérieur liées à l'animal et non à la terre, c'est-à-dire celles qui se font à l'ombre des murs, *totalement invisibles de l'extérieur,* dans la solitude de la besogne à réaliser, en dehors de toute gratitude même implicite, rien que par le regard que les autres jettent sur ce qu'on fait, regard de témoignage, à défaut d'être un regard de reconnaissance et, pourquoi pas, de considération. Les tâches de production se déroulent pour la femme comme si elle doit les assumer rien que par la valeur qu'elles détiennent en elles-mêmes, de manière intrinsèque, sans légitimation sociale extérieure. C'est au fond d'elle-même qu'elle doit puiser les raisons de son abnégation, elle doit être pour cela riche intérieurement, c'est-à-dire bénéficiant de cet auto-dynamisme intérieur qui, sur le plan psychologique des individus, démarque les êtres authentiques des êtres faux.

La deuxième différence, toujours dans la structure de production, réside dans le fait que l'homme se consacre plus que la femme au travail de la terre, alors que la femme se consacre plus que l'homme à la production liée à l'élevage. Il y a comme une spécialisation dans l'articulation terre-bête, l'homme se chargeant plus que la femme de la production en tant que spéculation, la femme plutôt à la production en tant qu'entretien des animaux. L'un se verse davantage dans la production réalisée dans un *rapport plutôt à l'inerte, l'autre dans un rapport plutôt au vivant.*

Si l'homme a, de tout temps, travaillé dans le cadre productif généré par le végétal et le minéral, la terre étant leur matrice, le lieu de leur genèse, la femme semble aujourd'hui investir les cadres productifs en s'investissant dans la production liée directement à l'animal. Sans aller jusqu'à chercher dans ces propos une justification à allure mythique, on peut dire que le partage sexuel tend à poser la relation entre le mari et sa femme dans un cadre qui dépasse le strict cadre familial, preuve, s'il en faut, que la question du genre est affaire tout autant de production, de reproduction que de mentalités et de mythologies, où les dieux sont tout aussi impliqués que les humains. La justification cesserait dès qu'on remarque que l'homme s'est occupé des éléments qui constituent le patrimoine (lié à la terre), tandis que la femme ne s'occupe que de ce qui est périssable (l'animal peut être vendu pour ses revenus en argent, il peut mourir). Alors que la terre reste un bien « inaliénable », l'animal peut être converti en « liquidités » consommables au quotidien des besoins du groupe.

La troisième différence réside enfin dans une sorte de partage injuste entre l'homme et la femme. Cette dernière se chargeant des tâches d'*exécution*, et de *routine* alors que son mari s'occupe des tâches techniques, des tâches de *conception* et d'*investissement*.

Les tâches de reproduction

La femme occupe une dominance manifeste et même écrasante dans les tâches de reproduction, du moment que sur 14 tâches elle en « accapare » 12, toutes réservées au renouvellement du groupe. Les statistiques suivantes le montrent : la préparation quotidienne des repas (99,25% contre 0% pour l'homme), la toilette des enfants (88,11% contre 1,25), la vaisselle (76,95% contre 0,5), la lessive (77,36% contre 0,45), la cuisson du pain (82,66% contre 0,95), la préparation du thé (79,21% contre 8,07), l'entretien du jardin potager (70,41 contre 20,27), la nourriture et les soins des adultes (83,5% contre 6,87), la corvée d'eau (47,55% contre 26,6), la corvée de bois (72,94% contre 16,62), le chauffage de la maison (82,09% contre 8,56), la préparation annuelle de la oula (83,40 contre 4,21).

Toutes ces tâches sont surtout des tâches qui se réalisent à l'intérieur de l'exploitation ou de la maison. Toutefois, dès que la tâche exige régularité, même si elle se fait à l'extérieur, la femme l'assure aussi, comme par exemple la corvée d'eau ou de bois. *Intérieur* et *régularité* des tâches, telle semble être la spécialité qui incombe à la femme dans le partage des travaux au sein de la famille. *Extérieur et irrégularité* (et quand il y a régularité, elle est comprise dans un temps long comme la moisson ou les labours ou les semailles qui se font une fois l'année) sont les deux traits qui caractérisent essentiellement les tâches dévolues aux hommes dans le partage des travaux au sein de la famille. L'irrégularité peut parfois s'estomper au profit du ponctuel et du sporadique.[21]

Que reste-t-il pour l'homme comme tâche de reproduction matérielle du groupe ? Il ne lui reste, en fait, que les tâches suivantes :

1- la vente des produits de l'exploitation au marché, (88,46% contre 6,66);

2- l'approvisionnement en produits alimentaires (75,32 % contre 12,97).

Le quasi monopole en termes de pourcentage qu'accapare l'homme dans ces deux tâches provient du fait qu'elles se définissent par leur *positionnement à proximité des sources du pouvoir*. Si l'argent est le moyen par lequel le sexe mâle trône dans la famille, c'est parce que certaines tâches lui sont réservées, parmi lesquelles les deux tâches de reproduction précédentes.

Les tâches politiques

La tâche politique par excellence est celle du contact avec les autorités locales. Elle assure la gestion civile de la société telle que le contact avec la police, la garde nationale, avec l'école où iront les enfants, avec l'administration où l'on ira enregistrer la nouvelle naissance, ou le poste de police dans sa fonction civile, celle qui consiste à constituer sa carte d'identité, etc. La tâche politique consiste aussi en la défense physique du groupe quand il est menacé. Toutes ces tâches touchent les domaines de souveraineté du groupe, de positionnement politique et de visibilité.

On peut ajouter à cela les tâches de représentation, mais aussi celles de négociation (quand il y a des projets de développement initiés par l'Etat en direction des paysans) et de gestion de la vie administrative du groupe (papiers d'identité, état civil, présence dans les registres officiels, municipaux ou autres, règlement de factures d'électricité ou d'eau, et tout contact avec l'administration et apparentés relevant en dernière instance des affaires de la cité, par opposition aux affaires domestiques, etc., *cette tâche a un contenu largement politique, du moment qu'elle touche à la souveraineté du groupe et qu'elle exige représentation et négociation*. C'est essentiellement l'homme qui se charge des tâches politiques.

Définition du modèle patriarcal

Pour les trois structures examinées, liées à la production, à la reproduction et aux fonctions politiques, le mari, en somme, tient les *tâches d'extérieur* (apparat, puissance sociale, source de pouvoir matériel grâce à l'argent que procurent les espaces d'extérieur, les tâches irrégulières dans le temps), *de représentation, de gestion et de puissance*, alors que la femme s'occupe *des tâches d'intérieur* et qui sont, pour la plupart, *régulières, quotidiennes* dans leur majorité. La régularité de la tâche est un critère de son volume de travail généralement plus important que les tâches irrégulières ou sporadiques. C'est aussi un critère qui statue sur la forte pénibilité des tâches qui incombent aux femmes, par comparaison à celles qui incombent aux hommes.

Le modèle patriarcal se définit par les caractères de pénibilité, de régularité, pour les travaux confiés aux femmes, contrairement aux travaux dont se chargent les hommes, outre les trois rapports qu'on a cités au début de ce travail : il est constitué des trois noyaux d'inégalité originels, et qui sont tous des *rapports,* celui des mâles aux femelles, celui des ascendants aux descendants, celui des plus âgés aux moins âgés. Le patriarcat, ce sont des rapports mais aussi des contenus de travail et de fonctions qu'on accorde respectivement aux deux sexes dans le sens de l'exploitation, de la domination et de la mystification dont sont objet les femmes, à l'opposé des hommes. Ces caractères permettent d'enrichir la perception à construire du modèle patriarcal que les chercheurs ont constamment à renouveler. Le modèle patriarcal génère sa propre continuité, y compris à travers la nouvelle génération : il ne faut pas oublier de mentionner la participation des enfants (surtout que les proches qui vivent sous le même toit sont rares, dans les exploitations agricoles familiales) aux tâches. Une reproduction de la même structure de production et de reproduction est à l'œuvre, véhiculée et transposée par les enfants. C'est dire que le modèle, qui a tous les caractères du patriarcat, n'est pas prêt à disparaître.

Tâches de reproduction et société civile : les qualités féminines

Les activités de reproduction, liées à la société civile, sont assurées sur le plan visible, par les hommes. Mais sur le plan du travail de préparation, pour bien s'acquitter de ces tâches, c'est la femme qui en est largement garante et parfois déterminante. Ces activités de reproduction concernent le rapport au marché, le rapport à autrui dans le sens que ce sont des personnes qui se trouvent physiquement en dehors de l'exploitation familiale (voisins et étrangers), même si ce sont des parents (lointains ou alliés, par exemple).

Nous allons montrer dans ce qui suit le rôle de la femme dans les questions relevant de la société civile (le rapport au marché, le rapport aux parents, voisins et étrangers et le rapport aux autorités locales en tant qu'institutions s'occupant, entre autres,[22] de fonctions civiles).

Le rapport au marché

Dans le rapport au marché, le rôle de la femme est prépondérant, il suffit de montrer toutes les activités qu'elle déploie dans les activités génératrices de revenu (AGR)[23] ou se produisant sur le terrain direct des activités matérielles touchant l'élevage (bovins, ovins, volailles), la production agricole, (jardin potager, participation aux travaux du champ avec son mari, tels que moissons, désherbage, etc.) et parfois travaux d'artisanat (pour produire des pièces tissées, de la poterie) ou toute autre production pouvant être vendue au marché.

Le rapport aux parents, voisins et étrangers

Rapport aux parents

Dans le rapport de la famille à son environnement social, la femme se charge des liens avec les parents, qu'ils soient consanguins ou alliés. Elle participe à l'insertion de sa petite famille dans l'univers élargi des deux familles alliées, que ce soit par les échanges qu'elle organise (visites réciproques, maintien des relations de solidarité parentale, soutien matériel lors des occasions de dépense telles que les fêtes, les événements malheureux comme la maladie, la mort, un accident, etc.). En cela, elle assure le ciment du lien solidaire et se montre gardienne des rites, du rituel, des coutumes. C'est elle qui conjugue la culture de la solidarité au quotidien. En cela, elle perpétue les aspects de la tradition qui confortent le groupe en tant qu'acteur solidaire. En somme, ce qu'on appelle tradition n'est rien d'autre que cette pratique de la solidarité égrenée par des repères établis, dont l'histoire remonte aux ancêtres, et qui dotent le groupe d'une profondeur historique, d'un fonds culturel, celui de la tradition à respecter.

Le rapport aux voisins

Le rapport aux voisins est lui aussi assuré, pour l'essentiel, par les femmes, surtout quand c'est un voisinage de proximité, entre deux exploitations par exemple. La femme paysanne assure le soutien lors des moissons, lors des labours, quand on a besoin de bras supplémentaires, ou aussi quand on a besoin d'ingrédients pour les repas et qu'il faut beaucoup de peine pour les chercher sur les étalages du commerce de détail, en ville ou à la cantine du coin (épices, ingrédients urgents, médicaments ambulatoires à usage fréquent, usage des services de transport quand le voisin est « motorisé » etc.

Ce soutien est maintenu grâce aux femmes qui l'entretiennent tout au long de l'année. Elles le traduisent en comportement inscrit dans la culture quotidienne. C'est un rapport qui se fonde sur les principes de réciprocité et les traditions du bon voisinage, sachant que c'est un exercice difficile à maintenir vivace dans le rapport au voisin, quand on n'en a pas le « doigté ». En effet, les maladresses à ce niveau sont mortelles. Car le rapport aux voisins relève des perceptions réciproques et croisées que se font les partenaires de leurs actions réciproques, avec parfois des moyens de jugement de l'action de l'autre fort différents pouvant conduire à des malentendus (une générosité exagérée, par exemple, peut être interprétée comme une volonté d'écraser l'autre), une retenue très poussée à établir des liens d'entraide avec le voisin peut être perçue comme une attitude d'hostilité. Ce sont les femmes qui sont les gardiennes de la Bonne Pratique du Don et de la Réciprocité. Cette Bonne Pratique suit un Code précis et délicat.

Rapport aux étrangers

Même le rapport aux étrangers est lui aussi codé. Cette codification est gardée par les femmes. L'hospitalité n'est rien d'autre que faire accéder un étranger au monde intérieur, celui gardé par les femmes, ce qui donne au gynécée un caractère empreint de « sacré », dont la femme est le dépositaire. On connaît la valeur de l'hospitalité dans les activités de don. C'est le don qui permet les liens durables avec l'environnement. Cette durabilité est tributaire du détachement avec lequel les parties entretiennent leur relation. Ce n'est donc pas l'intérêt qui est ici prégnant, mais le don comme vecteur d'un « commerce », d'un lien social durable avec les étrangers à convertir en partenaires ou en amis.

Conclusion partielle

En résumé, on peut dire que toutes ces activités de type économique (marché), social (lien avec les parents, les voisins et les étrangers) et politique (liens avec les autorités locales ou régionales représentatives du pouvoir, de l'Etat central, de la partie civile) sont la condition de réalisation des tâches de reproduction qu'assure l'homme à l'extérieur de l'exploitation. La femme, elle, assure le segment travail, fondement de la valeur. L'homme, quant à lui, assure son appropriation et sa fonctionnalisation au sein de la société. La partie *travail* de la reproduction inscrite dans les activités à l'extérieur de l'exploitation est assurée en grande partie par les femmes. C'est le reste de la reproduction qui est assuré par l'homme, la partie *visible*.

Il se dégage de ce qui précède que les tâches de reproduction sont départagées entre la femme et l'homme. Ce qui touche l'aspect visible des tâches reliées tout à la fois à la société civile ou la société politique relève des hommes. En revanche, tout ce qui touche à l'intensité du travail nécessaire à valoriser les fonctions assurées est l'apanage des femmes. Parfois dans une seule activité (ou tâche), on trouve imbriquées tout à la fois société civile et société politique. Par exemple les projets de développement : ceux-ci contiennent un aspect civil (octroi du crédit, instruction des dossiers des candidats aux projets, établissement du dossier de candidature, agréage des composantes des projets par les autorités locales aux paysans, suivi gestionnaire du projet) et un aspect politique. C'est une démarche de lobbying pour jouir du statut de bénéficiaire du projet de développement local ou régional auprès des pouvoirs politiques locaux, les contacts ont pour objet d'asseoir des formes d'allégeances à l'occasion de ces projets. C'est à ce prix que le paysan compte accroître les chances de succès d'obtention des soutiens financiers pour monter le projet.

Dans ces tâches s'effectuant dans les deux sphères (civile et politique), l'homme est visible ; ce sont des tâches qui lui reviennent, la société actuelle le lui reconnaît. Cette reconnaissance sociale est une façon de reconnaître le pouvoir aux hommes sur ces tâches. Mais si l'on observe la question sous l'angle du travail investi et des préparations préliminaires pour que ces opérations aboutissent, on voit la place décisive qu'occupent les femmes. C'est grâce aux femmes, rivées à la besogne de production et de reproduction au sein de l'exploitation familiale, que les projets réussissent. Autrement dit, la femme assure le caractère de production des facteurs de réussite et l'homme valorise cela sur le plan social et politique. La femme se charge du travail et de la valeur à donner à ce travail, l'homme se charge de son marketing que ce soit dans le domaine économique, social ou politique. Il y a là un rapport entre producteur de valeurs et de richesses (femme) et gestionnaire de cette production, en termes de pouvoir acquis (homme). Gestionnaire qui a tous les relents du spéculateur moderne, c'est-à-dire celui qui manie des valeurs sans qu'il les ait nécessairement lui-même produites. Après cet exposé, on peut déceler les grandes lignes des propositions sur *la femme alternative d'ensemble*.

Science politique et société politique

Il suffit par conséquent de mettre en exergue ces tâches comme étant dotées d'un contenu foncièrement politique et de leur donner le mot qui leur convient le mieux, à savoir le terme de « reproduction », pour qu'on voie dans tout son éclat l'apport de la femme sur le terrain direct de la « politique », dans le sens anthropologique et étendu du terme, comprise ici comme l'art, la science ou la praxis d'assurer au groupe social sa reproduction. Le terme « reproduction » convient mieux que le terme politique, car il jouit de deux mérites : celui de la description, mais aussi celui de la formalisation. Ces deux mérites le prédisposent à reprendre son statut en épistémologie, c'est-à-dire détrôner le concept de politique et le remplacer. C'est là une façon de désaliéner nos catégories mentales.

Le terme « politique », par les sens divers qui sont venus s'agglutiner et se coller au sens spécifique, a été galvaudé au point qu'il veut tout dire et, de ce fait, ne dit désormais plus rien. Il est aujourd'hui source de confusions ; c'est même devenu un voile qui nous empêche de voir. Pour les questions féminines qui exigent une clarté et une clairvoyance, le terme de « reproduction » est mieux à même de rendre compte des fonctions éminemment politiques assurées par les femmes au sein de la famille et en dehors de la famille.

La propension du terme « politique » à conquérir des espaces qui ne relèvent pas du contenu sémantique de sa compétence est en grande partie due au fait que, dans le modèle classique, les fonctions de reproduction sont à la charge formelle de l'Etat qui en assure la majeure partie de la réalisation. Une fois que les fonctions et les tâches sont exprimées en termes d'activités ou de tâches de reproduction, il est possible d'enlever au terme politique les contenus qu'il a confisqués. Cette remise en selle des contenus sémantiques montre par conséquent la possibilité de confier les deux ensembles de tâches en question (production et reproduction) à la société civile et de les retirer de la société politique. Ce serait l'alternative qui permettrait de concevoir une société où les fonctions de l'Etat sont réduites à leur plus simple expression. Exception faite de certaines fonctions liées à la canalisation de la violence au sein de la société et à sa gestion par des procédés divers qui n'excluent pas la constitution d'un corps policier armé veillant à l'application des lois de droit civil, privé et public. En effet, la dimension de répression ne peut pas sortir de l'ornière de l'Etat, dont il faudra d'ailleurs circonscrire les contours. Une des fonctions de l'état est la répression, c'est-à-dire la nécessité de punir quand il y a délit et de réprimer quand il y a usage excessif de la force de la part d'un acteur de la société civile.

Deux acquis scientifiques en sciences sociales nous permettent d'envisager ces modifications et amorces essentielles à introduire dans les prérogatives accordées respectivement à la société civile et à la société politique. Le premier consiste d'abord à maintenir les catégories conceptuelles proposées par Gramsci qui distingue « société civile » et « société politique », en des termes très précis et très nuancés. Nous citons pour cela la spécialiste italienne de Gramsci, celle qui l'a lu dans sa langue.[24]

Le deuxième consiste en la leçon d'anthropologie contenue, à notre avis, dans les thèses de E.E. Evans Pritchard sur les tribus soudanaises (les Nuer), qui montrent que la fonction de médiation pour résorber les conflits, conjurer les violences, résoudre des problèmes réels pour la subsistance du groupe, l'extension des aires de pâturages des troupeaux chameliers et bovins est une fonction qui n'est pas assurée par une institution ou un « poste » ou une administration quelconque qui se trouverait au-dessus de la société. Cette fonction est assurée par une personne émanant et demeurant au sein de la société (appelée « l'homme au léopard ») et dont la condition d'exercice de cette fonction informelle, c'est qu'il soit pacifique, calme, ayant une propension nette à résoudre les problèmes à l'amiable et les conflits avec sens de la négociation et de la douceur dans les rapports, pratique se situant aux antipodes de la violence et de l'usage de la force (Pritchard 1968).

Dans nos sociétés contemporaines, la généralisation des délits et des passe-droits est telle qu'on ne peut plus se passer d'un corps armé chargé de maintenir l'ordre dans la légalité et le respect des droits de chacun et de tous. Mais ce qui nous intéresse dans les travaux d'Evans Pritchard, et de beaucoup d'autres anthropologues, c'est qu'il ne place pas la sphère politique (ou l'Etat et ses fonctions) au-dessus des fonctions dont pourrait se charger la société ; plusieurs tâches aujourd'hui assurées par l'Etat peuvent être dévolues à la société.

Ces acquis montrent l'autonomie de la « société civile » (Gramsci), les illustrations vont des tribus (comme les *Nuer* du Soudan) jusqu'aux sociétés contemporaines où la violence peut avoir un caractère légitime (aspect relevé par les études wébériennes) dès qu'il s'agit de punir les délits et de réprimer les passe-droits.

C'est le même principe que nous retrouvons dans l'exploitation familiale. Celle-ci gère ses problèmes relevant de la reproduction en son sein ou au sein de la société civile sans avoir à faire avec le pouvoir politique, tel qu'on l'observe aujourd'hui doté d'une influence tentaculaire sur la société civile. Cela montre qu'à ce niveau l'alternative est prégnante à condition, répétons-le, de considérer les termes usités avec un regard nouveau. Ce regard nouveau a consisté à démontrer que les tâches dites politiques sont des tâches de reproduction.

Principe masculin et principe féminin

Les tâches de reproduction, une ventilation selon les sexes

Les tâches de reproduction se déploient sur deux volets ; précisons d'abord que le sens que nous privilégions ici est un sens étendu donné au terme reproduction.

Le premier volet réside dans la production de la progéniture, mais aussi les activités de maintien en vie du groupe par la subsistance et les tâches connexes : tant sur le *plan concret* : hygiène, santé, instruction, domesticité inscrite dans la fourniture de la nourriture, la femme étant la nourricière, etc. que sur le *plan culturel et symbolique* : la femme reproduit le groupe en étant la gardienne de la tradition du groupe, la tradition étant le fil qui rattache à l'ancêtre et fonde l'histoire et la mémoire au sein du groupe. C'est la femme qui s'en charge.

Le deuxième volet réside dans les tâches de défense du groupe, de souveraineté, de représentation et de recherches de projets de développement, sans oublier les tâches liées à la vente et à l'achat de produits divers, sinon aux opérations de réciprocité avec l'entourage parental, quand celui ci existe, ou avec le voisinage, pour les produits périssables et qui sont produits en grande quantité, sans que cela soit possible de les écouler sur le marché. Ce deuxième groupe de tâches de la reproduction est l'apanage des hommes dans l'exploitation agricole familiale.

Ordonnancement des rapports de genre dans le capitalisme et le patriarcat : les tâches politiques réservées aux hommes

Les tâches de ce deuxième volet, mentionné ci-dessus, sont ce qu'on appelle généralement les tâches politiques, dans l'acception classique du mot. De ce fait, selon cette même acception classique du politique, ces tâches ne peuvent être, dans l'ordre social actuel régi par le capitalisme et le patriarcat, que masculines. En effet, elles sont l'apanage des hommes. Le cas des liens avec le marché en dit long. Ces tâches impliquent la négociation à l'extérieur de l'exploitation, pour acheter et vendre les produits de l'exploitation. Elles exigent une virilité dans les rapports, la négociation se faisant dans un carré serré de marchandage et de valorisation des produits à la criée, sans compter l'allure belliqueuse qu'exige l'acte de vendre ou d'acheter dans les milieux paysans, le tout se faisant dans le caractère vigoureux du rapport social aux autres.

Mêmes qualités masculines exigées dans les tâches de défense du groupe à l'égard de toute agression venant du milieu, violation de l'espace de l'exploitation par le bétail du voisin, rixes à propos des clôtures, etc.

Les tâches de souveraineté et de représentation du groupe, elles aussi, procèdent d'un principe de force dans un milieu viril où tout signe de douceur est considéré comme un signe de mollesse, par conséquent, un signe de faiblesse. De cela on conclut que le rapport au marché, que la souveraineté, la représentation du groupe, la négociation au nom du groupe (ici la famille) sont des tâches qui procèdent toutes *d'un principe de force et de virilité*, les deux piliers du principe masculin. On remarque que le principe masculin touche les tâches de reproduction situées dans la partie plutôt « répressive » du segment.

Principe féminin

En revanche, le deuxième segment des tâches de reproduction est l'apanage des femmes. Ces tâches sont : l'entretien, le maintien et le renouvellement du groupe familial, tâches liées aux soins et à la bonne santé, à l'hygiène, à l'hébergement, à l'habillement, au toilettage, à la reproduction physiologique par le pourvoi en aliments consommables grâce à la préparation des repas, au maintien des assiettes et de toute la vaisselle c'est-à-dire tous les ustensiles en état de pourvoir les habitants de la parcelle en moyens techniques nécessaires pour la subsistance. Ces tâches qu'on qualifie de « domestiques » se font dans un rapport interne à la famille et se réalisent dans le lien affectif qu'a la femme avec les membres de sa famille. Le principe féminin procède de la douceur, de la négociation qui se fonde sur la persuasion et la conviction quand il y a désaccord, vacance, ou nécessité de charger un autre membre d'une tâche à réaliser, auprès des enfants par exemple.

Du fait qu'elle se charge de la vie du groupe dans ce qu'il a de plus vital, la femme est à pourvoir pour se charger de la dimension dite « politique » de la vie du groupe. Cette dimension, nous avons essayé d'en montrer le contenu qui est essentiellement celui de la reproduction, dont se charge en grande partie la femme (segment vital) plutôt que l'homme (segment répressif).

De cela on peut tirer la conclusion que, seulement dans une acception revisitée du « politique » à la lumière de la revalorisation des fonctions de « reproduction » telle qu'exposée ici, l'on peut comprendre la place centrale des femmes dans la vie du groupe entendue ici en tant que communauté (la famille). Cela fonderait et asseoirait la légitimité des femmes à se charger tout aussi bien de « l'économique » (le vital) que du « politique ». Que reste-t-il de la société quand les fonctions économiques et les fonctions politiques relèvent ainsi des femmes ? Le principe féminin consiste en fait en cette fusion des fonctions politiques et économiques entre les mains de l'acteur qui s'en est historiquement chargé et acquitté tout en étant dépouillé de tous les attributs que couronnerait ce principe féminin assumé dans les faits.

Les femmes ont été dépouillées de ces attributs, mais, plus que cela, leur rôle et leur place centrales sont demeurés longtemps non reconnus socialement, non rémunérés, non valorisés et laissés enfouis dans la catégorie de « travail domestique », travail invisible et non reconnu publiquement.

Principe féminin et cadre communautaire assoupli

Les tâches de production et de reproduction au sein de la société dans son ensemble ne peuvent être gérées, en dehors des rapports « positivistes » qu'on a stigmatisés plus haut, que si d'abord la citoyenneté (une nouvelle citoyenneté) n'est plus régie par un principe d'inclusion-exclusion (de la Grèce antique au traité de Maastricht instituant l'Union Européenne), ni par un principe individualiste, comme c'est le cas aujourd'hui, ni par un principe d'appartenance formelle à un territoire particulier. Cette nouvelle citoyenneté aura fatalement à composer positivement avec le caractère communautaire qui doit régir plusieurs de ces rapports inscrits dans une approche nouvelle. Le principe de communauté est à comprendre dans le sens d'une valorisation des mécanismes de solidarité, de compréhension de l'intérieur des rapports humains et non de les réduire à l'extériorité de leur manifestation technique propre aux sciences juridiques. L'aspect contractuel n'est pas à bannir, il constitue en même temps un renforcement des aspects volontaires, il permettrait d'asseoir des engagements collectifs plus enthousiastes à l'égard des défis qui secouent un groupe social. Que serait la citoyenneté sans le contrat social qui définit, entre autres, les devoirs, les responsabilités et les obligations de tous et de chacun ?

Ce cadre communautaire aura à être suffisamment souple pour coexister avec d'autres modes de traitement du groupe avec son milieu environnant, exigeant des rapports de marché ou des rapports de plan, pour reprendre les trois catégories de S. C. Kolm. En effet, cet aspect communautaire ne refuse pas de composer tout aussi bien avec un système économique fondé sur le marché du moment que les besoins non satisfaits par la production fournie par la parcelle ne peuvent être assurés que par le marché ou par les projets dont se charge une instance publique qui s'appelle aujourd'hui Etat et qui peut devenir par la suite une « société politique » dans le sens le plus réduit de l'Etat, juste le nécessaire pour conjurer la pauvreté, éloigner le sentiment du besoin, parer aux urgences (catastrophes naturelles, sécheresse, manquement inattendu de stocks, etc.). Il serait un outil qui sert le vivre ensemble dans la cité, dans un cadre municipal et hors les murs, dans un cadre villageois régi par un conseil des sages pétri d'un esprit communautaire.

L'Etat ou ce qui en tient lieu ne serait nécessaire qu'en tant qu'une nécessité d'organisation collective pour parer aux vicissitudes de la vie, aux imprévus et aux drames qui peuvent survenir à chaque instant, et non une structure inamovible, faite pour faire triompher les plus forts sur le compte des plus faibles tout en se targuant d'être neutre et un arbitre, au moment où il est un « troisième larron » juge et pas seulement partie.

Conclusion

Pour que « la démocratie »,[25] contenu et contours, dont on a montré le caractère imprécis, dépasse ses impasses historiques (dont par exemple les mécanismes d'inclusion des bons citoyens et d'exclusion d'autres comme non citoyens, les femmes et les étrangers en l'occurrence), rejoigne le sens pour lequel elle a été conçue et envisagée en tant qu'utopie salutaire, à promouvoir au rang pas seulement de la cité, mais de l'ensemble des nouveaux citoyens du monde, le principe féminin est à privilégier à l'encontre du principe masculin.

Disons qu'au moins, à côté du principe masculin gérant des espaces sociaux divers, (le marché, le politique dans son segment répressif), le principe féminin est à promouvoir pour dégager un autre rapport de citoyenneté fondé sur des rapports de persuasion et de coopération. La démocratie, telle qu'elle doit être révisée et conçue de nouveau, procèdera d'un principe féminin, car émanant des fondements communautaires du groupe. Celui-ci aura à se rapprocher de la famille qui sera le noyau dur de la société civile. Cette dernière, dans beaucoup d'approches en vigueur aujourd'hui, ne comprend pas la famille, la vie privée étant considérée en dehors des rapports entre citoyens. Dans l'approche de la citoyenneté en vigueur, dans les sociétés contemporaines, parmi celles considérées « démocratiques », le privé est séparé du public.

Cette séparation peut être considérée comme un acquis si l'on entend par cela la sacralité de la vie privée d'une personne. Mais si l'on entend par cela l'exclusion de la chose publique et de l'intérêt public de ce que peut contracter tout un chacun dans sa vie privée, cela relève d'une sous-estimation du bien public.

Pour que le principe féminin prenne toute son ampleur, la famille est à engager comme composante de la société civile. Cette dernière a besoin d'un souffle communautaire qui instituerait, à côté des principes du marché, les principes de l'échange réciprocitaire, sans exclure, dans les conditions actuelles, les actions d'un public nourri des valeurs qualifiées de « providentielles » en matière de lutte contre la pauvreté, d'un soutien aux plus démunis, mais aussi de la nécessité de parer aux urgences, qui ne peut être que l'émanation d'un pouvoir public. Celui-ci peut ne pas prendre la dimension tentaculaire de l'Etat dans ses formes actuelles. Mais les tâches que nous avons situées dans le deuxième segment du « politique » (tâches répressives ») montrent qu'on ne peut pas en l'état actuel de l'alternative se passer des services du politique. Ce politique, nous lui avons circonscrit ses vertus de reproduction. Cela permet, dans une étude prospective, d'approfondir davantage cet élément essentiel pour réduire autant que faire se peut le rôle de la société politique au profit de la société civile.

Notes

1. Ce texte est une explicitation et un prolongement théorique du texte produit en 2005 : Laroussi Amri, « La femme comme alternative d'ensemble », in *Les femmes entre violences et stratégies de liberté, Maghreb et Europe du Sud*, sous la direction de Christiane Veauvy, Marguerite Rollinde et Mireille Azzoug, Editions Bouchene, 2004, pp. 319-329. Nous ajoutons des paragraphes suite à la révolution tunisienne du 14 janvier 2011, afin de servir de textes de base pouvant alimenter les discussions en cours sur le type de société que nous voulons en Tunisie.

2. Nous sommes particulièrement sensible à cette exigence de dater et de localiser dès que la question concerne le concept « démocratie ». Car, sans cette exigence, il se prête à toutes les acceptions et devient un fourre-tout. Exception faite des disciplines comme la philosophie ou l'anthropologie, les deux disciplines qui l'ont pris pour objet d'étude en tant que concept abstrait, aspirant à l'universalité.

3. De cette première constatation on peut déduire que la démocratie, dans sa forme historique reposant sur le concept de citoyenneté, partant de la Cité grecque jusqu'à l'Union Européenne, ne se fonde pas sur un principe éthique, mais plutôt sur un principe consensuel.

4. Weber parlera de « neutralisme axiologique ».

5. Le positivisme a constitué le lit idéologique, sur le plan des sciences humaines et sociales notamment, qui a conforté le développement du capitalisme : valorisation de la matière, prééminence de l'observation et du concret au détriment de ce qui est abstrait et spirituel, célébration des valeurs de l'efficacité contre les principes de l'enchantement qui régissaient les rapports sociaux à l'intérieur des sociétés agraires (qualifiées de « pré-industrielles »).

6. Le verdict est sans appel : « il faut traiter les faits sociaux comme des choses », in Emile Durkheim, *Les règles de la méthode sociologique*. Dix-septième édition, Paris, PUF, 1968.

7. On lira avec intérêt leur ouvrage en commun : *La construction sociale de la réalité*, Traduit de l'américain par Pierre Taminaux, Paris, Méridiens Klincksieck, 1989.

8. Malgré la distance que nous observons à l'égard du positivisme tel que cela apparaît, il y a à préciser que le positivisme joue toutefois un rôle important dans la lutte, aujourd'hui encore, contre « l'obscurantisme » religieux, surtout dans les pays islamiques où cet obscurantisme religieux s'incarne dans les courants de pensée salafites. Ces aspects du positivisme ont déjà été mobilisés depuis le XVI è siècle en Europe contre l'Eglise. L'objectif ultime était d'instituer la séparation nette entre sphère religieuse d'un côté et toutes les autres sphères : étatique et même parfois sphère politique, sans parler de la sphère scientifique, surtout celle de la recherche. Le positivisme, en Europe, dans les pays de religion traditionnellement chrétienne, a joué un rôle décisif dans l'instauration de la laïcité dans l'ensemble de la société. Ce phénomène, la laïcité, grâce au positivisme est sorti de l'ornière individuelle et psychologique pour devenir une affaire de société et de progrès social fondé sur le principe de liberté du culte.

9. A ce niveau, notre programme de recherche en sciences sociales a comporté un diptyque, c'est-à-dire un registre constitué de deux orientations : 1-celle de la recherche en amont sur les diagnostics, les stigmatisations, les dysfonctionnements, disons le caractère « anomique » du social et que nous avons rassemblé sous le terme de «ruptures» au sein de la société, dont on a essayé de construire une sociologie : cf. notre thèse, sur la sociologie des ruptures, soutenue en 1991 à Jussieu (Paris VII) et déposée, depuis. 2-celle de la recherche des solutions et des alternatives, partant de la conviction que nous nous inscrivons dans une sociologie de transformation sociale, de laquelle n'est pas, pour autant, exclue la sociologie de la connaissance, deux « sociologies » qui sont, dans nos approches épistémologiques du social, loin d'être en opposition exclusive.

10. Pourtant c'est cette catégorie citadine des femmes qui a attiré le plus les écrits des chercheur(e)s, y compris féministes, des deux sexes.

11. L'utopie, terme aujourd'hui déclassé, est à remettre en selle, dans les études sur les transformations de la société. Mais la réflexion sur les alternatives ne doit pas rester au stade de l'utopie, dans le sens de rêves et de vœux pieux, elle est à concevoir dans des termes qui assurent la réalisation et le passage à l'action, dans une perspective visionnaire axée sur les possibles.

12. Cette première définition sera enrichie dans le paragraphe ci-dessous intitulé « définition du modèle patriarcal ».

13. Les sciences sociales se définissent d'abord par le caractère privilégié accordé au terrain comme source première de la connaissance.

14. Nous ne focaliserons pas notre intérêt sur ces atteintes touchant de plein fouet l'autonomie du groupe, atteintes dues à deux facteurs décisifs : celui de la dévalorisation des produits d'approvisionnement provenant du producteur direct qui sont à mettre au marché au service du consommateur direct, sans passer par les intermédiaires ; ensuite celui du rehaussement du plafond des besoins réels du groupe, dont les plus importants : les besoins physiologiques en alimentation et en santé. Outre les besoins réels, il y a un gonflement de la représentation des besoins de vie décente du groupe dû aux effets des médias et de la culture de la sur-consommation rampante, processus reposant sur une information provenant de l'extérieur du groupe et qui l'appelle à consommer, parfois au-delà du besoin strictement physiologique. Dans les économies de marché particulièrement centrées sur la consommation, le groupe (le ménage ici) est soumis à des campagnes publicitaires faisant partie des politiques de marketing des entreprises capitalistes qui structurent le marché de satisfaction des besoins et plus particulièrement la champ de la consommation et de la sur-consommation.

15. Nous aurons l'occasion de le montrer dans nos travaux ultérieurs.

16. Nous nous sommes tenu dans notre terminologie (parents voisins, étrangers) à un niveau anthropologique. Cela nous permet de transcender le niveau empirique spécifique pour atteindre une sphère réflexive traitant des abstractions et des catégories conceptuelles, en droite ligne de notre souci de saisir le réservoir « d'alternatives d'ensemble » enfoui dans l'approche genre en tant qu'utopie salutaire.

17. L'amont est constitué de segments divers dont évidemment l'économie, et l'économie politique. Ces deux segments se trouvent dans les dernières étapes de l'amont et débouchent directement sur l'aval qui est constitué, entre autres, de la science politique, c'est-à-dire la consécration des catégories des rapports de production dans les catégories du pouvoir.

18. Exploitation agricole familiale.

19. Cette tâche est assurée par les maris. Elle figure dans le canevas d'entretien que nous avons établi pour mettre en relief les tâches occultes. Nous la retrouverons plus loin quand on abordera les techniques qualitatives d'identification des tâches occultes de reproduction immatérielle du groupe familial.

20. Pour tous les pourcentages portant sur la répartition chiffrée des tâches, figurant dans cette étude entre le mari et sa femme, le lecteur voudra bien considérer que ce qui reste pour fermer le chiffre unitaire « cent » est l'apanage du troisième membre de la famille, les enfants.

21. Voir notre ouvrage : « La femme rurale », le tableau de centralité féminine, n° 72, p. 346.

22. On verra qu'elles s'occupent aussi de fonctions politiques, ce qui les fait appartenir tout à la fois à la société civile et à la société politique au vu des fonctions considérées. Cela prouve l'interpénétration entre société civile et société politique, tout en sous-scrivant à l'idée que ces institutions ont un aspect dominant qui les fait ranger soit du côté des institutions de la société politique, soit du côté des institutions de la société civile.

23. Le corpus des études sur les Activités Génératrices de Revenus est immense. Ce sont surtout les organismes internationaux de développement qui ont initié ce terme. On le considère comme un des thèmes favoris de la littérature grise. Il n'en demeure pas moins qu'il constitue une thématique fort révélatrice des activités féminines. Beaucoup d'études l'abordent sous la forme de « la débrouille » économique (souvent dans l'informel) au féminin.

24. Maria Antonietta Macciochi, *Pour Gramsci*, Paris, Editions du Seuil, Collection Points, 1974. « Gramsci opère une distinction aussi subtile que complexe entre 'société civile' et 'société politique' dans l'Etat de classe. L'Etat serait 'la société politique' et représenterait le moment de la force et de la coercition, tandis que la société civile serait le réseau complexe des fonctions éducatives et idéologiques, ce par quoi la société est non seulement commandée, mais encore dirigée ». On peut, écrit Gramsci, distinguer deux grands niveaux dans la superstructure, celui qu'on peut désigner comme 'société civile', c'est-à-dire l'ensemble des organismes habituellement appelés internes et privés et celui de la 'société politique' ou l'Etat, correspondant respectivement à la fonction d'hégémonie que le groupe dirigeant exerce sur l'ensemble du corps social et à celle de domination directe ou de commandement qui s'exprime à travers l'Etat et le pouvoir 'juridique' », p. 164.

25. En tant qu'utopie salutaire dont l'aspect réalisation n'est pas totalement épuisé malgré l'usage qui en est fait historiquement depuis Athènes jusqu'à l'Union Européenne, pour dépasser le cadre historique dans lequel elle a été emprisonnée par la truchement du positivisme, en tant que paradigme qui lui a assigné son contenu (réservé à une catégorie de citoyens).

Bibliographie

Amri, L., 2003, *La femme rurale dans l'exploitation familiale. Le N-O de la Tunisie. Pour une sociologie des ruptures,* Paris: L'Harmattan.

Evans Pritchard, E. E., *Les Nuer, Description des modes de vie et des institutions politiques d'un peuple nilote.* Traduit de l'anglais par Louis Evrard. Préface de Louis Dumont. NRF. Editions Gallimard, Paris, 1968 (1937 pour l'édition originale, at the Clarendon Press, Oxford).

Guinchard, S. ; Montagnier, G., 1995, *Lexique des termes juridiques,* Paris, Dalloz, 10e édition.

Kolm, S-Ch., 1984, *La bonne économie, la réciprocité générale,* Paris: PUF.

Macchiocci, M. A., 1974, *Pour Gramsci,* Paris: Editions du Seuil, Collection Points.

Marx, Karl, 1969, *le Capital,* livre 1, traduit par J. Roy, Paris: Garnier-Flammarion.

Veauvy, M. R. ; Azzoug, M., (sous la direction de), 2004, *Les femmes entre violences et stratégies de liberté,* Maghreb et Europe du Sud, Editions Bouchene.

2

Etat, mondialisation et citoyenneté multiculturelle : femmes bantoues et femmes pygmées face au genre et aux politiques publiques

Jacques Tshibwabwa Kuditshini

Introduction

L'objectif de cette réflexion est d'examiner la question de la citoyenneté multiculturelle et l'impact sévère qu'exercent les politiques publiques, la dynamique interculturelle et les phénomènes de mondialisation sur la construction de cette citoyenneté par rapport à deux catégories de femmes : les femmes pygmées et les femmes bantoues. Elle trouve son ancrage scientifique dans l'un des sous-thèmes du symposium sur le genre 2008 proposé par le CODESRIA, en l'occurrence, celui consacré à la « Dialectique des identités multiples et la citoyenneté à l'ère de la mondialisation ». Elle se ressource dans les faits empiriques modelés par la dynamique des relations de genre entre, d'une part, les femmes bantoues et les femmes pygmées, et, d'autre part, entre toutes les deux catégories de femmes réunies vis-à-vis des phénomènes de pouvoir, et en particulier ceux relatifs à la question de la citoyenneté féminine.

Les termes rapports de genre, en effet, mettent en corrélation plusieurs types de référents. Ce sont d'abord manifestement les rapports hommes/femmes. Ensuite, ce sont les rapports entre femmes et les rapports entre hommes. Finalement, les rapports sociaux de sexe comprennent également les relations de catégories de femmes avec les phénomènes sociaux (que ce soit l'Etat, la division du travail, le système éducatif, les relations économiques, les systèmes politiques ou autres) (Imam Mama et Sow 2004:19). Comment alors l'Etat gère-t-il la question de la citoyenneté par rapport aux deux catégories de femmes ci-dessus évoquées ? Ce premier questionnement place au cœur de l'analyse la nature discriminatoire des politiques publiques. Celles-ci seront donc convoquées dans cette réflexion.

Comment les femmes et les hommes (généralement bantous) qui animent les institutions politiques, administratives, économiques, etc. se comportent-ils vis-à-vis des femmes pygmées, et de leurs droits en particulier ? Le deuxième questionnement place les acteurs au cœur des conduites et relations sociales. Ici, les représentations, les croyances et les mythes, ainsi que les structures mentales à l'œuvre dans la construction de ces mythes et croyances par les acteurs (Touraine 1984) auront aussi un intérêt évident pour notre agenda analytique.

Quel est l'impact de la diversité culturelle, mieux, de la dynamique interculturelle sur les rapports de genre, sur les femmes bantoues et pygmées quant à leur accès à la citoyenneté féminine ? La troisième interrogation, qui met en interaction politique et culture, nous conduit directement vers la problématique du multiculturalisme. Cette interrogation a d'ailleurs partie liée avec la dernière préoccupation de cette recherche qui se propose d'analyser l'impact de la mondialisation économique et culturelle sur l'accès de deux catégories de femmes (bantoues et pygmées) à la citoyenneté.

Dans ce papier, la citoyenneté est définie comme l'ensemble des normes juridiques et des pratiques sociales qui fondent le statut de citoyen. Plus explicitement encore, il s'agit, selon Rodota (1999:181), de l'ensemble des conditions permettant à l'individu de jouir pleinement de droits fondamentaux et de participer au fonctionnement du système politique. Bien entendu, c'est davantage l'aspect participatif, celui qui désigne le citoyen politique, le citoyen engagé, qui est ici évoqué par ces deux définitions. Tout en les prenant en charge, notre réflexion va néanmoins au-delà et s'appuie sur un concept encore plus opératoire pour l'appréhension de notre objet de recherche. Il s'agit du concept de citoyenneté multiculturelle. Ce concept proposé par Will Kymlicka (1995:18-22) vise à dépasser l'opposition entre la conception républicaine de la citoyenneté et le communautarisme. La citoyenneté multiculturelle est une citoyenneté différenciée qui reconnaît l'appartenance des individus à des groupes différents du point de vue culturel (Alpe *et al.* 2005). La citoyenneté multiculturelle suppose que tous les groupes culturels soient socialement égaux. Ainsi l'apartheid en Afrique du Sud ne relevait pas de la citoyenneté multiculturelle. Comme précisé plus haut, ce concept sera appliqué aux relations entre femmes bantoues et pygmées, et à leurs relations avec les phénomènes de pouvoir.

De fait, depuis la mise en relief du genre à la fois comme une catégorie d'analyse des rapports sociaux et comme une approche incontournable dans la formulation des politiques publiques, la question de la citoyenneté féminine est toujours envisagée comme si elle ne concernait que l'émancipation politique des femmes bantoues, soudanaises et nilotiques qu'on trouve en RDC et en Afrique centrale en général. Les femmes pygmées sont exclues des débats sur la citoyenneté. Les luttes menées pour la conquête d'une citoyenneté féminine égale à celle des hommes ne semblent pas s'inscrire dans une logique multiculturelle, dans la mesure où les femmes pygmées, porteuses d'une culture minoritaire différente de celle des autres femmes, culture du reste souvent méprisée, sont souvent abandonnées sur les marges. Même le féminisme d'Etat n'échappe pas à cette critique.

Placé donc au cœur de la dynamique interculturelle, le débat sur l'accès sexué à la citoyenneté apparaît comme un objet d'étude encore limité aux rapports hommes/femmes, les hommes étant considérés comme jouissant d'une citoyenneté positive, différente de celle des femmes. Cette thèse est fondée et les dynamiques sociopolitiques à l'œuvre dans presque tous les Etats permettent de la légitimer. Il faut néanmoins aller au-delà de cette thèse et s'intéresser aux relations intra-sexuelles. Tel est le sens de notre démarche qui, faisant sien le concept de citoyenneté multiculturelle, vise à montrer que le discours actuel sur l'accès sexué à la citoyenneté féminine à l'ère de la mondialisation ne prend pas encore en charge l'ensemble des femmes de la RDC (et de l'Afrique centrale) prises dans leur diversité culturelle et identitaire. L'objectif de ce papier est donc de plancher sur cette dimension pertinence du genre.

Il est de ce fait divisé en quatre points. Le premier prend en charge les aspects théoriques et généraux, le deuxième examine la question de la citoyenneté féminine pendant la période coloniale, le troisième est consacré à la même question, mais après la colonisation, et le dernier point essaie de proposer quelques pistes de réflexion pour une citoyenneté politique féminine multiculturelle.

Considérations générales et balisage théorique

Genre et citoyenneté

Juridiquement, la citoyenneté est définie comme :

> La jouissance des droits civiques attachés à la nationalité. Aujourd'hui, on entend par là le droit de vote aux consultations politiques, l'éligibilité, l'exercice des

libertés publiques qui donnent sens à la participation politique, enfin l'accès aux fonctions d'autorité dans l'appareil d'Etat (Hermet *et al.* 2005:52).

Ce concept est lié originellement à la démocratie. Les monarchies d'ancien régime du Moyen Âge européen, les Empires de Chine, d'Inde ou d'Amérique précolombienne ne connaissaient que des sujets, essentiellement voués à l'obéissance. Avec les idées démocratiques de l'Antiquité grecque (VIe-IVe siècles avant notre ère) émerge l'idée de participation à la « chose publique » (en latin *res publica*). L'exaltation de la citoyenneté réapparaît au XVIIIe siècle avec les révolutions américaine et française. Elle s'inscrit dans une double perspective : opposition à l'allégeance de type dynastique qui suppose une dépendance de type personnalisé, et affirmation de l'autonomie de la sphère politique, notamment par rapport au religieux.

La citoyenneté n'est pas seulement l'appartenance à une nation. Elle fait référence à une égalité de droits entre toutes les citoyennes et tous les citoyens, mais aussi à la réalité de ces droits, à leur exercice ainsi qu'à la possibilité d'avoir les mêmes droits et devoirs. Elle englobe les relations affectives, civiques, économiques et sociales. La citoyenneté ne va pas nécessairement de pair avec la nationalité. On peut avoir une nationalité sans exercer la citoyenneté ; on peut, comme c'est maintenant le cas dans l'Union Européenne, avoir certains droits, tel celui de vote, sans être un(e) national(e).

Pourtant, la nationalité n'a pas toujours été définie ainsi, la citoyenneté grecque excluait les femmes, les esclaves et les métèques, la citoyenneté romaine excluait également les femmes et les esclaves, même si les esclaves mâles, une fois affranchis, pouvaient devenir citoyens romains. Ailleurs, si la citoyenneté n'était pas si exclusive, elle avantageait néanmoins les hommes par rapport aux femmes. Les démocraties américaine de 1776 et française de 1789 excluaient elles aussi les femmes, même si au niveau textuel, rien ne l'autorisait dans la Constitution américaine.

De fait, dans ces démocraties, on définit la citoyenneté par l'autonomie, la responsabilité et la raison (lire à ce sujet Lavau 1985 ; Gaudemet 1991 ; Finley 1985 ; Shklar 1991 ; Fustels de Coulanges 1985). En étaient donc exclues certaines catégories comme les enfants, les femmes, les aliénés, tout comme ceux qui, ne possédant pas les biens, dépendaient d'un autre pour leur subsistance journalière. Aujourd'hui, la citoyenneté, malgré sa vocation universelle, reste dans la démocratie moderne une construction masculine qui présuppose l'égalité de statut politique entre les individus. Demander aux femmes d'être citoyennes revient alors à leur demander d'être comme des hommes (Peemans-Poulet 1998 ; Bélanger 1992 ; Veauvy 1997).

Derrière le contrat social d'apparence égalitaire se profile un contrat sexué. Carole Pateman (1988), qui défend cette idée, développe donc la thèse selon laquelle la citoyenneté patriarcale est fondée sur une universalité abstraite qui pose en fait le masculin en norme de référence. Dans les systèmes androcentriques, dit-elle, les femmes sont acculées au mieux à une citoyenneté de seconde zone : soit elles sont intégrées à la citoyenneté en tant qu'individus et leur égalité les assimile aux hommes en niant et déniant leurs expériences et leurs vies de femmes, soit elles sont incluses à la citoyenneté en tant que femmes, la différence sexuelle entérinant la séparation entre le privé et le public. Les femmes restent définies par leur appartenance à la sphère privée, à la famille. Les Etats leur accordent souvent des droits sociaux avant de leur donner le droit de vote ou de les affranchir de la tutelle masculine.

L'assignation des femmes à la sphère privée et la construction hiérarchique de la différence des sexes remontent aux temps immémoriaux et sont perceptibles à travers les constructions conceptuelles et théoriques mises en route par des auteurs ayant contribué à la consolidation de l'histoire de la pensée intellectuelle, et particulièrement celle de la pensée politique. Revisiter l'histoire de cette pensée permet non seulement de comprendre à quel point ces rapports de pouvoir sont constitutifs du politique, mais aussi de mieux saisir que l'impensé du genre, faisant écran à la compréhension des enjeux politiques des temps modernes, contribue à la légitimation de toutes les formes de domination (Pisier et Varikas 2002:1).

A ce titre, et comme nous le rappellent les deux auteurs précités, Locke paraît avoir joué un rôle d'importance dans la construction hiérarchique des rapports sociaux de sexe pour avoir substitué au droit paternel le droit conjugal, un pouvoir naturel, extérieur et antérieur à la volonté des contractants. En effet, dans son œuvre fondatrice du contractualisme, *Traité sur le gouvernement civil*, Locke soutient que la puissance conjugale n'est pas une puissance politique. C'est l'argument central de Locke dont l'objectif est de réfuter une fois pour toutes l'identité ou même l'analogie entre le pouvoir exercé par le chef de famille et le pouvoir politique.

Adam n'avait pas sur Eve « le pouvoir de vie et de mort » qui est le propre du pouvoir monarchique, dit Locke. Le pouvoir d'Adam était tout au plus celui que tout mari détient d'ordonner les choses d'intérêt privé, en tant que propriétaire des biens et de la terre au sein de la famille, et de faire prévaloir sa volonté sur celle de sa femme dans toutes les choses qui sont de leur intérêt commun. A l'abri du contrôle politique, la famille devient le lieu d'une domination naturelle, et pour cela invisible, qui prive les femmes des attributs constitutifs de la liberté civile et politique : le droit de disposer librement de leur corps, de leur force de travail, de leurs biens, enfin le droit de résistance, critère ultime de la liberté politique chez Locke.

Fondée sur la sujétion naturelle des femmes, la distinction privé-public introduite par Locke dessine le périmètre dans lequel sera contenue la liberté des femmes en tant que sujets politiques dans les siècles suivants. Locke n'a certes pas thématisé, comme ses prédécesseurs Tyrell et Sidney, l'exclusion des femmes du politique. Ses allusions aux reines peuvent même laisser entendre qu'il n'est pas en principe hostile à la participation politique des femmes. Mais en recourant à la nature pour fonder la puissance conjugale, il affirme la supériorité générale de tout homme sur toute femme dans et en dehors de la famille, réfutant par là même l'égalité et l'indépendance de tous les individus (Pisier et Varikas 2002:5).

La remise en cause de la théorie contractualiste de Locke, et de manière générale celle des théories naturalistes et essentialistes par les féministes, se trouve au cœur non seulement du déplacement des débats sur la citoyenneté vers d'autres terrains épistémologiques et méthodologiques, mais aussi au centre de l'émergence même des études de genre. Comme le dit si bien Parini (2006:21),

> L'émergence du concept de genre est liée à la nécessité de se distancer du sexe comme fait biologique pour investiguer la signification sociale de cette appartenance biologique. Il s'agit de comprendre comment et pourquoi un fait, à première vue uniquement biologique, soit l'appartenance à l'un ou l'autre sexe, devient un enjeu de pouvoir pour le contrôle des ressources matérielles et symboliques.

Envisagé sous cet angle, le genre apparaît comme un remise en question de la théorie contractualiste de Locke fondée sur la survalorisation des éléments biologiques ou naturels dans l'"explication des phénomènes d'autorité ou de pouvoir et la division sexuée du travail ou du savoir. Le concept de genre, qui correspond chez les féministes francophones aux « relations sociales de sexe », induit donc, d'après Bisiliat (2000:23) :

- le rejet du déterminisme biologique sous-jacent dans le mot sexe, et dans l'expression inégalité sexuelle ;
- le regroupement de toutes les différences constatées entre les hommes et les femmes, qu'il s'agisse des différences individuelles, des rôles sociaux ou des représentations culturelles, c'est-à-dire le regroupement de tout ce qui est variable et socialement déterminé. Il est également affirmé que les femmes ne forment pas un groupe homogène, mais un ensemble traversé par des différences de classe, de race et d'ethnie;

- l'asymétrie fondamentale, la hiérarchie et les relations de pouvoir entre les deux groupes, les deux rôles, les deux sexes, les deux genres.

Le genre renvoie donc aux catégories sociales (féminin et masculin) et non aux catégories sexuelles (hommes et femmes). Il implique un savoir sur la différence sexuelle et reflète un pouvoir qui est aussi une manière d'ordonner le monde, inséparable de l'organisation sociale de la différence sexuelle. Le savoir n'est ni fixe, ni fini, il est variable et sujet à d'innombrables changements. Il en est de même pour les complémentarités et oppositions entre les genres qui peuvent se transformer, évoluer, c'est-à-dire s'inscrire dans le changement social. A la suite de Parini, le genre fait donc référence à un système social (système de genre) fondé sur des représentations et des pratiques qui ont pour objet de :

- définir la nature des femmes et des hommes et leurs différences (biologiques et psychologiques) ;
- déterminer sur cette base leurs places respectives dans la société ;
- créer les conditions institutionnelles de cette partition des territoires basée sur l'inégalité ;
- organiser la permanence de cette situation (pour le groupe dominant) ;
- contester cette situation en vue de la changer (pour le groupe dominé, cela est appelé le féminisme).

Défini sous cet angle, le genre en tant que ressource conceptuelle transversale, approche et catégorie d'analyse, devient un instrument d'importance pour l'examen renouvelé des phénomènes sociaux, et du domaine politique en particulier où les femmes ont encore des difficultés à accéder et où les rapports masculins/féminins restent problématiques. D'abord, comme le dit Freedman (1997:9),

> Il y a un décalage apparent entre le domaine politique et d'autres domaines sociaux – et plus particulièrement d'autres domaines professionnels – en ce qui concerne les rapports hommes/femmes. Tandis que les femmes, dans les cinquante dernières années, ont réussi à pénétrer dans beaucoup de sphères professionnelles le droit, la médecine par exemple, celles qui réussissent une carrière politique restent toujours très minoritaires.

De plus, affirme Freedman, la citoyenneté politique n'est pas construite de la même façon pour les hommes et pour femmes. Il existe des contradictions entre les représentations de la féminité et celles du pouvoir. Ainsi, la sphère du pouvoir politique est perçue comme un domaine masculin où les femmes n'ont pas de place. Bref, d'un côté, et comme dit ci-haut, de nouvelles possibilités s'ouvrent aux femmes, et elles bénéficient de plus d'égalité face aux hommes, mais, de l'autre, même si les rapports entre les hommes et les femmes sont beaucoup plus égaux, la construction sociale de la masculinité et de la féminité se fait toujours d'une manière qui sépare nettement les deux genres et qui prescrit aux hommes et aux femmes des normes de comportement assez strictes.

Ainsi, les femmes doivent faire face aux contraintes de la féminité. Elles apprennent dès leur plus petite enfance la nécessité de paraître « féminines », de se faire belles, de séduire les hommes. Le rapport de séduction entre les hommes et les femmes est en effet paradigmatique des contraintes imposées aux femmes par la construction sociale de la féminité. En séduisant, les femmes se réduisent à l'inférieur, à un niveau de faiblesse par rapport aux hommes. Ainsi, les contraintes auxquelles les femmes doivent faire face sont symboliques autant que matérielles.

L'ensemble des préoccupations ci-dessus soulevées par Freedman exerce un impact sévère sur le statut politique des femmes et sur le processus d'acquisition d'une citoyenneté politique féminine égale à celle des hommes. A ce titre, le concept de capacité citoyenne mis en relief par Aminata Diaw et Aminata Touré (1998:40-41) permet de mieux rendre compte des efforts que les Etats doivent fournir pour sortir les femmes de la situation de citoyenneté de seconde zone dans laquelle elles se trouvent.

Les deux auteurs soutiennent en effet que l'individu peut être citoyen formellement et être totalement dépourvu de capacité citoyenne. La reconnaissance par l'Etat de la qualité de citoyen n'entraîne pas *ipso facto* la mise en œuvre par l'individu de sa capacité citoyenne : il fera preuve de sa capacité citoyenne le jour où il sortira de l'âge de la minorité, comme le dit Kant. Et la capacité citoyenne suppose, selon elles :

• la responsabilité qui fait que l'individu se sente coresponsable de l'espace institutionnalisé de vivre ensemble ;

• l'autonomie qui, parce qu'elle conditionne la responsabilité, n'est pas comprise sous l'angle de la stricte indépendance des individus, mais sous le mode de l'intersubjectivité ; l'autonomie doit être comprise comme la soumission exclusive de l'individu aux valeurs républicaines.

Mais, comme le concept de citoyenneté multiculturelle évoqué dans cette étude, le concept de capacité citoyenne nous semble aussi interpeller les femmes, en tant que catégorie politiquement vulnérable, à être solidaires avec d'autres femmes pour que la recherche de la pleine citoyenneté féminine tant voulue et souhaitée par tous ne puisse pas concerner seulement une catégorie de femmes et en exclure une autre sur la base des considérations d'ordre identitaire, ethnique ou raciste, comme c'est malheureusement le cas avec la question des femmes pygmées sous examen.

Genre et citoyenneté multiculturelle

L'objectif de cette étude, comme signalé dans l'introduction, est d'examiner et d'analyser les rapports sociaux au sein ou à l'intérieur même d'un sexe. Il s'agit d'examiner la dynamique de construction des rapports entre deux catégories de femmes porteuses de cultures tout à fait différentes : les femmes bantoues et les femmes pygmées.

Les femmes pygmées (tout comme les pygmées de manière générale) sont caractérisées par les spécificités culturelles suivantes (Nkoy 2005 ; Mafoukila 2006 ; Manga 2009) :

- un attachement particulier à la forêt (on les appelle les rois de la forêt et leur mode de vie dans cette forêt est telle que les bantous ont souvent tendance à les considérer comme des peuples primitifs ou sauvages) ;
- une mobilité légendaire qui rend leur contrôle difficile ;
- l'hostilité vis-à-vis de l'école, et donc carence d'une élite intellectuelle pygmée aussi bien dans les rangs d'hommes que de femmes ;
- la petitesse de leur taille physique ;
- une certaine négligence dans leur façon de s'habiller ;
- un habitat très précaire. Dans la forêt, ils utilisent des huttes en feuilles pour se protéger contre des intempéries et agressions des animaux ;
- des habitudes alimentaires héritées des temps anciens.

La culture pygmée est une sorte de culture ancrée dans l'activisme forestier, une culture de repli sur soi, et donc d'absence d'ouverture à la modernité, bien que quelques femmes et hommes pygmées commencent timidement à s'intéresser aux produits tels que la bière, le tabac et même à l'école. Il faut noter que les femmes pygmées, faute d'éducation et d'instruction scolaire, sont dans l'incapacité de comprendre les enjeux politiques ou économiques liés à leur citoyenneté. Elles ne peuvent pas non plus accéder à l'espace politique et prétendre conquérir le pouvoir et l'exercer comme les femmes bantoues plus instruites qu'elles.

Donc, bien que toutes les femmes soient, de manière générale, marginalisées dans une société androcentrique fonctionnant selon les codes et schémas idéologiques de la masculinité, il s'avère que les femmes pygmées sont non seulement marginalisées, mais aussi et tout simplement exclues, de manière à peine voilée, de la communauté nationale.

Cette exclusion s'opère notamment à travers des politiques publiques et programmes dits de développement qui n'intègrent pas les préoccupations et la culture des femmes pygmées. Sur le plan politique, malgré la non-discrimination théorique et formelle vis-à-vis de ces femmes, elles ne jouissent pas des droits attachés à la citoyenneté politique. Les femmes pygmées sont exclues de la participation politique et sont introuvables dans les institutions politiques de représentation ou d'exécution, aussi bien à l'échelon local que sur le plan national ou même sous-régional et régional.

Les acteurs de cette exclusion sont bien sûr connus : il s'agit de l'Etat, des institutions politiques, de la société civile elle-même, des partis politiques, des seigneurs de la guerre et des sociétés multinationales. Mais au rang de tous ces acteurs, se trouve également une catégorie d'actrices qui nous intéresse particulièrement dans cette réflexion : il s'agit des femmes bantoues. Celles-ci ont contribué et continuent à contribuer, comme les autres acteurs, à la marginalisation politique de leurs compatriotes pygmées.

Si la lutte pour l'acquisition d'une citoyenneté concerne normalement toutes les femmes qui en sont privées et qui, de ce fait, devraient faire preuve de solidarité et d'unité, l'exclusion des femmes pygmées de la jouissance de quelques droits politiques déjà arrachés par les femmes relève alors d'un paradoxe et n'est compréhensible que si l'on considère les femmes comme une catégorie non homogène, divisée, poursuivant parfois des intérêts égoïstes, et traversée par des pesanteurs idéologiques, ethniques, racistes et culturelles. C'est cette trajectoire analytique que nous avons imprimé à la présente étude et qui nous a contraint à mobiliser le concept de citoyenneté multiculturelle, lui-même orienté vers la saisie des rapports entre les femmes bantoues et les femmes pygmées, et entre ces deux catégories de femmes vis-à-vis des phénomènes de pouvoir.

En effet, d'après Ayesha Imam, Amina Mama et Fatou Sow (2004),

> Les rapports sociaux de sexe comprennent également les relations de catégories de femmes avec les phénomènes sociaux (que ce soit l'Etat, la division du travail, le système éducatif, les relations économiques, les systèmes politiques ou autres), ainsi que les relations différentes de groupes d'hommes avec ces mêmes phénomènes.

L'analyse des rapports sociaux de sexe, ou analyse consciente du sexe ou analyse sexuée, peut être spécifiquement centrée sur les femmes (ou les hommes), mais de façon à reconnaître clairement les rapports sociaux de sexe qui construisent historiquement son sujet, comme dans l'analyse de N'dri Assié Lumumba (2004:305-307) sur l'éducation des filles et des femmes en Afrique.

Nous démontrerons tout au long de cette réflexion que la non prise en charge de la notion de citoyenneté multiculturelle, c'est-à-dire d'une citoyenneté différenciée qui reconnaît l'appartenance des individus à des groupes différents du point de vue culturel (Alpe *et al.* 2005) par l'Etat et les femmes bantoues dans l'élaboration des politiques publiques et programmes de développement, explique en grande partie l'infériorisation des femmes pygmées dans l'espace politique et leur incapacité à s'investir dans la lutte pour l'acquisition de leur citoyenneté politique.

Etat et problématique de la citoyenneté politique féminine : la période coloniale

La République Démocratique du Congo s'est dotée, depuis février 2006, d'une Constitution qui proclame, en son article 14, la parité. D'après cet article, les pouvoirs publics veillent à l'élimination de toute forme de discriminations à l'égard de la femme et assurent la protection et la promotion de ses droits. Ils prennent des mesures pour lutter contre toute forme de violences faites à la femme dans la vie publique et dans la vie privée. La femme a droit à une représentativité équitable au sein des institutions nationales, provinciales et locales. L'Etat garantit la mise en œuvre de la parité homme-femme dans lesdites institutions. La loi fixe les modalités d'application de ces droits.

Si la mise en œuvre de la parité constitue une avancée très significative pour les femmes congolaises, la jouissance des droits politiques attachés à la parité ne concerne jusqu'à preuve du contraire que les femmes bantoues qui, bien que n'ayant pas encore fait leur entrée massive dans des assemblées élues, sont cependant les seules à y occuper les sièges et à participer à l'élaboration des lois et autres politiques publiques. L'acquisition, par les femmes congolaises, des droits politiques est une invention très récente dont le processus remonte à 1967 sous le régime de Mobutu.

Pendant la période coloniale, tous les Congolais, hommes et femmes confondus, femmes bantoues et femmes pygmées, étaient exclus de la participation politique. La République Démocratique du Congo, contrairement à d'autres colonies, est née en 1885 sous la forme d'un Etat indépendant du Congo ; en réalité, il s'agissait d'une propriété privée du roi Léopold II des Belges. De 1885 à 1908 donc, c'est le roi lui-même qui dirige sa propriété selon ses caprices et ses orientations. C'est en 1908 que l'Etat Indépendant du Congo devient le Congo belge, suite aux graves violations massives des droits de l'homme commises par les fonctionnaires du roi dans la colonie et qui furent dénoncées par la communauté internationale (Hochschild 2007).

La politique belge au Congo est d'abord une politique de domination et de discrimination raciale qui place les Blancs au sommet de l'échelle et les Noirs, toutes races confondues, au bas de l'échelle sociale, économique, culturelle et politique. Le désir de concrétiser la supériorité de la race blanche et des Belges en particulier se matérialise, sur le plan politique et administratif, par la mise en place, dans la colonie, d'une administration directe. Contrairement donc aux colonies anglaises et françaises, le Congo belge fut administré directement par les fonctionnaires belges, aussi bien au niveau central qu'au niveau local. Le Congo belge fut donc dirigé par des fonctionnaires qui recevaient leurs directives et leurs instructions du Gouvernement de la Mère-Patrie.

C'est la Charte Coloniale qui constitue la loi sur le Gouvernement du Congo belge et est, par conséquent, la base même de l'organisation administrative de la colonie. Cette loi est en réalité la Constitution du Congo belge. Elle fut votée par la Chambre des Représentants le 20 août 1908, par le Sénat le 9 septembre de la même année, promulguée par l'Arrêté royal du 18 octobre 1908 et publiée au Moniteur les 19 et 20 du même mois.

Dans le chapitre II consacré aux droits des belges, des étrangers et des indigènes, on peut lire ce qui suit : « Les Belges, les Congolais immatriculés dans la colonie et les étrangers jouissent de tous les droits civils reconnus par la législation du Congo belge. Leur statut personnel est régi par leurs lois nationales en tant qu'elles ne sont pas contraires à l'ordre public. Les indigènes non immatriculés du Congo belge jouissent des droits civils qui leur sont reconnus par la législation de la colonie et par leurs coutumes en tant qu'elles ne sont pas contraires ni à la législation ni à l'ordre public. Les indigènes non immatriculés des contrées voisines leur sont assimilés. Il est institué une commission permanente chargée de veiller sur tout le territoire de la colonie à la protection des indigènes et à l'amélioration de leurs conditions morales et matérielles d'existence » (Delvaux 1945:17).

Il importe déjà à ce niveau d'attirer l'attention du lecteur sur la différence qu'établit la Charte entre les Congolais immatriculés et les indigènes non immatriculés, nous y reviendrons plus tard. Sur le plan administratif, la Charte institue une administration centrale coloniale constituée par le ministère des Colonies et qui se trouve dans la métropole. Le ministre des Colonies se voyait doté d'un statut identique à celui de ses collègues. Faisant partie du Conseil des ministres, il participait aux délibérations qui portaient sur la politique de la métropole aussi bien que de la colonie. D'autre part, conformément à la coutume, il soumettait aux délibérations du Conseil les affaires coloniales les plus importantes et il avait à se conformer aux décisions de ce dernier (Vanhove 1967:21).

A la tête du gouvernement de la colonie se trouve un haut fonctionnaire nommé par le Roi et qui porte le titre de Gouverneur Général. Le Gouverneur Général représente le Roi dans la colonie et est assisté d'un ou de plusieurs vice-gouverneurs généraux. Ce fonctionnaire, le plus élevé de la colonie, a la haute direction de tous les services administratifs et militaires établis au Congo belge. Il est chargé de l'exécution du budget de la colonie et de l'ordonnancement des dépenses, et soumet annuellement au gouvernement central ses propositions budgétaires. A la tête de chaque province – il y en avait six à cette époque – se trouve un Commissaire Provincial qui représente le Gouverneur Général.

L'organisation dite indigène est dominée par le territoire qui constitue la cellule de base de l'administration coloniale et c'est, par conséquent, l'Administrateur Territorial qui est en somme la pierre angulaire de tout l'édifice administratif. Son influence, comme le précise Delvaux, sera considérable auprès des populations indigènes, car les rapports constants qu'il aura avec les autorités indigènes et avec les populations feront qu'il sera considéré comme le représentant de l'Etat.

Outre la politique indigène qu'il exercera dans son ressort, il lui incombera de veiller à la bonne marche des tribunaux, à la perception des impôts indigènes, au recrutement pour la force publique ; il assumera les fonctions de gardien de prison, d'immigration, de réglementation en matière de main-d'œuvre et d'inspecteur de l'industrie et du commerce, tout en ayant aussi dans son ressort la politique économique, la politique routière, la politique agricole et l'établissement des centres commerciaux et des marchés. Jusqu'à la veille de l'indépendance, aucun Noir n'a pu accéder à ce poste stratégique, pourtant le plus bas dans la hiérarchie administrative. Quand on sait que la politique coloniale belge était très ségrégationniste, l'on mesure l'étendue des dégâts que l'action de ces administrateurs territoriaux belges aux pouvoirs énormes a engendrés tant sur la nature des relations sociales entre Blancs et Noirs que sur la construction des conditions matérielles, spirituelles et intellectuelles pouvant contribuer à l'épanouissement des Congolais.

En effet, malgré les dispositions de la Charte Coloniale, la société coloniale était une société régie par un pouvoir raciste ayant fait de la discrimination raciale son cheval de bataille et son référent dans la gouvernance politique, économique et culturelle. De toutes les politiques publiques discriminatoires secrétées par le pouvoir colonial et qui expliquent la position d'infériorité des congolais vis-à-vis des Belges, et celle des pygmées vis-à-vis des populations bantoues, figurent en bonne place celles relatives à l'enseignement, à l'emploi et à la participation politique.

Comme la plupart de puissances coloniales, la Belgique n'a jamais associé les Congolais à la gestion de l'Etat. Ils ont donc été exclus de la participation politique jusqu'en 1957, date à laquelle les premiers autochtones ont eu à voter pour la première fois. La première politique discriminatoire est celle qui a donc exclu les Congolais de la participation politique. Parlant dans un article publié en 1951 au sujet des droits politiques des congolais, Pierre Wigny, qui fut ministre des Colonies de 1947 à 1950, s'exprimait en ces termes : « Un citoyen participe à la souveraineté nationale. Par son vote, il choisit ses représentants responsables devant le corps électoral ». Ceci – au Congo – n'est pas encore possible. Nous avons de la démocratie une conception réaliste. Il ne suffit pas de former artificiellement quelques chefs, il faut éduquer la masse capable de les contrôler. Mais, dès à présent, il faut encourager la participation à des conseils de territoire ou de district, au gouvernement des centres extra-coutumiers ou des villes, bref à ces assemblées primaires qui là-bas comme ici doivent être des écoles d'apprentissage politique.

D'après donc Wigny et malgré tout le mouvement vers l'indépendance qui se dessinait dans d'autres pays colonies, l'éducation politique au Congo belge devait commencer par la base. Jean Stengers (2007:245-246) constate qu'en réalité, non seulement l'autorité coloniale ne se hâte pas, mais elle ne se préoccupe que fort peu de tracer des plans pour l'avenir. Pas question de la moindre planification, même à moyen terme, de l'émancipation politique. Dans les milieux universitaires, on remue parfois quelques idées générales, quelques projets ; cela ne va pas au-delà de la discussion académique. Cette exclusion des Africains congolais de la politique aura des répercussions plus tard sur l'accès des femmes à l'espace politique post-indépendant, et en particulier des femmes pygmées.

Le deuxième site de discrimination et de politique raciale, c'est l'enseignement. La discrimination dans le secteur de l'enseignement est importante à analyser parce que ce secteur est en interaction avec le domaine politique. On ne peut en effet comprendre comment les femmes pygmées sont exclues aujourd'hui de la citoyenneté politique sans interroger leur passé colonial et post-colonial dans le secteur de l'enseignement parce que la constitution d'une élite politique féminine est très tributaire des possibilités d'accès des femmes à l'instruction.

Au Congo belge, il existait pendant la période coloniale des écoles pour enfants européens (pour garçons, pour filles et mixtes), des écoles officielles pour enfants indigènes et des écoles pour mulâtres. Evidemment, les programmes étaient différents dans les unes comme dans les autres. Aux enfants européens on dispensait des enseignements de qualité pour leur permettre de poursuivre leurs études universitaires en Belgique après les humanités. Il existait donc en 1928 pour les enfants européens 18 écoles publiques et 2 écoles privées, comprenant un personnel enseignant de 100 unités, religieux et religieuses, laïcs et laïques, et une population scolaire de 1617 unités, soit une augmentation de 27 pour cent sur l'année précédente.

On prévoyait l'ouverture de deux nouvelles écoles à Buta et à Kamina. Les internats ont joui d'un succès considérable et partout dans les écoles officielles ou subsidiées, le programme était le même que dans la métropole. Il faut y ajouter les écoles spécialisées pour Européens, notamment l'école de musique d'Elisabethville et les écoles industrielles d'Elisabethville et de Jadovithville (spécialement pour jeunes gens et adultes) qui, toutes trois, étaient subventionnées par la colonie.

Les écoles officielles pour enfants indigènes comprenaient :

Ecoles pour garçons :

- une école pour garçons à Léopoldville-ouest, dirigée par les Frères des Ecoles Chrétiennes et comprenant quatre primaires, quatre années de travail du bois et mécanique, et notamment mécanique auto ;
- une école pour garçons à Boma dirigée par les Frères des Ecoles Chrétiennes et comprenant six primaires et quatre moyennes ;
- une école pour garçons à Coquilathville dirigée par les Frères des Ecoles Chrétiennes et comprenant six primaires et quatre moyennes ;
- une école à Stanleyville dirigée par les Frères Maristes et comprenant six primaires, quatre années de menuiserie et quatre années de forge ;
- une école pour garçons à Buta dirigée par les Frères Maristes et comprenant six primaires, quatre moyennes, quatre années de travail du bois et quatre années de travail du fer ;
- une école pour garçons à Lusambo dirigée par les Frères de la Charité et comprenant six primaires, quatre moyennes, cinq années de travail du bois et cinq années de travail du fer.

Elles comprenaient au total 3942 élèves (Delvaux 1945:114-117).

Ecoles pour filles :

- une école pour filles à Léopoldville-ouest dirigée par les dames Chanoinesses de Saint Augustin et comprenant de la troisième à la 6e primaire. Au total 180 élèves. Il y avait aussi 15 écoles ménagères comprenant, en 1938, 393 élèves. L'enseignement ménager était essentiellement pratique et adapté à la fonction de bonne mère.

Comme on peut le constater, il ressort de ces statistiques que l'enseignement pour indigènes était très rudimentaire et qu'il était très professionnalisé ; il était conçu dans le sens de ne pas permettre aux Congolais de poursuivre leurs études universitaires, d'ailleurs il n'existait même pas d'universités jusqu'en 1953. Par ailleurs, il existait très peu d'écoles pour filles et mixtes, et l'Etat colonial avait mis en œuvre une politique scolaire destinée à former davantage des ménagères. Mais ce qui est important à relever à ce niveau, c'est que l'école pour fille citée ci-haut ainsi que les écoles ménagères et mixtes se trouvaient pour la plupart dans des centres urbains occupés par les autochtones bantous, et donc très éloignés des sites occupés par les femmes pygmées.

Le postulat belge de base dans le domaine de l'enseignement était : « pas d'élites, pas d'ennuis ». Il fallait donc éviter de former l'élite pour garantir la stabilité de la colonie. A ce titre, on peut dire à la suite de Stengers (2007:217)

> Que dans la formation des élites par l'enseignement, il y a eu de la part de l'autorité coloniale des mesures de freinage par lesquelles on a délibérément ralenti l'évolution. On a freiné lorsqu'on a refusé à de jeunes Congolais les moyens et l'autorisation de poursuivre des études à l'étranger, ou dans la métropole. L'étranger ou la métropole, c'était en tout cas l'Europe, c'est-à-dire, aux yeux de l'autorité coloniale, un lieu de perdition pour les jeunes Congolais : ils risquaient de devenir communistes comme les Africains déambulant à Paris sur le boulevard Saint-Michel, ou anticolonialistes comme ceux fréquentant en Angleterre la London Schools of Economics.

On a freiné aussi lors de la création de la première université congolaise, celle de Lovanium, en 1954. Le projet des promoteurs était d'organiser aussi dès le début, à coté des études de médecine, d'agronomie et de sciences administratives, des études de droit. L'administration coloniale s'y est opposée. Former des avocats, selon elle, c'était préparer des agitateurs politiques, « fabriquer des révolutionnaires ». Le droit à Laudanum ne pourra être créé que deux ans plus tard, en 1956, après que cette opposition eut été vaincue. Les conséquences de la discrimination dans l'enseignement sont telles qu'à l'accession du Congo belge à l'indépendance, on ne pouvait pas dénombrer 10 universitaires, et même pas une femme universitaire.

Le problème de l'accès à l'emploi et des règles discriminatoires dans la législation du travail au Congo est lié de près à celui de l'enseignement. Le statut des fonctionnaires en vigueur jusqu'en 1959 mentionnait quatre catégories ; les trois catégories supérieures et la moitié supérieure de la quatrième exigeaient un diplôme universitaire. Les employés non spécialisés, tous Congolais, jouissaient d'un statut spécial d' « auxiliaires ». De ce fait, les Belges touchaient de très hauts salaires ; c'était nécessaire, disait-on, pour pouvoir recruter du personnel qualifié en Belgique (Young 1965:62).

Mais ces politiques discriminatoires étaient appelées à connaître des limites, avec l'apparition, après la Deuxième Guerre mondiale, d'une élite africaine instruite. Il fallait lui accorder un statut satisfaisant dans la société congolaise pour tempérer des revendications qui avaient déjà commencé à voir le jour. Pour faire face à ce défi, des mesures furent prises en deux étapes. Dans la première, de 1945 à 1952, on s'efforça de définir, pour l'élite, un statut légal privilégié par rapport à la masse. Cela se traduisit finalement par le décret d'immatriculation de 1952, en faveur des évolués. Mais les difficultés qu'il y avait à préciser la nature et l'extension exacte de cette réforme faisaient prévoir son échec. Dans les années qui suivirent, l'effort se porta sur une déségrégation au petit bonheur selon les secteurs où elle semblait le plus urgente (Young 1965:48).

L'immatriculation est un processus par lequel une personne dénommée « évoluée » accédait à un statut différent de celui de la masse ignorante qui le rapprochait du Blanc et lui donnait droit à accéder à des milieux généralement réservés aux Blancs comme les cinémas ou les bars par exemple. L'évolué immatriculé pouvait également accéder à une classe intermédiaire dans les transports en commun, trains et bateaux, avoir des chambres à part dans les hôpitaux, et ne pas subir le fouet en prison. L'immatriculé était censé avoir adopté la « civilisation européenne » pour accéder à ce statut.

La magistrature était chargée de se procurer toutes les informations désirées sur le récipiendaire, et l'on affichait des bans au siège territorial le plus proche. Un essaim d'administrateurs belges faisait une descente à la résidence du candidat de la façon décrite par un de ces candidats qui se l'était vu refuser pour manque de maturité, Patrice Lumumba. « Toutes les pièces de l'habitation, à partir du salon, chambre à coucher, cuisine jusqu'aux WC, sont explorées de fond en comble, dans le but de déceler tout ce qui est incompatible avec les exigences de la vie civilisée ».

Ce tableau indique clairement que la société coloniale était une société fondée sur la discrimination raciale et sur la domination des Belges sur les Noirs. Toutes les stratégies avaient été mises en place par l'Etat colonial pour maintenir la supériorité de la race blanche, et même des femmes blanches sur les femmes noires : bantoues et pygmées. Comme toutes les sociétés coloniales, la société coloniale était une société multiculturelle. Les politiques publiques de racialisation, de racisme et de discrimination décrites dans les trois grands domaines de la vie ci-haut ont fait de l'Etat colonial un acteur constructeur d'une citoyenneté féminine déséquilibrée. On trouvait donc au sommet de l'échelle des femmes blanches jouissant d'une citoyenneté de premier rang, suivie d'une citoyenneté de second rang détenue par les femmes bantoues qui, vis-à-vis des femmes pygmées d'ailleurs invisibles dans la société, bénéficiaient encore d'un peu plus d'estime.

Le maintien des femmes noires dans la situation des dominées n'a pas été seulement l'œuvre de l'autorité coloniale. A la manière des rapports inégalitaires existant aujourd'hui entre les femmes bantoues et les femmes pygmées et qui résultent des rapports de pouvoir entre ces deux catégories des femmes, l'Union coloniale des femmes belges (UFC) a aussi contribué à la construction des rapports d'inégalité et d'asymétrie entre les femmes belges et les femmes noires. Catherine Jacques et Valérie Piette nous retracent l'itinéraire de ce groupement féminin qui a énormément servi la cause coloniale. L'étude de l'UFC permet d'appréhender partiellement les valeurs collectives véhiculées au sein du milieu colonial dans sa composante féminine. Elle permet de dépasser l'image classique de la coloniale et de son expérience individuelle et de tenter ainsi de saisir les différents éléments qui participent à la construction d'une identité collective (Jacques et Pierre 2004:95-96).

Fondée en 1923 à Bruxelles, l'Union des femmes coloniales se donne comme objectif « de fortifier l'esprit de solidarité parmi les coloniales belges ». Un comité exécutif se met en place et les membres sont des femmes ayant fait un séjour au Congo et souhaitant partager leurs expériences avec les futures coloniales. L'UFC, dont les membres sont pour la plupart issues de la moyenne bourgeoisie, entretient des liens étroits avec les milieux féministes réunis autour du Conseil national des femmes belges (CNFB). Les fondatrices et dirigeantes de l'UFC ont une conscience forte de la « mission civilisatrice » de la Belgique à l'égard du Congo. Issues en majorité des milieux où se recrutent les cadres supérieurs masculins coloniaux, elles envisagent difficilement leur action sans la comparer avec celle de leur conjoint ou de leur père. Ces femmes, comme le disent Jacques et Piette, représentent en quelque sorte le versant féminin du cadre idéologique de l'œuvre coloniale belge.

Imprégnées des valeurs morales occidentales chrétiennes, les dirigeants de l'UFC ne parviennent que très rarement à se dégager des préjugés raciaux de leur époque. L'objectif principal de l'Union des femmes coloniales est la « recherche du progrès constant des conditions de vie féminine et familiale au Congo tant pour la société indigène que pour la société européenne ». Au Congo même, les autorités coloniales demandent à la coloniale de « civiliser » l'Africaine, ce qui signifie en clair : transformer la femme africaine en une bonne mère, dans le cadre d'une famille nécessairement monogame (car l'apport de la cellule sociale monogame est le fruit le plus élevé de la civilisation chrétienne), lutter contre la dépravation (la polygamie et la prostitution) et, en dernier lieu, développer la scolarisation des jeunes filles.

L'action la plus visible de l'UFC est la création d'ouvroirs pour femmes africaines dans les principaux centres urbains du Congo. En 1925, l'UFC ouvre « des centres éducatifs » destinés aux femmes africaines. L'objectif de ces ouvroirs est explicite : ils se veulent « une véritable école de colonisation par l'influence que la femme européenne peut avoir sur l'éducation générale de la femme indigène ». Ces ouvroirs (couture, raccommodage) se transforment peu à peu en de véritables « Foyers sociaux pour femmes » dans le courant des années 1930. Comme l'affirment les deux auteurs précités, l'instruction des petites Congolaises n'est certes pas réclamée dans une perspective émancipatrice, mais dans le but avoué de mieux les intégrer au sein de l'organisation coloniale. Il est impératif de les soustraire à l'influence néfaste des structures coutumières qui constituent une entrave au développement de la colonie.

D'après les mêmes auteurs, l'UFC ne s'est jamais distanciée des intérêts propres au monde colonial : elle demeure avant toute chose une association d'épouses de coloniaux ou d'agents du gouvernement colonial, alors que le Bulletin renseigne les femmes coloniales sur les avancées féministes dans la métropole ou ailleurs. Quand la Commission « Travail » du Conseil national des femmes belges sollicite l'avis de l'UFC pour formuler des vœux relatifs au travail des femmes indigènes, ses membres se dérobent, estimant la question prématurée : « Nous n'avons aucune suggestion à faire valoir auprès des législatures en ce qui concerne cette question ». Elles se bornent à signaler l'interdiction de la récolte du copal par les femmes et les enfants et omettent de mentionner l'ordonnance du 5 octobre 1935 relative au travail de nuit pour certaines catégories indigènes qui, dans son article premier, interdit le travail aux femmes et aux enfants entre « huit heures du soir et six heures du matin ».

A travers l'action de l'UFC dont la trajectoire nous est rapportée par Catherine Jacques et Valérie Piette, se dégagent quelques idées qui nous semblent centrales. La première, c'est le rôle joué par cette institution coloniale féminine dans la construction et la structuration ou la hiérarchisation des ordres de citoyenneté féminine pendant la période coloniale dans une société multiculturelle. Mais l'UFC co-agit avec l'autorité coloniale qui, à travers des politiques tout aussi discriminatoires fondées sur des différences communautaires et identitaires, est partie prenante dans ce processus de hiérarchisation de la citoyenneté. Ici intervient l'opérationnalité du concept de citoyenneté multiculturelle.

La deuxième idée-force, c'est le lien qu'il faut établir entre les catégories d'analyse que sont la race, la classe et le genre dans sa dimension intra-sexuelle pour mieux appréhender les non-dits de certains discours obscurantistes, mais qui se présentent comme des canaux véhiculant des valeurs diverses. L'articulation de la conscience de genre avec celles de classe et de race montre comment peut se former une identité collective dont les membres poursuivent à la fois des intérêts divergents et convergents, les derniers pouvant être court-circuités par les premiers lorsque les enjeux se situent dans des registres idéologiques contradictoires. C'est notamment le cas de ces femmes, membres de l'UFC impliquées dans un mouvement féministe en Occident où elles sont censées normalement défendre les intérêts de toutes les femmes, fussent-elles celles de couleur (conscience de genre oblige quand même), mais qui se refusent d'inscrire leur action dans ce schéma parce que les intérêts de classe et de race les orientent vers la négation de ceux de genre.

L'ensemble de ces facteurs est tel que pendant toute la période coloniale, les femmes noires (bantoues et pygmées) n'ont pas eu l'opportunité de participer à la politique en tant que citoyennes, sujets de droits politiques et civils. Il faudra attendre la fin de la période coloniale pour voir l'Etat post-indépendant mettre en place des politiques publiques sexuées destinées à reconnaître le rôle que les femmes congolaises peuvent jouer dans le domaine politique. Le ton sera donné par le régime de Mobutu qui autorisera les femmes à voter et à se faire élire pour la toute première fois en 1967.

Malheureusement, comme pendant la période coloniale, tout en octroyant aux femmes ce droit qui les avance vers la conquête de leur citoyenneté, l'Etat se révèle être aussi l'artisan principal des politiques publiques qui ne propulsent pas les femmes pygmées vers cette citoyenneté. Les femmes bantoues qui auraient pu remédier à cette défaillance vont aussi se comporter comme les femmes membres de l'union des femmes coloniales, en élaborant des programmes, des lois ou des projets qui ne tiennent pas compte de la culture et des besoins des femmes pygmées. A ces deux facteurs vont s'ajouter les effets pervers de la mondialisation.

Etat postcolonial, dynamique de genre, citoyenneté multiculturelle et mondialisation

La prise du pouvoir par le président Mobutu en 1965 après cinq ans d'une première République caractérisée par les soubresauts sociopolitiques en tous genres (1960-1965) consacre le début de la deuxième République et l'avènement d'un Etat développeur mais autoritaire. Sur le plan des rapports sociaux de sexe, le régime de Mobutu a imprimé une nouvelle trajectoire à la problématique de la citoyenneté politique féminine et à celle de l'éducation des femmes congolaises.

Alors que les femmes sont restées en marge de la participation politique pendant toute la période de la première République dont les institutions politiques étaient pourtant issues des premières élections démocratiques, libres et transparentes, organisées peu avant l'indépendance par l'autorité coloniale, c'est le régime de Mobutu, issu d'un coup d'Etat militaire, qui sera le premier à accorder aux femmes le droit politique le plus élevé : le droit de vote et d'être élues. Grâce à cette acquisition politique, les femmes participeront pour la première fois à un référendum constitutionnel organisé par le nouveau régime en 1967.

Déjà en 1966, c'est-à-dire juste une année après son accession à la magistrature suprême, le président Mobutu venait de nommer au poste de ministre des Affaires sociales une femme, Sophie Kanza Lihau. C'est la toute première Congolaise qui a occupé le poste politique le plus élevé en RDC. Le régime de Mobutu est celui qui a placé la question de la promotion de la femme au cœur de son agenda programmatique et institutionnel, même si au finish il est quand même demeuré un régime patriarcal.

Tout est parti de la création en 1967 du Mouvement Populaire de la Révolution (MPR). Ce parti unique se veut à l'époque un parti de mobilisation des masses populaires, et particulièrement des femmes congolaises autour des tâches de développement national et de reconstruction de l'unité et la concorde nationales. « Otumoli ba mamans, otumoli Mobutu, disait-on à cette époque (quiconque provoque les mamans, s'en prend à Mobutu lui-même). Cette expression est la traduction des relations de fidélité politique qui existaient entre Mobutu et les mamans. Dans presque tous les meetings politiques, les conférences, les manifestations du parti où Mobutu était appelé à prononcer un discours, il s'arrangeait toujours pour parler de la femme africaine et congolaise en particulier, qu'il voulait toujours authentique et valorisée.

Dans tous les congrès du MPR, parmi les points inscrits à l'ordre du jour, celui relatif à la promotion de la femme revenait avec une fréquence très remarquable. Lors du 3e Congrès du MPR par exemple, quelques-unes des recommandations avancées :

- rendaient hommage au Président-Fondateur du Mouvement Populaire de la Révolution pour avoir permis à la Maman Zaïroise de recouvrer sa dignité et la jouissance de la plénitude de ses droits ;

- chargeaient le Comité exécutif de consolider les acquis de la politique d'amélioration de la condition féminine ;
- invitaient tous les organes du MPR à mettre à la disposition de la Maman Zaïroise les moyens lui permettant d'améliorer sa capacité de production dans tous les domaines ;
- demandaient au Comité exécutif ainsi qu'au Conseil exécutif d'intensifier les programmes d'éducation et de formation de base en matière scolaire non discriminatoire à l'égard des filles;
- recommandaient au Comité exécutif et au Conseil exécutif de mettre tout en œuvre pour faire disparaître des mentalités, les us et coutumes qui dévalorisent la femme, et promouvoir l'éducation morale chez les parents et les jeunes filles ;
- invitaient la Citoyenne Zaïroise à se sentir davantage responsable de sa promotion et à prendre conscience de l'importance du rôle capital qu'elle est appelée à jouer dans la communauté en général et dans le foyer en particulier ;
- demandaient à la Citoyenne Zaïroise de faire montre de fierté nationale et de libération culturelle.

Lors de ses différentes sessions et rencontres, le congrès du MPR est souvent revenu sur la question de la femme congolaise avec la même rigueur et vigueur. Dans un système autoritaire et totalitaire où il n'y avait pas à l'époque d'espace d'expression pour les mouvements féministes qui n'existaient même pas, cette démarche politique effrénée visant à conférer à la femme congolaise une pleine citoyenneté avait tout l'air d'un féminisme d'Etat à peine voilé.

Il faut remonter à la création même du MPR en 1967 pour en comprendre le sens et la signification. Quand le MPR a été créé, il a en effet reçu l'appui de tous les anciens mouvements féminins qui préexistaient et qui ont carrément été incorporés dans le MPR. Au fil du temps, les femmes vont se révéler être des militantes assidues et finalement incontournables pour Mobutu qui était à la recherche de bases sociales solides pour asseoir son pouvoir. C'est ainsi qu'il intègre certaines femmes dans les organes dirigeants du parti et de l'Etat. Malheureusement, malgré l'activisme politique des femmes congolaises et leur soutien au régime de Mobutu, elles n'ont pas été nombreuses à occuper des postes de responsabilité dans le parti. La plupart des postes de conception et de commandement sont restés sous le contrôle d'hommes.

Par ailleurs, comme nous l'avons dit dans notre mémoire de DEA consacré à l'étude du militantisme féminin en RDC, les femmes ont été à cette époque utilisées comme des militantes de seconde main, leur militantisme étant façonné par les hommes et finalement mis sous la tutelle et le contrôle de l'élite politique masculine qui pilotait un Etat patriarcal. La division du travail au sein de ce parti était telle qu'aux femmes étaient souvent réservées des tâches qui les rapprochaient davantage de celles exécutées dans la sphère privée (Tshibwabwa 2006a).

Vers les années 1980, Mobutu va initier sa politique d'émancipation de la femme congolaise matérialisée en 1985 par la création du Département (Ministère) de la condition féminine et famille (Condiffa en sigle) dont les objectifs étaient :

- lutter contre l'analphabétisme ;
- alléger les tâches féminines par le moyen de technologies appropriées ;
- élargir les programmes de formation et de vulgarisation agricole qui impliquent la participation des femmes ;
- développer des infrastructures propres à aider les femmes dans leurs travaux.

La politique mobutiste d'émancipation féminine ne put atteindre les objectifs qu'elle s'était assignés. Aucun des projets soumis par la Condiffa dans le cadre du premier plan quinquennal (1986-1990) ne fut retenu. « Des recommandations officielles à leur mise en pratique, il y a tout un fossé dont la profondeur se mesure à la futilité du discours politique », s'exprimait Gertrude Mianda à propos de cette politique d'émancipation.

Cette politique d'émancipation de la femme congolaise initiée par le régime de Mobutu a été une production sociale nécessitée par la mise en œuvre d'une stratégie destinée à incorporer les femmes dans le MPR pour en faire des militantes de seconde zone, pour en faire des soutiens du régime. La césure entre l'énonciation des discours officiels sur les femmes et la réalité politique de leur instrumentalisation est un paramètre important qui permet de cerner l'orientation patriarcale des politiques en faveur des femmes en RDC (Tshibwabwa 2006a:139).

Malgré l'échec de la politique d'émancipation mobutiste, il ne fait néanmoins l'ombre d'aucun doute que par rapport à la période coloniale, son régime a énormément contribué à avancer la cause de la femme congolaise et en particulier à la rendre, dans la mesure du possible, visible dans l'espace public. Mais comme on va le voir dans les lignes qui suivent, la femme dont il s'agit ici, c'est surtout en particulier la femme bantoue.

Cette politique de visibilisation de la femme dans l'espace public, et politique en particulier, se double d'une politique scolaire qui a permis aux filles congolaises d'accéder massivement à la scolarité. En effet, c'est au régime de Mobutu qu'appartient aussi le mérite d'avoir contribué à l'augmentation des effectifs scolaires et estudiantins féminins en RDC. En 1960, il n'y avait que 418 500 filles dans l'enseignement primaire sur un ensemble de 1 550 000. Cinq ans plus tard, en 1965, les effectifs des filles ont augmenté de 248 865, soit plus de la moitié. En 1976-1977, selon les statistiques de l'UNESCO, ces effectifs sont passés à 1 590 113. Aussi peut-on dire en chiffre absolu que l'augmentation des effectifs s'est traduite par un apport de 1 171 613 unités, soit un accroissement moyen annuel de 8,7pour cent.

Pour l'enseignement secondaire, l'augmentation s'est traduite par un apport de 227 691 unités. Alors qu'en 1960, il n'y avait que 13 154 filles dans l'enseignement secondaire, en 1977-78, elles sont passées à 240 845, soit plus de 18 fois l'effectif de 1960, avec une croissance annuelle de 18,6 pour cent. Quant à l'enseignement supérieur, en 1960, sur 774 étudiants, il n'y avait aucune fille. Il a fallu attendre l'année académique 1961-1962 avec la création de l'Institut Supérieur Pédagogique de la Gombe (ISP/Gombe), anciennement appelé Ecole Normale Moyenne pour jeunes Filles de Kalinab, pour voir cinq filles dans l'enseignement supérieur au Zaïre.

L'année d'après, la première fille zaïroise a été inscrite à l'Université Lovanium et progressivement, le taux de participation des femmes à l'enseignement supérieur s'est accru, surtout avec la création des instituts supérieurs destinés uniquement aux filles : l'institut Supérieur des Arts et Métiers (ISAM) et l'Institut Supérieur des Techniques Médicales(ISTM). Aussi de cinq filles en 1961, l'effectif des filles est-il passé à 3.086 en 1978-79, soit un taux de croissance annuel de 45 pour cent. C'est une progression spectaculaire, comme le constate Mweze (1984:112-113), qui a fourni ces statistiques.

Malheureusement, toutes les statistiques ci-dessus ne concernent que les femmes bantoues, ce sont elles qui finalement ont été favorisées par ces politiques d'éducation et de participation politique. D'ailleurs, les écoles et instituts supérieurs pour filles dont il est question ci-dessus n'ont été construits que dans des centres urbains et les sites occupés par les populations bantoues, et assortis des programmes qui ne tenaient pas compte de la culture des populations pygmées. Il n'a pas été mis en œuvre des programmes de développement pouvant favoriser le désenclavement des pygmées et leur intégration socioéconomique et politique dans la communauté nationale.

Le ministère de la Condition féminine et de la famille évoqué dans ce travail n'a pas eu d'autres politiques que celles destinées à raffermir davantage le pouvoir des femmes bantoues vis-à-vis des femmes pygmées. D'ailleurs, aucune femme pygmée n'a eu l'opportunité de faire partie de ce département situé à Kinshasa, alors que les pygmées habitent des sites éloignés de la capitale. Tout comme l'Etat patriarcal, les femmes bantoues ne se sont pas servies de la sphère d'autorité qui était la leur (si minime soit-elle) pour concevoir des politiques de libération des femmes pygmées longtemps marginalisées par le pouvoir colonial.

Elles ont en revanche travaillé dans le sens de consolider le régime patriarcal animé et dominé par des hommes, contribuant, de ce fait même, à la pérennisation du régime. Il est certes vrai que les femmes ne disposaient pas de pouvoirs de décision sur les matières les plus importantes pour sortir leurs compatriotes de l'obscurité et les conduire vers l'acquisition d'une véritable citoyenneté, mais il est tout aussi vrai qu'elles les ont exploitées chaque fois qu'il était possible pour protéger leurs intérêts égoïstes et mieux se positionner sur l'échiquier politique.

La longue période de transition politique (1990-2006) a été caractérisée en RDC par la violation massive des droits de l'homme qui ont eu des répercussions néfastes sur la question de la citoyenneté des femmes, surtout dans les territoires occupés par les pouvoirs rebelles qui ont géré des espaces territoriaux depuis 1998 jusqu'en 2002. Pendant toute cette période, les femmes congolaises ont participé à presque toutes les rencontres politiques organisées dans le but de mettre fin aux conflits armés et rétablir la paix en RDC. Mais leur lutte est allée aussi dans le sens de reconquérir leurs droits et libertés remis en cause par la dynamique des conflits armés.

C'est ainsi que lors de la mise en place des institutions de la transition post-conflit (2003-2006), les femmes réussiront à imposer aux entités impliquées dans le partage du pouvoir la prise en compte du système de quotas qui, malheureusement, n'a pas été respecté. Lors de l'élaboration de la Constitution de la IIIe République, il sera prévu le fameux article 14 évoqué déjà dans cette étude, qui consacre le principe de parité homme/femme. Pour un pays ayant obtenu l'indépendance en 1960, cette évolution est spectaculaire même si on en est encore au plan formel.

Certes, après les élections organisées en 2006, c'est-à-dire au lendemain de l'adoption par référendum de ladite Constitution qui consacre la parité, la représentativité des femmes dans les institutions politiques, tant nationales que locales, est très faible. A titre illustratif, lors des élections présidentielles, la

Commission Electorale Indépendante (CEI) avait enregistré 33 candidatures, dont 29 masculines et 4 féminines pour un seul siège présidentiel. Pour les élections législatives, elle a enregistré 9 709 candidatures, dont 8 389 masculines, 1 320 féminines pour 500 sièges. Quant aux élections provinciales, sur 13 474 candidatures enregistrées par la CEI, 11 943 ont été déposées par des hommes, 1 531 par les femmes pour 690 sièges, dont 632 soumis au vote et 58 soumis au système de cooptation. Pour les élections sénatoriales, il a été enregistré 1 127 candidatures, dont 1 023 masculines et 104 féminines pour 108 sièges. Au niveau des entités territoriales soumises aux élections comme les provinces, il a été enregistré 76 candidatures, dont 74 masculines et deux féminines pour 11 sièges.

Après les scrutins, les résultats suivants ont été enregistrés : 0 femme élue pour les élections présidentielles, 42 femmes élues sur 500 sièges du Parlement, 43 femmes élues sur 632 sièges dans les provinces, Une femme chef coutumière cooptée sur 48, 5 femmes élues aux élections sénatoriales sur 108, 0 femme élue sur les 22 gouverneurs et vice-gouverneurs qui animent les provinces aujourd'hui. Dans le gouvernement post-élection, l'on dénombre 9 femmes ministres et vice-ministres sur 60, pour le gouvernement provincial de la ville de Kinshasa, 2 femmes ministres sur 8 et 9 femmes députées provinciales sur 48.

Au regard de ces résultats très défavorables pour les femmes, l'on ne peut s'interdire de constater, comme je le faisais remarquer dans une autre étude, que la parité n'est pas nécessairement et exclusivement un problème juridique. La Constitution de la IIIe République et la loi électorale n'ont rien changé à la situation des femmes qui demeurent toujours minoritaires dans les instances d'élaboration des politiques publiques, malgré la proclamation de la parité. La parité nous semble être à la fois une problématique juridico-politique et socio-psycho-culturelle parce qu'elle requiert à la fois la constitution d'une élite politique féminine, d'un leadership politique féminin et un travail intense d'éducation à la perception et la promotion par le corps électoral (tous sexes confondus) d'une citoyenneté sexuée et non discriminatoire, à travers les suffrages qu'il est appelé à adresser aux candidats et aux candidates (Jacques Tshibwabwa 2006b:31).

Il faut faire remarquer que dans toutes les candidatures enregistrées pour les différentes élections évoquées ci-dessus, comme dans les résultats des scrutins et dans les institutions gouvernementales nationales et locales, on ne signale pas la présence d'une femme pygmée. Tous les sièges et postes sont occupés par des femmes bantoues. L'analyse des statistiques de tous les régimes politiques qui se sont succédé en RDC s'inscrivent dans la même lignée. Seul le concept d'exclusion politique peut rendre compte de la situation politique des femmes pygmées (même des hommes d'ailleurs), qui ne sont citoyennes que de nom. Si les femmes bantoues sont en partie responsables de cette exclusion et discrimination, il est important de mobiliser, dans un cadre intersectionnel, la combinaison des différents types de rapports sociaux (de race, d'ethnie, de classe, etc.), et surtout de culture, dans l'explication du processus de marginalisation des pygmées.

Dans une autre livraison scientifique que nous avons coécrite avec Catherine Odimba, nous avons essayé de mettre en relief les facteurs ayant contribué et contribuant à la marginalisation des pygmées, de manière générale, de la politique et de l'économie. Il semble, disions-nous, que la dynamique d'interactions interculturelles exerce un impact sévère sur la situation des pygmées et explique en premier lieu la discrimination dont ce peuple, pourtant autochtone, est l'objet aujourd'hui. Le mode de vie des pygmées est souvent perçu par les Bantous comme une forme infra-humaine de vie et d'existence et sur la base de cette perception ou représentation collective, des stéréotypes et des clichés allant jusqu'à assimiler les pygmées aux sauvages ont été développés et alimentés au fil du temps.

Ils se sont bien sûr ressourcés d'abord à l'anthropologie coloniale qui avait tout l'air d'une science de dénigrement des Africains et surtout des pygmées, ensuite ces préjugés ont connu, à travers les différentes temporalités historiques de la RDC, une trajectoire mouvementée dont, malheureusement, le point d'achèvement n'a pas été leur éradication. Ces clichés développés par les corps sociaux à partir de ce mode de vie ont connu un relief particulier lorsqu'on les a transposés dans la sphère publique, et particulièrement dans le domaine de la gestion de l'Etat et de ses institutions (Tshibwabwa et Odimba 2008:8).

En effet, la non prise en charge de la « culture pygmée » dans l'élaboration des politiques étatiques d'intégration nationale, de la réduction de la pauvreté et de la protection des droits de l'homme est un élément fondamental d'explication. Il met en interaction la dynamique interculturelle et les politiques étatiques. Erigée en référent dans l'élaboration des politiques publiques, la culture bantoue fait figure d'autorité et même d'autoritarisme qui montre que le débat relatif à la hiérarchisation des cultures et à la supériorité des unes par rapport aux autres est encore loin d'être clos, malgré les rassurantes productions de bonnes paroles des auteurs tels que Claude Lévi-Strauss (2001) ou Edgar Morin (1997).

Cet élément montre également comment la diversité ethnique ne coïncide pas nécessairement avec la diversité culturelle lorsqu'elle s'applique au domaine de la gestion ethno-politique de l'Etat. En effet, dans la gestion de l'Etat et du pouvoir, les bantous, qui dominent le champ politique, ne se comportent pas, face aux pygmées, comme des gens appartenant à plusieurs cultures qui épouseraient les contours de leurs ethnies respectives. Ce que l'on aperçoit plutôt dans la gouvernance politique et économique, c'est seulement l'existence de deux cultures malgré la diversité ethnique : d'une part, la culture bantoue et son emprise autoritaire sur la conception et l'exécution des politiques étatiques et, d'autre part, une culture pygmée marginalisée, ignorée et dominée par la première. Les politiques étatiques apparaissent donc comme des politiques fortement monoculturelles à cause de la nationalisation de la culture bantoue, malgré la dynamique interculturelle et multiculturelle (Tshibwabwa et Odimba 2008).

La dynamique actuelle de la mondialisation explique aussi la marginalisation des pygmées. La mondialisation, on le sait, tend à occidentaliser toutes les cultures de la planète, et dans cette mouvance d'occidentalisation, les pygmées, qui ne participent pas à la gestion de l'Etat et à l'élaboration des politiques publiques, assistent impuissants à la destruction de leurs substrats culturels à la fois par les bantous et par les forces de la mondialisation. Les multinationales minières et forestières impliquées dans la déforestation et l'exploitation minière, et donc dans la destruction de l'environnement et sites naturels habités par des pygmées, contribuent largement à la destruction de la culture pygmée, à l'accroissement de leur pauvreté et à la violation de leurs droits économiques et sociaux et ceux relatifs au développement.

Le processus actuel de mondialisation est le deuxième facteur qui explique la marginalisation des pygmées. Les études récentes réalisées sur la situation des populations autochtones dans le monde montrent que ce processus de mondialisation, porteur de violence, se manifeste notamment à travers ce que l'on peut appeler le développement agressif. Le développement devient agressif lorsque les populations touchées en sont les victimes et non les bénéficiaires, lorsque ces populations sont mises de côté au moment de la planification du développement et ne sont pas considérées comme des partenaires du développement, et lorsque, plutôt que d'être au centre du développement, elles sont considérées comme de simples ressources dans un processus axé sur le profit (The Philippine Alliance of Human Rights Advocates, 1996).

Le développement agressif entraîne des violations des droits fondamentaux des peuples autochtones parce qu'il dénigre et en détruit les pratiques de développement et les systèmes autochtones. Il viole ces droits dans toutes leurs dimensions : économique, sociale, culturelle, civile et politique. Il repose souvent sur l'idée de départ selon laquelle les façons de faire de la société dominante sont intrinsèquement supérieures à celles des autochtones. La mise à exploitation des sites miniers et forestiers des populations autochtones à travers notamment des grands projets dits de développement tels que l'extraction minière, pétrolière, forestière, les plantations agricoles ou la construction des barrages est à la base des migrations forcées de populations autochtones et des pertes de leurs terres traditionnelles.

Vers une gouvernance multiculturelle citoyenne

A travers tout ce qui vient d'être développé ci-dessus, se dessine clairement toute la problématique de la gouvernance qu'il importe d'invoquer aussi dans cette étude. Il s'agit bien sûr ici d'une gouvernance qui tienne compte de la dynamique des rapports sociaux de sexe dans l'espace politique et qui débouche sur la construction d'une citoyenneté inclusive. En tant qu'acteur principal impliqué au premier chef dans l'élaboration des politiques publiques de participation et éducatives, l'Etat est interpellé. Il doit mettre en place des stratégies de développement et de définition d'une citoyenneté sexuée qui permettent à toutes les catégories des femmes de jouir de leurs droits politiques, économiques et sociaux.

Cela suppose bien sûr que les femmes pygmées soient instruites de la même manière que les femmes bantoues. Toutes les études menées jusqu'à ce jour montrent clairement que les pygmées tiennent à la sauvegarde de leur culture et de leur environnement (la forêt) considérée comme leur mère nourricière. Il est donc possible de les intégrer dans les structures sociopolitiques de la RDC tout en leur garantissant une certaine autonomie culturelle en tant que peuple minoritaire, au lieu de chercher à les assimiler à une culture bantoue dans laquelle elles ne se retrouvent pas.

Le calendrier scolaire en vigueur en RDC est un exemple éloquent de l'emprise presque autoritaire de la culture bantoue sur la culture pygmée. Au rang de ces facteurs qui expliquent la non scolarisation des femmes pygmées, se trouve également l'inadéquation entre le calendrier scolaire et le mouvement saisonnier des peuples autochtones concernant la chasse et la cueillette. En effet, la carte scolaire ne prend pas en charge le rythme des différentes saisons et des ressources naturelles qu'y tirent les peuples autochtones et auxquelles ils sont attachés. Il n'est donc pas étonnant de les voir abandonner les salles de classe pendant ces saisons pour se lancer à la recherche des chenilles, champignons, végétaux, miel, etc. L'organisation de la scolarité basée sur le sédentarisme est en effet en contradiction avec le mode de vie des peuples autochtones pygmées essentiellement basé sur le nomadisme, bien que quelques-uns d'entre eux soient en train de se sédentariser.

L'importance de la culture et de l'identité, surtout en cette période de mondialisation hégémonique, est de plus en plus mise en exergue par plusieurs auteurs. En fournissant des répertoires d'action et de représentation à nos choix, la culture, la tradition et les processus d'identification remplissent une fonction de boussole ou d'orientation (on peut dire aussi de mise en rapport ou de médiation). Nous définissons comme orientation la capacité que possède la culture à établir des rapports significatifs entre les éléments de l'environnement : personnes, institutions, événements. La culture est une capacité à mettre en œuvre des références, des schèmes d'action et de communication. C'est un capital d'habitudes incorporées qui structure les activités de ceux qui le possèdent ; c'est ce qui permet à un Eskimo, à un Parisien ou à un pygmée d'établir un rapport significatif entre les choses et les personnes, et de ne pas partir à la dérive dans le monde, comme l'affirme Jean-Pierre Warnier (2004:11).

Une bonne gouvernance étatique devrait tenir compte de ce paramètre, surtout dans le domaine de l'éducation des femmes pygmées. A ce niveau, et comme le souhaite l'UNESCO qui tient à la protection de la diversité culturelle et aux droits culturels, la question de l'éducation et de l'alphabétisation dans les langues autochtones est d'une importance capitale. Dans sa résolution 1997/14 du 22 août 1997, intitulée « Groupe de travail sur les populations autochtones », la Sous-Commission des droits de l'homme de l'ONU a prié le Secrétaire général de transmettre le rapport du Groupe de travail aux organisations autochtones, intergouvernementales et non gouvernementales et à fournir des informations et des données, en particulier sur tout ce qui concerne le point intitulé : « Les peuples autochtones : éducation et langue ».

Ce rapport ayant trait à l'esquisse méthodologique relative à l'aménagement linguistique en faveur des langues autochtones invite les gouvernements et d'autres acteurs à concevoir et à élaborer le schéma directeur d'une opération de réforme linguistique, à engager une action de formation des agents de la réforme (maîtres, futurs maîtres et futurs cadres d'enseignement), à mettre en place des structures de conception, de production et de diffusion d'instruments pédagogiques en langues autochtones et sur ces langues, et, enfin, à mettre à l'étude un cadre juridique, administratif, financier et technique dans lequel la réforme peut effectivement être lancée et développée.

L'Etat doit donc s'inscrire dans le sillage de ces recommandations parce qu'enseignement autochtone et autodétermination des autochtones sont intimement liés. Un véritable enseignement autochtone ne peut être dispensé que lorsque les autochtones ont un réel pouvoir d'intervention dans le processus d'éducation, comme le montre Jack Beetson, président de la Fédération of Independent Aboriginal Education Providers d'Australie (2007:7). Mais les programmes ne doivent pas non plus confiner les autochtones dans les ghettos, ils doivent les rendre capables d'assimiler les connaissances à partir de leurs cultures tout en leur ouvrant des horizons larges qui les intègrent dans la communauté nationale et internationale, et leur permettent aussi d'accéder à la citoyenneté internationale. On ne peut en effet, à l'ère de la mondialisation, concevoir une école ou une éducation qui isole davantage les pygmées du reste de la société.

D'après Céline Saint-Pierre (2001:279), c'est à ce niveau qu'apparaît aujourd'hui le rôle de l'école. Après avoir identifié quatre phénomènes qui posent actuellement des défis majeurs aux sociétés démocratiques dans la société-monde et servent de points de repère dans l'examen de la mission de l'école en tant qu'institution, elle se propose d'examiner comment l'école est interpellée en tant qu'institution organisatrice de la citoyenneté. Il est attendu, dit-elle, de l'école qu'elle soit en mesure, d'une part, de concilier l'appartenance commune et la diversité culturelle et sociale et, d'autre part, d'apprendre aux élèves le « comment vivre ensemble » dans un espace sociopolitique pluraliste.

Dans ce rôle d'éducation à la citoyenneté, l'école doit aller au-delà de la transmission de savoirs et de valeurs et adopter un nouveau modèle pédagogique qui favorise l'interaction, la participation, l'entraide, le respect de la diversité des points de vue et des capacités de chacun. Au Québec, dit-elle, cette vision se traduit, par exemple, par l'enseignement coopératif, la pédagogie par projet et la pédagogie de la découverte. Dans les écoles secondaires, sont mis sur pied des conseils d'élèves, des projets communautaires et des activités de coopération internationale, qui répondent aussi aux exigences d'une citoyenneté ouverte sur le monde (Saint-Pierre 2001:281).

Dans les milieux où les femmes pygmées vivent avec les femmes bantoues, l'Etat doit favoriser la création des écoles devant promouvoir un enseignement tel que celui évoqué par Céline. En effet, un des facteurs qui empêchent aujourd'hui les femmes pygmées (et tous les autochtones pygmées en général) d'aller à l'école, là où elles en ont l'opportunité, est le dénigrement et la discrimination dont elles sont victimes de la part des élèves bantous et des enseignements bantous. Catherine Odimba rapporte que dans une école où un pygmée était admis comme élève, l'enseignant (bantou) de la classe où se trouvait ce pygmée avait pris l'habitude de poser des questions toujours à ce dernier pour le voir échouer et le ridiculiser publiquement en ces termes : vous les pygmées, vous n'êtes pas intelligents, votre place ne se trouve pas ici.

Et quand l'élève pygmée réussissait à certaines des questions difficiles qu'il lui posait, il s'étonnait de voir un pygmée être aussi capable d'assimiler des savoirs scientifiques. Finalement, indisposé et découragé, ce pygmée a fini par abandonner les études. On voit comment la formation à une citoyenneté sociale ouverte sur l'importance de la diversité culturelle ou du multiculturalisme culturel apparaît dans ce contexte comme un impératif catégorique pour la réussite de la scolarisation des femmes pygmées. D'où, également, le rôle que doivent jouer des maîtres et futurs maîtres formés aux langues autochtones et à la culture des populations pygmées comme suggéré par le rapport du Groupe de travail sur les populations autochtones de la Commission des droits de l'homme de l'ONU évoqué plus haut.

Outre l'implication de l'Etat dans la gouvernance, celle des femmes bantoues elles-mêmes en tant qu'agents de promotion de la citoyenneté de leurs compatriotes pygmées est très sollicitée. Penda Mbow (2006:14) constate à ce sujet que « si la dimension concrète des exigences des femmes est clairement perçue, il leur manque, cependant, une perception juste des enjeux politiques, une cristallisation à la fois d'une conscience citoyenne égalitaire et d'une conscience nationale ». On voit à travers cette importante remarque de Penda qu'il manque aux femmes une conscience égalitaire dans la mesure où elles ne luttent pas pour l'acquisition d'une citoyenneté féminine égale pour toutes les femmes, et à l'échelle nationale. L'analyse des interactions entre les femmes bantoues et pygmées sous examen va dans ce sens.

Les femmes bantoues impliquées dans les institutions de gouvernance doivent orienter leur gouvernance dans le sens de permettre à d'autres femmes défavorisées de devenir de véritables sujets politiques. C'est dans ce sens qu'il faut comprendre la question de Penda Mbow ci-après : « quel sens les femmes peuvent-elles donner à la bonne gouvernance pour un plein exercice de leur citoyenneté ? ».

C'est par ce plein exercice de leur citoyenneté acquise massivement et de manière inclusive que les femmes réussiront à se construire un pouvoir non seulement d'influence, mais aussi de décision. Le même auteur s'exprime dans une autre réflexion en ces termes : « c'est en démêlant les relations qu'elles entretiennent aussi bien avec les hommes que les unes avec les autres que l'on peut comprendre comment un pouvoir féminin se construit à l'intérieur d'un système de rapports inégalitaires » (Penda 2005:2).

Mais les hommes qui, finalement, occupent une place centrale dans les institutions de la gouvernance sont doublement interpellés. Leur rôle dans l'exclusion politique des femmes, aussi bien bantoues que pygmées, est très évident. Etudiant la question du genre et de la gouvernance au Maroc, Malika Benradi (2002:203) constate que

> l'accès des femmes à la représentation politique reste l'un des domaines où l'écart entre normes constitutionnelles, aspirations collectives et pratiques sociales demeure plus marqué. Malgré une conviction forte partagée par les deux sexes de la nécessité d'impliquer les femmes dans le champ politique, l'évolution vers une plus grande mixité apparaît bloquée par les structures masculines du jeu politique et par l'auto-exclusion des femmes.

La responsabilité des hommes est aussi mise en relief par Onalena Doo Selolwane (2006:19) qui, constatant le taux de représentation féminine très faible au sein de la législature du Botswana (5%), la plus vieille démocratie de la région australe, estime que «la question directe que les femmes africaines devraient se poser dans le cadre de leur recherche de légitimité politique consiste à se demander comment démocratiser à la fois le fonctionnement interne des partis politiques et les systèmes électoraux nationaux, afin d'améliorer la représentation intégrante ».

Nous espérons que le nouveau ministère de Genre, femmes et familles créé en République Démocratique du Congo, au lendemain des élections de 2006, et qui est dirigé par une femme, essaiera de jouer un rôle cardinal dans l'émancipation politique des femmes en général et dans celle des femmes pygmées en particulier, en se servant de ces quelques pistes de solution ouvertes par notre recherche.

Conclusion

Cette réflexion a eu le mérite de plancher sur la question de la citoyenneté féminine, et en particulier de celle des femmes pygmées. Le concept de citoyenneté multiculturelle a été placé au centre de nos analyses. Il s'agit d'une citoyenneté qui promeut aussi bien les hommes que les femmes concernées ici, dans leurs diversité et pluralité culturelles. Une citoyenneté multiculturelle n'abandonne pas d'autres femmes sur les marges, elle est inclusive.

Mais tout en promouvant la citoyenneté des femmes bantoues et pygmées dans leurs diversités identitaires, la citoyenneté multiculturelle n'est pas une forme de citoyenneté de repli sur soi, elle doit permettre aux femmes pygmées de s'ouvrir à la communauté nationale et au monde. A ce titre, elle est proche des concepts de « pleine citoyenneté » ou de « nouvelle citoyenneté » dont parle Céline, où l'on voit une approche susceptible de faire face à la crise d'une participation sociale active et responsable et aux difficultés de répondre aux exigences du « vivre ensemble ».

La mise en œuvre de cette pleine citoyenneté conduit à la création d'un nouvel espace d'appartenance et de reconfiguration de l'identité de chaque individu, espace dans lequel celui-ci apparaît en tant qu'acteur social. Le champ de la participation sociale est ainsi redécoupé. Elle ne se limite plus à la communauté locale, régionale et nationale. Elle fait appel à une conscience citoyenne qui inclut la coopération et la solidarité internationales comme contrepartie de la compétitivité internationale et de la globalisation des marchés (Saint-Pierre 2001:278-279).

La nouvelle citoyenneté implique le passage d'un homme éclaté à un homme moderne capable de réaliser la synthèse de sa vie personnelle, familiale, sociale, professionnelle. Passer d'un citoyen éclaté à une nouvelle citoyenneté réalisant la synthèse du sujet politique, du sujet producteur et du sujet citadin - usager-consommateur. Passer du citoyen de l'Etat-nation à la fois au citoyen planétaire et au citoyen du local. Telles sont les exigences aujourd'hui (Lefebvre 1991:13). La nouvelle citoyenneté peut donc être définie, d'après Lefebvre, pour chaque individu et pour chaque groupe social, comme possibilité (comme droit) de connaître et de maîtriser (personnellement et collectivement) ses conditions d'existence (matérielles et intellectuelles), et cela en même temps comme acteur politique, comme producteur et comme citadin-usager-consommateur, dans son lieu de résidence, dans sa cité et sa région, dans ses activités professionnelles comme dans les domaines du non travail, mais aussi dans sa nation et dans le monde.

A travers cette étude, se dessine aussi toute la nécessité de susciter des recherches sur les rapports sociaux intra-sexuels, comme celle qui concerne les rapports entre femmes bantoues et femmes pygmées, tout comme des études entre hommes bantous et hommes pygmées. Les hommes peuvent s'exploiter entre eux, tout comme les femmes. A cette préoccupation se trouve celle qui consiste à articuler, dans les analyses, rapports de sexe avec rapports de genre, rapports de classe, rapports de race et rapports de religion.

Bien que la lutte pour la conquête de la citoyenneté soit une lutte commune à toutes les femmes, elle est perçue par les différentes catégories de femmes de manières différentes. Ainsi, les femmes bantoues, qui animent les institutions étatiques et sont dans les couloirs du pouvoir, ont tendance à privilégier les intérêts de la classe dirigeante à laquelle elles appartiennent, tout en reléguant au second plan les intérêts des autres femmes. On voit comment la conscience de classe peut constituer un obstacle à l'émergence d'une conscience de genre, au sein même d'un sexe où une catégorie peut utiliser d'autres comme escalier, mieux, comme escalator politique ou économique.

Bibliographie

Alpe *et al.*, 2005, *Lexique de sociologie*, Paris: Dalloz.

Assié-Lumumba, N., 2004, « Education des filles et des femmes en Afrique : analyse conceptuelle et historique de l'inégalité des sexes », in Ayesha, I., Mama ;A. et Sow, F. (dir.), *Sexe, genre et société. Engendrer les sciences sociales africaines*, Dakar: Séries de livres du CODESRIA.

Delvaux, R., 1945, *L'organisation administrative du Congo belge*, Anvers: Editions Zaïre.

Benradi, M. et M'chichi Alami, H., 2002, « Genre et gouvernance : analyse des comportements politiques des hommes et des femmes au Maroc. A propos d'une enquête de terrain. », in AFARD/AWWOORD, *Genre, intégration économique, gouvernance et méthodes contraceptives*, Dakar: Série des livres AFARD.

Belanger, A.J., 1992, « La démocratie libérale comme règle du jeu », in Boismenu, G. (dir.), *Les formes modernes de la démocratie*, Montréal-Paris: L'Harmattan.

Diaw, A. et Touré, A., 1998, *Femme, Ethique et Politique*, Dakar: Fondation Friedrich Ebert.

Beetson, J., 1998, *Les peuples autochtones et leur droit à un système d'éducation autochtone indépendant*, Genève: Haut Commissariat aux Droits de l'homme.

Bisiliat, J., 2000, « Luttes féministes et développement : une perspective historique », in Bisiliat, J. et Verschuur, C., (dir.), *Le genre : un outil nécessaire. Introduction à une problématique*, Paris-Canada: L'Harmattan-L'Harmattan Inc.

Finley, M., 1985, *L'invention de la politique. Démocratie et politique en Grèce et dans la Rome républicaine*, Paris: Flammarion-Champs.

Fustels de Coulanges, N.D., 1985, *La Cité antique*, Paris: Hachette.

Freedman, J., 1997, *Femmes politiques : mythes et symboles*, Paris-Canada: L'Harmattan -L'Harmattan Inc.

Gaudemet, J., 1991, *Les institutions de l'Antiquité*, Paris: Montchrétien.

Hermet, G. *et al.*, 2005, 6è édition, *Dictionnaire de science politique et des institutions politiques*, Paris: Armand Colin.

Hermet, G. *et al.*, 2005, *Dictionnaire de la science politique et des institutions politiques*, Paris: Armand Colin.

Hochschild, A., 2007, *Les fantômes du roi Léopold. La terreur coloniale dans l'Etat du Congo. 1884-1908*, Paris: Tallandier.

Imam, A., Mama, A. et Sow, F., 2004, *Sexe, genre et société. Engendrer les sciences sociales africaines*, Paris-Dakar: Karthala et CODESRIA.

Jacques, C. et Piette, V., 2004, « L'union des femmes coloniales (1923-1940). Une association au service de la colonisation », in Hugon, A., *Histoire des femmes en situation coloniale. Afrique et Asie, XXe siècle*, Paris: Karthala.

Kymlicka, W., 1995, *Multicultural citizenship. A liberal theory of minority rights*, Londres: Clarendon Press.

Laufer, J., 2005, « Domination », in Maruani, M., (dir.), *Femmes, genre et sociétés. Etat des savoirs*, Paris: La Découverte.

Lavau, G., 1985, « La démocratie », in Grawitz, M. et Leca, J., (dir.), *Traité de science politique*, Vol. 2, Paris: PUF.

Lefebvre, H., 1991, *Du contrat de citoyenneté*, Paris: Editions Sylepse-Periscope et transeditions Archipel.

Levi-Strauss, C., 2001, *Race et Histoire*, race et culture, Paris: Albin Michel/Editions UNESCO.

Mafoukila, C.M., 2006, *La scolarisation des enfants pygmées au Congo. Evolution historique et perspectives*, Yaoundé, Presses Universitaires d'Afrique. Est du Cameroun, Paris: L'Harmattan.

Mossuz-Lavau, J., 2005, « Parité : la nouvelle « exception française », in Maruani, M., (dir.), *Femmes, genre et sociétés. L'état des savoirs*, Paris: La Découverte.

MPR/Secrétariat Général, 1988, Rapport au IVe Congrès du Mouvement Populaire de la Révolution, Kinshasa, N'sele, 16 mai.

Mweze, B., 1984, « L'éducation des femmes au Zaïre et leur accès à l'emploi », in IPN (éd.), *Colloque sur l'apport de la femme dans le processus de développement national*, Kinshasa: Centre de recherche et de pédagogie appliquée, 24-26 juillet.

Nkoy Elela, 2005, *Situation des autochtones pygmées (batwa) en RDC. Enjeux de droits humains*, Kinshasa: Chaire Unesco de l'Université de Kinshasa.

ONU/Commission des droits de l'homme, 1998, Examen des faits nouveaux concernant la promotion et la protection des droits de l'homme et des libertés fondamentales des autochtones : éducation et langue.

Pateman, C., 1988, I. Stanford: Stanford University Press.

Parini, L., 2006, *Le système de genre. Introduction aux concepts et théories*, Zürich: Editions Seismo, Sciences sociales et problèmes de société.

Peemans-Poulet, H., (dir.), 1998, *La démocratie à l'épreuve du féminisme*, Bruxelles: Louvain-la-Neuve (Université des femmes).

Pereira-Marques, B., 2002, Le genre et les travaux anglo-saxons sur la citoyenneté, Communication faite au Colloque AFSP, *Genre et Politique*, 30 – 31 mai.

RDC/CEI, 2006, Constitution de la RDC, Kinshasa, Mars.

Selolwane, O.D., 2006, « Les femmes et la construction de la légitimité électorale », in *Bulletin du CODESRIA* : La femme africaine, Numéro spécial 1 et 2, juin.

Tshibwabwa, K., 2006(b), Genre, élections et construction des institutions politiques de l'Etat de développement démocratique en RDC, Communication faite au CODESRIA, Caire, Egypte.

Tshibwabwa, K., 2006(a), Femmes et action politique : pour une histoire politique relationnelle et genrée du militantisme partisan en RDC. De l'indépendance (1960) à 2004, Mémoire de DEA défendu à l'Université de Kinshasa, Département des Sciences Politiques et Administratives.

Tshibwabwa, K. et Odimba, K., 2008, «Dynamique interculturelle, politiques étatiques et processus de mondialisation : regard sur les minorités autochtones pygmées», in *Cahiers de la Chaire UNESCO* de l'Université de Lyon. (Article sous presse).

Penda, M., 2006, « Femmes, citoyenneté et gouvernance », in *Bulletin du CODESRIA* : La femme africaine, Numéro spécial 1 et 2, juin.

Penda, M.(dir), 2005, *Hommes et femmes entre sphères publique et privée*, Dakar: Série sur le Genre du CODESRIA 5.

Pisier, E. et Varikas, E., 2002, De l'invisibilité du genre dans la théorie politique. Le débat Locke/Astell, Communication faite au Colloque AFSP, *Genre et Politique*, 30 – 31 mai.

Rodota, 1999, *La démocratie électronique. De nouveaux concepts et expériences politiques*, Rennes, Editions Apogée.

Saint-Pierre, C., 2001, « Eduquer autrement pour un monde complexe et pluraliste », in Mercure, D., (dir.), *Une société-monde ? Les dynamiques sociales de la mondialisation*, Laval: Les presses universitaires de l'université Laval.

Stengers, J., 2007, Congo, *Mythes et réalités*, Bruxelles: Racine.

Touraine, A., 1984, *Le retour de l'acteur*. Essai de sociologie, Paris: Fayard.

Vanhove, J., 1967, *Histoire du Ministère des colonies*, Bruxelles: Académie Royale des Sciences d'Outre-mer.

Veauvy, C. et Pisano, L., 1997, *Paroles oubliées. Les femmes et la construction de l'Etat-nation en France et en Italie*. 1789-1860, Paris: Armand Colin.

Warnier, J.P., 2004, *La mondialisation de la culture*, 3e édition, Paris: La Découverte.

Young, C., 1965, *Introduction à la politique congolaise*, Kinshasa-Kisangani-Lubumbashi: Editions universitaires du Congo.

3

Masculinities, Femininities and Citizen Identities in a Global Era: A Case Study of Kiambu District Kenya, 1980-2007

Felix Kiruthu

Introduction

Globalisation has vastly increased the interconnections among peoples across the globe, and influencing the construction of gender and citizenship identities. Since the first United Nations Conference on Women, held in Mexico City, in 1975, there has been an evolving consciousness among scholars and civil rights activists that development is a gendered process (Woodhouse, 2003; Berry 2009). Consequently, a focus on gender, as opposed to women, as a category for analysing how economic, political, social and cultural systems affect men and women differently, has gained recognition among scholars (Elson 1995). This is informed by the understanding that gender is socially constructed whereas sex is determined by one's biology: people see themselves either as masculine or feminine based on the ideological and social constructs that shape their reality either as men or women (Praechter 2003). Unfortunately, for a long time, attention has been directed at women as the singular group that is discriminated against and disenfranchised, while men have been kept in a straitjacket as the perpetrators (Bannon and Correia 2006).

Research trends in social sciences have, therefore, begun to shift focus towards men, due mainly to the realisation of the need to also appreciate the challenges men face, for a more holistic understanding of society. This entails a critical exploration of issues of masculinities as they interact with the development process. Unfortunately, even here, there has been a tendency to focus on the hegemonic masculine identity, which tends to overlook the subtle variations within masculinity, and which works against vulnerable men and boys (Bannon and Correia 2006). Ratele *et al.* (2007) point out that masculinity has not undergone the kind of scrutiny given to femininity. For a long time, few studies interrogated the complex ways in which men and women negotiate their relationships. This underscores the need to focus on the particularities of different contexts in order to understand the vulnerabilities of both men and boys. Their situation has been obfuscated or ignored due to the dominant view of men as oppressors (2007:3). This is particularly important given the pervasive impact of globalisation.

Globalisation is a system of domination and disempowerment which impacts social groups differently (Olorudi 2003). By dissolving geographical borders between states, these forces erode the autonomy of the nation-state, politically, economically and culturally. Consequently, constructions of citizenship and gender identities are reshaped and reconfigured in multiple ways by these dynamics. Since gender is socially constructed, these forces have challenged the dominant constructions of femininity and masculinity by deconstructing the socio-cultural and economic roles prescribed by society for both men and women. This calls for both a clear analysis on the impact of globalisation on gender relations, and an examination of the different kinds of masculinities, namely, the relations of domination, alliance and subordination in our societies resulting from globalisation, in the context of a particular space and time (Bannon and Correia 2006).

This study analyses how globalisation has impacted on the construction of citizenship and gender identities in Kenya from 1980 to 2007. As Elson (1995) observes, a gender perspective on development is crucial as it facilitates the design of more nuanced and human-centred development strategies. The particular ways in which Kenyan citizens in Kiambu District have attempted to deal with the realities of marginalisation and social exclusion accompanying the forces of globalisation are interrogated in the study, using the lens of masculinities. This is critical, given that men and women are subordinated by these dynamics in different ways at different historical times and spaces. Data for this study were collected between 2002 and 2007 as part of a larger research study undertaken by the author entitled: 'The History of the Informal Enterprises in Kenya: A Case Study of the Jua Kali Sector of Nairobi, 1899-1998'. The study employed a variety of multidisciplinary approaches, including oral interviews of 150 respondents who were identified through purposive sampling. Secondary literature was also used as well as observation schedules focusing on socio-economic activities of both men and women in Nairobi and Kiambu District. Another important component of data was obtained from Kikuyu popular culture. This included listening to local songs, watching and listening to local narratives, both in video and compact disc recordings of local drama such as *Machang'i*, *Kihenjo* and *Githingithia*, which depict the day-to-day struggles and events in the people's lives.

Background to the Introduction of SAPs in Kenya

Globalisation is a system that creates new challenges for citizenship, both in established Western democracies and in the less developed countries of the world (Castles and Davidson 2000). In Africa, the advent of colonialism from the late 19th century marked the onset of a remarkable stage in the globalisation process in the region. While the goal of colonialism was capital accumulation, the policies pursued by the state had a differential impact on African men and women (Visram 1988). This was because it accommodated certain traditional patterns of power and authority as long as they served the colonial goal of capital accumulation. In Kenya, patriarchal traditions characterised most communities including the Kikuyu, and were fully exploited by the colonial authorities whenever it served their needs, especially for enforcing social control (Robertson 1997). Most of the colonial administrators and Christian missionaries in Kenya were men whose ideologies were informed by the ideas of the late Victorian era, which they promoted in the colonies. Among these were the European biases of male superiority, grounded on the view that men were the 'breadwinners' while women belonged in the home (Visram 1988:80). Consequently, the colonial labour force was predominantly African men forced to enter the labour market through coercive measures including land alienation, taxation and forced labour (Elson 2004). In this way, men were encouraged to join the commercial economy as workers either on white settler plantations, urban centres or in the public sector, while women remained in the subsistence sector. Moreover, colonial education and land policies enhanced a gendered, capitalist division of labour, characterised by domination of wage labour by men (Elson 2004; Wangui *et al.* 2005).

After independence in 1963, the Kenyan state was very much the progeny of the colonial state. Male domination continued to be pervasive in all the structures of power (Staudt 1987). The symbol of the Kenya African National Union (KANU), the political party that came to power at independence, was the cockerel, which symbolised masculinity. This illustrates the mindset of the male elite who took over political power from the British. Consequently, although a Bill of Rights was passed that affirmed that all citizens were equal before the law, women were underrepresented at all levels of the economy, politics and social development. However, as Ratele *et al.* point out, men's structural and more immediate dominance is produced and reproduced by the domination, oppression, violence, abuse, deprivation and damage of some men by other men (2007:23). Thus, whereas the men who had acquired Western education and those who inherited the reins of power from colonialism prospered by acquiring large farms, senior ranks in the public service and private sector, the majority of Kenyan families continued to struggle for their livelihood as peasants. Therefore, in addition to the large number of women who were politically, socially and economically sidelined by the state after independence, some men were similarly marginalised, subordinated and socially excluded by poverty (Hearn 2007). Such exclusion undermines people's rights as citizens to influence decisions that determine their lives.

It must be noted that some women were beneficiaries of the system, as class interests supersede women issues. Since the male-dominated state in Africa virtually blocks the majority of women from joining the ruling class, some women have aligned themselves with powerful men. They constitute the 'femocracy' according to Amina Mama (Nasong'o and Ayot 2007). This confirms that gender relations should be understood as dynamic and historical rather than static; they are relations that are continually subject to decomposition and recomposition in planned and unplanned interactions between people and institutions (Elson 1995:1852).

Throughout the first decade of President Daniel arap Moi, who succeeded Jomo Kenyatta in 1978, Kenya's major exports suffered considerable price fluctuations with serious consequences for economic growth. Then there was the recurrent drought between 1979 and 1994. These factors created a serious food shortage that necessitated large imports of grain including the yellow maize, which was acquired from the USA. The 1980s were also bad for the coffee sector, which had been the single most important foreign exchange earner for the country (Ikiara 1991). This was attributed to a combination of factors, ranging from the domestic politics of the industry, to the suspension of the International Coffee Agreement. These challenges affected the majority of citizens adversely, especially in Kiambu District, which is predominantly a coffee-producing region. It was in this environment that the SAPs were imposed by multilateral donors led by the International Monetary Fund and the World Bank, and by Western bilateral donors. These policies were influenced immensely by the neoliberal counter-revolution of the newly elected governments of the North headed by Margaret Thatcher in Britain and Ronald Reagan in the USA. The SAPs entailed the liberalisation of the economy, retrenchment of public servants, and introduction of cost-sharing policies in schools and hospitals as well as the devaluation of the local currency (Gilpin 2000).

The implementation of the SAPs translated into a reconfiguration of social, political and economic power in favour of the rights of owners of large-scale money capital, from international financial institutions like the Bretton Woods institutions to capitalised traders in the newly liberalised markets in developing countries (Elson 2004). As a consequence, globalisation led to the marginalisation of millions of citizens, both men and women. Discussing the timing of SAPs on African countries in the 1980s, Bayart *et al.* (1999) argue that the importance of the continent was devalued in the estimation of the great powers, not only due to the resolution of the East-West rivalry during the Cold War, but also due to the peace negotiations between Israel and its Arab neighbours. Hitherto, these conflicts enabled the African elite to gain substantial political rent, and also enhanced Africa's importance to the West in general (Muuka 1998). The international environment suddenly turned hostile. As critics of SAPs in Africa have observed, the strings attached to loans worsened human wellbeing in terms of the deterioration of social conditions involving the basic human rights to food, education, employment, shelter and health, a clean environment and security of persons. This in turn impacted on citizenship identities in a differentiated manner. Trade liberalisation meant the renewed influx of manufactured goods from industrialised countries into Africa. This resulted in deindustrialisation in parts of the continent, with job losses and greater vulnerability for many families. The leading garment and textile firms in Kenya such as the Kisumu Cotton Mills (KICOMI), Rift Valley Textiles (RIVATEX), Mountex, Raymonds and Yunken were all closed down (Kinyanjui 2003; McCormick and Rogerson 2004). The leather industry was not spared either – Tiger Shoes and Bulleys Tanneries collapsed. These industrial closures caused the loss of earnings for the workers, especially men who dominated the sector.

Since the donors also recommended the privatisation of poorly performing government bodies as part of the SAPs, several parastatals in Kenya were earmarked for privatisation. These included: Kenya Airways, East African Bag and Cordage Company, and Kenya Power and Lighting Company. Given that local investors were not capitalised enough, it was mainly foreign investors who acquired the privatised firms, usually in collaboration with the local elite. This trend is particularly important if we are to fully comprehend the impact of globalisation on citizenship identities and the magnitude of the masculinity vulnerabilities experienced in Kenya since the 1980s.

Muuka (1998) observes the consensus that SAPs have mostly bolstered the fortunes of the wealthy citizens with ill-gotten property and quick-yielding speculative investments. For the poor workers, life became almost unbearable as most received only a token payment on retrenchment. By 2001, the Kenyan government had retrenched about 60,000 civil servants, two-thirds of which were men serving in the lowest cadres (Kiruthu 2007). Most of the workers were devastated since they had neither accommodation nor a source of livelihood. Those who opted to take their families back to Kiambu had to manage the small ancestral pieces of land and contend with hostility from relatives who were already using the land. These conditions inevitably caused a lot of stress not only in gender relations, but also among extended family relations.

Several other aspects of the SAPs contributed to strains on citizens and ultimately created more vulnerability for the already suffering Kenyans. For instance, as part of the focus on reforms on good governance, the international donor community demanded political pluralism. This in turn motivated the political elite to grab state assets such as land and government houses, which were then given out or sold to obtain funds and largesse with which to bribe voters during elections. Thus, economically disadvantaged citizens had their votes undermined by wealthy politicians through vote buying, and other forms of corruption. In particular, men and boys could be bought with money or beer to scuttle meetings and shout insults at political competitors. Secondly, the reduction of government funding for health and education ensured that parents continued to shoulder an even larger responsibility for their own lives, the lives of their children, as well as the lives of their extended families. This resulted in an increase in the labour burden shouldered by women as they had to step in and provide some of the care services previously provided by government hospitals and other institutions (Terisa and Brownhill 2001; Elson 2004).

Kenyans responded to the SAPs in several ways. In Kiambu District, those who were retrenched either from the public or from the private sector engaged in activities such as poultry farming. Unfortunately, the great number of poor people desperately seeking a means of livelihood became engaged in similar economic activities. Consequently, as Nairobi and local markets were flooded with eggs and chicken, many of these small entrepreneurs could not break even. These and other frustrations contributed significantly to economic and social vulnerability among both men and women, thereby creating new strains in gender relations. By 2004, only 1.8 million of the 11.4 million people in the labour force were employed formally, with 70 per cent of women employed in the informal sector as opposed to 40 per cent of men (ICA 2004).

It should be noted that a good number of men and women were bold enough to venture into spaces traditionally regarded as exclusive for the opposite sex. Some men started selling used apparel, popularly known as *mitumba* in Kenya. Whereas this business was traditionally regarded as female in the 1980s, by the mid-1990s there were more young males in it than women. A number of middle-aged women and girls joined the *matatu* taxi sector either as drivers or conductors. Out of about 100 Nissan taxis on the Nairobi-Thika route in 1990, 20 were ran by women (Kiruthu 2007). The SAPs ultimately changed the community's order of gender relations, especially among the men who stopped being the main breadwinners for the household. This confirms the argument by Loizos (1994) that masculinity is not a stable essence, present throughout a lifetime or a stage of life, but a series of negotiated identities, acts of will, assertions, performances, fragments of a person who at other times and in other contexts may have other gender attributes.

The Impact of Globalisation on Cash Crop Farming in Kiambu

Kiambu is one of the seven districts that constitute the Central Province of Kenya, the ancestral home of the Kikuyu people. The district covers 1,329 sq. km. and is the smallest district in Central Province (Government of Kenya 2005). It is on the border of Nairobi, the capital city; therefore, many of the residents are greatly influenced by activities in the capital, not only in terms of business opportunities but also in terms of social and political activities. The district also shares a border with Kajiado District to the south, Nakuru District to the west, Nyandarua District to the northwest and Thika District to the east. In general, Kiambu has good rainfall and fertile soils that enable farmers to produce not only food crops but also cash crops such as tea and coffee. Consequently, the district has a high population density. In most regions and land has been fragmented into small pieces resulting in a decline in productivity over time. However, the climate in the district is not uniform. For instance, the more westerly parts are colder and receive more rain than the southern and northern parts (Muchoki 1988). This could explain its diversity in terms of economic activities and differentiation in the standard of living. It should be noted, therefore, that masculinities and femininities are shaped by many factors, including the distinctive regions and contrasting production regimes in particular spaces at different historical periods (Laizos 1994). This is to say that even in Kiambu, it is not possible to talk of a uniform impact on gender relations.

The collapse of cash-crop agriculture contributed significantly to the weakened masculinity in Kenya, given that the sector was predominantly controlled by men in most of the country (Nyamongo 2006). A number of politicians, especially from Kiambu, had tried to block President Moi's ascension to political power in Kenya following the demise of Jomo Kenyatta in 1978 (Nasong'o 2007; Mueller 2008). Therefore, the new president created his power base in the Rift Valley Province in order to entrench his own political hegemony. Consequently, Moi (of Kalenjin origin) deliberately weakened the existing political and economic power structures. He started by removing Kikuyu technocrats from influential government positions (Munene 2006). He then turned to agricultural institutions and destabilised them with a view to destroying the economic strength of the Kikuyu community, including replacing the Kenya Farmers Association, which was dominated by Kikuyu cash crop farmers, with the Kenya Grain Growers Association (Mueller, 2008). Consequently, many prominent Kikuyu businesses collapsed in the second half of the 1980s, including the Rural-Urban Bank, whose chairman was a former Nairobi Mayor, Andrew Ngumba. Other businesses that went bankrupt due to political interference included the Southern Credit Finance, and the Continental Bank. As that these businesses were owned by Kikuyu men, their collapse greatly eroded Kikuyu male hegemony.

Therefore, by the time SAPs were introduced, the main agricultural institutions that had supported central Kenyan small-scale farmers were already down. The liberalisation of the agricultural sector in Kenya therefore exacerbated the situation in Central Kenya. Among the agricultural institutions that were weakened by the SAPs were the Pyrethrum Board of Kenya (PBK) and the Kenya Planters' Cooperative Union (KPCU). The collapse of these institutions heralded the death of the farmers' cooperatives that hitherto provided logistical and financial support, and contributed significantly to masculinity vulnerabilities in Central Kenya in several ways. First, the cooperatives used to give loans to farmers to enable them to discharge their domestic obligations such as payment of school fees and hospital bills based on the amount of produce delivered to the producer cooperatives by each farmer. Such liquidity enabled small-scale farmers to enjoy stable family life. Secondly, cooperatives used to acquire agricultural inputs such as fertilisers and pesticides on behalf of farmers on credit and the beneficiaries were then expected to pay for the inputs upon receiving payment for their produce.

Unfortunately, the changes brought about by globalisation were too harsh for the producer cooperatives in Kenya and subsequently led to the death of the cooperative movement. With the advent of SAPs, even the government was unable to subsidise the prices of agricultural inputs at a time when the cost of living was rising. The extent of the crisis is perhaps best illustrated by the fact that in Kiambu District, the earnings from one kilogram of milk declined from Ksh18.70 in the 1980s to Ksh15 in 2005. In contrast, over the same period, the cost of a bag of cattle feed rose from Ksh300 to Ksh 900 (Nyamongo 2006). Similarly, the pyrethrum sector collapsed with the advent of the SAPs. Although Kenya was one of the world's largest producers of pyrethrum with 17,710 tonnes of dry flowers in 1992/93, accounting for 65 per cent of global production, this declined to approximately 7,000 tonnes in 1997/98. The gravity of the situation was illustrated by the fact that up to December 2007, some pyrethrum farmers had not been paid for deliveries dating way back to the 1990s when the industry began to experience problems. This implies that the farmers who would otherwise have benefited from growing this cash crop in Kiambu and elsewhere are still suffering because of the lost opportunities to make a decent living. It is noteworthy that most of the small-scale farmers in the high altitude regions of the district such as Limuru, Githunguri and Kiambaa Divisions depended on pyrethrum and dairy farming for their livelihood. The decline of the sub-sector left many families devastated, especially the men who had been controlling cash crop production in most of Central Kenya.

With the liberalisation of the economy, the main pillars that supported coffee and tea farming were similarly weakened. For instance, more coffee millers were allowed to compete with the KPCU, such as the privately owned Thika Coffee Mills and some multinational coffee growers in the country. This was in spite of the fact that most of the small-scale coffee growers had developed their farms with the financial and logistical support of the KPCU for many years. Kisero (2008) observes that while Kenya exported 130,000 tonnes of coffee in 1988, by 2008 the country exported less than 55,000 tonnes. Unfortunately, the Kenyan political elite did not seem to recognise the link between successful small-scale agriculture and national security and stability. The disruption of the sector has devastated entire families especially in Central Kenya ever since, with terrible consequences. One of the immediate responses of the men to the crisis was to abandon cash crop farming, especially coffee, pyrethrum and tea. In essence, the farmers had no means of income at a time when the economy was experiencing a serious depression and there were few chances of getting employment. Many of them became idle and unproductive. The scale of the crisis is perhaps illustrated by the fact that many of the small shopping centres in Central Kenya acquired a new name, *mung'etho*, meaning 'a place for idlers'. This was in view of the fact that most of these shopping centres were devoid of much economic activity due to the collapse of the rural economy and most men would hang around at such centres. Thereafter, rural women shouldered most of the burden on the farms. Cash crop farms that were abandoned by men were now being taken over by women who were working against all odds to try and make a living.

Commenting on the situation in Maragwa District, also in the Central province of Kenya, Terisa and Brownhill (2001) have observed that since 1985, women small-scale coffee farmers in the area had uprooted coffee trees and replaced them with bananas and vegetables. Previously, many husbands had encroached on women's food plots to plant coffee for more income when it was paying well. However, since the mid-1980s when commodity prices began to decline in the global market, many local youth, men and women joined hands in replacing coffee with bananas and other locally tradable crops. In essence, this meant that women took control of their labour, the crops that they were producing, as well as their family land. They began to rebuild a subsistence political economy, which supported their own families' welfare.

This situation was fertile ground for domestic disputes. Men would stagger home at night to demand food from the already frustrated women. On many occasions, wives in collaboration with their children would beat up husbands. Several serious injuries and even deaths were reported as a result of these domestic fights. As a consequence, several families became separated, with devastating effects on the mothers, and the children who had to abandon school.

As already observed, many men spent a lot of time in the shopping centres. While at face value this could be dismissed as a sign of laziness, one must remember that most of them were traditionally socialised to believe it is out of order for mature men to hang around the house, especially when not involved in economic activities. This is because culturally, the house is regarded as the 'woman's space'. The shopping centres would, therefore, provide some psychological relief for the idle males. Occasionally, they would secure some pocket money, free liquor and a chance to earn some money from politicians. The impact of this on the male ego cannot be underestimated. Although some theorists have attributed symptoms of the masculine crisis such as drunkenness, violence and drug abuse to the socialisation of boys in masculine values, Taylor Gibbs and Merrighi emphasise that pressures of underachievement are felt all the more keenly among groups of men who are already marginal. Giving examples of the African American community in the USA, they argue that since the 1980s, globalisation has dealt men a number of blows: it has made them more vulnerable to unemployment, homelessness and depression (Heartfield 2002).

An informant from Kiambu narrated his predicament. Having been retrenched by the government, he had to vacate his government house in Nairobi and bought a small plot in Kiambu near his ancestral home, where he built a small, semi-permanent house for his family as he struggled to obtain an alternative means of livelihood. In the meantime, the firstborn son who had just completed secondary school certificate examinations could not enrol in college on account of inadequate funds though he had done well in the exams. Within a few weeks, the man noted that his son was becoming rude and would not even run errands for his father. On one occasion, he did not only refuse to run errands but also asked how come his father could afford to smoke but could not raise school fees? A daughter who was suspended from school in Form Two got pregnant, and to make the matters worse, the man found out that his wife was sleeping with a rich businessman in the neighbourhood. Similar experiences drove many males into drugs, alcohol and depression. Indeed, cases of depression have been on the increase in Kiambu since the 1980s.

As Baker and Ricardo (2006) observe, a near universal feature of manhood is that it must be achieved. Moreover, manhood in the African setting presumes that males must behave and act in specific ways in the eyes of their social group. In essence, this implies that other men and women in society judge whether one has achieved manhood or not. In Kiambu, the situation was perhaps worsened by the Kikuyu community's emphasis on monetary accumulation as an important feature of manhood. Unlike in other parts of

Kenya where ownership of a large piece of land and head of livestock earns men special recognition, in Kikuyu, land and especially Kiambu, this is not the case. The Kikuyu people are on record as being among the most capitalist society in Kenya, probably due to their unique colonial experience under the British government. This could explain the great economic pressure on the men in Kiambu that created a lot of disharmony in the family during the SAP era.

The District Strategic Plan (2005-2010) indicates that the population of primary school children was relatively high compared with that of secondary schools, which indicates that many children were unable to proceed beyond primary school mainly due to lack of school fees in 2002. Further, it observes that secondary school enrolment rate for boys as at 2005 was 46.4 per cent, compared to a 53.3 per cent enrolment rate for girls. This implies that more boys likely joined the unemployed youths in the shopping centres of Kiambu. Indeed, out of 35,508 boys who fell within this age group, only 16,379 were enrolled in secondary schools by 2005 (Government of Kenya 2005). Moreover, since 2005 the number of girls completing the Kenya Certificate of Primary Education (KCPE) has consistently been significantly higher than that of boys in the whole of Central Kenya, including Kiambu District. The rise in school dropout rate among boys in the region paved the way for an even more serious masculinity crisis in the district, manifested in unemployment, abuse of alcohol and drugs such as opium, as well as violence (Kinyanjui, 2008).

These new challenges encountered by the society were bound to create a lot of stress not only on gender relations, but also on inter-generational relations. As Nyamongo (2006) points out, the erosion of men's customary roles and economic disempowerment led to their withdrawal from playing an active role in household planning and provision. Consequently, the resulting strains are reflected increasingly in the levels of domestic conflict, especially violence against women. Men's social status and their sense of manhood suffer especially when they are unable to get gainful employment. Studies among the Yoruba in Nigeria have documented accounts of women belittling husbands who are unable to provide financially for the family. In such situations, the relationship between couples is likely to be strained (Cornwall 2003). Indeed, such marital disharmony is reported to have contributed to the increase in the rate of extramarital affairs among men and women in Kiambu. The increasing number of single women welcomed men who failed to get sexual fulfilment at home. In several instances, these were unemployed husbands who no longer commanded respect from their wives. These circumstances partly explains the high rate of HIV&AIDS infections in Central Kenya during the 1980s and 1990.

Apart from the strains in relations between husbands and their wives, the economic challenges that accompanied liberalisation created a lot of conflict between parents and their children. In Kenya, where well-connected citizens are able to secure either business opportunities or jobs for their children, other youths in the society are left in a state of hopelessness. In such a situation, conflict arises especially between male youths and their parents. Some of the youth in Kiambu, for instance, began to demand that family land be partitioned so that they could get a means of livelihood. However, there is a serious scarcity of land in Kiambu and such demands were bound to cause bitter family feuds, some of which resulted in bloodshed and several cases of suicide. Indeed, the mainstream media in Kenya reported several cases of suicide among males in Central Kenya between the 1980s and 2008. Although research has not been conclusive, it can be argued that there is a strong connection between the crises of masculinity and the economy and the suicide phenomenon. Thus, economic crisis in Kenya during the globalisation era has significantly undermined the sense of citizenship among disadvantaged members of society who experience economic and social deprivation in contrast to the opportunities enjoyed by wealthier people.

Unlike the men in Kenya, women have developed new survival strategies in the face of globalisation. Munguti (2002) calls the Kenyan women's new survival strategies 'invisible adjustment'. She adds that women are capable of making adjustment policies socially possible by increasing their own economic activities and working harder and by abnegation. They have also developed an elastic concept of time, whereby they work for long hours while doing many things at the same time (2002:15). Similarly, Kinyanjui (2008) observes that Kenyan women have used their strong social and religious networks to overcome socio-economic hardships, especially pressure to fulfil subsistence and domestic obligations. Such women networks range from prayer groups and 'merry-go-round' to business support groups, among many others. These support networks facilitate women's participation in socio-economic and political spheres. It is curious that men have not made similar efforts, especially in the rural areas of Central Kenya. This could partly explain the magnitude of the masculinity vulnerabilities both economically and socially, as men struggle to make ends meet in the absence of a good social support network like that of their women counterparts.

From the 1990s, some women in Kiambu began to make a radical move that would have been unthinkable in the traditional past. They paid dowry to their parents, implying that they had given up on marriage. This gesture has important implications for the construction of both gender and citizenship in the globalisation era. First, contrary to Kikuyu traditions that expect men to pay dowry, women can now pay dowry as long as they are economically stable. This means that women can be masculine in terms of performance, and therefore masculinity should not be understood only in terms of biological attributes. Secondly, and even more importantly, Kikuyu women have given men a strong signal that contrary to societal expectations, marriage is just one option for women – they can equally choose to remain unmarried. Some women, especially from the evangelical churches, obtained visas to travel to the US especially in the 1990s on the pretext that they were going for evangelical training. A majority of such women have remained in the diaspora, taking advantage of globalisation to escape from the social and economic frustrations in Kenya arising as a result of the same globalization process. As Okemwa (2009) observes, gender-focused research in Kenya tends to obscure the diffusion of developments that have emerged as a consequence of economic crisis and SAPs, leading to the social and economic vulnerability of a large group of men.

A large number of men have responded to the new challenges by increasingly turning to the consumption of the illegal and cheap brews in a bid to drown their frustrations. Moreover, as part of strategies to make an income during the SAP era, Kiambu traders, both men and women, began to brew cheap liquor. There were reports that for the liquor to ferment quickly, the unscrupulous brewers used potentially harmful chemicals to accelerate the rate of fermentation. So potent were these brews that within a minute or two of consuming a glass, many drinkers would black out. This annoyed many women not only in Kiambu but also all over Central Kenya and in the slums of Nairobi where the brews were being consumed. Several demonstrations were organised by the women to the district headquarters to complain against the brews. Women, supported by children, led itn the campaign to beat up the brewers and to pour the liquor away. The men who consumed these brews did not only become economically unproductive, but also lacked the stamina to fulfil their conjugal duties and women complained that the liquor had destroyed their manhood. Ironically, some of the traders who popularised these brews were men and they made a lot of profit at the expense of the health and social wellbeing of other males.

Reporting on the Kiambu women protests against the illegal brews, the *World Media Watch* of 20 August 20 stated that a group of Kikuyu women protested against the home-made alcohol, and even blocked the busy Nakuru-Nairobi highway for an hour to demand tougher laws against the people behind the brews. Some of their placards said that women were being denied their conjugal rights as their husbands had been reduced to 'zombies'. The consequences of drinking these brews were disastrous and caused untold misery to members of the community. For instance, on 22 November 1998, six people were charged to court for brewing and distributing illegal alcohol and thereby causing the deaths of 140 people in Nairobi and the neighbouring Kiambu District. During the same month, another 20 people became irreversibly blind as a result of consuming the liquor, while 400 people were admitted to hospital suffering from alcohol poisoning (Ahmad 1998). Experts explained that the brews were laced with methanol to enhance their potency, which poisoned vital organs in the body, causing blindness and impairing the kidneys and the liver. While the women accused the government of failing to take action against the merchants of death who brewed and supplied the liquor, President Moi blamed the problem on the repeal of the Chief's Act in 1997, which reduced the powers of the provincial administration. As Ratele et al. (2003) point out, men's structural and more immediate dominance is produced and reproduced by oppression and abuse of fellow men.

The great masculine dilemma experienced in Kiambu during the globalisation era is perhaps best illustrated by the case of a cobbler, Kamangu Ndimu, the late husband of the tele-evangelist Bishop Margaret Wanjiru of the Glory is Here Ministry in Nairobi. Kamangu is reported to have become a drunkard during the economic downturn of the 1990s, as a result of which the couple separated. However, Wanjiru worked hard and did not lose hope. Starting as an untrained church pastor, she excelled, using both local and global networks to become an internationally acclaimed tele-evangelist. When Kamangu went to court to stop Wanjiru from remarrying, he got support from several men who also contributed funds to help meet his legal fees. Indeed, Kamangu became a national celebrity and featured prominently in Kikuyu talk shows. Eventually he tragically passed away in 2009, apparently due to alcohol-related damage to his liver and kidneys. Meanwhile, Wanjiru won the closely contested Kamukunji parliamentary seat in Nairobi. The high mortality rate among men in Kenya is therefore directly connected to the new challenges facing masculinity. Reverend Timothy Njoya (2010), states that 75 per cent of the Kenyan men who head families are dysfunctional and that by age 60, 89 per cent of them are already dead.

Another danger that accompanied the increasing rate of alcoholism in Kiambu District was the increase of HIV&AIDS infections. The connection between the disease and substance abuse has been confirmed by experts.

According to Bannon and Correia (2006), men are known to constitute a larger proportion of the people who abuse drugs and are, therefore, more likely to engage in reckless sexual behaviour. The Kiambu District Strategic Plan (2005-2010) confirms that HIV&AIDS is a major health problem in the district, especially in the coffee- and tea-growing zones. The prevalence rate of the disease in 2001 was averaging 34 per cent, which was very high in comparison with the national prevalence rate of 14 per cent. Moreover, 60 per cent of inpatients were hospitalised for HIV&AIDS-related complications in 2002. More seriously, the most of those infected were between 25 and 34 years of age, the most productive members of society. This resulted in a sharp increase in the number of HIV&AIDS orphans and the obligation to direct family income towards care for HIV-positive family members. Most informants were categorical that the main causes of the spread of the disease in the district included unsafe sexual behaviour, drug abuse, alchoholism, peer pressure and family breakdown.

The enormous economic strain experienced by most citizens following the introduction of SAPs led to the reconfiguration of relationships not only between men and women but also between the rich and the poorer classes, especially in Central Kenya and the main urban centres such as Nairobi. From the 1980s onwards, the general state of insecurity rose, especially due to v i o l e n t robberies. Given the high rate of unemployment, many young men became sophisticated criminals. Although the police and other security forces tried to contain the situation, over the years, many incidents of robbery and violence have occurred. Some of the best known criminals in the country included Wanugu, Rasta and Wacucu. Another notorious criminal was Matheri from Gachie village in Kiambu. According to Gibbs and Merrighi (2002), the pressures of underachievement are felt more keenly among groups of men who are already marginalised, and they are more likely to engage in criminality. Since the 1990s, most of the vehicles that were stolen in the capital, Nairobi, eventually resurfaced in Kiambu, or were taken across the border to Tanzania and South Africa, through sophisticated, international criminal networks.

One of the most unfortunate developments during the SAP era was the emergence of a militia largely comprising Kikuyu men, known as *Mungiki*. The group has been most active in Central Kenya, Nairobi and some parts of the Rift Valley Province. The name *Mungiki* is derived from Kikuyu language, meaning: 'we are the public'. According to one of its spokesmen, Ndura Waruingi, the militia aimed to assert the rights of a social class among the citizens that felt acutely deprived and marginalised in a rapidly globalising world (Kagwanja 2003: 29). Although initially posing as a socio-religious group, the fact that it attracts the membership of marginalised groups in society such as the unemployed, hawkers, touts and *jua kali* (informal sector) artisans cannot be downplayed. Indeed, it can be argued that the economic downturn following the liberalisation of the economy caused the rising scale of criminality and insecurity. Analysing the possible causes of the emergence of the militia, Mueller (2008) traces its roots to the presidency of Daniel arap Moi, whose strategies to consolidate political power during the globalisation period entailed destroying Kikuyu hegemony and dismantling the economic foundations of the Kenyatta state, including Kikuyu agricultural associations. She argues that it was in this milieu of decay that criminal gangs began to appear as significant actors (2008:192)..

The *Mungiki* militia stated categorically that it would reclaim prime land, housing estates and other up-market property in Central Kenya and Nairobi for the exclusive use of its members (*Daily Nation* 17 April 2007). It took issue with what it considered the criminalisation of poverty as evident in the eviction of squatters from forestland in Kiambu and elsewhere among the Kikuyu, as well as the eviction of kiosk owners from up-market estates and hawkers from the streets of Nairobi. It should be noted that all this happened at a time when the rich were grabbing public land with impunity, especially during the Moi era, up to 2002. Concurring with Kagwanja (2003), Mueller (2008) argues that the militia operated almost as a shadow state in some Nairobi slums, as well as in some parts of the countryside such as Kiambu and other Kikuyu districts. The close proximity of Kiambu to Nairobi and the high levels of unemployment experienced by young men, made the district one of the strongholds of the militia. *Mungiki* members took control of several businesses such as the commuter transport industry, otherwise known as the *matatu* sector – *matatus* are privately owned taxis. The gang demanded 'protection fees' from *matatu* operators and other businesses in most of Central Kenya and on some routes in Nairobi. Their activities culminated in April 2007, when members of the militia set fire to *matatus* and houses after touts and drivers from Githunguri and Banana Hills in Kiambu resisted paying extortion fees (*Daily Nation*, 17 April 2007). In both instances, villagers joined the fight in support of the matatu operators and in the chaos, a lot of property was destroyed, and several deaths and injuries were reported. Although the Kenyan authorities have sought to eradicate the militia by arresting and shooting some of its members to death, it has survived over the years, mainly because its grievances have never been addressed adequately. It is argued here that the militia is symptomatic of the masculine crisis created by the globalisation process, which has reconfigured citizenship and gender relations globally.

Conclusion

The chapter has demonstrated that there is a strong connection between globalisation and the construction of masculine and feminine identities in Kenya since colonial times. The commercialisation of land and male labour, hand in hand with the persistence of patriarchal traditions in most African communities, led to greater economic and political subordination of women during colonialism. However, globalisation impacted on citizens in a differentiated manner. Men who failed to acquire land, Western education and other advantages were also subordinated in various ways. At independence, the African male elite that acquired political power did not deconstruct the colonial state. Rather, women continued to be side-lined from the centre of political, economic and social development. Men controlled the most lucrative sectors of the economy, including senior positions in the public service, industries and cash crop farming, while most women remained in subsistence farming.

With the onset of the new phase of globalisation in the 1980s, the economic and political landscape was transformed, especially in Central Kenya. The collapse of cash crop farming and related industries created unprecedented economic vulnerability, especially among men. The masculinity crisis that ensued was manifested in unemployment, abuse of drugs and alcohol, mental depression, and a high mortality rate among men, especially in Kiambu and other parts of Central Kenya. Many Kiambu men lost industrial jobs or substantial revenue from the sale of cash crops. However, some men and women, such as Bishop Margaret Wanjiru, used global networks to become wealthy. The political class, for instance, collaborated with international capital to acquire privatised government firms and buildings, confirming the view of Cornwall and Lindisfarne (1994) that masculinity is not a permanent attribute. While many men became despondent due to the decline in their self-esteem in the face of economic depression, women coped much better, using their social networks such as women groups. This underscores the importance of using masculinity as a tool to analyse societal dynamics in a more nuanced manner. This is one of the ways that we can comprehend threats to national and international security posed by different forms of masculinity – related issues include terrorism, emergence of militia, armed robbery and other forms of criminality and social problems associated with men.

References

Ahmad, K., 1998. (http://www.ndc hrblancet pdf.2000).

Anderson, D.M., 2002, 'Vigilantes, Violence and the Politics of Public Order in Kenya', *African Affairs*, No. 101.

Baker, G. and Ricardo, C., 2006, 'Young Men and the Construction of Masculinity in Sub-Saharan Africa: Implications for HIV/AIDS, Conflict and Violence', in Bannon, I. and Correia, M., eds., *The Other Half of Gender: Men's Issues in Development*, Washington DC: World Bank.

Bannon, I. and Correia, M., 2006, *The Other Half of Gender: Men's Issues in Development*, Washington DC: World Bank.

Bayart, J.F. *et al.*, 1999, *The Criminalisation of the State in Africa*, Indianapolis: Indiana University Press.

Berry, M., 2009, 'A Woman's Worth: Accounting for Women in the Global Market', *The Denver Journal of International Law and Policy*, Vol. 1, No. 37, p. 3.

Bigsten, A. and Kayizzi-Mugerwa, S., 1997, 'Economic Liberalisation, Growth, and Poverty Reduction', in Kifle, H., Olukoshi, A.O, and Wohlgemuth, L., eds, *A New Partnership for African Development*: Issues and Dimensions, Uppsala: Nordiska Afrikainstitutet.

Castles, S. and Davidson, A., 2000, *Citizenship and Migration: Globalisation and the Politics of Belonging*, New York: Routledge.

Cornwall, A. and Lindisfarne, N., 1994, 'Dislocating Masculinity: Gender, Power and Anthropology', in Cornwall, A. and Lindisfarne, N. (eds.), *Dislocating Masculinity: Comparative Ethnographies*, New York: Routledge.

Daily Nation, 17 April 2007, '*The Mungiki Menace*', Editorial, Nairobi: *Daily Nation*.

Elson, D., 2004, 'Social Policy and Macroeconomic Performance: Integrating the Economic and the Social', in Thandika Mkandawire, ed., *Social Policy in a Development Context*, Basingstoke: UNRISD/ Palgrave Macmillan.

Elson, D., ed., 1995, *Male Bias in the Development Process*, Manchester: Manchester University Press.

Gibbs, J.T. and Merighi, J.R., 1996, 'Young Black Males', Quoted in James Heartfield, 2002, 'There is no Masculinity Crisis', Genders Online Journal, Issue 35, http://www.genders.org/g35/g35_heartfield.html.

Gilpin, R., 2000, *The Challenge of Global Capitalism*, Princeton: Princeton University Press.

Government of Kenya, 2005, *Kiambu District Strategic Plan*, 2005-2010, Nairobi.

Heartfield, J., 2002, 'There is no Masculinity Crisis'. *Genders Online Journal*, Issue 35, (http://www.genders.org/g35/g35_heartfield.html)

Ikiara, G.K., 1991, 'Policy Changes and the Informal Sector: A Review', in Coughlin, P. and Ikiara, G.K., eds., *Kenya's Industrialisation Dilemma*, Nairobi: East African Educational Publishers.

Institute of Economic Affairs, 2004, *Mainstreaming Gender in National Budgets: The Gaps in the Kenya Budget Process*, Nairobi: Institute of Economic Affairs.

Kagwanja, P., 2003, 'Facing Mount Kenya or Facing Mecca: The Mungiki Ethnic Violence and the Politics of the Moi Succession in Kenya, 1987 to 2002, *African Affairs*, Volume 102, No. 456.

Kinyanjui, M. N., 2010, 'Social Relations and Associations in the Informal Sector in Kenya', Social Policy and Development Programme Paper, (E-Paper, No. 43, January UNRISD).

Kinyanjui, M. N., 2008 'Informal Enterprise is a Path to Urban Dynamism in Nairobi', Working Paper Presented to the International Development Centre, Open University, UK.

Kinyanjui, M.N. and Kiruthu, F., 2007, 'Super-Imperialism: A Perspective from East Africa', in Bowles, P. *et al.*, eds., *Regional Perspectives on Globalisation*, New York: Palgrave Macmillan.

Kinyanjui, M.N., 2003, 'A Gender Analysis of Small-Scale Garment Producers' Response to Market Liberalisation in Kenya', *African Geographical Review*, 22: 49-59.

Kisero, J., 2008, *Daily Nation*, 30 July.

Leys, C., 1975, *Underdevelopment in Kenya: The Political Economy of Neo-Colonialism* London: Heinemann.

Loizos, P., 1994, 'A Broken Mirror: Masculine Sexuality in Greek Ethnography', in Cornwall, A. and Lindisfarne, N., eds., *Dislocating Masculinity: Comparative Ethnographies*, New York: Routledge.

McCormick, D. and Rogerson, C., 2004, *Clothing and Footwear in African Industrialisation*, Pretoria: African Institute of South Africa.

Munene, M., 2006, 'Conflict and Conflict Management in Kenya from 1963 to 2005', in Kamenju, J. and Godfrey Okoth, P, eds, *Power and Power Politics in Kenya: An Interdisciplinary Discourse*, Nairobi: SRIC.

Muchoki, F.M., 1988, 'Organisation and Development of Kikuyu Agriculture 1880-1920', MA Thesis, Kenyatta University.

Mueller, S.D., 2008, 'The Political Economy of Kenya's Crisis', in *Journal of East African Studies*, Vol. 2, No. 2, 185-210.

Munguti et al., 2002, 'The Implications of Economic Reforms on Gender Relations: The Case of Poor Households in Kisumu Slums', in *Gender, Economic Integration, Governance and Methods of Contraception*, Dakar: AAWARD/AFARD.

Muuka, G.N., 1998, 'In Defense of World Bank and IMF Conditionality in Structural Adjustment Programs', *Journal of Business in Developing Nations*, Vol. 2, Article 2.

Murunga, R. and Nasong'o, S., 2007, 'Prospects for Democracy in Kenya', in Murunga, R. and Nasong'o, S., eds., *Kenya: The Struggle for Democracy*, Dakar: Codesria.

Njoya, T., 2010, *The Masculinity as Flawed Social Construct"*, Unpublished Paper, Presented to Young Women's Leadership Institute, 8 April.

Nyamongo, M.A. and Francis, P., 2006, 'Collapsing Livelihoods and the Crisis of Masculinities in Kenya', in Bannon, I. and Correia, M. (eds.), *The Other Side of Gender: Men's Issues in Development*, Washington DC: World Bank.

Okemwa, S.N., 2009, 'Enduring Passions: The Fallacies of Gender-Fused Development in Kenya'. http//apad.revues.org/document 255.html.

Olurodi, L., 2003, Gender, Globalization and Marginalization in Africa', *Africa Development*, Volume XXVIII, Nos. 3 and 4.

Oyugi, W., 2003, 'The Politics of Transition in Kenya, 1992-2003: Democratic Consolidation or Deconsolidation', in Oyugi, W. O. *et al.*, eds, *The Politics of Transition in Kenya: From KANU to NARC*, Nairobi: Heinrich Boll Foundation.

Praechter, C., 2003, 'Learning Masculinities and Femininities: Power, Knowledge and Peripheral Participation', *Women Studies International Forum*, Vol. 26, No. 6, pp. 541-552..

Ratele, K., Shefer, T. and Strebel, A., 2007, *From Boys to Men: Social Constructions of Masculinity in Contemporary Society*, Cape Town: University of Cape Town Press.

Staudt, K., 1987, 'Women's Politics, the State, and Capitalist Transformation in Africa', in Markovitz, Irving, ed., *Studies in Power and Class in Africa*, Oxford: Oxford University Press.

Terisa, E. and Brownhill, S.L., 2001, 'The African Jubilee: Mau Mau Resurgence and the Fight for Fertility in Kenya', *The Canadian Journal of Development Studies*, Volume xxii, 2001.

Visram, M., 1988, 'Gender Politics and the State: A Study of Kenya and Zimbabwe', MA Dissertation, Department of Political Science, James Fraser University, Canada.

Wangari, E., Kamau, W. and Kinyua, A.M., 2005, 'Globalisation and Its Impact on Women in the Third World', in 'Gender Discrimination: A Global Perspective', Forum on Public Policy 290, Volume 1, No. 3.

World Mediawatch, 1999, http:// news.bbc.co.uk.

Woodhouse, M., 2003, 'Gender Mainstreaming into Poverty Reduction Strategies: Reflections from Oxfam and Civil Society', paper presented at Siem Reap, Cambodia, 17-18 September 2003.

4

The Acquisition of New Citizenship in the Global Village through the Emerging Female Chieftaincy and Notability in Bangwaland, Cameroon

Prudentia Tamonkeng Fonkwe

Introduction

When the struggle for women's emancipation and gender equality reached the peak of international attention with the holding of the four world conferences on women in Mexico (1975), Copenhagen (1980), Nairobi (1985) and Beijing (1995), some women hoped that gender barriers would be dismantled and women would start getting into male-dominated spheres; perfect gender equality would then be celebrated. It did not take long to discover that as women got into those male spheres, fluid and hidden bureaucratic gate-keeping regulations, conditions and mechanisms kept surfacing to keep women's progress in check. A practical example in Cameroon is the accession of Bangwa women to chieftaincy positions originally reserved for men. As women pioneers break gender barriers to obtain hitherto 'male' titles, one would have expected a transformation in gender and power relations in the institution. However, gender discrimination and discrepancies persist.

Historically, some outstanding women dotted across Africa have either been vested with or have attained traditional, political, administrative and military authority. Qunta (1987:23-46) and Awe (2005) cite women such as Queen Mother Yaa Asentewa of Asante (Ghana) (1840-1921), Queen Hatshepsut of Egypt (1508-1458 BCE) who ruled their countries brilliantly as kings, chiefs, diplomatic and military leaders either to bring remarkable development, liberate their countries, repel foreign invaders or conquer more territories. However, African women lost these privileged positions to the colonial, Eurocentric, patriarchal and masculinist onslaught that relegated women to the backyard and tore African men and women from their cultural roots. Mazrui (1999) holds the colonialists responsible for the oppression, marginalisation and loss of visibility of the African woman. He posits that in Kenya, nobody owned land but it was controlled by women. However, when the colonialists came, they assumed that all land was owned by men and so they issued title deeds to men and dealt only with men in the public sphere. The best documented female paramount chief in Cameroon is Mrs. Assiga, née Marie Thérése Atangana (Chef Supérieur des Ewondo) chief of the Ewondo of the Centre Region of Cameroon. The Ewondo council of kingmakers elected her to succeed her father (Chief Charles Atangana) as their paramount ruler in 1996. She exercises her functions with impartiality, diligence, efficiency and commitment, qualities that have earned her national and international admiration and recognition.

Bangwa, known by the indigenous appellation *MbenWeh* (the people of Nweh) is a cultural configuration of nine autonomous states (clans) that constitute the Menji and Alou sub-divisions in Lebialem Division in the South-West Province of Cameroon. The clans (*fondoms*) are Njorgwi, Essoh-Attah, Lebang, Lewoh, Ndungatet, Nwametaw, Nwangong, M'muockmbie and M'muockngie. Each clan is headed by a paramount traditional ruler. Apart from Njorgwi and Essoh-Attah, which have not yet crowned female chiefs and notables, all the others have gone into history as reformists who heeded the call for gender equality in all spheres of life by crowning women notables and chiefs. As women enter the privileged patriarchal sphere, they are expected to enjoy the patriarchal dividends that go with elevated citizenship status. But this expectation has not materialised.

This chapter attempts to address some pertinent questions relating to female chiefs' citizenship and globalisation. For example, is the crowning of female chiefs and notables a demonstration of gender sensitivity on the part of traditional authorities or is it a fallback strategy in the modernisation/globalisation era of increased costs of human development? Is it a demonstration of good governance as advocated by developed democracies and international organisations since the world has become a global village? Is the admission of women into the male mainstream a deconstruction of decades of cultural constructions or is it a mere camouflage aimed at adapting to changing circumstances in order to avoid the cul-de-sac syndrome? Is it really a cultural transformation or a decline? Is it a strategy for the superstructure to divide and rule women in the light of the increasing feminist activism and advocacy for women's empowerment, emancipation and gender equality? In short, what has globalisation got to offer this new breed of citizens – female chiefs? Another concern is that as women negotiate entry into the public sphere/masculine space, what happens to those hegemonic constructions of masculinities? Do they collapse or are new forms of male power created? As women enter what were areas of male privilege, competition for control of the public sphere will certainly threaten male hegemony. But can women change the *status quo?*

The main thrust of this chapter is that in spite of the cultural, economic, social and political ramifications of globalisation as an international development discourse, there has been no visible transformation programme to bring women into the men's club. In other words, the admission of the namely, women into the male-dominated public sphere is not an indication of the deconstruction of decades of cultural construction. Instead, the kingmakers (local and global) seem to be willing to integrate women into the men's club (a mere window-dressing attempt to adapt to the changing rhetoric) because of the apparent immediate benefits that such outreach may bring them (the men, superstructure). I have drawn on social dominance and contemporary citizenship theories to show that globalisation, like citizenship is gendered male. For instance, how can men and women, the haves and have-nots, be equal citizens when they have different access to and control over land, labour, credit, education, decision making, technology, information and so on? Therefore, just as the world's poor and marginalised people (especially women) are helping to sustain globalised patriarchy by filling in its loopholes (in their subordinate roles), so are the Bangwa female chiefs and notables crowned to prevent endangered cultural values and dynasties from disintegrating. Through the acquisition of female chieftaincy titles, the women are lulled into believing that they are at the centre of power and decision making, whereas they are still in the periphery.

Primary data was collected qualitatively through interviews while secondary data was collected from reviews of literature and documentation. Informants for the study were: three female sub-chiefs, eight female notables, five kingmakers (males), five ordinary men and five ordinary women. The youngest female chief was 32 years old and the oldest was above 60 years old. One of the cheifs was married with children while two were divorced without biological children. All the eight female notables were married with children.

Apart from the youngest female chief, all the other female chiefs and notables had an independent source of income. The youngest female notable was about 50 years old. One of the female chiefs and three of the female notables traced their genealogy to the paramount chief's palace, while five traced theirs to subchiefs' palaces. Two female chiefs acquired their titles through purchase. We can conclude that age, wealth and birth are the main determinants for the acquisition of status in the Bangwa chieftaincy and notability institution.

This chapter is divided into six sections. The first section introduces the work, the methodology and thrust of the argument. The second section discusses the theoretical and conceptual frameworks that define the concept of gender, globalisation and citizenship and their interconnectedness. Section three focuses on social stratification in the Bangwa cultural setup, demonstrating the privileged position that men occupy in society in relation to women. Before the conclusion, the fourth and fifth sections analyse, discuss and describe the roles of gender, globalisation and citizenship in Bangwa and how the interface between the three concepts affects women in general and the female chiefs in particular.

Theoretical and Conceptual Framework

The core issue under discussion here is the interface between gender, citizenship and globalisation as an unfinished agenda in the African development discourse. As Africa enters the 21st century, it faces enormous challenges as well as new opportunities to harmoniously and equitably blend the three concepts in order to minimise the bitter effects and derive the maximum advantages in terms of economic growth and development. Gender is the culturally defined group of attributes, behaviour and roles ascribed to men and women based on their perceived sex (Humm 1997). To this definition, Ogundipe (2007:12) adds that, 'Women and men are born as biological females and males but are constructed by their societies into what the specific society thinks constitutes a woman or a man.' Societal constructions of biological females and males into socio/cultural women and men forms 'gender politics', which 'refers to the interactions of men and women and the relations of power between them at all levels of society' (Ogundipe, *op cit.*:12). Gender politics becomes strongly linked to citizenship because it creates boundaries of inclusion and exclusion which, according to Nyamnjoh (2004), can be political, social, cultural, and above all material. Therefore,

> How well we succeed in claiming and realising our citizenship – global, national
> or otherwise – and in what form or forms, depends very much on how we are able

to negotiate away the boundaries of exclusion of which we are victims (Nyamnjoh, *op. cit.*:39).

Basically, citizenship refers to the pride, rights and obligations that one enjoys or exercises in space and time, and the feeling of satisfaction that one belongs, is protected and accepted socially, legally, politically, culturally and economically by a society. This concept of citizenship denotes an inevitable relationship between the superstructure and the base, the state, government and the governed. Most state constitutions provide that all their citisens, regardless of race, religion, sex and religious belief are equal before the law and possess inalienable rights. In practice, however, it is glaringly visible that other variables such as age, location, gender, education, wealth, marital status, social status and birth determine one's class/level of citizenship. Osaghae (2004) admits that the question of citizenship has a strong link with rights discourse but posits that 'notwithstanding the evolving modes of and concern with global and cosmopolitan citizenship, citizenship remains a within-state variable'. This is because 'it is within states that equity, universality and inclusion are sought and struggled for and the survival of the state remains as important as the survival and living of its (equal) citizens and constituents'.

It becomes evident that citizenship boundaries are not only defined, prescribed and imposed by the state but also informally through traditions and attitudes through the dynamics of gender politics. Therefore, citizenship itself can generate 'legitimate' social inequality depending on the political and social climate of a nation. Through the pre- and post-independence struggle of African countries, Neocosmos (2007) has illustrated the inbuilt, exclusive and inclusive character of citizenship and has come out with the concept of active and passive citizens. He postulates that during the struggle for independence, the popular upsurge and liberation, the oppressed/freedom fighters transform themselves into inclusive moral communities of active citizens taking their destiny into their hands; but after the struggle, they metamorphose into an exclusive, essentialist community, with a passive, state-imposed conception of citizenship and of indigeneity, 'approving of the chauvinism which systematically excludes a large number of foreigners and 'others'. Such a change indicates the collapse of the moral order necessary for a national and independent popular emancipatory politics. From the emancipatory perspective, citizenship should not be about subjects bearing rights conferred by the state, but rather about people who think about exercising their active political agency, i.e. 'becoming agents through their engagement in politics as militants/ activists' and not necessarily as politicians' (Neocosmos *op. cit.*:46).

Mies and Reddock (1982) have taken the example of women's active participation in the national liberation struggles of Algeria, Zimbabwe and Mozambique to illustrate that after the struggles, the fruits of liberation were never shared equally between sexes. The women were simply ushered back to the kitchen. While male heroism was praised and rewarded, women freedom fighters' heroism was disparaged and whittled down to harassment, humiliation, and they were rejected as women who had handled guns and so could not make good wives. Lazreg (1994:146) sums up the fate of Algerian women involved in the national struggle, noting that, 'women as a group were seen as necessary to the building of the state, but as contributors not participants. Sacrifice, not duty complemented by right, was the corner stone of the new state's view of women'. Women's marginalisation in post-war/independent countries ties in strongly with the perspective of the social dominance theory of citizenship.

According to sociologists such as Zanden (1990), only power can determine which group subordinates the other, meaning that one group uses power to achieve domination and subjugation. In most societies, power is determined by factors such as sex, age, birth, wealth, influence, level of education and status. Those who control power are those favoured by these factors and by that token, they enjoy more privileges, prestige and power in their societies than the rank and file. As a result of these privileges, the power wielders become the norm and the pacesetters. They feel superior to the others and their status stands out as the standard for the rest of society to strive to attain. In addition, through the gate-keeping, screening process, some people are either kept out or admitted to the dominant class. Most people in the position of dominance are the untouchables, the 'patriots' of society who own and control others; whereas Njoya (2003:13) believes that 'to dominate is not to govern'.

The social dominance theory stratifies society hierarchically, ascribing power and citizenship vertically from the bottom to the top (the power triangle). Within these societies, what one has, and when and how he/ she got it, depends on age, birth, wealth, and one's sex and the prevailing gender roles, among other factors. Gender roles are a fundamental source of social inequality because they establish a framework within which men and women gain their identities, their access to and control over resources, their decision-making roles and their visibility. In this light, the social, political, economic and cultural structures of most human societies favour men over women. By extension, those discriminatory structures determine one's citizenship status. Thus, men generally enjoy better citizenship status than women. Men generally justify their dominance on three main counts. The first is their resort to the myth of creation in the Bible where God made man but created woman to be man's helper. The second is their physical strength in that men are generally physically stronger than women in some respects and it is 'just obvious' that the powerful should dominate the weak. The third count is biological. They argue that while men have x and y chromosomes that determine the sex of the baby, women have only two x chromosomes. Men should, therefore, determine who owns what in society because their role in procreation is assumed to be more important than that of females. A Burundi proverb explicitly states that 'woman is only the passive earth; it is the man who provides the seed' (Berger 2005: 148). We can draw some logic from the dominance perspective to inform our appreciation of female chieftaincy and issues of citizenship in a highly gendered, globalizing world.

Bensaid (2004:323) has observed that many states are facing a crisis of national sovereignty in their present concept of citizenship and nationality, which are 'increasingly dissociated from one another as the public sphere is increasingly privatised in multinational political entities'. Bensaid (*op. cit.*) suggests that the failure of the equation of nationality and citizenship creates the need to radically redefine citizenship in two broad categories: the citizenship of residence, referring to one's citizenship of country of birth; and community citizenship, being an organised form of plural group membership. Community citizenship could be more important than national (residence) citizenship and may 'provide a solution to the choice between abstract universalism and vindictive communitarianism'.

The concept of globalisation has diverse usage. To many social scientists, it is a key part of an international development rhetoric that refers to the interdependence and interconnectedness of world systems enabling the direct interaction of people across state frontiers even without state consent (Anuguom 2007; Mkandawire 2002; Nyamnjoh 2004; Vinay 2006). It is the driving force affecting many global issues, ranging from migration to fair trade and debt relief. Giddens (1990) defines globalisation as a process that involves 'the intensification of worldwide social relations which link distant localities in such a way that local happenings are shaped by events occurring many miles away and vice versa'. This definition seems to suggest a symbiotic relationship between the world's nations. But critics of globalisation from the South (developing world) such as Rodney (1974), Allen and Hamnett (1995), Ihonvbere (1996, 2000) and Aina (1995) argue that globalisation flows are not mutual but a top-down, one-way traffic from the developed North to the peripheral South, which was integrated in the world system as an appendage.

This uneven playing field created by globalisation has bred resistance, conflicts, exploitation and contestation in the developing countries. This observation corroborates Aiyedun's (2004) view of globalisation as a universalisation concept that transcends geo-political boundaries, penetrates sovereign nation-states to construct and deconstruct objects, practices and value systems. Aiyedun (*op. cit.*) further emphasises the element of power relations among global actors in the economic, political, cultural and social fields. Within the domain of power relations lie structures of domination, oppression, marginalisation, exploitation, polarisation and, inequalities – in short, binaries and asymmetries.

Mohammed (2004) traces the historical evolution of globalisation in Africa back to the colonisation and partition of Africa and the introduction of a capitalist economy by the colonial powers. That foreign incursion introduced the principle of division of labour and incorporated Africa into the capitalist world economy by assigning it the role of supplier of raw materials and, cheap labour, markets for manufactured goods and investment outlets for the industrialised countries. The various conferences on Africa's economic reform programmes, good governance, capacity building, poverty reduction, democracy and so on are pure echoes of the Berlin conference resolutions that partitioned Africa. Sceptics strongly assert that globalisation can only impoverish, exploit and marginalise Africa.

The shortest and most recent route of globalisation to Africa was through the economic reforms of the 1980s, the famous structural adjustment programmes (SAP) with their disastrous consequences for the poor, weak, vulnerable and marginalised. Among other drastic measures aimed at economic recovery, SAP emphasised the dominance of market forces, reduction of state expenditure; currency devaluation; privatisation of state-owned corporations; massive retrenchment of workers and salary cuts, all of which had a traumatic effect on the population. Africa was thus already incapacitated on the terrain of globalisation. Africa's socio-economic and even political policies are almost always externally directed. Unable to determine either the sales or purchase price of any product on the world market, or initiate or negotiate any international development programme, Africans are really not equipped to withstand the competition challenges posed by globalisation. This view is succinctly expressed by Cheru (2008:38):

> 'Globalisation, with its contradictory tendencies, poses a great challenge to African countries. Africa has been ill-prepared to simultaneously adjust itself to complex global dynamics, exploit new opportunities or manage internal and external threats.'

In one perspective, global interconnectedness should break all barriers of age, sex, race, tribe, class and so on, and level the playing field for free and fair competition for development. However, Randriamaro's (2002) assessment of globalisation is that it is built on a history of slavery, racism, colonialism, exploitation, inequalities, domination and discrimination, especially against women and other marginalised or oppressed groups.

In short, little has been done by the 'grandmasters' of globalisation to empower states and international institutions to assume the heavy responsibilities and obligations enshrined in United Nations resolutions and international conventions. The one positive thing that SAP did was that it made it clear to African men that they were not as powerful as they had thought they were. When prices of cash crops that were controlled by men (the division of labour gave food crop production to women and cash crops to men) fell drastically in the 1980s, men became 'castrated' and whole families survived on the proceeds from food crops. The value of women's work became visible and most of them gained self-confidence, courage and assertiveness, which gave them some level of empowerment and liberated them to venture into male-dominated activities such as cash crop production and pig rearing.

Bleak as the negative picture of globalisation painted by its critics may be, Mkandawire (2002) and Nyamnjoh (2004) have credited it on many counts. Globalisation leads to greater economic welfare and rewards factors of production according to their productivity. It gives individuals and nations the opportunity to fully exploit their 'comparative advantages' and potential. Furthermore, it frees individuals from the shackles of local tyranny, tradition and provincialism' (Mkandawire op. cit.: 2). Other proponents of globalisation argue that since it breaks down physical and social boundaries of inequality, it empowers individuals. In addition, it 'accelerates flows and fluidity across physical, economic, social and cultural boundaries in ways that turn individuals into veritable melting pots of plurality and diversity'. Prencipe (2004:255) sees globalisation as a product of a confluence of three factors:

(i)   Expansion of transaction space through the integration of new countries (new players);

(ii) Globalisation of large enterprises organising their research, procurement, production, and sales activities on a global level (new games);

(iii) Growth in trade as a result of liberalisation and deregulation (new rules of the game).

But Prencipe (*op. cit.*) is quick to observe that the globalisation of wealth, from which the dominant social strata of poor countries also benefit, is tantamount to the 'globalisation of poverty that afflicts vast segments of the population of rich countries, most notably persons of foreign origin' and illegal immigrants in particular. This category, alongside the poorly or uneducated workers forms a reservoir of cheap and exploitable labour force. Globalisation therefore creates

> ...inequalities because it does not take place in a just and equitable manner. In spite of the greater economic and technological interconnectedness that has led to economic growth and poverty reduction, 'globalisation has widened the income gap between rich and poor, ignited conflicts in poorer regions and led to rapid degradation of the environment in some parts of the world' (Bhargava and Gurkan 2006: 413).

Social Stratification in the Bangwa Cultural Milieu

Bangwa society is stratified, with culturally defined roles, rights and duties. One is born into a family as a boy or girl and upward mobility can be obtained either through inheritance, personal achievement, or royal lineage (conferment) by those culturally empowered to exercise that prerogative. There is no chieftaincy by election as is the practice in some traditions.

Originally, the only traditional female titles were those of Mafua and *Ankwetta* (royal princesses). The titles were conferred by a dying monarch alongside that of his successor. The princesses were collaborators of the reigning chief and they had specific roles to play for the smooth functioning and sustainability of the monarchy institution. Today, things are taking a different turn – women are bearing male titles, hence the phenomenon of 'female masculinity'.

Looking at the royal cabinet from a gender perspective, it appears to have a gender balance in the sense that the paramount ruler is flanked by two male assistants (princes) and two females (royal princesses). However, the roles they perform in the administration of the clan reflect their sex role socialisation. In addition, while Nkwetta and Asaah are entitled to become sub-chiefs (Befua-Nka-Ngeh) after their mandate expires, Mafua and Ankwetta cannot; that reveals the gender bias in the cultural set up.

The genealogy of most Bangwa royal dynasties can be traced back beyond eight generations. For example, Essoh-Attah has ten (Fomin, undated). However, the only well documented royal princess (mafua) is Mafua Nkengafac (1893-1985), the royal princess of the Fuantem Asonganyi and Fuantem

Broad stratification of the Bangwa traditional society

The broad structure of social stratification in Bangwa society is as follows:

Paramount ruler/Fon/His Royal Majesty

- Ankwetta (1)
- Mafua (1)
- Attendants/retainers
- Bekem Atem Mangwar (5)
- Befua Nteuh (2) — a, b
- Nkwetta
- Asaah
- Secret cult/kingmakers/council of nine
- Befua (chiefs)
- Befua Nka-Ngeh (3) — a, b
- Bekem Nteuh (6)
- Quarter heads
- Commoners
- Befua-seh (4) — a, b

Fuo = chief
Befuo = chiefs
Nkem = notable
Bekem = notables

(1) Female posts in the royal throne, crowned at the same time as the paramount ruler/chief.
(2) Notables directly crowned by the paramount ruler.
(3) Semi-autonomous sub-chiefs who lost their paramount status to another paramount ruler and have become subjects of the paramount lineage.
(4) Sub-chiefs from the paramount lineage.
(5) Sub-chiefs who have acquired titles through purchase or accomplishment.
(6) Notables of lower rank crowned by sub-chiefs.
◊ Used to be purely male spheres but they are now accommodating women.

Defang dynasties of Fontem-Lebang who was crowned in 1935 and reigned until her death in 1985. She was crowned chief posthumously in 1985 during her burial. The title was automatically conferred on her successor. In addition to her productive and reproductive roles, Mafua Nkengafac did a lot for the community at the political, economic and social levels, even breaking gender barriers. For example, she was the only female customary court judge among paramount rulers in the Bangwa Native Court at Azi-Fontem. She was also her father's solace and emissary and ably represented him in foreign diplomacy. Alemanji (2006:119) confirms that 'she carried out all the major important duties in the palace including dealing with the European administrators and other foreign dignitaries'. She was also a peacemaker and a women's and community leader. She was highly respected for her hard work, honesty, impartiality, selflessness, generosity, intelligence, strong sense of commitment and devotion to her family, community and humanity. It is noteworthy that Bangwa society is patrilineal and male preference is an open practice. Succession is by inheritance and the unwritten rule is that only males inherit thrones. It would be an exception for a female to take over even her poor peasant father's lineage when he has sons.

However, as already said, women are breaking into the chieftaincy institution which has no history of female chieftaincy. But since the advent of the 20th century, that privileged male sphere in Bangwa land has witnessed an unprecedented expansion to accommodate a few women. Those women (now traditional female elite and cultural custodians) experience upward social mobility and of course enjoy higher citisenship of women status than peasant men and ordinary women. At first glance, the accommodation of women in the men's club looks like a transformationof power relations but a closer look at the setup reveals that female chiefs are still deprived of some of the attributes enjoyed by their male counterparts even though they perform the same traditional functions.

For the African continent as a whole and the Bangwa in particular, the corrosive effects of globalisation on its culture are devastating. To the diehard masculinists and patriarchists the world seems to be falling apart, especially as traditional markers of masculinities and status indicators that strongly favoured men appear to be giving way to new indicators such as the acquisition of formal education, and economic and political power. The fear is that some marginalised social actors can move up the social ladder to challenge the established *status quo*. In the current dispensation, many modern women have broken new ground and are competing well with men. Consequently, some of the hitherto marginalised women with second-class citizenship status are now deemed useful for the role of custodian of disappearing cultural values in the face of globalisation. However, it is neither obvious nor even imaginable that they can ever rise to the apex of traditional authority and the power triangle.

Gender, Globalisation and Citizenship in Bangwa

All reviewed literature on gender and holistic development points to the fact that in almost all human societies, women as a sex category fall in the subordinate and marginalised class and by extension, are treated as inferior or second-class citizens (Anderson 1983; Jackson et al. 1993; Larson et al. 1998; Lips 1999; Zewde 2003; Arnfred 2006). The position of women is even more precarious in a complex global age that has as its driving force the implantation of global capitalism and profit maximisation. In this much talked about global capitalist village, citizenship is determined by one's answer to the question, 'who are you?'; meaning 'what economic, political, social and cultural power do you wield in the society?'

The answers to the above questions are very much conditioned by one's sex, where the male sex is considered superior in almost all societies. By implication, a male is a superior citizen relative to a female. Since independence, women have increasingly broken into men's clubs in the public sphere and are struggling to exercise their rights there. This social mobility has been made possible because of women's increasing access to formal education and formal sector employment, leading to their visibility in the public sphere. However, inasmuch as the increasing global activism for gender equality, women's empowerment, poverty reduction, women's public visibility, women's agency and so on seem to be creating crevices in the otherwise solid walls of entrenched masculinities and structural obstacles to accommodate a few token women, the practical fruits of globalisation have not transformed the citizenship status of the women masses in Bangwa. This is because globalisation and citizenship are still top-down concepts. From an emancipatory perspective, Neocosmos (2007) posits that citizenship is not a top-down process of rights being conferred by the state or superstructure on its subjects but about acquiring and exercising active agency such that subjects become active agents of their own development and not just passive participants. This leaves a lot to be done in Bangwa in terms of awareness raising, sensitisation and policy implementation.

The agenda of the neoliberal economic policy, which is the core of globalisation, is to entrench trade liberalisation and economic stabilisation in order to strengthen profit-driven markets and the accumulation of private property. Randriamaro (2002) states that under such marketised governance, the main responsibility of the state is no longer to ensure and protect the social and economic rights of its citizens but to facilitate the establishment of 'an enabling environment for free trade and foreign investment as prescribed by the international financial institutions and imposed through the WTO regime'. Parpart *et al.* (2000:67) postulate that the catechism of global capitalism has not produced global uniformity within or between nations. Instead, globalisation has produced 'a characteristic unevenness, as some nations, regions, genders, ethnics groups and classes advance while others are subjected to new forms of subordination and generate new forms of resistance'. From their disadvantaged position, Africans in general and women in particular have to run faster and faster to follow the development trend, yet remain on the same spot because they are overstretched on the unequal playing field. Globalisation works to maintain the poor in their 'proper' position so that the rich continue to exploit their cheap labour in order to maximise profit accumulation. On the globalisation ladder, Bangwa women are at the bottom; and that position embodies their global citizenship.

The rural Bangwa woman of the study area lives on agriculture. She is responsible for all the production stages up to consumption and marketing. Add to this her reproductive and community roles and we can imagine what the woman goes through. Paradoxically, she remains unentitled to land ownership, inheritance and top leadership positions. Even with primitive production tools, when she has produced surplus crops and wants to sell them for cash, she loses a good amount of it for reasons beyond her control: either inexistent or very poor farm-to-market roads; archaic and inefficient storage methods and facilities; low selling prices because markets are saturated with the same food items. She also has to battle it out with animal and insect pests. Little or no attention has been paid to the commercialisation of the food grown by women; and with little or no education, lack of credit facilities and appropriate technology, they often run at a loss. In the meantime, her task of fetching water, firewood, and finding fertile farmland becomes even more difficult as trees and water catchment areas are cleared for competing uses. With increasing environmental degradation and loss of fertile topsoil, and with no access to fertiliser, she also has to increase her farm size (which implies working longer hours than before) to make ends meet; and the result is a drop in the standard of household well-being, with negative effects on long-term economic growth and development as a whole.

For those women who venture into the private informal sector, their growth and performance is hindered by numerous obstacles such as lack of education, no access to credit and harmful cultural practices. Most of them just resort to small-scale petty trading and retail, locally called '*buyam-sellam*'. These rudimentary activities cannot adequately equip women to face the fierce, global capitalist competition monopolised by transnational corporations. In that international exchange, it is the sophisticated industrialised and technological products that matter, not fresh tomatoes and perishable cocoyam produced by African women in general and Bangwa woman in particular. Lowy and Betto (2004) have summarised the globalised neoliberal scale of values held deep in the heart of Western capitalist civilisation into the dollar, the euro and the yen. Human values naturally meant to be qualitative have been quantified and given monetary values in such a way that a person who has say a billion dollars, euros or yen is worth more than the person who has only a million, and so on down the scale of 'net worth'. It goes without saying that if a person has little or no money, he/she is worth nothing; and if one is worth nothing then he/she is outside the civilized world market, as if he/she never existed. This is the hard reality that confronts the poor every day in the global village. Economic capacities and incentives are strongly gender differentiated to the disadvantage of women. However, Bangwa men and women have refused 'to celebrate victimhood' (Nyamnjoh 2004:37) and have developed their own strategies for surviving in their own way within the system. One of those strategies is to make gender boundaries more flexible and accommodating. McNeil (2001) outlines a three-part strategy to promote gender equality and engender development:

- Reform institutions to provide equal rights and equal opportunities for men and women;
- Foster economic development to strengthen incentives for more equal access to resources and participation;
- Take active measures to redress persistent disparities in command of resources and political voice.

So far, however, McNeil's proposal has not translated into reality in Bangwa land. The statistics provided by Amoros (2004) shows that '80 out of every 100 poor are women' and that 'throughout the world women hold only 1 per cent of positions of responsibility' this holds true for the Bangwa woman. This is not to say that nothing has changed in the lives of Bangwa women. Things are changing but women are not the active agents of those changes.

There has been a conscious attempt by the government to address five of the eight Millennium Development Goals (set at the United Nations Millennium Summit in 2000, with a target date of 2015). The goals that are being addressed are: reduce extreme poverty and hunger; achieve universal primary education for all; reduce child mortality; improve maternal health; and combat HIV/AIDS, malaria and other diseases. There has been a marked increase in agricultural productivity through the dissemination of improved and adaptable seeds/seedlings and the creation of agricultural outposts with extension agents who advise the farmers. Increased agricultural productivity increases income from sales (supplemented by the export of food crops to neighbouring countries), reduces poverty, hunger and hunger-related diseases (Kabeer 2003). In addition, the establishment of more medical centres for the rural population has reduced infant mortality and improved maternal care while endemic diseases such as smallpox, river blindness, polio, and sleeping sickness have virtually been eradicated. Garba *et al.* (1997) and Visvanathan *et al.* (1997) affirm that with the eradication of endemic diseases, better nutrition and available (though not always affordable) medical services, women's reproductive role as caregivers becomes easier. This means that more time can be dedicated to other productive activities and community services, even leaving some time for leisure (a necessity for human well-being). There is also a higher level of educational attainment for both boys and girls due to the establishment of many primary, secondary and technical schools in Bangwa land. The ordinary Bangwa man and woman have also been exposed to modern gadgets such as the cell phone, cable television, video films, foreign dressing and electricity. Movement and transportation have been facilitated by cheap Chinese motorcycles (locally known as *okada*) used for local commercial purposes. Even though not everybody can afford these luxuries and facilities offered by modernisation/development and globalisation, Nyamnjoh (2002b) posits that because of African cultural values of fraternity, sociability and conviviality, it is possible for the have-nots to benefit from the haves. For example, whole communities assemble in the homes or business places of those who have TV sets to watch interesting programmes such as football matches. Cell phone owners have become communication nodes for their communities – some run 'call boxes', charging for phone calls while others simply act as relays for communication with relatives, even those on different continents. Furthermore, like nation-states that have grouped themselves into blocs and interconnected networks in order to face the challenges of globalisation, Bangwa women have also seen the need to belong to local social groups. They rely on these groups for their social security insurance and other self-empowering services and activities that the state cannot deliver.

Notwithstanding this trickle-down impact of globalisation on the population, globalisation has not been engendered. If globalisation is to be engendered, it must make provision for a gender budget, increase investment in female education and health, expand access to services and assets, and remove legal and regulatory constraints on women's opportunities. And as Aruna *et al.* (1991:4) suggest, 'so that the fruits of development must be consciously distributed for specific purposes to specific populations', they should not simply trickle down. This point of view rejects the one-size-fits-all gender-blind (neutral) principles of globalisation.

Globalisation, with its primary motive being material accumulation, profit maximisation and capital expansion, is certainly taking place in a socio-economic and cultural context characterised by hierarchies and inequalities. A development project with that foundation certainly hurts the poor and as Krishna (1983), Garba *et al.* (1997) point out, any development policy that marginalises the poor and vulnerable will hurt women even more. This is because women have been identified as the poorest of the poor in almost all human societies to the extent that poverty has been seen as 'feminised' as if to say 'poverty, thy name is woman' (Garba *et al. op. cit.*; Kabeer 2003).

In the absence of a development ideology based on shared objectives of equity and equality, globalisation will continue to make some people feel that they are at the mercy of unpredictable forces because they are inadequately prepared and equipped to participate fully in and consequently benefit from the process.

Gender, Globalisation, Citizenship and Female Chiefs in Bangwa

Just as the globalisation terrain is not level for the North and South, rich countries and poor countries, there are also inequalities between men and women within a cultural community such as Bangwa. While the principle of globalisation enables corporate bodies based in industrialised countries to seek more profitable outlets in all parts of the world, in practical terms, economic and cultural capacities and incentives are strongly gender-differentiated, and grossly to the disadvantage of women. In spite of all the merits of globalisation, it has not resulted in a revolutionary transformation of power and gender relations as gender inequalities persist in all spheres of human activity. In this state of inequality, 'might' is often considered right and the appropriate model. In such a situation, the weak are usually marginalised and exploited. Bangwa women in general and the female chiefs in particular, like most women around the world, find themselves in this category of the weak and marginalised and relegated to invisibility in the private sphere, at best playing only marginal roles in public life and decision making.

The public sphere is the sphere of power/authority, knowledge, decision making, command and control, and patriarchy makes men visible and audible in that sphere while women are kept invisible in the private sphere (Visvanathan 1997; Cornwall 2005). However, post-modernist feminists such as Mohanty (1988), Barriteau (1992), Nicholson (1990) do not see power as something held only by the men or the ruling class, but as something diffused through society, exercised in many different ways by different people (men and women) and closely tied to control over knowledge and discourse, in attitudes, perceptions and behaviours. Conferring male titles on women looks like an attempt to redress inequalities at the level of cultural rights, a direct challenge to and deconstruction of conventional assumptions about masculinities and, by extension, citizenship. Unfortunately for women, since citizen boundaries are fluid, as they obtain male titles and are supposed to leave the periphery to join the centre, they soon discover that the boundaries have shifted, leaving them still at the periphery – a situation of hope and disappointment, inclusion and exclusion, empowerment, yet enslavement. Now that women are being given male titles which make them visible in the public sphere, they can exercise their active agency and power by expressing their will even when others oppose them; given that chieftaincy perpetuates class dominance, inequalities and, especially, the marginalisation of women.

A number of factors have militated in favour of women's entry into the men's club of chieftaincy and notability. First of all, status indicators, concepts of wealth and variables of masculinity have changed. Pre-colonial masculinity defined masculine power in terms of man being a warrior, bread provider, violent, possessing many wives and children, physical manhood, and having a large compound, land and dependents to take care of (Lindsay and Miescher 2003; Larson *et al.* 1999; Anderson 1983; Jackson *et al.* 1993; Arnfred 2006.) Today, there are alternative routes to the acquisition of masculine power through the socio-economic, political, formal educational and legal changes brought by the colonial administration that gave subordinates (women and other marginalised people) the opportunity for autonomy and status. By the neo-liberal and globalisation catechism, hegemonic masculinity today is defined in terms of capital expansion, accumulation of wealth and profit maximisation. By these criteria, many women are qualified to accede to the positions of notables and chiefs in their societies. Tazi's (2006:133) reflection on the place of women in Bangwa land today is that 'women are just as deserving of chieftaincy today as men are'. His backup argument is that if in the past chiefs were community development agents and leaders, collected taxes, heard disputes and shared out farm lands (functions that have almost died out today); then a woman who brings development or scores a great accomplishment should deserve an important recognition as her male counterpart who does the same thing'.

One of the generalised consequences of economic crisis and structural adjustment programmes for African societies is that the government no longer takes full responsibility for the socio-economic development of its citizens. Various categories of people have developed survival strategies to counter the effect of economic hardship. Kingmakers in favour of female chieftaincy explained that with the dwindling family sizes, increasing rural exodus, lineage disintegration, increasing cost of living, poverty and increasing demand for contributions towards self-help community and development projects and so on, it is necessary to extend male titles to women who can contribute towards the unity and sustainability of royalty on the one hand and community development on the other. Globalisation operates on a similar principle that enables international corporate bodies to seek more profitable outlets all over the world. One of the respondents asked, 'what is the worth of a chief without wealth (money?); money talks and opens all doors these days'. Another respondent expressed the opinion that the polarisation of class around economic interests and the emergence of women as salaried workers have made them visible in the public sphere, so why not in the traditional sphere? If the government can elevate women to the rank of minister and senior military officer, then why should the traditional society not recognise them also?

Most importantly, by conferring a title on a subordinate, the superior authority secures that subordinate's support, loyalty and service on all occasions. The covert objective of granting titles to subordinates seems to converge with the dependency theorists (Amin 1974; Gunder 1979) of development who see the North (metropolis, men, haves, etc.) as having created a situation of dependency in the South (periphery, women, have-nots, etc.) that it exploits to enrich itself. In addition, the conditions for the acquisition of titles have been narrowed down to purchase deals over the counter. If a woman is the highest bidder she should get the title – and there are many women who have the money to pay and meet other conditions such as 'feeding' the other chiefs and notables of their rank and contributing their quota for all traditional and modern development dues.

Besides, one kingmaker disclosed that it does not cost the chief anything to crown somebody. Instead, it enriches him. This is because in the old days, title was accompanied by gifts as royal symbols of authority, land and in some cases a princess for a wife. Today, however, there are so many chiefs that a majority of them are landless and without territorial jurisdiction. This is the time when women are brought in, perhaps because there are no more 'men of substance' without titles. The kingmakers are not really interested in the empowerment of the female chiefs but the assurance that their loyalty and service are used in the interests and support of the system.

As with her male counterpart, a female chief or notable is a cultural custodian. She is a development agent, a peacemaker, mediator and a judge who resolves conflicts and settles disputes. As a leader, she is a role model and incarnation of the right mode of conduct. All chiefs and notables give material and financial support and advice to sustain the authority that crowned them. This financial and material support to sustain royalty is an added expenditure on the women who are already identified in most societies as the poorest of the poor. Although most of these functions are just an extension of women's community role, they demand extra effort and sacrifice to perform them well, given the fact that women still have to perform their productive and reproductive roles efficiently.

The strong force that favours female chiefs and notables is that in purely traditional matters, traditional authority is not contested. Even if somebody is against having a female chief, he/she cannot influence the traditional authority that conferred the title to withdraw it. Because of that respect for the culture, all female notables/chiefs interviewed reported that they were respected by men and women who were superior, equal and inferior to them in rank. They also reported that in the exercise of their cultural duties, they did just what tradition required, forgetting they were women. Publicly, they do not go unnoticed, because their attire resembles that of male chiefs. They distinguish themselves from the rank-and-file by their expensive and gorgeous traditional regalia befitting their status, which makes it possible for everyone to recognise them even from afar. That regalia alone is a 'hard passport' (Nyamnjoh op. cit.) that permits them to receive V.I.P treatment in public.

In a patriarchal society, it was never foreseen that women could command authority in the public sphere, not to talk of having power over their husbands. So with the entry of new players onto the playing field, new rules of the game have to be set. When the impossible becomes possible, a compromise has to be sought. To balance the equation therefore, their spouses' statuses too are raised. Asked whether the exercise of their traditional authority did not negatively affect the relationship between them (female chiefs) and their spouses, the respondents said, 'No'. They reported that on the contrary, their husbands were very supportive and were doing everything possible to help them succeed. Such support stems perhaps from the fact that as the women return home, they hang the 'public coat and hat' in the wardrobe and assume their full functions as housewives and mothers, submitting themselves to their husband's authority. They also revealed that their husband's opinions are always sought before their wives are given titles, which means that if they oppose, the proposal would be dropped. In contrast, no woman is ever consulted before her husband is given a title.

Geisler (1995) and Ottosson (1998) agree that women in politics always enjoin other women to obey their husbands, keep their homes neat and play their reproductive roles well. Loutfi (1985:13) shares a point of view similar to that of Geisler and Ottosson stating that, 'given the structure of rural society as it affects women, the strategies of obedience, self-sacrifice and submission seem the most likely to provide them some guarantee of security', and hence power. Loutfi adds that it is not uncommon for many women who have broken traditional constraints to attribute a greater part of their success to enlightened, supportive fathers, brothers and husbands, rather than to their own efforts.

One could even say that female chieftaincy titles inadvertently clip those women's wings – they all reported that not only do they not challenge their husbands at home but they also do everything not to project a negative image for fear of discouraging kingmakers from crowning other women. Thus, while male chieftaincy relies on home support for its strength in the public sphere, the domestic sphere disempowers female chiefs who cannot exercise their active agency for fear of violating cultural norms. Gender remains one of the staunchest areas of exclusion and hindrance for women and its hard boundaries have not been demolished by the powerful forces of globalisation. In Bangwa, a female chief who is higher than her husband in public cultural rank returns home to be submissive to him.

The female chiefs reported some of the difficulties and challenges they were facing in asserting their full authority as compared to their male counterparts. One of the areas where they still felt marginalised is in the presentation of a traditional dance called *Nkweh*. It is a warrior dance, a symbol of power and conquest reserved for the 'who is who' in the clan. By these criteria, no female chief has proven her prowess such that they can qualify to own that dance cult. It is like those United Nations member countries without veto powers. The respondents reported that they were still negotiating for that authority. But the negotiation will take a long time because no woman is in the village Central Committee of Nine which takes final decisions that the paramount ruler only implements. This Central Committee of Nine can be equated to the Group of Eight countries in world politics. Thus, what obtains at local level seems to be a microcosm of global arrangements and forces. Aiyedun (op. cit.) suggests that if Africa is to be an effective actor in the globalised world, major structural changes must be effected. As new entrants into chieftaincy, women went in without negotiating the terms of inclusion. They were simply integrated and accommodated without a transformation of the structures to mainstream them. Chieftaincy, like globalisation, is not a liberal flow as its advocates propound; it has structural inequalities and imbalances embedded in it, to the advantage of the strong minority.

Married female chiefs have not been able to secure a piece of land for their *lefem* (sacred groves/shrines) at the entrance to their palaces. This is because the compounds belong to men. Even though some male chiefs also do not have the *lefem*, if they wanted to, they would create space in their compounds. Women, however, do not have that free hand. They are landless chiefs. The issue of land ownership has direct bearing on status and citizenship. The problem of women's non-entitlement to land (an important factor of production and indicator of wealth) has been one of the contributory factors to women's poverty and marginalisation. Since Bangwa society is an agrarian one, those who own land are the privileged while the landless poor, according to Lowy and Betto (2004) are the 'nobodies'. The fact that female chiefs are so few in number, and that they lack experience as well as resources (*e.g.* land), contributes to their marginalisation inside the mainstream of chieftaincy. The fate of female chiefs reflects that of developing country producers of agricultural raw materials in competition with the world's economic and technological giants who are the proponents of globalisation – there is ostensible inclusion as citizens and members of the globalised world and at the same time exclusion because of economic and social insignificance.

Another area involving uneasy power relations is the constitution of the female chief's cabinet and the crowning of their own subordinate notables. Two of the three chiefs have put in place a cabinet and crowned a few notables but even these executive members are not proud of the titles. They are ashamed that the recognition has come from the weaker sex, symbolising inferior citizenship. Just as the forces of globalisation pull weaker entities towards them (especially Europe and North America), human beings from weak countries are in mad rush in search of strong European/American identities and citizenship. It is profitable to identify with the strong, not with the weak. In the same light, some staunchly masculinist opponents of female chiefs confessed that inasmuch as they cannot openly challenge the traditional rulers who adulterate the culture by awarding male titles to women, personally they would not invite those female chiefs to their palaces on any occasion. They have accused globalisation (or Westernisation) of disrupting their cultural cohesion and they lump together female chieftaincy and the deviant and unnatural sexual/cultural orientation of the international gay and lesbian movement and see them as part of the fallout from globalisation. As globalisation gives voice to the voiceless, even prostitutes have transcended their denigrated and ignominious status to claim workers' rights as 'sex workers' (Ghosh 2004).

In the old days, a man's rank and status in society were determined by the human (wives, children, slaves, etc.) and material resources (wealth) that he commanded. Today, many chiefs are monogamously married with just a few children. However, no chief (some succeeded their father very young) worthy of his salt is without a palace (even if it is just one roofed house) and a wife. As women enter that male sphere, should they too marry wives and build their own palaces? Unmarried respondents without biological children admitted that they had already married wives who were bearing children for them. They justified their strategy as one that would perpetuate their dynasties. Another married chief and some notables too expressed the desire to marry their own wives who would bear them children whom they would lord over as their fathers; after all, they had paid the bride price for the women. However, one senior female notable was against the idea of 'woman-to-woman' marriage. She said it was not only illegal but also oppressive and dehumanising and would encourage prostitution. In addition, one would be 'fathering' children without having blood affinity with them. Moreover, any cloud on parentage may be punishable by the Cameroon Penal Code, which stipulates that each child must have a biological father.

The problem of woman-to-woman marriage is so complex that in trying to solve one problem a new one is created. For example, which of the children (those to whom she is mother or those to whom she is father) would inherit her throne? Do they have the same rights and status? Can they make the same claim to her inheritance? We must not forget that if a married woman contracted for joint property with her husband upon their marriage, then in the event of the death of one party, the other has the pride of place to control and inherit the estate. The confusion will be chaotic. Whatever the case may be, some of those children would feel marginalised by the arrangement. Furthermore, if the children's biological fathers claimed their children before a court of law, they would be handed to them.

The female chief/notables were divided on the sex of their successor. They said it would depend on the child who is most responsible and capable of uniting and protecting family values and interests. However, one respondent favoured a female successor so that the institution of female chieftaincy should not disappear. Female chiefs who succeeded their fathers, have had to wrestle it out with their half-brothers (who were babies at the time their father passed away) who claimed that their sisters were only regents and should hand over the throne to them now that they were grown up, because succession is for males. One case was resolved at an enlarged family meeting and the female chief was confirmed, while another case ended up in the law courts. The males lost the case on the grounds that every child has equal rights of inheritance over their father's property. Statutory law can do a lot to enforce gender equality and citizenship status. However, one must have the courage, education, resources and information in order to fight for, obtain and defend those rights.

Another dimension of power is in the booty and other advantages enjoyed by those who wield it. The female chiefs/notables reported that they enjoyed no extra financial and material advantages. Apart from the long traditional caps and beads they wear (which earn them respect) and the fact that there are special seats reserved for them at all occasions and the privilege of eating first, before the crowd, there are no other advantages. We noticed a general tendency to glorify traditional titles – men and women, literates and illiterates, the rich and the poor, etc., all seem under pressure to acquire titles by any means and at all costs. Yet, the economic rewards are not evident.

Most migrants seeking citizenship in Europe and North America live in the dream and illusion that acquisition of that status is the final solution to all their problems of poverty, marginalisation and general existence. However, disillusionment sets in when they discover that new obstacles such as race, level of education, high level connections come into play and again relegate them to the periphery of pauperism. Chieftaincy thus gives females some degree of cultural and social rights but denies them economic rights; yet, the neo-liberal doctrine of globalisation is founded on capitalism. So the female chiefs are living in the age of globalisation but are not in the mainstream and consequently, are not enjoying its fruits.

However, those female chiefs who come from royal palaces admitted that they had some meagre share of the bride price paid by bridegrooms to marry princesses and other female relations. In the final analysis, is that all about female chieftaincy/notability? The answer is simple. Acquiring the position of chief indicates achievement; a feeling that a woman has raised her head above the crowd; a feeling that she has arrived, that she belongs and has an edge over others. In short, one feels that one is an incarnation of the correct social values and has the power to shape and determine other people's destinies and citizenship.

As with power, citizenship and globalisation have exerted an osmotic rather than a symbiotic force on the general populace and are sapping the resources from those who are not comfortable with where they belong. Thus, some poor families have committed financial suicide and have into abject poverty by liquidating or mortgaging all their assets to send their beloved children to Europe and America. Some aspirants for rank and titles in Bangwa land have also auctioned family assets and given the proceeds to traditional rulers to acquire titles. The title distributors (sellers) collect the money to develop their families while their clients do not get richer in their newly acquired status. Instead, they spend the rest of their lives making contributions befitting their rank in order to maintain their position and prestige in the power triangle and help sustain the superstructure. The award of titles has become a lucrative business to the superstructure (the monarchy) but a financially unprofitable yet desirable one for the base – a replica of what obtains in the UN, the World Bank and IMF between the highly industrialised and the developing world countries.

Conclusion

Through an examination of the complexity of women's entry into the traditional male sphere of chieftaincy in Bangwa, we can say that men and women are players in the globalising world but the terrain is still unfavourable for women. As in all power and decision-making structures at national and international levels, women are largely under-represented in the chieftaincy. As a result, they cannot effectively influence policies that discriminate against women. Since women are entering this male sphere from a weaker and less privileged position due to the gender biases that play against them, it is imperative to engender globalisation and citizenship.

As women (new players) negotiate their entry into the men's club in Bangwaland, we expect a transformation of the structures (new rules) to accommodate all actors equally. However, by every indication, male bias is still strong since the status quo has not changed. A look at the power relations inside chieftaincy leads to the conclusion that far from concerning themselves with challenging the patriarchy for the purpose of cultural transformation, the kingmakers incorporate a few women in order to tap from their resources. Hence, the cultural democratic space that crowns female chiefs and incorporates them as citizens in the male club eventually excludes them because of their sex. This reflects the fluid, inclusive and exclusive nature of citizenship, as Nyamnjoh (ibid.) posits. The token female chiefs and notables in the club can be said to have a bit of access to the hitherto exclusively male club but not control. The bulk of resources, empowerment and decision-making power are concentrated at the level of the state, from which women have been largely excluded. For globalisation to be integrated, holistic, equitable and sustainable, it must have a gender component/dimension. Engendering globalisation involves the use of gender-disaggregated data and more gender-sensitive indicators to assess its impact on men and women (Beck 1999). In order to assess the degree of gender mainstreaming in the globalisation process, we need to address questions such as 'who is doing what; for who; with what; why; in what conditions; for how much; how does it affect him/her?' It is necessary to address them because just as the globalisation terrain is not equally level for the North and the South, so are there inequalities between men and women. This is because men and women (especially in sub-Saharan Africa) have different access to and control over vital resources such as land, labour, credit, infrastructure, education, health, technology, information and time.

Even though the female notables and chiefs foresee a bright future for female chieftaincy, we did not see the concrete strategies for making that happen as these females have simply fitted themselves into male frames. In such a situation, de Beauvoir (1947:15) remarks that 'women have only gained what men have been willing to grant; they have taken nothing; they have only received'. An osmotic relationship (where a stronger, dominant solution pulls the weaker one towards it and exploits it) can be used to explain women's entry into the men's club, rural exodus, migration from the South (poor, less developed countries) to the North (rich, developed countries) and other related phenomena such as citizenship. The result is the dissolution of smaller entities and identities into global ones. When an individual or a minority loses his/her economic, cultural, social and political autonomy by being submerged in a larger and stronger whole, he suffers from identity and citizenship crisis. Female chiefs in Bangwa seem to be at a cultural crossroads as they attempt to be women and men at the same time. Such a situation neither contributes to their empowerment nor reduces their triple role burden. Instead the burden is increased as they operate as 'masculine females'. Why can the women not set their own pace and norms and break new ground by crafting a politics of their own and growing in it to the summit? Why must the weak, oppressed and marginalised people in general and women in particular always try to walk in the shadows and according to the dictates of the strong, dominant, oppressor, especially men?

The Bangwa kingmakers should be thinking of designating other titles and nomenclature of recognition not necessarily 'Fuo' (chief) or 'Nkem' (notable) that are already saturated and rapidly losing their value. Lawrence (1955:41) denounced such a situation of absolutes and affirms that 'once and for ever, let us have done with the ugly imperialism of absolute. There is no absolute good; there is nothing absolutely right. All things flow and change, and even change is not absolute'. We must, however, commend the dynamic, progressive and forward looking effort of the kingmakers who are adapting to the wind of change by admitting women into previously exclusively male chieftaincy positions. We also laud those courageous and assertive women who venture into such masculinist spheres. That token gesture is a glimmer of hope for the world's men and women who are concerned with gender equality and equity.

Bibliography

Achankeng, F. and Nkemnji, F., eds., 1999, *Lebialem issues And Challenges At century end*, Madison: Nkemnji Global Tech.

Aina, T., 1995, 'Globalisation and Social Policy in Africa, Dakar: CODESRIA Working Paper Series, 6/96.

Aiyedun, Ernest, 2004, 'Nature and Meaning of Globalisation', in Odama, J. and Aiyedun, E., eds., *Globalisation and the Third World Economy: Impacts and Challenges in the 21st Century*, Lagos: Malthouse Press, pp. 19-29.

Alemanji, A., 2006, *In Defence of a Tradition: the Legacy of Mafua Nkengafac Fuantem Asonganyi*, Wandsbeck: Reach Publishers.

Allen, J. and Hamnett, C., eds., 1995, *A Shrinking World? Global Unevenness and Inequality*, Oxford: Oxford University Press.

Alubu, O., 2004, 'Citizenship and Nation-Making in Nigeria: New Challenges and Contestations', *in Identity, Culture and Politics*, Vol 5, Nos. 1 & 2, pp. 135-161, CODESRIA and ICES.

Amin, S., 1974, *Accumulation on a World Scale*, Brighton: Harvester Press.

Amoros, C., 2004, 'Feminism and the Three Enlightenment Ideals, in Fisher, W. and Ponniah, T., eds., *Another World is Possible*, Black Point: Fernwood Publishing.

Anderson, M., 1983, *Thinking About Women: Sociological and Feminist Perspectives*, New York: Macmillan.

Annan, K., 2000, *Millennium Address to the UN General Assembly*. (http://www.un.org/millenium/sg/report/state.htm.)

Arnfred, S., ed., 2006, *Rethinking Sexualities in* Africa, Uppsala: Nordic Africa Institute.

Atem, G., 2006. *The Lebialem struggle: The Political Evolution of Nweh-Mundani* (1922-1992). Buea.

Awe, B., 2005 '*The Iyalode in the Traditional Yoruba political system*' in Cornwall, A., ed, Readings in Gender in Africa. London: The International African Institute.

Barriteau, E., 1992, 'The Construct of a Post-Modernist Feminist Theory for Caribbean Social Science Research', *Social and Economic Studies*, Vol. 41, 2, pp. 1-43.

Beck, T. 1999, *Using Gender Sensitive Indicators: A Reference Manual for Governments and Other Stakeholders*. London: The Commonwealth Secretariat.

Berger, I., 2005, 'Rebels or Status Seekers? Women as mediums in East Africa' in Cornwall, A., ed 2005 *Readings in Gender in Africa*. London: The International African Institute.

Bhargava, V. and Gurkan, I., eds., 2006, *Global Issues For Global Citizens: An Introduction to Key Development Challenges*, Washington DC: World Bank.

Cheru, F., 2008 *Africa's Development in the 21st Century: Reshaping the Research Agenda*. Uppsala: The Nordic Africa Institute, Current African Issues No. 41.

Cornwall, A., ed., 2005, *Readings in Gender in Africa*, London: International African Institute.

de Beauvoir, S., 1949, 'The Second Sex', in Nicholson, L., ed, *The Second Wave: A Reader in Feminist Theory*, London and New York: Routledge.

Fomin, S., (undated), *A Handbook on Essoh-Attah chiefdom*. Essoh-Attah Development and Cultural Association (EDCA).

Garba, P. *et al.*, 1997, *Women and Economic Reforms in Nigeria*, Ibadan: Institute of African Studies.

Geisler, Gisela, 1995, 'Troubled Sisterhood: Women and Politics in Southern Africa: Case Studies from Zambia, Zimbabwe and Botswana', *African Affairs*. Vol. 94, No. 377, pp. 545-78.

Ghosh, S., 2004. 'The Shadow Lines of Citizenship: Prostitutes' Struggle over Workers' Rights', *Identity, Culture and Politics*, Vol. 5, Nos. 1 & 2, pp 105-123.

Giddens, A., 1990, *The Consequences of Modernity*, Cambridge: Polity.

Gunder, F., 1979, *Dependent Accumulation and Underdevelopment*, New York: Monthly Review Press.

Ihonvbere, J., 1996, 'Africa and the New Globalisation: Challenges and Options for the Future' in Didsbury, H., ed, *Future Vision: Ideas, Insights and Strategies*, Bethesda: World Future Society.

Ihonvbere, J., 2000, *Africa and the New World Order*, New York: Peter Lang.

Jackson, S. *et al.*, eds., 1993, *Women's Studies: A Reader*, Cambridge: Cambridge University Press.

Larison, A., *et al.* eds., 1998, *Changing Gender Relations in Southern Africa: Issues of Urban Life*, Lesotho: ISAS.

Lawrence, D.H., 1955, *Why the novel matters in selected literacy criticism*, London: Heinemman.

Lindsay, L. and Miescher, S., eds., 2003, *Men and Masculinities in Modern Africa*, Portsmouth: Heinemann.

Lips, H., 1999, *A New Psychology of Women: Gender, Culture and Ethnicity*, London: Mayfield.

Loutfi, M., 1985, *Rural Women: Unequal Partners in Development*, Geneva: ILO.

Lowy, M. and Belto, F., 2004, 'Values of a New Civilisation' in Fisher, W. and Ponniah, T., eds., *Another World is Possible* Black Point: Fernwood.

Lynda, R., 1994, 'The Evolution of Female Chiefship during the late nineteenth-century wars of the Mende', *The International Journal of African Historical Studies*, vol 27 no 3, pp 481-503.

Mazrui, A., 1999, *Cultural Forces in World Politics*, London: Heinemann.

McNeil M. ed., 2001, *Development Outreach: Promoting Gender Equality*, Washington DC: World Bank.

Mohanty, C., 1988, 'Under Western Eyes: Feminist Scholarship and Colonial Discourses', *Feminist Review*, Vol. 30, pp. 61-88.

Nicholson, L., 1990, *Feminism/Post-Modernism*, New York: Routledge.

Njoya, T., 2003, *The Divine Tag on Democracy*, Yaoundé: Cle-cipcre.

Nyamnjoh, F., 2004, 'Globalisation, Boundaries and Livelihoods: Perspectives on Africa', in *Identity, Culture and Politics*, Vol. 5, Nos. 1 & 2, pp. 37-59.

Ottosson, Ase, 1998, 'At Least Our Voices Are Now Heard': Changing Meanings of Gender and Power in Rural Uganda', Masters Thesis in Social Anthropology, Stockholm University.

Parpart, J. *et al.*, eds., 2000, *Theoretical Perspectives on Gender and Development*, Ottawa: IDRC.

Qunta, C., 1987, 'Outstanding African Women, 1500 BC-1900 AD', in Qunta, C. ed., *Women in Southern Africa*, London: Allison and Busby, pp. 23-61.

Randriamaro, Z., 2003, 'Gender, Neoliberalism and the African State', Paper prepared for the ILRIG Globalisation School 2002, Cape Town, South Africa 30 September- 4 October 2002.

Rodney, W., 1974, *How Europe Underdeveloped Africa*, London: Bogle L' Ouverture.

Rowbotham, S., and Linkogli, S., eds., 2001, *Women Resist Globalisation: Mobiliszing for Livehood and Rights*, London: Zed Books.

Tazi, P., 2006, 'Traditional leadership in Lebialem: A Pragmatic Approach', in Achankeng, F., ed., 2006, I, Madison: Nkemnji Global Tech., pp. 117-133

Visvanathan, N. *et al.*, 1997, *The Women, Gender and Development Reader*, London: Zed Books.

Zanden, J., 1990, *Sociology: The Core*, New York: McGraw-Hill.

Zewde, B., ed., 2003, *Land, Gender and the Periphery: Themes in the History of Eastern and Southern Africa*, Addis Ababa: OSSREA.

5

Globalisation, Masculinity, and Citizen Migration: Rethinking Gender in the Twenty First Century Zimbabwe

Ivan Marowa

Introduction

The twenty first century has witnessed an increase in citizen migration; particularly from developing economies to 'stronger' economies in the Third World and to developed economies of the North. This migration is not only a product of globalisation that has ushered in an understanding of interconnection between and among different countries of the globe, but also has other factors connected to it. Much of the citizen migration occurs in Africa where populations are constantly moving at national, regional and international levels. This movement of populations is necessitated mostly by the unfavourable conditions that obtain in African countries, especially economic disintegration and political instability. However, within Africa, in Southern Africa especially, only people from low performing economies like Zimbabwe have been moving, usually to Botswana and South Africa (Cheater and Gaidzanwa 1996).

In Zimbabwe, for example, the census of 2002 estimated that the country's population numbered about 15 million but only 12 million were resident in Zimbabwe. The remainder were living and working in other countries, the majority being in South Africa, Botswana and the United Kingdom (UK). Globalisation has also allowed such people the opportunity to acquire citizenship in different countries. Apart from that, globalisation has also facilitated the export and import of skills and labour across national and international borders. Within this context, Zimbabwe has been greatly affected by brain drain to the extent that its economy became quite dysfunctional in the last decade until the formation of an inclusive government in February 2009, following the disputed 2008 presidential elections. Most sub-Saharan African countries have not been spared the same fate, as their persistent economic problems have shown.

Globalisation is a refined term that sounds good but is in fact rooted in concepts of colonialism and patriarchy. It encapsulates capitalism, masculinity and patriarchy in one apex structure that controls the globe; what has changed is the form and its packaging. Jansen *et al.* (2002) argue that globalisation is not new though its dynamics may have changed over time. The globalisation process started many years back with the slave trade, the partitioning of the African continent, colonial governance, externally-imposed economic systems and so on (Jansen *et al.* 2002:2). Obiora (2004) emphasises the same point, arguing that the integration of the Africa into the global economy dates back to the days of slavery through to the contemporary phase of capital-led integration.

The term globalisation is widely known and talked about but it actually has no clear definition. As Jansen *et al.* and Obiora note, globalisation is understood in relation to interactions between societies, economies, technologies and cultural advancement (Jansen *et al.* 2002:2; Obiora 2004:6,7). The societies which developed the concept are patriarchal; hence globalisation is a product of patriarchal thought. The concept is a link between the strong and the weak, and the idea of one global village is false because there are a few members of the globe who are more equal and have more powers than the others. In the fundamental multilateral organisations – World Bank, International Monetary Fund (IMF) and World Trade Organisation (WTO) – voting is weighed according to financial contributions, therefore most countries of the Third World, particularly those in the African continent, do not have the voting strength to exert any influence on major decisions that affect the world. Their presence is felt only in the United Nations (UN) General Assembly, which practises one country one vote. However, the UN does not have the same kind of influence and impact in matters of international and domestic trade, finance and economic policy as the Bretton Woods institutions and the WTO.

Castells (2001) points out that this new global economy does not mean the entire world is one single economic system, and that not everything is global. For example, most jobs are not global and not all markets are free (Castells 2001: 3; see also Jansen *et al.* 2002:3). Castells further argues that international financial institutions such as the IMF make the rules of the game and also make sure developing countries follow the rules – and to be in the global 'club', a country has to accept the rules (*ibid*:6). This makes globalisation masculine – some members judge others and consider them unworthy markets or governments.

This paper argues that globalisation is much more masculine in its ideology than gender neutral. From all appearances, globalisation has given women a greater opportunity to participate in the economies of their countries and the world. What has in fact happened is the further entrenchment of patriarchal values as women have become more and more tied to the household and their movement has been back and forth for the family. This is as a result of the disparities that have existed since the slavery and colonial periods when women had to carry the burden in the home. Globalisation is a new and modern form of slavery and slave trade with an internationally legitimate and legalised system that in fact suits only the powerful. Just as the slave trade plundered the young and strong men and women, retarding development in Africa because of the removal of able-bodied citizens, today globalisation is taking the best brains and skills out of the developing economies to the developed ones. Jansen *et al.* (2002) argue that the labour market has remained segmented; unskilled labour continues to be immobile while skilled labour tends to flow from the poor countries to the rich ones (Jansen *et al.* 2002:3).

Globalisation has continued the relationship of domination between the metropolis and the periphery, just as with the 'horse and the rider' of colonial capitalism. Ntarangwi argues that capitalism and masculinity are structured in a way that opposes feminism and, specifically, gender equity (Ntarangwi 1998:19). So, if globalisation includes capitalism, then criticisms that have been raised against capitalism are relevant to it. In addition, globalisation has also entrenched and continued what Gwaunza (1998) calls 'commuter family arrangements' which began nationally during colonialism and is now manifested on a global scale. The phenomenon of commuter families, particularly in Southern Africa, started to become evident with the discovery of minerals in South Africa in the second half of the nineteenth century. Men from Zimbabwe, Malawi, Zambia and Mozambique became part of the migrant labour that shuttled between their workplace and homes, a practice that was not open to women. Cheater and Gaidzanwa (1996) make a crucial point that ideas about space, presence and mobility are gendered and also influenced by race, class and age (Cheater and Gaidzanwa 1996:191). In its purported endeavour to build interconnectedness in the world, globalisation is working to increase the gap between the few rich and the many poor and instead of interconnection, the economies of poor countries are being submerged.

The twenty first century has been seen as a renewed opportunity to address gender equity issues, particularly the continuing effort to empower women. This is meant to close the gap created by the traditional notions of the public and private spheres. The public domain which wields power and control is seen as the preserve of men while the private belongs to women. The UN has shown a clear recognition of this challenge by identifying it as the third major objective to be achieved in the Millennium Development Goals (MDGs). Hence, MDG 3 points up the need to 'promote gender equality and empower women'. These MDGs were developed possibly as an afterthought in recognition of the fact that globalisation was failing to address gender in its development and integration process. According to Ntarangwi, women are seen as a cultural construct and potential competitor in the male-dominated sphere of capitalism and thus are restrained from entering the public space of capitalism through images of re-invented morality and tradition (Ntarangwi 1998:19).

The first pointer to masculinity is seen in the creation of the powerful and powerless or the wealthy and the poor, where the wealthy and powerful control the transformation process of globalisation, be it political, economic or social. The situation is one of conditioned dependency, following the inequality caused by the historical exploitation of poor countries by the rich and powerful nations (Offiong 2001:44-45). Pettman (1999) points out that globalisation is not a uniform or unidirectional process because it has a differing and uneven impact on different regions, classes and people. O the contrary, globalisation, today, is marked by growing disparities in terms of wealth between the nations of the North and South. Cox (1996) argues that power and wealth are concentrated among the triad of North America, Western Europe and East Asia (Pettman, 1999:209). Also, Wallerstein notes the division of the world into three categories, the core, the semi-periphery and the periphery, with Africa being at the periphery that is responsible for supporting the development of the core. Pettman further adds that while no region or state can escape the impact of the capitalist world market, whole states and regions, notably in Africa, are bypassed except as suppliers of raw materials or migrant labour for the rich states and regions (Pettman 1999:209).

As already noted, there is no clear definition of globalisation. This paper analyses the concept in general, highlighting its structures and operations and how they work to connect the world in the sectors of economy, information and communications technology and so on. It then brings out some of the positive contributions that have come from globalisation, even if cosmetic and mostly to the benefit of those who control the process. The paper proceeds to give an overview of the Zimbabwean context, tracing the historical background of migration and mobility, showing that the pattern has not shifted much since colonial times, and then examines the contemporary situation. It argues that globalisation, together with some internal factors, has contributed to the migration of Zimbabweans to countries of the North and other relatively developed Third World nations, as almost the entire population of skilled personnel have left the country. In the final section, the paper analyses the gender dimension of the migration process, emphasising how women have been negatively affected while their male counterparts took advantage of the opportunities presented by globalisation. The section also analyses the impact of technology (especially the Internet) on keeping the migration pattern composed mostly of men, showing how women have found themselves in a quagmire in the wake of the establishment of interconnected economies, trade and labour market structures.

Understanding the Parameters of Globalisation

According to Offiong (2001:1), 'globalisation is the consummation of the international capitalism and its associated institutions and the subjugation of peoples of the globe which began centuries ago'. The statement identifies two crucial things in the two-tier concept of Globalisation. That is, it is first an ideology or philosophy; and secondly it is a process. Obiora divides globalisation into five structures, namely, ideology, capital flows, trade, culture and politics (Obiora 2004:9-11). This division fits the two categories highlighted above. Proponents of globalisation argue that there should be development of elements of commonalities in the various sectors of significance to human existence, particularly economics and politics. As an ideology, globalisation is just like any other concept that came before it and underwent changes such as slavery, imperialism, colonialism and neocolonialism. Obiora notes that globalisation places absolute value on the operation of the market and subordinates people's lives (*Ibid*:9). Castells argues that globalisation is a code word for the new system emerging in the world and at the same a banner to rally the determined march of global corporate capitalism (Castells 2001:3).

This ideology is based on the concept of strong and weak, rich and poor and, in that context, it is endowed with masculine thinking, where some nations have the power to dictate what should be done and what should not be done while other nations (the majority) are not part of the decision-making process at all except, of course, to comply with the agreed terms. This is similar to the divide between the public and private spheres. If Obiora is correct in arguing that the political structure today is not as influential in the globalisation process as capital flows, trade, as well as cultural and economic structures, then it explains the calls for allowing women into politics as that would sway their energies towards the less important structure in globalisation. The result is that men continue to influence crucial areas of global economy through organisations such as the World Bank and IMF.

In terms of processes, globalisation emphasises transformation that builds integration and development between and among nations of the globe. Offiong notes that globalisation emphasises multiplicity of linkages and interconnectedness that surpasses nation-states by setting up a process through which events, decisions and activities in one part of the globe have consequences for communities in very distant parts of the world (Offiong 2001:1). The major component of the process is the movement of goods, services, information and technology and of people by means of migration. The process is centred on trade and investment in which the terms are set by the rich and powerful who own and control capital. In analysing globalisation, there is a need to distinguish between the ideology and the process while recognising that the two concepts help to explain the gendered nature and consequences of globalisation.

Globalisation calls for the removal of the various forms of isolation that are apparent around the world. It is a concept that presents the world as one village, advocating for integration and development, from national and regional to international level. As an ideology, globalisation stresses domination and that is why it emphasises oneness while understanding that there is a difference between the developing and developed economies of the world. According to Pearson, globalisation is a new era that promises integration and development for all, with technology, investment and trade overcoming geographical and economic isolation (Pearson 2000:10). Isolation is replaced by interconnection and liberalisation ranging from economic, technical and financial to cultural aspects. The argument of globalisation is that the world should have a common understanding and vision. The Secretary-General of the United Nations Conference on Trade and Development (UNCTAD), commenting on the economic aspects of globalisation, observed that 'it is a process whereby producers and investors behave as if the world economy consisted of a single market with regional or national sub-sectors' (Pearson 2000:10). This means that globalisation is a process that is realised through transformation from an inward-looking to an outward-looking and all-encompassing understanding of economics, as well as financial and technical transactions.

The transformations, particularly of interconnectivity, that are espoused by globalisation are realised through developments in technology and communications that bring the world into a 'globalised market'. Such a market no longer 'recognises' borders or boundaries between nations, regions and continents. Pettman (1999) makes this point clear by arguing that 'almost nothing is simply 'domestic' anymore as the globalised market impacts on individuals as well as states' (Pettman 1999:209). The result of creating a globalised market has been the free exchange and movement of raw materials, goods, services, capital and human resources across boundaries. The significant factor that has given the globe a sense of oneness is the Internet and the sophisticated technologies associated with it to disseminate information.

Castells (2001) argues that the organisational form and value of all kinds of businesses is based on information technologies which the Internet organises (Castells 2001:2). McGrew also notes that the extended awareness of global interconnectedness is enhanced by the electronic media that bring distant events to the instant attention of their audiences, creating a sense of global connectivity (see Offiong 2001:1). This has led to the further development and growth of those companies referred to as transnational corporations (TNCs), which are engaged in transnational productions that give them a domestic presence in many different countries. They include bottling companies such as Coca Cola and processing companies. These TNCs are the best movers of human capital, skills and financial capital across boundaries that make them change and acquire new citizenship. Pettman illustrates this by pointing out that transnational production is spread over different sites and states and new corporate management strategies now link different parts of the globe, independent of state boundaries and agents (Pettman 1999:208-209).

Apart from economic considerations, globalisation has also caused some social transformation in the world. The idea of a global village has led to the emergence of the concept of universal citizenship where people are free to acquire any citizenship of their choice. This citizenship entails identifying with the group, community or state an individual would have joined. According to Meer and Sever, citizenship is about membership of a group or community that confers rights and responsibilities as a result of such membership. (Meer and Sever 2004:2). So when people talk of universal citizenship, it is about equal rights in all spheres of life without considering race, class or gender. However, there are shortcomings in globalisation both as an ideology and as a process.

Commenting on citizenship, Meer and Sever make a critical observation that can also be applied to globalisation. They point out that the concept of membership by definition means some are included and some are excluded; and for people the world over, citizenship has been about exclusion (Meer and Sever 2004:6). The relationship among nations of the world – whether economic or social – is one of exclusion rather than inclusion, especially when one looks at the ever-widening gulf between developing and developed economies. This point can best be illustrated by the African economies and the brain drain that characterises such economies. Instead of creating the intended global village, the world has actually been divided into two camps. Calhoun *et al.* argue that although the world has been knit closely, there has been a division of the population of many countries into winners and losers and there has also been a division of the regions of the world into winners and losers and Africa is a loser region (Offiong 2001:3).

Mazrui argues that the economic and social disparities between the First and Third Worlds have created frustrations among the educated in developing countries and that has increased the temptation to seek fulfilment abroad (Mazrui 2002: 86). For example, Zimbabwe has been going through an economic recession since 2000. By the 2008 elections, it had an inflation rate well above 165,000 per cent. The World Bank and the IMF has refused to bail Zimbabwe out of its economic crisis to the extent of even stopping loan facilities to the country. On the other hand, the First World countries have been busy recruiting skills from Zimbabwe, depleting the country's labour skills reservoir. Within the broad context of existing international relations globalisation works more for the exclusion of developing economies to the benefit of the developed economies. It is an expression of masculinity in terms of who owns what, controls what and has power to control such things. There is no doubt that globalisation is a social construction just like masculinity and femininity. Although globalisation is viewed more in economic terms, it is about control and power to control in a global relationship designed by the IMF and World Bank and the World Trade Organisation. For Mazrui, brain drain in Africa or the Third World has been a product of two interrelated forces: uneven development between the global North and South and the new levels of mobility fostered by globalisation (Mazrui 2002:86). In this regard, globalisation should be viewed as responsible for maintaining the prevalent masculine and feminine thinking in patriarchal communities, and gendered citizen mobility, mostly in a one-way direction – from developing to developed economies.

Globalisation and Citizen Migration in Zimbabwe

The issue of citizen migration is not a new phenomenon in Zimbabwe. During colonial times, men migrated to urban areas, mines and farms for work within the country or to the South African mines. Only males were allowed to move and women could not follow their husbands to their workplaces. There were numerous legal restrictions employed by the colonial government to curtail unwanted movement but this changed in the later part of the twentieth century as women increasingly and 'illegally' entered the restricted areas. With independence, movement between rural and urban areas became free, though migration remained modest. That did not change the gendered nature of migration. It continued, with women commuting between the towns or their husband's workplaces and the rural areas, as most women are supposed to look after the home. Pointing to the gendered nature of mobility, Cheater and Gaidzanwa (1996:191) argue that history shows a sharp contrast between men's mobility and women's immobility. While today it is common to talk about movement of goods and services and even people among nations as part of the concept of oneness, Cheater and Gaidzanwa make a crucial point that this assumption needs explicit qualification because ideas about space, presence and mobility have continued to be gendered and are also influenced by race, class and age (*ibid.*).

As women began to acquire some education and professional qualifications, they managed to break into the economic sphere as employees and later as owners of companies. While the Constitution bestows rights on everyone, inasmuch as everything is made free and accessible, there are still unwritten expectations attached to the rights, particularly those relating to gendered assumptions; thus, in practical terms, the playing field is not even. Nonetheless, there has been a great presence of women in most crucial areas of Zimbabwe's economy and, lately, politics, pointing also to the increased presence of women in urban areas. The change in the economic and political landscape that occurred in Zimbabwe from 2000 created a new wave of citizen movement and migration from rural areas to towns, further into the region and across the region. The volume of internal rural-urban migration increased dramatically as conditions worsened but the full extent, as Crush argues, will remain unclear until a census is conducted. The increase affected not only rural-urban migration but also the volume of cross-border migration into neighbouring states for informal trade and business and to search for employment opportunities. The disparities in levels of development in Southern Africa, the South African economy being a vehicle for the penetration of modernisation, have caused a leakage of people into stronger economies in the region (Cheater and Gaidzanwa 1996:190; Crush and Tevera n.d.). The good thing is that as the economy faced difficulties, women, especially those unemployed, grabbed the opportunity and ventured into cross-border trading, even influencing other women to leave their jobs to join informal trading.

The migration started slowly in the 1990s as signs of economic contraction set in and skilled labour which was internationally marketable left the country. It gained momentum in 2000 and Zimbabwe became a significant exporter of mainly skilled labour (Crush and Tevera n.d.) and other non-skilled migrant labour as economic conditions deteriorated. In African countries, globalisation introduced itself through structural adjustment programmes (SAPs). These were policies that called on African countries to liberalise their economies, letting market forces dictate the pace of development in terms of prices, supply, demand and movement of goods and services. The SAPs were the first stages of facilitating growth in foreign trade, movement of goods and services, as well as capital and labour. This was part of the modernisation theory which stressed that ideas, especially beliefs and values, have transforming power (Offiong 2001:25). As Offiong notes, the modernisation theory argues that the West must play an important role in the economic development of poor countries (*ibid*:39) and this should have been the context in which SAPs were developed and exported to Africa as a way of creating conditions for development in African countries. However, the SAPs did not produce the anticipated and desirable results. Boutros Boutros Ghali in 1996 highlighted the fact that globalisation was failing to reach all peoples in a positive way and that many people in the Third World were excluded, unable to access the prosperity offered by globalisation (Offiong *ibid*:4). Another critical aspect of these SAPs was the reduction of government expenditure (also on its workforce), envisaging a situation where employment would be created following effective implementation of the SAPs. Zimbabwe is one such African country that tried structural adjustment and the effects proved disastrous. According to Hammar and Raftopoulos, the effects of SAPs in Zimbabwe included increases in interest rates and inflation, deindustrialisation marked by a 40 per cent decline in manufacturing, with company closures and massive job cuts and a fall in real wages and overall standards of living (Hammar and Raftopoulos 2003:6).

The SAPs as implemented in Zimbabwe played a significant role in the disintegration of the country's once strong economy. The way these SAPs were brought to developing countries, especially in the case of Zimbabwe, shows that globalisation as an ideology is neither neutral nor equitable but promotes a skewed relationship centred on exclusion rather than inclusion. Its inherent characteristics are masculinity. R. W. Connell argues that masculinity recognises dominance and subordination and that these relationships (of masculinities) are constructed through practices that exclude and include, intimidate and exploit, and so on (Connell 2006:37). The excluded are seen as the 'other' and that points to the belief in the presence of differences between the included (rich) and the excluded (poor), between men and women or the dominant and the dominated. Pearson illustrates the thrust of the SAPs very well. She argues that the 1980s to 1990s was an era dominated by economic policies designed to compel indebted developing countries to restructure their economies and become solvent within the world economy (Pearson 2000:12). The basis of the SAP package was to engineer economic restructuring for financial assistance and credit from the World Bank, IMF and bilateral creditors - a situation that underpins dominance and subordination. In Zimbabwe, the SAPs disrupted the economy and set the process of citizen migration in motion. Here, it is important to consider the political crisis that erupted during the same period and the international resistance to the government of President Robert Mugabe (McGregor 2009:186). The result was a dramatic increase in trans-border migration (ibid.) away from a highly volatile political environment in which members of the opposition party, Movement for Democratic Change (MDC) and other innocent people were being hunted down. As McGregor aptly puts it, the launch of the 'third Chimurenga' in 2000 and the return by ZANU-PF to the wartime rhetoric of 'enemies' and 'sell-outs' together with the violent occupation of farms, and brutal assaults forced many people into exile (McGregor 2009:190).

By 2004, the United Kingdom (UK) had become known to Zimbabweans as 'Harare North'. This term developed from the understanding that the UK was attracting a lot of Zimbabwean migrants. Unfortunately statistics about Zimbabweans who have migrated to the so-called 'greener pastures' were not well kept and updated. However, in 2002 the United Nations Development Programme (UNDP) contracted the Scientific and Industrial Research and Development Centre (SIRDC) in Zimbabwe to carry out an analysis of the causes and effects of brain-drain in the country. SIRDC established that there were about 479,348 Zimbabweans in the diaspora; mainly in the UK, Botswana and South Africa (Chetsanga 2005:4). That was just an estimate;

the actual figure is believed to be greater. The UK attracted the larger share of Zimbabwean migrants at that time because up until November 2002, Zimbabweans did not experience the visa restrictions that were the lot of other Africans who wanted to go to the UK. According to Pasura the UK Home Office in 2006 was working with estimates of 200,000 Zimbabwean asylum seekers (see McGregor 2009:186).)

As the conditions worsened at home, more Zimbabweans migrated from the country. Women in the informal sector moved mainly because they needed income for their livelihood and to send their children to school. However, the major markets were not near home, so hundreds of women and women networks spread out across the Southern African region (Cheater and Gaidzanwa 1996:192).

Cleaver (2002:2) speaks of new analyses which recognise that men and women may be disadvantaged by social and economic structures, and that both have the right to a life free from poverty and oppression, a condition offered by globalisation in theory. For many Zimbabweans, globalisation offered an opportunity to escape poverty and economic meltdown, particularly in the post-2000 period. According to Chetsanga, more than half of the 479,348 people emigrated due to work-related factors while 8 per cent mentioned political factors (Chetsanga 1989:4), following the emergence of the Movement for Democratic Change (MDC) as the first strong and real opposition party on the Zimbabwean political landscape.

Zimbabwe's economy created its own problems after 2000 (though not devoid of international interference) such as low salaries, a skyrocketing inflation rate, unemployment above 80 per cent and widespread poverty. Many people searched for alternative sources of livelihood, career advancement and survival opportunities. Chetsanga points out that the brain drain in Zimbabwe (and Africa) is caused by the human quest for better opportunities in life (Chetsanga 1989:5). The figures from SIRDC were not disaggregated so it is difficult to analyse the figures with a gender perspective. What is certain is that the problems affected everyone across the gender spectrum. Africans in the diaspora contribute to the underdevelopment of Africa by their absence, thereby contributing to the great economic and social disparities between the developed and developing economies. Mazrui points out that the globalised labour market has substantially improved intercontinental mobility for certain economic and social classes (Mazrui 2002:86).

The free movement of goods, services and human resources has never been wholly accepted globally. While peoples of different nations have found employment in international organisations and financial institutions due to their expertise, they are sometimes seen as a threat at the national level. Hence, visa restrictions have continued to be imposed on foreign nationals, and prospective migrants are diligently screened

In the 1990s, at the height of the Zimbabwean crisis, the then South African Home Affairs Minister, Mangosuthu Buthelezi, commented that:

> South Africa is faced with a threat, and that is the SADC ideology (occurring within the ideology of globalisation) of free movement of people, free trade and freedom to choose where you live or work. Free movement of persons spells disaster for our country.... (Sachikonye 1998:i)

Inasmuch as nations welcome globalisation, they also pick the aspects that benefit them and exclude those that hamper their progress and development. Therefore, the developed countries maintain their visa restrictions, and the rigid and tiresome process of applying and acquiring citizenship, where first and foremost an individual is identified as 'alien'. For Zimbabweans, this has resulted in tighter immigrant visa conditions and increased deportations from the UK. With regard to South Africa, Zimbabweans have resorted to illegal means of getting into the country. Medical personnel such as doctors and nurses, technicians, university lecturers and researchers from Zimbabwe have entered the global labour markets. Lecturers and researchers moved mostly to the UK, United States and South Africa while doctors and nurses were destined mostly for Australia, New Zealand and the UK. The former Minister of Health and Child Welfare, David Parirenyatwa, while addressing an association of Zimbabwean midwives, acknowledged that the country had trained 6,000 midwives but that only 400 were currently working in the country's health sector (Zimbabwe Broadcasting Corporation TV News, 28 July 2008). Movement has not only occurred across labour markets but also internally. The exit of university lecturers and researchers for better opportunities left gaps that lectures from colleges and polytechnics had to fill, where possible. This created a shortage in colleges, which some qualified secondary schools teachers moved up to fill. The movement continued in a cycle as better opportunities opened up, creating serious labour mobility within the country, in the southern African region and internationally.

Globalisation: The Gender Dimension of Migration

The global labour market has continued with the gendered patterns in terms of employment as it gives more opportunity to men than women while the men avoid taking on jobs that have been traditionally defined as women's work. Brodie (1994) argues that global deregulation and restructuring re-privatise tasks and spaces, and push women back 'home' even though about a third of households do not have a male breadwinner and more women work outside the home (Pettman 1999:212). This point emphasises the argument by Cheater and Gaidzanwa that ideas about space, presence and mobility have remained gendered.

The global labour market has no defined policies that favour women although there has been an improvement in employment of women in different national economies. The majority of women have remained immobile because the desired job market is located far away from them and they cannot leave their families or the conditions are not compatible with the presence of women. According to Ntarangwi, the opportunities and tools that enable one to participate fully in the free market are all influenced by gender, class, race and so on; and hence are restricted (Ntarangwi 1998:21). Pearson emphasises that while globalisation has resulted in women's increasing involvement in production and paid employment, most are retaining their reproductive duties in an increasingly unstable world (Pearson 2000:13-14).

Women make up 52 per cent of the population of Zimbabwe, possibly due to two factors; that is, the higher death rate among men compared to women or that more men have emigrated than women. This is just speculation, as no explanation has been offered to explain the difference. Gaidzanwa believes that migration and trade have been gendered processes because of the social roles assigned to people in different communities. For instance, from colonial times migrant labour in Africa was seen as men's preserve because the men tended to move around in search of work (Gaidzanwa 1998: 84). Ntarangwi adds that the practical dimension of women taking up jobs outside the home contradicts their socially sanctioned role of mother and home maker (Ntarangwi 1998:21). This refers us back to the divide between the public and private spheres.

According to Meer and Sever, this divide sees women's roles and responsibilities as family care and child rearing while men's roles are decision making, formal politics, economics and the workplace (Meer and Sever 2004:18). The continued salient belief explains the gendered nature of citizen mobility anywhere. In Zimbabwe, the medical profession is probably the hardest hit by emigrant women, first because it is one of those professions with a higher proportion of women than others and, secondly, because of the brain drain. The medical field has seen more female nurses migrate to the UK, New Zealand, Australia, South Africa, Botswana, especially with the upsurge of home-based care centres, and Zimbabwe has good expertise in this field. Female teachers have not migrated much because of certain hindrances in their profession such as pre-requirements such as language skills, pre-tests, and challenges of getting work permits. Those who have migrated have gone mostly to Botswana and South Africa, with a few trying Mozambique where English was recently introduced in schools.

Most women in Zimbabwe are active in the informal sector which is largely populated by uneducated people. Their numbers have been swelled by the influx of public sector and manufacturing workers thrown out of jobs as unemployment rates rose above 80 per cent. Where women are employed, in most cases they are involved in low-paid jobs that do not offer any social security on retirement. This acts as a hindrance to women's mobility because they lack enough income to finance their emigration and their lack of skills also makes it difficult to find employment in other countries. Pettman observes that state formation processes are also gendered because women are already positioned differently from men in matters of the state, citizenship and the labour market, hence women are disproportionately represented among state workers in areas such as health and education (Pettman 1999:212). The first disadvantage women face in migration is the bottleneck structure of access to economic and political participation, which is a major hindrance to their mobility while men's mobility is relatively limitless.

Another economic subsector that has seen a growth in women's involvement is international transport, tourism and entertainment industries. Pearson argues that the growth is partly due to the increase in the trafficking of women for sexual services (Pearson 2000:13). Women see it as a means of gaining freedom from the oppressive male or family control, and re-appropriate their position in the society. Zimbabwe's border ports such as Beitbridge and Chirundu and tourist centres such as Kariba and Victoria Falls and other areas with increased international transport business such as Hwange have a large number of women ready to offer sexual services to those in the transport sector and tourists. This is also a consequence of gendered migration as women only can work with what is closest to them because of the family and a lack of professional or technical skills. Currently organisations such as the Aids Network in Zimbabwe are involved in HIV&AIDS education in such areas..

The Influence of Technology on Migration

Improvements in technology and communications have been an integral part of the globalisation process and have had an impact on the gendered nature of citizen migration. For Zimbabwe, these technical improvements have resulted in enhancing what Gwaunza calls 'commuter family arrangements' in her analysis of the impact of migrant labour in colonial Zimbabwe. Technological developments have become central to the integration process in the world economy and these technological changes have enhanced and supported citizen migration. Technology has also helped TNCs to transcend national and continental boundaries in their operations.

Pearson argues that the new computer and telecommunication technologies, including the worldwide web have facilitated the spread of new services and processes such as data entry, e-commerce, call centres and various consumer services, so neither production nor consumption of such services are constrained by geographical boundaries or distances (Pearson 2000:11). Technological advancement has thus benefited citizen migration as immigrants could use electronic transaction services to send money or to get the relevant information for decisions to stay or move and what precautions to take. It is against this background that this paper has borrowed Gwaunza's concept of 'commuter family arrangements'. Commenting on the impact of labour migration on family organisation in Zimbabwe, Gwaunza argues that domestic labour migration contributed significantly to the shaping of family arrangements (Gwaunza 1998: 49). She further notes that the changes in socio-economic conditions affected traditional practices and the extended family. However, they did not collapse or disintegrate – members become physically and geographically displaced or separated (Gwaunza 1998:49). The development of a cash economy during the colonial period saw men (married and unmarried) leaving their rural homes to seek employment in the towns and mines and commercial farms, separated from their families. The 'rural-urban commuter family arrangements' are still evident today (Gwaunza 1998:50).

While modern technology helps the male emigrants reach their foreign destinations and maintain communications with home, such arrangements (just as in colonial times) have continued to dislocate families. According to Gwaunza, 'the commuter family arrangements are not good for the core group of mother, father and children, or indeed, for the family as a whole' (Gwaunza 1998:53). While some men use electronic money transfers, emails and mobile phones to stay in touch with their families, others (including women) take advantage of the separation to develop sexual liaisons. Such effects of citizen migration may result in the break-up of families, the spread of sexually transmitted infections (STIs) and HIV&AIDS, or may even fail to address the poverty that pushed them abroad to find better opportunities. In the end, the improved technology of globalisation facilitates the free movement of capital, services, goods and human resources but the negative effects of citizen migration are virtually insurmountable. Women are the most affected as globalisation has not occurred in a neutral environment but one that is firmly rooted in patriarchal thinking where femininity is solely to serve the aspirations and interests of masculinity.

Conclusion

Globalisation is a concept and a process for the integration of national economies into a global economy linked by information and communications technology. The technological developments have reduced the importance of national borders in the movement of services and goods and skilled labour across countries and continents. However, little has been achieved with respect to the integration of African economies into the global economy as equal partners. Secondly, globalisation has not changed anything in terms of gender discrimination as it has not given equal opportunities to both women and men. As this paper showed, globalisation is an ideology and a process that is new in name only; its agenda has remained the same from the days of slavery and colonialism till now. The capitalist and patriarchal ideas of globalisation have resulted in entrenched class, race and gender spaces.

Zimbabwe has been particularly affected by migration but with little benefit. The country has lost skilled labour to develop other economies at the expense of the local economy. Although the migration is partly linked to the political and economic crisis, the country has not received assistance from the international community particularly the World Bank and IMF, of which Zimbabwe is a member. The stance taken by these bodies (Zimbabwe is not the only victim) simply highlights the fact that globalisation is not about integration and development of weak economies but about exploitation and continued marginalisation of the weak and poor countries of the globe. In Zimbabwe, some companies connected with the industrialised North were instructed to stop their business in Zimbabwe; some companies were placed under a trade ban, clearly against the concept of integration of global economies.

The whole process has affected women greatly as they failed to break out of the patriarchal structures. The persistence of rigid notions of 'femininity' has had an influence on migration and the conduct of societies. Instead of bringing about benefits to the world as a whole, globalisation has further divided the world into the rich and the poor and that gap is not closing but widening. In that respect, it is correct to argue that globalisation has not done anything towards achieving its claimed objective. Obiora (2004) asked an ominous question when he said:, 'What is our future?'

There is an urgent need to reorganise and re-examine the concept of globalisation as far as it aims to integrate national economies. This re-examination would address not only the widening gap between the North and the South but also the fact that globalisation policies have remained gender insensitive and that its unwritten attitudes and beliefs control the pattern of conduct in the social, economic and migration areas.

References

Castells, Manuel, 2001, 'The new global economy', in Muller Johan, Cloete, Nico and Badat Shireen eds., *Challenges of globalisation: South African debates with Manuel Castells*, Cape Town: Maskew Miller Longman, pp. 2-21.

Cheater, A.P. and Gaidzanwa, R., 1996, 'Citizenship in neo-patrilineal states: Gender and mobility in Southern Africa, *Journal of Southern African Studies*, Vol. 22, No. 2, pp. 189-200.

Chetsanga, C.J., 2005, 'An analysis of the cause and effect of brain drain in Zimbabwe', in Palmberg Mai and Primorac, Ranka eds., 'Skinning the skunk: facing Zimbabwean futures', Discussion Paper 30, Uppsala: Nordiska Afrikainstitutet.

Cleaver, F., 2002, 'Men and masculinities: New directions in gender and development', in Cleaver, F. (ed.), *Masculinities matter: Men, gender and development*, London: Zed Books, pp. 1-27.

Connell, R.W., 2006, *Masculinities*, Cambridge: Polity Press.

Gaidzanwa, R.B., 1998, 'Cross-border trade in Southern Africa: A gendered perspective', in Sachikonye, Lloyd, ed., *Labour Markets And Migration Policy in Southern Africa*, Harare: Sapes Books, pp. 83-94.

Gwaunza, Elizabeth, 1998, 'The impact of labour migration on family organisation in Zimbabwe', in Sachikonye, Lloyd (ed.), *Labour markets and migration policy in Southern Africa*, Harare: Sapes Books, pp. 49-55.

Hammar, Amanda and Raftopoulos, Brian, 2003, 'Zimbabwe's unfinished business: Rethinking land, state and nation', in Hammar, Amanda, Raftopoulos, Brian and Jensen, Stig (eds.), *Zimbabwe's unfinished business: Rethinking land, state and nation in the context of crisis*, Harare: Weaver Press, pp. 1-47.

Jansen, Eduard, Mwapachu, Juma and Semboja, Joseph, 2002, 'Introduction', in Semboja, Joseph, Mwapachu, Juma and Jansen, Eduard eds., *Local perspectives on globalisation: The African case*, Dar es Salaam: Mkuki naNyota Publishers, pp. 1-9.

Mazrui, Ali A., 2002, 'Brain drain: Between Counterterrorism And Globalisation', *African Issues*, Vol. 30, No. 1, pp. 86-89.

Mbiba, Beacon, 2005, 'Zimbabwe's global citizens in 'Harare North': Some preliminary observations', in Palmberg, Mai and Primorac, Ranka eds., 'Skinning the skunk: facing Zimbabwean futures', Discussion Paper 30, Uppsala: Nordiska Afrikainstitutet.

McGregor, JoAnn, 2009, 'Associational links with home among Zimbabweans in the UK: Reflections on long-distance nationalisms', *Global Networks*, 9, 2, pp. 185-208.

Meer, Shamim and Sever, Charlie, 2004, 'Gender and citizenship: Overview report', in BRIDGE *(development-gender)*, Institute of Development Studies, Brighton: University of Sussex.

Ntarangwi, Mwenda G., 1998, 'Feminism and masculinity in an African capitalist context: The case of Kenya', *SAFERE: South African Feminist Review*, Vol. 3, No. 1, pp. 19-32.

Obiora, Ike F., 2004, 'The impact of globalization on Africa: A call to solidarity and concern', in Obiora, Ike F., ed., *Globalization and African self-determination: What is our future?* Enugu: CIDJAP Publications, pp. 1-20.

Offiong, Daniel A., ed., 2001, *Globalisation, Post-Neodependency and Poverty in Africa*, Enugu: Fourth Dimension Publishing.

Pearson, Ruth, 2000, 'Moving the goalposts: Gender and globalisation in the twenty-first century', I, Vol. 8, No. 1, pp. 10-19.

Pettman, Jan J., 1999, 'Globalisation and the Gendered Politics of Citizenship', in Yuval-Davis, Nira and Werbner, Pnina eds., *Women, citizenship and difference*, London: Zed Books, pp. 207-220.

Sachikonye, Lloyd M., 1998, 'Introduction: Labour Markets and Migration Policy in Perspective', in Sachikonye, Lloyd, ed., *Labour Markets and Migration Policy in Southern Africa*, Harare: Sapes Books, pp. i-x.

Internet Source

Crush, Jonathan and Tevera, D., 'Zimbabweans who move: Perspectives on international migration in Zimbabwe', Migration Policy Series, No. 25, http://www.queensu.ca/samp/sampresources/samppublications/policyseries/policy25.htm.

6

The Body as a Tool: Female Youth in Nigeria Negotiating the New Global Order*

Mfon Umoren Ekpootu

Introduction

Economic liberalisation and the compression of the global market has led to the exclusion of a large number of people from basic needs and resources, thereby questioning notions by which rights and entitlements are allocated. The retreat of the state from social service delivery; the insistence on market transactional mechanisms to access social services; the food crisis which has resulted in the high cost of staple foods; and the current global economic crisis; have a disproportionate impact on certain members of society. The pressures, constraints and contradictions of globalisation and the burdens of adjustment to economic restructuring are localised among the poor in both rural and urban areas. At one end of the spectrum, the educated, high-income, socially and politically empowered groups stand to benefit from the changes brought about by trade liberalisation. At the other end, however, the dispossessed strata are inhibited in terms of securing such benefits and tend to be marginalised as the economic space becomes more aggressive and competitive. Data supplied by the World Bank reveals that, in 2001, over 1.1 billion people around the world were living in extreme poverty, with a projected reduction to 0.6 billion in 2015. Conversely, in sub-Saharan Africa, the number of poor people has been on the increase, from 227 million in 1990 to 313 million in 2001, with an expected rise to 340 million by 2015 (World Bank 2006). In recent times, the global recession has thrown individuals and states into economic distress and tightened the noose of economic exclusion around the necks of the poor.

Encouraged to desire the goods available to their peers in the more affluent Western countries, most Nigerian youths are unable to actualise these wants. The promise of infinite opportunities as promoted by globalisation clashes with the reality of rising unemployment, widespread insecurity, food crisis, widening disparity of wealth and intense poverty.

At the same time, new opportunities are provided by accelerated communication and information technology, enabling new vistas of relationship, which have expanded the scope of the use of the female body for various forms of trade celebrating consanguinity over the traditionally acceptable conjugality. It has enabled the procurement of sexual services through the internet and enhanced the practice of transnational and secondary prostitution (where the person has another occupation or activity besides sex work). The promotion of individualism and the negation of communal ties ensure that the individual becomes the sole agent in negotiating the opportunities and dangers of the capitalist-driven consumer society. Traversing these spaces, female youths in Nigeria are constrained to devise their own means of survival. With the loosening of societal constraints and the expanded field of permissible sexual expression, some young Nigerian females are increasing employing their bodies as tools to gain access to resources. This choice has been strengthened by the increased knowledge about reproduction and the use of contraceptives. The *Nigerian Demographic and Health Survey (NDHS)*) shows that one-third of the female population aged 25-49 years have had sexual intercourse by the age of 15 years and the number increases to more than three-quarters of women by the age of 20 (NDHS 2003:88-9). Awareness and knowledge of family planning methods are also rising – about 8 in 10 women are knowledgeable about family planning methods, with pills and injections being widely used (NDHS 2003:62-3). Sexual realities of women and girls in Nigeria challenge nationalist understanding and cultural practice.

This chapter explores the engagement of Nigerian female youths in the sex industry as a remedy to deprivation and marginalisation. It questions how globalisation, global consumerism and the neo-liberal mantra of individualism shape the activities of young female Nigerians in their negotiation of the economic space through the use of the body as a tool. It also explores the impact of this negotiation of sexuality and agency on female citizenship and discusses whether the celebration of the self and exercise of agency has translated into political agency and the claiming of space in the public sphere. The chapter is divided into five sections, beginning with a background study of the status of women in Nigeria. Women in Nigeria continue to be discriminated against and they lack full citizenship rights. This section will highlight the role of women in the Nigerian society, their entitlements and their rights. Section two gives a theoretical perspective that draws from feminist readings of the body, sex work and citizenship. Subsequent sections will discuss prostitution and situate it in a historical and socio-cultural context for a more nuanced understanding. The dynamics underlying sex work and the divergent of markets in female sexual labour and what impact these have on women's claim to citizenship will also be examined.

Background

The pervasion of poverty and the widening disparities in income as the country is polarised into those integrated into the globalisation process and the marginalised, remain a major challenge to Nigeria. A long history of political and democratic deficits – over 25 years of military dictatorship, macroeconomic instability, and pandemic corruption – has deepened poverty in Nigeria. The *Nigerian Human Development Report* of 2007/2008 shows an increase in income poverty. The number of Nigerians living below the poverty level of US$1 per day has risen from 70 percent in 2003 to 70.8 percent and for those living below US$2 per day from 91.5 per cent to 92.4 per cent (UNICEF 2005; NHDR 2007/8). Despite government attempts to improve educational services with its Universal Basic Education Scheme (UBE), the benefits are felt more at the primary level. The primary school gross enrolment ratio from 2000-2006 was 111 for males and 95 for females. However, there was a sharp decrease at secondary school level within the same period with a gross enrolment figure of 37 for males and 31 for females (UNICEF 2007). High dropout rates and, low quality of education haves meant that despite a high literacy rate among youths – 87 per cent for males and 81 percent for females – recorded from 2000-2006 (UNICEF 2007), the majority of them lack basic skills and are incapable of making the transition from school to work. This dysfunctional education has kept the youths largely marginalised and incapable of accessing the opportunities in a technology-driven, globally integrated economy.

Literature on globalisation indicates its asymmetric impact on men and women and the intensification of the latter's marginalisation fuelled by gendered social, economic and political structures (Guuttal 2000; Hogan 2001; Lim 2002; Ongile 2004; Phalane 2004). The differentials in impact on both sexes are premised on the fact that women are situated differently from men in the capitalist reproductive process. In its 2007 Annual Report, the United Nations Development Programme illustrates the growing global marginalisation of women despite the increase in the number of women in the workforce. According to the Report, women constitute 60 per cent of the world's 1 billion poorest people (*www.undp.org*). Women generally have a lower level of educational attainment and this affects the types of employment open to them. One cannot discuss the impact of trade liberalisation on women without considering the whole gamut of gender stereotyping, articulated by patriarchy, which carries with it certain socio-cultural expectations.

Theoretical Framework

The chapter employs the feminist analysis in the reading of the female body which foregrounds it within the larger context of unequal power relations (Brook 1996; Davies 1997; Conboy *et al.* 1997). A woman's reproductive capacity intertwines her closely to the body which, in line with body-mind dualism, is constructed as the 'other' of the mind. The latter, allied with reason, stands apart from the body, which, according to Susan Bordo is,

> apart from the true self…undermining the best efforts of the self. That which is not-body is the highest, the best, the noblest, the closest to God; that which is body is the albatross, the heavy drag on self-realisation (Bordo 2003).

This construction of gender which positions a woman as inferior to the mind is a historical construct that has been given credence by medical discourse over the years (Sanchez-Grant 2008) and this has catapulted the body to the forefront of feminist debate as a site of male oppression. Jackson and Scott (cited in Sanchez-Grant 2008) argue that bodies acquire meaning in a socio-cultural context, in interacting with others. Control of the body, therefore, is instrumental to female liberation. The assertion that, 'the personal is political', is a rebuttal of the separation of the public sphere from the domestic. The female body as a social construct derives from a normative discourse that excludes women and demands a re-reading with the intent to dismantle and re-assemble by women themselves.

In recent decades, the female body has become a site for contestation as the gains achieved by women's movements around the world become more apparent. With shifting gender roles and new sexual freedoms, a lot of women are making efforts to construct a life imbued with their own meaning. One important aspect is controlling their sexuality. Sexuality is acknowledged as an integral part of human experience and sexual rights as deriving from fundamental and universal human rights. At its 14th World Congress of Sexology held in Hong Kong in 1999, the World Association of Sexual Health (WAS), adopted several sexual rights including: the right to sexual freedom; the right to sexual autonomy; the right to sexual privacy; the right to sexual pleasure; and the right to emotional sexual expression (WAS 1999). This implies a notion of the body that is individualistic and, according to Izugbara and Undie (2008), incompatible with social realities in many African countries. Drawing from a study of two societies in South-Eastern Nigeria, the authors argue that ownership of the body is communal and this is important in the brokering of sexual rights. The social construction of sexuality highlights the importance of local discourses of the body in female expression of sexual rights. In Nigeria, this communal claim on the body is more prevalent in rural societies and ensures a repression of female sexual rights reinforced by male-privilege social controls of sexual intercourse inhibiting women from expressing their sexuality.

In urban centres, the communal hold on an individual's body is loose. Women have developed resistance to traditionally acceptable sexual behaviour, enhanced not just by the spatial separation but the agents of modernity – the consumerist culture; the sexual revolution; advances in contraceptive technology; and education – all of which have enabled the young Nigerian woman to exercise more control over her sexuality. The exchange of sex for money by some female youths in Nigeria could then be read as an act of re-appropriation. The body becomes the means by which these women exert control over their own sexuality, a site of power, contestation and patriarchal control.

Feminists reject the classical liberal representation of citizenship as being individualistic and rights based. Contrary to its universalistic language, citizenship, according to feminists, excludes women and is represented 'through codes of a phallocentric discourse' (Jones 1990) Women's sexual independence, it has been asserted, poses a threat to the nation, citizen, home and family (Jamal 2006). In the dominant discourse, the public/political sphere is seen as male. If public space and citizenship entitlements are seen as dominant male arenas, prostitution and its claim to rights could prove disruptive of traditional spaces of reproduction and heterosexuality within which citizen rights and obligation are ensconced and could be read as a display of 'irresponsible citizenship or no citizenship at all' (Alexander 1997, cited in Jamal 2006). This gendered discourse on citizenship forestalls the achievement of real gains by women in their negotiation of citizenship irrespective of their ability to lay claim to the public/political sphere (Keller 1988, cited in Jones 1990).

For Pateman (1988) the relationship between men and women has historically been underwritten by a sexual contract. Thus negotiation for any form of citizenship by the sex worker cannot be realised because her work subjugates her and her body. The woman in commercial sex trade sells not just sex but her identity (Anderson 1993; Pateman, 1988). This analysis of the sex trade has been criticised by Kempadoo (2001) as overlooking the complexity of the global sex trade by ascribing monolithic explanations of its violence and risk. Satz (1995) argues for the recognition of internal hierarchy in prostitution and differentials in the markets for female sex labour. From the streetwalker to the high-priced courtesan, the determining factors are varied and an understanding of these is imperative in trying to grapple with the complexity of the sex trade.

Such gradation of the sex industry is visible in Nigeria and it would be erroneous to group the diverse practices of prostitution under one theoretical basket. Be that as it may, the forces of demand and supply remain constant in the economics of the sector. In analysing the engagement of Nigerian girls in the sex industry, the chapter draws on the social exchange theory as explored by Baumeister and Vohs (2004) in their work on sexual economics as an analytical tool. The heterosexual community is examined as a market place where female sexuality is imbued with value by society while the man's sexuality is seen as worthless. Sexual relations become an unequal exchange in which the woman gives away something of value in return for nothing. Equality is attained only when the man relinquishes something valuable that is non-sexual. Sex thus becomes a female resource that can be traded for non-sexual material resources.

For numerous female youths in Nigeria, their bodies are the only resources that can be exchanged for access to economic and societal resources. This act could be motivated by the need to survive or a thirst for materialism. Then again, it could as well be the need to satisfy sexual desires without encumbrances, an expression of sexual freedom.

Contextualising Prostitution

Some feminists have attempted to locate prostitution empirically. Bernstein (1999:94) for instance, argues for the need to historically and culturally situate prostitution, as a prerequisite to discerning what is 'wrong or right with it'. In this statement, she echoes Shrage (cited in Berstein 1999:95) who posits that different social meanings attached to prostitution in diverse cultures could elicit different feminist reaction. Debra Satz (1995) highlights the internal hierarchy within prostitution and notes that the motive for engaging in commercial sex determines what is wrong or right about a woman selling sex. She goes on to reiterate the choice of prostitution by some women as a profession instead of other alternatives. This is especially true for the more educated, higher priced prostitute.

Prostitution is an economic transaction and the profit constitutes an important motivational factor in an impoverished society such as in Nigeria. Young women faced with few opportunities for direct access to income and other resources, and who are increasingly called upon to contribute to family income, barter their bodies in exchange for a degree of financial empowerment. Sex for sale becomes a desirable choice when earnings from it are higher than from the few other financial opportunities. The urban, upwardly mobile, blue-collar young man; the wealthy businessman; and the rich and influential politician symbolise a source of wealth, prestige and power for the female youths and a medium for means of escape from the poverty trap. The older clients are variously labelled – 'sugar daddies', 'uncles', 'aristos' or 'mugus'.

Factors which shape the decision of some young Nigerian women to enter into the sex trade are more complex and dynamic than conventional wisdom allows. The effects of globalisation cannot be ignored. Economic globalisation; structural adjustment programmes; the erosion of the welfare state; the widening disparity between the poor and the rich exacerbated by pandemic corruption have led to a feminisation of labour and a commodification of human beings. It has seen the negation of the negotiating power of women.

Technology and the internet have aided the industrialisation of sex and a widening of the permissible field of sexual expression. The female body has become demystified and female agency highlighted. However, the choice to trade her body as a marketable product cannot be analysed outside the value society places on female sexuality. As illustrated by Baumeister and Vohs (2004), sex is a female resource culturally endowed with value that can be used for exchange and negotiation. The female body becomes an object for male pleasure, deriving from a hegemonic patriarchal ordering which in itself cannot be divorced from the differential power and autonomy inherent in male/female productive labour and accruable income. It could be argued, therefore, that prostitution of female youths in Nigeria developed from the symbolic meaning that Nigerian culture assigns to gives the female being.

As pointed out by Hollibaugh and Moraga (1983), female 'sexual values are filtered through a society where heterosexuality is the norm'. In tandem with the societal conception of their sexuality, female youths put their sexual demands within these boundaries to elicit male responses. This sexual objectification of the female is discursively produced as the norm and sustained by the sexual domination implicit in media representations of women. Visible in many newsstands across the country are sexually graphic magazines and pornographic videos that can be accessed by the young and old. Media adverts are projected with sexually coded language. The representations of women as objects of desire go hand-in-hand with images of the sexy, chic woman.

With overwhelming media images telling women how to look and act, it becomes easy for them to perform the scripted roles. Further, fashion and beauty, as argued by Hyndman (2006), have been manipulated by men to keep women in a subjugated state. Young Nigerian women try to make their appearance conform to the dictates of society and in the process are kept reliant on male care to keep them in the socially prescribed state. Beauty is measured by the man and it is to attract male attraction that the female adorns her body. Even when some would argue that beautification gives self-satisfaction, such self-satisfaction is primarily derived from being found desirable by others.

In the case of the female sex worker, her perception of her body as an economic tool shapes her attitude towards it. As a source of capital, the body needs to be advertised to increase its market value and stimulate male interest. This puts her under pressure to measure up to societal perceptions of beauty and fashion. Being scantily and alluringly dressed could be viewed as a rational strategy used by the women to optimise their product value. Efforts to attract the male gaze have contributed to a flourishing market in second-hand clothes known in the Nigerian parlance as *okrika*. Their affordability has made them the common choice for young women and, indeed, a large number of Nigerians who want to dress in high-fashion, Western-style attire.

The Sex Trade

Transnational Sex Work

The transnational sex trade has continued to be utilised as a means of migrating to wealthier countries. There are in fact considerable numbers of Nigerian sex workers in African countries such as Mali, South Africa and Côte d'Ivoire. For this chapter, however, the focus of attention is on transnational sex workers in Europe. The interconnectedness of countries has brought the West closer to

Nigerians and romanticised it as a haven of wealth, with emigration perceived as the ticket to sharing in that wealth. The 'success' of some commercial sex workers in Europe expressed in lavish displays, with some investment in real estate and businesses on their return to Nigeria only strengthens the notion of the viability of sex work in the West despite its inherent exploitation.

Human trafficking has been defined by the Trafficking in Persons (Prohibition) Law Enforcement and Administrative Act 2003 of Nigeria as:

> All acts and attempts involved in the recruitment, transportation within or across Nigeria borders, purchases, sales, transfer, receipt or harbouring of persons involving the use of coercion, deception or debt bondage for the purpose of placing or holding the person whether for or not in involuntary servitude (domestic, sexual or reproductive) in force or bonded labour or in slavery-like conditions. (Ndaguba 2005a:1-2)

It is estimated that Nigerians account for about 80 percent of sex workers in Europe (UNICEF Nigeria Fact Sheet 2002:1). Data from research conducted in 2005 by the National Agency for the Prohibition of Trafficking in Persons and Other Related Matters (NAPTIP), extending over 20 selected states in southern and northern Nigeria, show that many more girls than boys are trafficked, at a ratio of 7:3 (Ndaguba 2005b:1). Italy is the most important destination country for women and children trafficked from Nigeria; it is identified as a source, transit and destination country *(www.naptip.gov.org.)* Sex workers dominate the northern region of Turin, and Rome and Naples in the South (Carling, 2006). However, Nigerian sex workers in Norway have been on the increase since 2004 and presently make up the second largest group of foreign sex workers in the country (Carling 2006). Other destinations in Europe include Spain, Belgium and The Netherlands, while Saudi Arabia is notable in the Middle East.

Debates about prostitution and the underlying questions of morality, exploitation, contestation and power continue to engage feminist attention. Modernist feminists emphasise the violence and danger to women implicit in prostitution. Prostitution, according to this approach, perpetuates sexual discrimination against women and continues to marginalise women, defining them as passive receptacles of men's desire (MacKinnon 1989; Pateman 1988). With prostitution, the woman sells not just sex but also her self, unlike other forms of labour that can be contracted out independent of the contracting self (Pateman 1988, cited in Bernstein 1999:96).

Others try to normalise sex work in an attempt to gain access to the rights enjoyed by other workers. McClintock (1993) argues that 'society demonizes sex workers because they demand more money than women should for services men expect for free'. Most of the trafficked depend on such avenues to reach Europe. They take personal decisions to migrate overseas for prostitution despite reports of the risks and problems of such work. They are motivated by several factors: to escape from pandemic poverty and marginalisation; the hope to strike it rich and emulate the financial success of older prostitutes; and pressure from family members who see them as an escape route from deprivation and marginalisation. Exploitation in this case is not necessarily an inherent element. In an interview, Eunice, an employee of CARITAS, a religious organisation concerned with the rescue and rehabilitation of Nigerian prostitutes in Turin, Italy, noted that the girls see the madam as a benefactor and the ability to travel to Europe is sufficient compensation for whatever hardship they encounter in the process. This is especially so for new recruits from rural communities with limited exposure to urban lifestyles. To them, the white man epitomises wealth and sophistication. Most of the recruits are enticed with false promises of employment in Europe.

Trafficking of Nigerian women and children often involves several layers of recruitment – (i) the local recruiters who get hold of the women and children, most of whom are kinfolk and acquaintances; (ii) the 'trolleys' or agents who accompany the new recruits to the designated destination points; trolleys could be more than one in the long haul from source to destination country; (iii) the madams who are the sponsors and are mostly resident in Europe. Occasionally, the madam, often a retired prostitute, undertakes the local recruitment in person (UNODC/UNICRI 2004:4). Trafficking routes are usually by air, land and sea depending on the ease of transportation and the money paid by the trafficked (UNODC/UNICRI 2004:4-5).

Lagos is the primary departure point for those travelling by air and the northern states of Katsina or Borno for those travelling by land through the Sahara desert (UNODC/UNICRI 2004:5). Certain neighbouring countries, especially Ghana, Mali and Côte d'Ivoire (and as far away as South Africa in some cases) serve as points of transit *en route* to Spain and Italy by sea (Germano 2001; UNICEF Fact Sheet 2002:5). Travellers to Saudi Arabia move from West Africa through Libya (UNICEF Fact Sheet 2002:2). Bilateral agreements between Nigeria and countries such as Italy have made entry difficult, especially by air, and pushed a lot of the traffickers to use the land route through the Sahara desert. From 2007 Morocco, with its proximity to Spain became a breeding ground for kidnappers who made huge sums of money kidnapping trafficked girls for ransom demanded from sponsors.

Attracted by the huge financial benefits, many young men migrated to Morocco. This trend, according to a 'madam's boy', an undergraduate student in the University of Port Harcourt, necessitated the search for safer routes and turned attention to the South African route.

In Europe, the girls are delivered to their sponsors and become virtual prisoners, forced into prostitution until debts incurred are fully paid. There are varying accounts of amounts paid by a trafficked prostitute; however, most reports cite US$40,000 to US$50,000 (Germano 2001; Benzi 2001; UNODC/ UNOCRI 2004). Aside from the seizure of their travel documents, and in many cases being given room and board by the madams, compliance and repayment of debts are further secured by the enactment of *juju* rites prior to embarking on the journey. During such rites, the new recruits are forced to give some hair from the head, armpit or pubis (Benzi 2001:177-8). In some cases, their nail clippings and menstrual blood are added. These are all tied up in a bag and used for *juju* rites. The psychological impact on the girls is tremendous and contributes to the refusal by most of the girls to divulge the names of traffickers or testify against them in court.

The upsurge of prostitutes from Eastern Europe into countries such as Italy, Spain and Holland has reduced the demand for Nigerian girls and caused a fall in client fees. The estimated daily income of prostitutes in the 1990s ranged from US$300 to US$500 on a busy night (*Newswatch* 26 July 1999). By the time of the field survey in 2004, daily income had dropped to about US$100-US$150. The need to generate income daily induces some desperation – prices are lowered rather than lose a client because of the need to 'make returns' to the madams and bosses. Furthermore, engaging in group sex, fetish sex and animal sex attracts higher remuneration. It could take from one to three years to pay back debts owed the madam and while still indebted, the sex worker has almost no access to her earnings. In spite of this, they find ways of sending money back home.

The diverse ways in which transnational prostitutes create meaning in their lived experiences reveal the error in ascribing monolithic characteristics to Nigerian sex workers in Europe. One of the ways of exercising her agency, as argued by Carling (2006), is by circumventing the control mechanisms imposed by the madam to keep her financially disempowered. She utilises social networks to retain part of her earnings, most of which is remitted home to family members and for investment. A lot of the trafficked women subsequently become sponsors and years of 'working the beat' can be viewed as an internship period. The possibility of eventually reaching the status of madam acts as an incentive to bear the hardships faced. Hence, in this case, the sex worker is not a victim, but is navigating the sexual economic space guided by her goals.

The unprecedented rise in transnational prostitution in Nigeria, the huge profits derivable and the dent in the country's image have attracted government attention and placed issues of trafficking for prostitution at the forefront of government policies. However, migrant prostitution is only one aspect of the sex industry.

Campus Runs/Clubbing

With growing sexual liberalisation in society, prostitution has become manifest in more clandestine spatially mobile forms. It has come to encompass women (sometimes known as secondary prostitutes) who are engaged in other activities – for example, school or waged employment – while also doing sex work. Nyamnyoh (2005) observed in a study of consumerism among the youths in Dakar the accelerated commoditisation of sex in the face of exclusionary consumerism. Conditioned by global consumerism but largely unequipped to partake in it, the youths create their own means, exchanging sex for 'consumer opportunities and consumer citizenship'. They are known in local parlance as '*disquettes*', young trendy 'consumer zombie'. The linkage to a computer diskette lies in the girls' compactness and like a diskette, the girls can be sexually 'formatted' and 'reformatted', their availability appropriated by different users. The targets or clients of the *disquettes* are the '*thiofs*' who epitomise a revered fish. The '*thiofs*' differ in range and the 'grand' or '*super thiofs*' constitute the apex of the local elite including foreigners.

In Nigeria, some university students are engaging with greater frequency in such forms of prostitution. Their clients are the sugar daddies who are the equivalents of the Senegalese *thiofs*. The young womens' sexual liaisons with older, often married partners for monetary and other material benefits are termed 'runs'. Other remuneration aside from cash can be a rented house/apartment for the young woman, buying her a car, or setting her up in a business (such as a boutique, hairdressing salon, a bar or a night club). Some of these clandestine relationships, especially those involving foreigners or *oyigbos*, sometimes result in marriage.

For many of the female youths attending tertiary institutions, 'runs' have become a major avenue for accessing societal resources. Clients are solicited through pimps, some of who are the 'big girls' on campus. These are young women with access to wealthy business men, government officials and oil company workers. They are responsible for arranging for the girls and presenting them for selection by the 'aristos' at parties and functions organised by an 'aristo'. Compensation for sexual services would be given in an envelope, popularly called, 'thanks for coming'. The amount ranged from N20,000 to N250,000, depending on the value of the man and the services rendered or not rendered. Sexual activities are varied depending on the inclination of the client and could include group sex.

Developments in information and communication technology have facilitated the procurement of sexual services through the internet and enhanced the practice of transnational and secondary prostitution. Free access to the internet prompts the youth to explore their sexuality in new ways. There are websites where sex movies and nude pictures can be viewed and downloaded. The trendy, alluring, sexy female is portrayed as the 'modern' lady where modernity celebrates the self. For the woman, then, the body is no longer the last frontier subjected to patriarchal control, but can be self-appropriated and disposed of as desired.

Conclusion

The acknowledgement of sex outside the realms of conjugal relations has brought with it attempts at containment and control, and an emphasis on the risks and dangers of sex. The negative approach to sex has been combined with stereotypical representations of gender. In the discourse on commercial sexual relations, sex workers are constructed as a homogenous and victimised group, and resistance modes and experiences are ignored. However, sex workers are not a homogenous group, but differ in age, social class, sexual orientation and work (O'Neill 1996). Routes into prostitution are also varied. Not all are coerced into it, but some make independent decisions due to the economic realities in the face of poverty, unemployment and marginalisation. Others drift into it through peer pressure as well as the desire for financial independence and acquired tastes. The coercion dominant in human trafficking is not typical of the sex industry. Indeed there are prostitutes who, forced by economic necessity, cannot withhold consent as they like. This is not slavery which entails absolute subservience to a controller, but socio-economic imbalances in society capable of forcing any worker to accept objectionable conditions (Bindman 1997:2d).

The HIV/AIDS epidemic has enforced the linkage of sex with risk. The dangers inherent in commercial sexual liaisons are commonly believed to erode the women's voice. Challenging this representation of commercial sex workers as helpless victims, which ignores how the latter construct risks associated with sex work, Izugbara (2005) illustrates the strategies employed for managing such risks by female sex workers in Aba, a commercial city in south-eastern Nigeria. They set the parameters, prior to sexual relations, such as: selection of workplaces; types of clients; hours of work; number of clients per day; permissible sexual acts; payment before sex; indulgence in drugs and alcohol; and prompt medical attention. The use of *juju* is a major feature in the sex industry and is used for varied reasons including protection, to enhance market value, to exert control over clients, and to remain competitive.

In interrogating the commoditisation of the female body, commercial sex has been read as locking women further into male-defined sexual practices, a social mechanism of a phallocentric society used for the subjugation of the female. In her sale of sex, the female youth on the one hand circumvents patriarchal control by reclaiming her body and exercising her rights to sexual expression. On the other hand, she endorses societal perception of the female body as consumable and remains tied to its hegemonic grip. Analysed differently, for female agency to have meaning, it needs to be articulated within the space of female marginalisation. She therefore puts her sexual needs within such boundaries to thwart male control. As argued by Andrea and Jolly (2006:5), it is only in taking control of her body either 'to protect its integrity or enjoy its pleasures' that the female can partake in other benefits of development.

Note

* This paper is part of a larger study on prostitution in Nigeria and is drawn from a field study conducted in three major cities in southern Nigeria – Calabar, Port Harcourt and Lagos. These areas were chosen because they constitute some of the melting pots of diverse ethnic and occupational groups in Nigeria. Participants in diverse practices of prostitution – 'campus runs', clubbing, streetwalkers – were interviewed. It was more difficult to interview the latter and male assistant researchers acting as clients had to be utilised in some cases. The interviews were easier in the first two activities, especially as the researcher is a lecturer at the University of Port Harcourt.

References

Bamgbose, U., 2002, 'Teenage Prostitution and the Nature of the Female Adolescent in Nigeria', *International Journal of Offender Therapy and Comparative Criminology*, 46(5), pp. 569-585.

Baumeister, Roy F. and Vohs, Kathleen D., 2004, 'Sexual Economics: Sex as a Female Resource for Social Exchange in Heterogeneous Interactions', *Personality and Social Psychology Review, 8(4), pp. 339-363.*

Benzi, Don Oreste, 2001, 'Report on Nigerian Prostitute in Europe', *Proceedings of the First Pan-African Conference on Human Trafficking*, Abuja, Nigeria, 19-23 February.

Bindman, Joe, 1997, 'Redefining Prostitution as Sex Work on the International Agenda', Commercial Sex Information Service, http://www.walnet.org/csis/papers/ redefining. html#2c

Bordo, Susan, 2003, *Unbearable Weight: Feminism, Western Culture and the Body*, London: University of California Press.

Brook, Babara, 1990, *Feminist Perspectives on the Body*, New York: Pearson Education Inc.

Carling, Jorgen, 2006, 'Migration, Human Smuggling and Trafficking from Nigeria to Europe', Geneva: International Organisation for Migration.

Conboy, Katie *et al.*, 1997, *Writing on the Body: Female Embodiment and Feminist Theory*, New York: Columbia University Press.

Cornwall, Andrea and Jolly, Susie, 2006, 'Introduction: Sexuality Matters', *IDS Bulletin* 37(5), pp. 1-11.

Davies, Kathy, ed., 1997, *Embodied Practices: Feminist Perspectives on the Body*, London: Sage Publications.

Germano, Giovanni, 2001, 'Human Trafficking as a Transnational Problem: The Responses of Destination Countries, Proceedings of the First Pan-African Conference on Human Trafficking, Abuja, Nigeria, 19-23 February.

Guttal, Shalmali, 2000, 'Women and Globalisation – Some Key Issues', Paper presented at the conference, 'Strategies of Thai Women's Movements in the 21st Century', 28-29 March.

Hogan, Goretti, 2001, 'How Does Globalisation Affect Women?', *International Socialism Journal* (92) Autumn.

Hollibaugh, Amber and Moraga, Cherrie, 1983, 'What We are Rolling Around in Bed With: Sexual Silences in Feminism', in Ann Snitow *et al.* eds., *Powers of Desire: The Politics of Sexuality*, New York: Monthly Review Press.

Hyndman, Aynsley, 2006, 'Female Modification through Time', http://www.ecclectica. ca/ issues/2006/1/index.asp?Article=23

Izugbara, C.O. 2005), '"Ashawo Suppose Shine Her Eye": Female Sex Workers and Sex Work Risks in Nigeria', *Health, Risk and Society*, Vol. 7, No. 2, June, pp. 141-159.

Izugbara, C.O. and Undie, Chi-Chi, 2008, 'Who Owns the Body? Indigenous African Discourses of the Body and Contemporary Sexual Rights Rhetoric', *Reproductive Health Matters*, 16(31), pp. 1-9.

Lim, Y., 2002, 'The Effect of the East Asian Crisis on the Employment of Women and Men: The Philippine Case', I 28 (1).

Ndaguba, Carol N., 2005b, 'Re: Formal Presentation of Nigeria's Combined First and Second Country Periodic Report on the Implementation of the Convention on the Rights of the Child (CRC) to the UN CRC Committee at the United Nations Office, Geneva', Paper presented at the United Nations Office, Geneva 26 January.

Ndaguba, Carol N., 2005a, 'Human Trafficking: The Woman/Child Rights', Paper presented at the Centre for Policy Study and Resource Development Seminar, Abuja, 18 October.

Nyamnjoh, Francis, 2005, 'Fishing in Troubled Waters: Disquettes and Thiofs in Dakar', *Africa: Journal of the International Africa Institute*, 75 (3), pp. 295-324.

O'Neill, Maggie, 1996, 'Prostitution, Feminism and Critical Praxis: Profession Prostitute', *The Austrian Journal of Sociology* (special edition on Work and Society), Winter.

Ongile, Grace, 2004, 'Globalisation, Trade and Gender – The Key Concerns', *Gender, Economies and Entitlements in Africa*, CODESRIA Gender Series 2, Dakar: CODESRIA.

Phalane, Manthiba, 2004, 'Globalisation and the Feminisation of Poverty: A South African Perspective on Expansion, Inequality and Identity Crisis', *Gender, Economies and Entitlements in Africa*, CODESRIA Gender Series 2, Dakar: CODESRIA.

Sanchez-Grant, Sofia, 2008, 'The Female Body in Margaret Atwood's "The Edible Woman and Lady Oracle"', *Journal of International Women's Studies*, Vol. 9, No. 2, pp. 77-92.

UNICEF, 2002, *Child Trafficking in West Africa: Policy Responses*, Florence: UNICEF Innocenti Research Centre.

7

Genge Videos? Struggles over Gender and Citizenship in Kenya

Hezron Ndunde Otieno

Introduction

Citizenship has become a very popular subject of debate in the recent past, appropriated nationally and internationally, both by the Left and the Right, as well as by feminists. In the most general sense, citizenship is about membership or belonging (Delanty 2000). The interest in citizenship is not just in the narrow, formalistic sense of having the right to carry a specific passport. It addresses an overall concept encapsulating the relationship between the individual, the state and society. Beyond the formal definition of citizenship, that is, membership in a nation-state, modern theories of citizenship have drawn their inspiration from Marshall (1950, reprinted in 1992).

Marshall defined citizenship as 'a status bestowed on those who are full members of a community; and those who possess this status are equal, with respect to the rights and duties with which the status is endowed' (Bulmer and Reese 1996). These include civil, political and social rights, and obligations. Marshall defined social rights as 'the whole range, from the right to a modicum of economic welfare and security to the right to share ... in social heritage and to live the life of a civilised being according to the standards (of) society'. According to Sweetman, this view of citizenship goes beyond the concerns of politics, national government and legal systems to the interaction of individual people's rights with collective groupings at all levels (Sweetman 2003).

Yuval-Davis (1997) agrees that Marshall's definition provides the framework to analytically discuss citizenship as a multi-tiered construct which applies to people's membership in a variety of collectives – local, ethnic, national as well as transnational status – and considers this multi-tiered approach important because neo-liberal states have redefined and reprivatised their tasks and obligations. It is no longer defined by nationality and the nation-state, but has become de-territorialised and fragmented into the separate discourses of rights, participation, responsibility and identity. Cosmopolitanism has increasingly become a significant force in the world due to new expressions of cultural identity, civic ties, human rights, technological innovations, ecological sustainability and political mobilisation. Citizenship is no longer exclusively about the struggle for social equality but it has become a major site of battles over cultural identity and demands for the recognition of group difference. Delanty (2000) argues that globalisation both threatens and supports cosmopolitan citizenship. Critical of the prospects for a global civil society, he defends the alternative idea of a more limited cosmopolitan public sphere as a basis for new kinds of citizenship that have emerged in a global age.

This chapter examines patterns of gender struggles over citizenship among the youth in Kenya by investigating the discourse of music videos, particularly the locally produced videos known as *Genge*. As such, it seeks to illustrate how global, national, and local cultural flows from various information and communication technology (ICT) genres are reworked in the emerging romantic and sexual contours of Kenya's future generations as represented in these music videos. The thrust of this study is to raise the level of public dialogue and debate about the way women are depicted in the oftenmisogynistic lyrics and images of popular culture.

DeLauretis has used the term 'technologies of gender' to refer to ways in which film and other such media participate in the cultural construction of what it means to be male or female. She argues that far from being a biological construction, gender is produced and shaped by social discursive practices (de Lauretis 1987). This paper argues that music is foremost among cultural 'technologies of the body', and that it is a site where we learn how to experience socially mediated patterns of kinetic energy, emotions, desire, pleasure and much more. Connected to the idea of specific entertainment value and demand associated with music videos, the images of gender (attractiveness, decorative role, and sexuality) that are frequently used to sell certain lifestyles or ideals are central to this study.

Recent scholarship in the field of popular culture has paid a lot of attention to issues of audience interpretation or construction of meaning (Griswold 1987; Liebes and Katz 1990; Shivley 1992). The issue of cultural use has similarly garnered attention (Beisel 1992; Corse 1997; Griswold 1987). The two literatures obviously intertwine since people's use of culture influences their interpretation of it. Little of this research, however, has seriously considered systematic differences in how men and women view images through highly patterned, gendered lenses and, simultaneously, how the process of interpretation allows men and women to construct various identities

At a different level, however, research in traditional forms of popular culture has an established history in the field of African studies. There is a growing interest in studying the emergent cultural and ICT genres such as music (Hofmeyer, Nyairo and Ogude 2003; Larkin 2004); films (Diawara 2003); popular magazines (Nuttal 2003); and television (Barnet 2004). Such intensified research and analysis are as significant in Kenya as elsewhere in the world since this is intertwined with global cultural flows and the public space of nations, facilitated by the proliferation of new ICTs. Indeed, the Kenyan scene is replete with examples of music being used as a cultural form. For instance, politicians reworked popular music from artistes such as GidiGidi and MajiMaji in the run-up to the 2002 elections to enthuse the populace to vote for particular parties (Hofmeyer, Nyairo and Ogude 2003).

Lukalo (2006) discusses various notions of culture, politics and youth music in the Kenyan context during former President arap Moi's rule. Moving away from the notion that youth activities can be equated with idleness and acts of terror, he examines the historical centrality of music and politics in Kenya. To enhance the discussion, politics and the urban context serve as the basis for interrogating youth involvement through music in the political space in Kenya. So, music is a critical component of peoples' lives and identities in societies throughout the world (Grosssberg 1989; Hall 1981) especially the youth, who are particularly voracious consumers and producers of popular culture (Lipsitz, Maira and Soep 2004; Wills 1990). Although the youths' ability to consume popular culture is largely dictated by their economic means and, in some cases, constrained by religious or cultural norms, the products of the ICT-obsessed world shape the imaginative landscape of the youths' lives (Dolby 2001).

In the last two decades, newer varieties of modern popular music have arisen in Kenya, which are mostly local derivatives of Western hip-hop and rap. They include the sub-genres *Genge* and *Kapuka* beats. These have revolutionised Kenyan popular music and created an industry dominated by the youth. Most artists affiliate themselves with a production house which serves the same function as a recording company.[2] The music videos produced by the youths, especially young women, are fraught with contestation over belonging. Comparatively few women have ventured into the realm of the *Genge* and *Kapuka* music genres in the country and this has compelled them to construct an alternative space in a male dominated field. Men have always assumed dominant roles and females have always been featured subordinately. Female perspectives have always been infused, but within the realm of representation as sexual objects.

Of Identity, Citizenship and Popular Flows: Some Contextual Reflections

There exists a lacuna in the study of music, both secular and gospel, with regard to the issue of gender identities and citizenship struggles, whereas the Kenyan music space, as inany other African country, offers a striking example of a field where contestation between ethnic, gender and national identities isexpressed. This study analyses contestation over gender and citizenship in Kenya as depicted in the locally produced music videos known as *Genge* by both young men and women. *Genge* video images may reveal the strategies that young women use in challenging the hegemonic tendencies of the music industry in the country, and at the same time provide insights into how both local and global cultural flows, in terms of music videos, are reconfigured by the youths.

The global media disseminate a non-local identity, but one directed at the global youth, and mediated largely by music videos. Music videos create and reinforce a stereotypical and *status quo* view of gender, which places limitations on women's social roles (Signorielli 2001). Social cognitive theory suggests that the more people watch television, the more likely they are to view the real world in terms of television images (Bandura 2002). This tendency emphasises the importance of media images and their effect on viewers. Cultivation theory is also concerned with how television, as a system of messages, creates a social reality or view of the world over time (Gerbner, Gross, Morgan, Signorielli and Shanahan 2002). Describing music video content provides a crucial foundation for understanding what messages are communicated, and consequently what images are not presented. Although this study is not an assessment of the effects of stereotypical images of gender on society directly, it presupposes that these images are not contributing to a broad understanding of the variety of roles females play within society. The limited depictions of females are perhaps visually provocative and perceived as standard features or 'must haves' in the minds of producers, artistes, and audiences; however, these images necessitate questions about the standardisation of gender for the sake of perceived and perhaps actual marketability in the current global media systems. As a post-modern commercial art form, music videos change as music evolves, which emphasises the mutability of this particular type of popular media. This evolution capability suggests the potential diversification of music video images of gender. The cultural entwinement of music and video images embodies popular media in an advanced sense, and requires analysis of the influential factors of image production and audience perception.

At a different level, global media content reaches the youth in Kenya through imported programmes that inundate Kenyan television screens. The emergent cable and satellite providers supply specialised music video channels across a variety of genres and languages, which reflects the popularity of this type of media for both audiences and musicians. This technology has transformed the parameters of television viewership in the country. Multichoice Africa, based in South Africa, broadcasts both video and music channels in Kenya through programmes on DSTVs' such as *M-Net* and *Channel* O, giving urban youths an opportunity to listen to music and also watch music videos. *MTV* Base is another programme that is frequently watched by youths in Kenya. In early 2007, a new entrant into the satellite broadcast field was G-TV and it has several music video channels such as *Kiss, Afro Music Channel and MTV Base*. [By the time of writing this paper, Gateway Company that owned G-TV had collapsed due to the global economic recession]. The youths then strive to configure their music videos with a local identity infused with these global cultural flows. The local electronic media have not been left behind either. The state broadcaster, Kenya Broadcasting Corporation (KBC) has *Club One*; Citizen TV has *Xtreem Music*; and Kenya Television Network (KTN) has *Vibe City*, while Nation Television (NTV) has *The Beat* and *ReUp*. Radio Africa Group of companies has recently established a channel, Kiss TV, dedicated solely to music videos.

The chapter explores the various effects these one-sided images have on the society. It endeavours to empower readers to voice their concerns and encouraging people, especially those in the music industry, to work towards a balanced portrayal of women's character in music videos. The aim is not to censor or point fingers at individual artists, but to raise consciousness and encourage consumers and producers of music to use alternatives to the predominant representation of women as hypersexual objects.

Viewing media productions as sites of struggle through which identity is constantly renegotiated and contested, this study moves beyond a conventional feminist reading of the videos to consider the ways they serve to subvert traditional restrictions placed upon female expressions of sexuality. With the advancement in information communication technology, there has been an increase in images that are degrading to women. The global trend in consumerism has created a climate in which advertisements and commercial messages portray women as sexual objects and target young girls inappropriately. The lack of gender sensitivity in the media is evident in public and private, local and international media.

The global Framework Number 33 of the Beijing Declaration, (United Nations 1995) observes in part that the media have great potential in promoting the advancement of women and the equality of men and women by portraying women and men in a non stereotypic, diverse and balanced manner and by respecting the dignity of the human person. Baudrillard suggests that current systems of production and consumption seduce subjects into representing their bodies as capital or a fetish consumer object. Those who lease their bodies then become patriarchal, cultural or corporate signifiers, rather than retaining ownership of the commodity (Baudrillard 1998). As such, the nature and presumed effects of images of women in the media, particularly in advertising, have been the subject of numerous studies and intense debate for several decades (Plous and Neptune 1997).

This paper considers the ways that such images subvert traditional gender roles by voicing a raw form of sexual expression that has historically been exclusive to masculine discourse. To fully understand all the dynamics involved in select *Genge* videos by female artistes, this study considers both the ways in which such representations appeal to female audiences and the inter textual elements that nuance these particular songs. The intention of study is notto dispute that such videos should be heralded as a token of female empowerment, but simply to illustrate that such videosreflect a great deal more than mere patriarchal oppression. This study contributes its findings to the field of cultural studies, studies in youth cultures, ICT and sexual identity formation. Kenya is an important area of study, as is reflected by the growing interest in issues of gender, citizenship and the proliferation of ICTs.

Authority, Music and the Body

Balliger (1999) discusses how political ideology is played out in cultural productions. Balliger argues for 'tracing a definition of politics that moves from formal political structures to power relations in everyday activities'. This approach borrows from Gramsci's concept of hegemony which breaks with the idea of rule as enacted through purely state and political forms because, in his view, domination saturates the whole social process'. Plato, on the other hand, observes that '... music is something to beware of as a hazard of all our fortunes, for the modes of music are never disturbed without unsettling the most fundamental political and social conventions'.[3] Plato tolerates music only when it serves as a vehicle toward some hegemonic, political end. His apprehension about music clusters around two principal issues – contempt for law and seduction of the body – both of which are reproduced virtually every time a controversy concerning youth culture appears. He observes in his Laws that:

> Music has given occasion to a general conceit of universal knowledge and contempt for law, and liberty has followed in their train....liberty is nothing in the world but reprehensible impudence.[4]

What remains suitable for the Republic then are genres of music dedicated either to the martial discipline of the Spartans or to the moderate exchange of ideas through rhetoric. In designing the perfect state, for example, Plato wanted clear restrictions placed on musical composition. He directed that music 'be preserved in [its] original form, and no innovation made... for any musical innovation is full of danger to the whole state...When modes of music change, the fundamental laws of the state always change with them' (*The Republic* IV, 424c).Denouncement of these twin threats, subversion of authority and seduction by means of the body recur constantly throughout history. Saint Augustine of Hippo, who indulged prodigiously in the pleasures of the flesh when he was young, was bound to abolish music not only for himself but his entire flock. He writes concerning the effects of music in the context of liturgy.

> I realize that when they are sung, these sacred words stir my mind to greater religious fervor and kindle in me a more ardent flame of piety than they would if they were not sung...But I ought not to allow my mind to be paralysed by the gratification of my senses, which often lead it astray. For the senses are no content to take second place. Simply because I allow them their due, as adjuncts to reason, they attempt to take precedence and forge ahead of it, with the result that I sometimes sin in this way.[5]

In Saint Augustine's view, while music serves to amplify holy words, its mere presence can distract the attention from the spiritual realm and direct it back to the 'sensual body'. Note especially the slippage between the body and sin narratives in Saint Augustine and elsewhere in Christian writings in which the most innocuous of sensory responses seem to allude to the spectre of unbridled sexuality.

In a culture rigidly structured in terms of a mind and body split, then the appeal of music to the body predisposes it to be assigned to the 'feminine' side of the axis. For instance, theologian John of Salisbury's harangue [with its before-singing, counter-singing and in-between singing] with the 12th century polyphony (the practice whereby several voices in the all-male choir sing different parts simultaneously) presents a veiled depiction of illicitly intertwining male bodies (Holsinger 1993). For Plato, John of Salisbury and Saint Augustine, nothing other than masculinity itself is at stake and by extension, the authority of the church, state and patriarchy. Music is analysed as part of the terrain on which social and moral struggles are enacted. Thus, as in feminist discourses, the personal becomes political because cultural productions reinforce power relations in everyday life.

Recognising representation of identity as a political process capable of reinforcing power relations in society, this paper considers the ways that patriarchal conceptions of women are both reinforced and challenged by representations in music images. Here, we seek to illustrate how women are contesting limited and limiting social and cultural spaces; we observe women looking for recognition and respect in social interactions, women fighting invisibility, clamouring for empowerment. In performing these songs, women are simply reasserting their presence; they are highlighting their edifying attributes of being loving, dependable and compassionate. Any close analysis of the rich repertoire of women's music uncovers an array of songs that not only problematises women's innumerable struggles and muted locutions in a globalised world, but that also critically interrogates women's marginalization, patriarchal dependence and social entrapment. The songs provide a psychological and intellectual public sphere through which gendered, social and political identities are constructed, contested, shaped and manipulated.

Women's 'inability' to exploit the music as a site for articulating feminist issues, alluded to in a number of studies, has always been a misperception, given that the articulation has always been there in the public domain; it is the appreciation that has been wanting. Clory has argued that images of females on television may adversely affect the way women see themselve sand what they can and should aspire to (Clory 2001). Moreover, society views masculine traits more positively, and sexist views may affect career choices (Sideman, 1992). Botta's (1999) study indicate that female adolescents look to media images and their representations as a way to gauge what one should look like, and may adopt behaviours to meet these ideals.

Popular Cultures

Popular cultures can be understood as a collective space where identities are constructed, enforced, and negotiated. The discourse on global cultural forms has thus pushed the study of popular music to centre stage in scholarly research and activism. This is because popular music has always subverted the notion of national boundaries, transcended them and transformed them into new conduits and spaces that allow for the emergence of new identities. Put simply, music is an integral part of popular culture and a central stage on which identity formation and negotiation is played out.

Since popular music is defined by industry norms, Western definitions of what constitutes 'music', and representations of race, class, and gender, we might best think about music and politics as an activity embedded in relations of power. The struggle over the body and the music that incites it has always been the centre of cultural contestation in Western discourses. Hence, to assess music from the outside as though it were but one commodity among many, or as though its meaning resides solely within its lyrics, is to fail to locate its pleasures, its means of manipulation and, therefore, its politics of gender.

Struggles over Gender and Citizenship in Music Videos and Lyrics

The gender politics represented in *Genge* or *Kapukamusic* videos, then, are not irrelevant or inconsequential; rather, they contribute to the larger discourse of cultural hegemony. In *Music and Male Hegemony*, Sheppard (1987) explores a psychodynamic paradigm of male domination. Sheppard argues that the momentary role of the male in sexual reproduction creates a psychological deficit that creates the need to control the means of cultural reproduction: 'Control of cultural reproduction compensates [for] a lack of centrality in biological reproduction'. Since women are believed to factor centrally in human social relations, the male psyche seeks to subordinate women, and thus sustain the illusion of male centrality. Sheppard explains: 'as reflections of the male desire to control the world, women must be controlled and manipulated. This is accomplished by means of their isolation and objectification. The conceptualisation of people as objects decontextualised from social relations implies the possibility for uncontested, unilateral control'. Within the confines of patriarchy then, women are essentially delineated in one of two roles in popular culture:nurturer or sex object. Sheppard argues that female musicians are always representative of this dichotomy. Male hegemonic conventions prevent women from assuming full human status in popular music: 'In order to be 'successful' in a male-dominated society', women 'must package themselves... as objects amenable to control by men'. Unlike the assertive, autonomous sexuality expressed in 'cock rock', sexualised representations of women are necessarily a portrayal of subordination structured so as not to offend the fragile male psyche.

The potential for contestation is built right into the definition of 'hegemony' itself. Balliger explains: Hegemony, while saturating all arenas, is, however, never complete because oppositional practices affect and shape the hegemonic process. Oppositional forces played out in popular music videos are among the most effective means of contesting cultural hegemony, because music defies the fixed and closed meanings required for absolute authority. Sheppard (1987) observes that 'the existence of music, like the existence of women, is potentially threatening to men to the extent that it insists on the social relatedness of human worlds...music reminds men of the fragile and atrophied nature of their control over the world'.

This perception of music as inherently more dialogical than most other cultural productions can be attributed to the work of Marshall McLuhan (1969), which situated cultural communication within a dichotomy of oral/aural and visual culture, each of which embodies distinct modes of consciousness. While visual culture is preoccupied with ordering the world into rigid categories, oral/aural culture is subjective, unfixed, mythological, and participatory. Unlike visual space that 'allows us not only to distance ourselves from the phenomena of the world but also to interject ourselves into the world at a distance', auditory space is 'a sphere without fixed boundaries... It is not pictorial space, boxed in, but dynamic, always in flux, creating its own dimensions moment to moment.' A medium that privileges the aural realm is thus less authoritative, more subjective, and capable of portraying alternative and subversive meanings. Since 'male hegemony is essentially a visual hegemony', the aural/oral consciousness embodied by music poses a threat to patriarchal ideology.

McLuhan considered television a 'cool' medium; meaning that it requires active participation on the part of the viewer in order to complete the message. He therefore situated the psychic effects of television, the medium of the music video, within the dynamics of aural culture. By McLuhan's logic, then, the music video genre creates a psychic space in which male hegemony can be challenged on many levels. Incorporating the double forces of sound and image, the music video is rich in the potential to create multiple, sensory, and emotional meanings that undermine patriarchal rationality.

A number of rappers of the *Genge* genre in Kenya have usedexplicit lyrics. Some of their videos have also raised eyebrows. Thus, Lady S's (Sharon

Wangwe) *Ukimuona (If You See Him)* text provides fertile ground for considering Gramsci's 'dialectical view of cultural struggle'. In light of the dialectal nature of hegemony, and the participatory nature of aural/oral media productions, a post-feminist or neo-feminist reading of Lady S's text is also possible. She sings about dumping her lowlife boyfriend (who she scolds in the video for having cheated on her), female empowerment and sisterhood while exposing her body provocatively to viewers. She tells in the lyrics of how she loves and misses him, yet she also says that she is going to dump him! (After releasing the single, she actually parted ways with her boyfriend.)

I refer here to the academic definition of post-feminism which sees the post- as a process of ongoing transformation and change rather than assuming that patriarchal discourses and frames of reference have been replaced or superseded. Of most relevance to Lady S's video is Projansky's definition of 'sex-positive post-feminism', which 'embraces a feminism focused on individuality, independence and women's 'choice' to engage in heterosexually attractive bodily display'. A post-feminist reading of her text contests Sheppard's insistence that such representation always indicates the subordination of women to the male gaze. In privileging the views of Lady S's female fans, who take pleasure in identifying with these representations, the post-feminist approach creates the potential of examining cultural texts beyond the lens of patriarchy altogether. No longer do we need to begin all critiques of representation with a preoccupation with what they *mean to men*. Although female performers indeed work within patriarchal conventions and industry norms, many of them have a great deal of control over the cultural productions they create, and many such creations are largely marketed to a female audience. Employing an extended definition of what constitutes 'text', we can consider how Lady S's assertive vocal style, the video's visual symbolism, and the song's inter-textuality lays the foundation for an alternative reading of *Ukimuona*. Consider the excerpt:

Kiswahili	Translation
Ukimuona mwambie namtaka	*If you see him tell him I want him*
Ukimuona mwambie namhata	*If you see him tell him I miss him*
Mara ajuena mpenda!	*Let him know I love him!*

In his essay *Text*, Sheppard (1999) calls for an expanded conception of what constitutes the textual elements of a song. The 'meanings' embodied by a musical piece cannot be uncovered simply by considering the musical notation or lyrics, but the contextual implications of voice inflection, beat, rhythm, performance and imagery which reveal social meanings that operate 'behind the back of language' must also be considered. Sheppard employs an extended definition of text to reinterpret Tammy Wynette's song *Stand by Your Man* and illustrate the ways these elements undermine the reassertion of patriarchal gender roles implied by the lyrics. Wynette's increasingly assertive voice, which does become harder and more uncompromising can be read to be symptomatic of the strength necessary to support weak men rather than showing weakness in the face of male superiority'. A comparison can be made here with Wahu, another female artist in Kenya, who deploys fierce and passionate vocals in her song *Sitishiki (I Am not Afraid)*. Consider the following excerpt:

> *Sitishiki nawewe hunitishi nahizo helazako ooh haunitishi*
> *Siisubahi haunisubaishina hizo helazako ooh haunitishi*

Translation

> *I'm not afraid and you can't make me afraid with your money; ooh can't threaten me*
> *I'm not confused because of your money; ooh can't threaten me*

Here, the force of her performance implies self-assuredness, autonomy, and even authority, which function to undermine the objectification she seems so eager to provide visually in yet another single, *Little Things You Do*, featuring Boby Wine, a singer from Uganda. She tells him, while making provocative dance moves in the video,

> *Let me show you what a Kenyan girl can do; every little thing you do, makes me go oooh; boy you turn me on.*

This is not the Wahu whose music lyrics have always emphasised women's empowerment, independence and family values as in her previous singles like *Sitishiki, Liar,* and *Sweet Love,* which won her the best female award at the MTV African Music Awards (MAMA) in Abuja, Nigeria in 2008. Some respondents termed the video controversial, that it made them squirm when they watched it. Indeed, the lyrics and the accompanying video of *Little Things You Do* contain many contrasting elements; it is at once reminiscent of Sheppard's 'woman the sex object', and expressive of a fierce sexual autonomy that flaunts the very real fact that men ultimately cannot control female sexuality. A number of critics in the areas of embodiment theory, post-colonialism and feminism have noted the links between naturalisation of 'woman' as 'other' and 'notions' of 'raced' otherness. Through the examination of music videos, it may well be possible to study the ways in which the body of the woman is inscribed with and transformed by political, gendered, social and sexual meanings.

Another instructive video is by Amani, a female artiste, in her song *Bad Boy*, featuring Nyashinski of the Kleptomaniacs, an all-male group. *Bad Boy* certainly provides us with multiple representations that fit Sheppard's critique. Gyrating, scantily dressed female dancers fill the screen and move their bodies in a sexually suggestive, perhaps even explicit, manner. The video is a voyeuristic form of the male gaze. Laden with scantily clad female bodies, sexual images and provocative dance moves, such videos send out worryingly mixed messages about a female's position in the world to men and women alike. Are these women empowered or objectified? Are they expressing their sexuality or conforming to patriarchal expectations and wishes? Are they even doing both? Consider the extract below:

Kiswahili	English (translation)
Njarozako tayari nimekanywa	*Your character, I have already been warned*
Penzi lako nanambiwa nibalaa	*Your love i'm told is precarious*
Namibado siweziku kuacha	*But I don't want to leave you*
Nifanyeje? Naroho ishapenda.	*What should I do? Yet my heart loves you.*

The text seems to consciously subsume within itself a discourse on sexuality and, by extension, masculinity. The video to the song appears simply to naturalise the sexual objectification of women and subordinates femaleness to the dominance of the male gaze. Textually, she is incapable of making a choice between the advice given to her against the 'bad boy' and the love she has for him. It does not seem likely that female fans 'read', these highly sexualised representations of women in music videos as portraits of objectification. Indeed, some authors have suggested that women in their teens and twenties view hegemonic femininity differently compared to middle-aged women and to the feminist interpretation of it (Winship 1985; Skeggs 1993). Younger women are said to view images identified with hegemonic femininity not as signs of weakness and passivity in women but as indications of being 'in control' of their sexuality.

Belly dancing representsa modification of socio-cultural expectations of appropriate modes of bodily movement for women. It represents a breach of dominant patriarchal discourses, which demand that women attempt to control the perceived excesses of their bodies. Most notably, belly dancing destabilises the social assumption that women should not shake, wobble or draw attention to their breasts, hips, abdomen and especially their pelvises. Key to anexamination of belly dance or any other dance style as a site for contestation is the notion that the dancer's ability to move her torso, hips, and pelvis independently from the rest of the body produces a sense of ambivalent desire in the viewers. On the one hand, the explicit flexibility of belly dancing is constructed as highly desirable, since flexibility in women is frequently linked with innuendos of sexual prowess. On the other hand, however, the exhibition of female flexibility threatens the stability of patriarchal standards of female 'normalcy'. She is threatening precisely because she premeditatedly moves her body in a transgressive manner. The traditional standards of feminine demeanour, according to which women are expected to be constrained and passive but not sexually available, constitute a form of hegemony that might be characterised as 'traditional' hegemonic femininity.

Henley (1977) shows that norms for nonverbal behaviour are different for each gender. Women, as a consequence of their perceived inferior status, are expected to occupy less space than men and to exert greater control over their bodies and facial expressions. This is seen in the expectation that clothing should be neat and well put together and limbs placed in disciplined postures. Women's legs are supposed to be closed rather than apart and arms should be close to the sides of the body. Nudity and displays of breasts and genital areas are also defined as inappropriate.

At the time of writing this paper, at least two female music artists from East Africa had posted their nude images on the internet. This caused a huge storm within the music industry but ironically, the Ugandan artist was hotly sought after and immediately offered a job as a radio show host. The Kenyan has also been successful, appearing on several music videos by Kenyan male artists. This fact points to the legitimate possibility that such constructions are created, at least in part, to appeal to women's own idealized and hyper sexualised image of themselves. La Sara attributes such representations to an emerging 'fearless feminism'.

> I say fearless feminism, because this new feminist genre is based not in the propagation of the myth of victimisation... but in the true strength and liberation of being who we are, who we want to be. This new feminism does not disallow and disavow lipstick and bras, but encourages a creative mix of sexy and strong, saucy and strident (La Sara 2002).

Amani's 'fearless feminist' symbolism is rather simplistic and clichéd, such as her more frequent presence and exaggerated appearance in the video as compared to her male counterpart. An analysis of the meanings embedded in Amani's *Bad Boy* video would be incomplete without a brief note on some of the video's intertextual elements. The male rapper who appears in the video is a *Genge* star, Nyashinisky, whose rap style is uninhibited and aggressive. His 2006 song *Twendeleeama Tusiendelee*, (*We Go On or We Stop*) was a scathing attack against another male artist, Bamboo, who is currently based in the USA for his little escapades with women. The lyrics to the song incorporated violent metaphor and crude allusions to his sexual exploits. Consider the excerpt below'

> *We tabiayako nikumanga nakilama halikama mbuzi, si rap tulianza zamani…hip hop ni culture ya love, kaani kutusindioujilikane…?*

Translation
> *Your behaviour is to have sex everywhere like goats, we started rap long time ago… hip hop is a love culture must you be abused to be popular…?*
> *(From Ogopa DJs Recording Company)*

Nyashinisky's work is neither 'gangsta' rap nor driven by misogynist themes, but rather utilises street slang, commonly known as *sheng*, and sexual metaphor in an aphoristic and figurative style characteristic of early 1990s East Coast hip-hop, a genre prevalent among Black Americans. His lyrical style employs violent and sexual symbolism as a means of illustrating his own assertiveness, invincibility and male prowess. A most crucial point about Nyashinisky's style is that it represents a form of discourse that remains almost exclusively the domain of men. Employing this semantic style is problematic for the female performer because misogynist connotations are embedded in the very essence of violent and sexual semantics that connote a phallic superiority. Even within hip-hop culture across the Atlantic, there are few female artists who borrow heavily from this style (although rap artist Lil' Kim presents a notable exception to this pattern). Although *Bad Boy* does not represent Nyashinisky's 'dirtiest' lyrics, it is a song that remains true to his anarchic themes such as when he informs Amani,

> *Najua unaipenda unaitaka pianaeza tell na design*
> *unaiangaliaa ahasiimakosayako…*

Translation
> *I know you love it and need it I can tell by the way you are looking at it;*
> *aaha it is not your mistake…*

This promotes hedonistic abandon and reckless aggression. Such lack of inhibition is not a virtue traditionally encouraged, or even tolerated, by female artists or women. But then, Amani responds to Nyashinisky with the same words. The videos under discussion create a space in which feminine representations of sexual desire, vanity and prowess can be expressed. Responding in tune with Nyashinisky's assertion, Amani effectively contributes to a dialogue that has traditionally excluded women's participation; she is calling upon her 'girls' to crash the male-dominated sphere of social inhibition and control and tell them, *'they love it and need it …it is not their mistake'.* It must be taken into consideration that Nyashinisky is the *Bad Boy* that Amani wants to fall in love with. This implies the 'feminine' strength that she possesses to overcome the masculine tendencies inherent in the *Bad Boy*.

The study of popular music is a relevant and consequential project capable of revealing the ways hegemony is reinforced through culture. Incorporating a wide array of symbolic practices, including lyrics and visual imagery, rhythm, beat, pitch, tonality, editing effects, and montage, the music videos are rich in potential to connote cultural and ideological propositions. The medium of the music video, the primary promotional vehicle for the music industry today, is an especially rich space to explore the ways in which race, gender, class, and sexuality intersect in the construction and proliferation of ideologies of citizenship in the mass media and popular culture.

Even though *Genge* music can, and often does, reinforce the interests of patriarchal ideology, it carries within itself the seeds of opposition and contestation. Meanings in popular music are never fixed, absolute or definitive; rather they call upon the listener/viewer to participate in their completion. Female-centred, female-marketed texts such as Lady S's *Ukimuona* can no longer be understood simply as evidence against patriarchal dominance. The pervasiveness of hypersexual representations of women in this music connotes a great deal more than mere 'objectification'. The ongoing and dialectical struggle between woman and patriarchy is constantly renegotiated in cultural productions. Rather than serving only to disseminate the ideas of male hegemony, popular music videos serve as a stage upon which the many nuances of an emerging female identity in Kenya are played out.

Conclusion

This study set out to examine patterns of gender struggles over citizenship among the youth in Kenya by investigating the discourse of music videos, particularly the locally produced videos known as *Genge*. It sought to examine the gendered representation of women and to illustrate how global, national, and local cultural flows from various ICT genres are reworked in the romantic and sexual contours of Kenya's future generation as represented in a cultural form, music video.

Without a doubt,the artists presented here are only a small representation of the contradictory messages regarding the female that flood the music industry both local and globally. Women still inhabit an uneasy social zone in which they are more empowered, but still not empowered enough to overcome pre-existing stereotypes. The female body remains an object to be looked at – by the 'male gaze'. It elicits as much interest from feminist critics as it does from the general public. These mixed messages, then, are perhaps unavoidable. Whenever a female artist makes a music video, it is inevitable that she is presented to be viewed and consumed by the TV audience. The mainstream music video remains a genre in which the female is objectified, sexualised and usually submissive and most female artists are content to conform to these constraintsif it sells a few more records. While a few artistes in Kenya, especially on the gospel and Afro-fusion scene, are making headway by refusing to conform, these artistes are significantly outnumbered by ones who are willing to 'sex it up'. And, as long as the music industry demands that women say empowering words while looking sexy in their videos, these artistes will continue to send out mixed signals to young women. These signals will create yet another generation of women who are confused about their identity, their bodies and how to relate to the world.

Regardless of personal interpretations as to the social value, the prominence of such female-centred, hypersexual texts in the media does illustrate a fundamental change in gender politics. Although the artists certainly provide us with many conventional images of women-as-sex-objects, it is imperative that students of cultural studies are fully aware of the meanings such a text carries for its target female audience, and that we recognise how this text represents a development in the articulation of female voice. This paper has argued that the videos should not only be heralded as tokens of female empowerment, but also that they reflect a great deal more than mere patriarchal oppression.

The fundamental contribution of cultural studies has been to illustrate the ways in which cultural hegemony is perpetuated in representations of popular culture. Music is not a transcendent, natural, or universal art form, but rather a social construction shaped by structural forces, dominant ideologies, and the conventions of information technology, globalisation and the hegemonic values of white, Victorian patriarchy. Even as such social factors are naturalised upon the stage of popular music, they are also challenged, undermined, subverted, and renegotiated.

Notes

1. The term 'technologies of gender' is originally from Michel Foucault, 1979, *Discipline and Punish: The Birth of the Prison*, Trans. Alan Sheridan,New York: Vintage Books, p.24. My use of the term is informed by de Laureti's reworking of Foucault's models of both disciplinary and sexual technologies.
2. The popular production houses include Ogopa DJ's, Homeboyz, Mandugu Digital and Calif Records. Popular artists include Nameless, Redsan, Necessary Noize, Nonini, Juacali, Kleptomaniax, Longombas, Suzzanna Owiyo, Achieng' Abura, Rat-A-Tat, the late Lady S and Amani. Their compositions run the gamut from reggae/ragga and pop to Afro-fusion, rap and hip-hop. Many Kenyan artistes mix different languages in a single song, usually English, Swahili and their mother tongue or *Sheng* (a hybrid of Kenyan languages and English/Swahili). This serves to reach a wider audience.
3. *Ibid.*
4. Plato, *The Republic*, 424 BC, quoted in Weiss, Pierroand Taruskin, Richard, eds.,1984, *Music in the Western World: A History in Documents*, New York: Schimer Books, p.7
5. Saint Augustine (354-430),1961, *Confessions*, trans. R.S. Pine-Coffin, Harmondsworth: Penguin Classics, quoted in Weiss and Taruskin, op. cit., p.29.

References

Balliger, Robin, 1999, 'Politics', in Horner, Bruce and Thomas Swiss eds. , *Key Terms in Popular Music and Culture*, Malden: Blackwell Publishers Inc., 1999.

Bandura, A., 2002, 'Social Cognitive Theory of Mass Communication', in Bryant, J. and Zillmann, D., eds, Media *Effects: Advances in Theory and Research*, Mahwah: Lawrence Erlbaum Associates, pp. 121-154.

Baudrillard, J.,1998, *The Consumer Society: Myths and Structures*, London: Sage Publishers.

Barnett, C., 2004, 'Yizo and Yizo: Citizenship, Commoditization and Popular Culture in SouthAfrica', *Media, Culture, and Society*, , Vol. 26, No. 2.

Beisel, Nicola, 1992, 'Constructing a Shifting Moral Boundary: Literature and Obscenity in Nineteenth Century America', in *Cultivating Differences: Symbolic Boundaries in the Making of Inequality*, Larmont, Michele and Fournier, Marcel, eds, Chicago: University of Chicago Press..

Bulmer, M. and Rees, A. M., eds, 1996, *Citizenship Today: The Contemporary Relevance of T. H. Marshall*, London: University College London Press.

Corse, Sarah, 1997, Nationalism and Literature: The Politics of Culture in Canada and the United States, Cambridge:Cambridge University Press.

Clory, M.N. Sr., 2001; 'A Personal Reflection on Television's Messages and Images, and a Challenge to Future Practitioners', in Toth, E. L. and Aldoory L., eds, *The Gender Challenge to the Media*, Cresskill: Hampton Press..

Deranty, Gerald, 2000, Citizenship in a Global Age: Society, Culture and Politics, Buckingham: Open University Press.

Diawara, M., 2003, 'Towards a Regional Imaginary in Africa', in Kumar, A., ed., *World BankLiterature*, Minneapolis: University of Minnesota Press, 64-81.

Dolby, N., 2001, *Constructing Race: Youth, Identity, and Popular Culture in South Africa*, Albany: State University of New York Press.

de Lauretis, T.,1987, *Technologies of Gender*, Bloomington: Indiana University Press.

Duffy, Dennis,1969, *Marshall McLuhan*,Toronto: McClelland and Stewart Limited.

Fletcher, Phoebe,' Lecture Six: Women in/and Advertising', *Film, TV & Media Studies Lecture Resource*, (n.d.). (http://www.arts.auckland.ac.nz/ ftvm/110/110week3c.htm). Accessed 10 July 2008.

Gerbner, G., Gross, L., Morgan, M., Signorielli, N. and Shanahan, J., 2002,'Growing up with Television: Cultivation Processes', in Bryant, J. and Zillmann, D., eds., *Media Effects: Advances in Theory Research*, Mahwah: Lawrence Erlbaum Associates.

Grossberg, L., 1998, 'Pedagogy in the Present: Politics, Postmodernity, and the Popular', in Giroux, H. and Simon, R., eds., *Popular Culture, Schooling, and Everyday Life*, Granby: Bergin and Garvey.

Hall, S., 1981, 'Notes on Deconstructing the Popular', in Samuel, R., ed., *Peoples History and Socialist Theory*, London: Routledge and Kegan Paul.

Henley, Nancy M., 1977, *BodyPolitics: Power, Sex and Nonverbal Communication*, Englewood Cliffs: Prentice-Hall.

Hofmeyer, I., Nyairo, J. and Ogude, J., 2003, 'Who Can Bwogo Me?' Popular Culture in Kenya', *Social Identities,* Vol. 9, No. 3.).

Frith, Simon, 1987, 'Towards an Aesthetic of Popular Music' *inMusic & Society*,Richard Leppert and Susan McClary, eds., Cambridge: Cambridge University Press.

Foucault, M., 1979, *Discipline and Punish: The Birth of the Prison*, Sheridan, Alan, trans., New York: Vintage Books.

Griswold, Wendy, 1987, 'The Fabrication of Meaning: Literary Interpretations in the USA, Great Britain and West Indies, *American Journal of Sociology*, No.5, pp.1077-1117.

Kruse, Holly, 1999, 'Gender', in *Key Terms in Popular Music and Culture*, Horner, Bruce and Swiss, Thomas, eds., Malden: Blackwell Publishers Inc.

Larkin, B., 2004, 'Bandiri Music, Globalisation, and Urban Experience in Nigeria', *Social Text*, Vol. 22, No. 4.

LaSara, W. 'Outrageous Roots and a Bright Future.' *Soapbox girls: the Sexuality Issue.* (July 2002). (http://www.soapboxgirls.com/jul102/articles/ outrageous4.html). Accessed on 10 July 2008.

Liebes, Tamar and Elihu Katz, 1990, *The Export of Meaning: Cross Cultural Readings of Dallas,* New York: Oxford University Press.

Lipsistz, G., Maira, S. and Soep, E., 2004, *Youthscapes: The Popular, the National, the Global,* Philadelphia: University of Pennsylvania Press.

Lukalo, F. K., 2006, 'Extended Handshake or Wrestling Match? Youth and Urban Culture Celebrating Politics in Kenya', Discussion Paper No. 32, Uppsala: NordiskaAfrikainstitutet.

Marshall, T.H.,1950, *Citizenship and Social Class and other Essays,* Cambridge: Cambridge University Press (reprinted 1992).

Meyers, M., 1997, *News Coverage of Violence against Women*, Thousand Oaks: Sage.

Nuttall, S. 2003,' Self Text in Y Magazine', *African Identities*, 1(2).

Plous, S. and Dominique Neptune 1997, 'Racial and Gender Biases in Magazine Advertising', *Psychology of Women Quarterly*, 21: 627-644.

Population Reference Bureau, 2000, *Social Marketing for Adolescent Sexual Health. Results of Operations Research Projects in Botswana, Cameroon, Guinea and South Africa,* Washington DC: Population Reference Bureau.

Ross, Andrew and Ross, Tricia, eds., 1994, *Microphone Fiends: Youth Music and Youth Culture,* New York and London: Routledge.

Sheppard, John, 1987, 'Music and Male Hegemony', in Richard Leppert and Susan McClary, eds., *Music & Society*, Cambridge: Cambridge University Press.

Sheppard, John, 1999, 'Text', in Bruce Horner and Thomas Swiss, eds.,Key *Terms in Popular Music and Culture,* Malden: Blackwell Publishers.

Shivley, JoEllen, 1992, Perceptions of Western Films among American Indians and Anglos, *American Sociological Review*, Vol. 57, No. 6, pp. 725-734.

Signorielli, N., 2001, 'Television's gender role images and contribution to stereotyping', in D.G. Singer and J.L. Singer, eds., *Handbook of children and the media*, Thousand Oaks:Sage.

Skeggs, Beverly, 1993, 'A Good Time for Women Only', in Fran Lloyd, ed., *Deconstructing Madonna*, London: B.T. Batsford.

Sweetman, C., 2003, 'Editorial', *Gender and Development*,Vol. 11, No. 3, November.

United Nations Department of Public Information, *Fourth World Conference on Women, Beijing, China 4-15 September 1995, Platform for Action and the Beijing Declaration No.33.*

Weiss, Pierro and Taruskin, Richard,(eds.), 1984, *Music in the Western World: A History in Documents*, New York: Schimer.

Wekesa, P., 2004, 'The Politics of Marginal Forms: Popular Music, Cultural Identity and Political Opposition in Kenya', *Africa* Development, Vol.XXIX, No.4, Dakar: CODESRIA.

Wills, P., 1990, *Common Culture*, Milton Keynes: Open University Press.

Winship, Janice,1985, 'A Girl Needs to Get Street-wise, Magazines for the 1980s', Feminist Review 21: 25-46.

Yuval-Davis, N., 1997, 'Women, Citizenship and Difference', *Feminist Review*,No. 57, Autumn.

8

Citoyenneté et développement humain au Maroc face aux différentes formes d'exclusion: une approche genre

Mustapha Ziky

Introduction

L'objectif de ce papier est de mettre en évidence les effets des inégalités de genre sur la citoyenneté et le développement humain au Maroc. La participation de tous les citoyens sans exclusion à l'œuvre du développement de la société est un principe démocratique et une exigence en matière de droits humains. La réalisation du développement humain et l'émancipation de la citoyenneté exigent un dépassement de l'objectif classique de l'accroissement économique *stricto sensu* pour se fixer un but essentiellement démocratique, celui de réaliser l'équité et l'égalité entre hommes et femmes.

L'absence d'une telle vision au Maroc a handicapé le développement et favorisé l'exclusion de la femme, provoquant une crise de citoyenneté et même parfois d'identité chez celle-ci. En effet, bien que l'article 8 de la Constitution postule l'égalité des droits entre les femmes et les hommes, les faits révèlent diverses formes d'exclusion par le genre. Elles se manifestent par le taux d'analphabétisme relativement plus élevé chez les femmes, leur intégration insuffisante aux activités économiques et des inégalités réelles en matière d'accès aux opportunités, aux rémunérations et d'accès aux postes de responsabilité. En plus, la participation de la femme aux rouages politiques demeure marginale et on observe même un déficit flagrant en matière d'autonomisation et de participation aux décisions touchant même à leur existence en tant que femmes.

Certes, ces différentes formes d'inégalités et la crise de citoyenneté qui en découle entravent l'émancipation de la femme et sa participation active à la réalisation du développement humain. Cette problématique de l'inégalité par le genre et de ses répercussions se pose aujourd'hui avec acuité, suite à une nouvelle détérioration enregistrée en matière de développement humain, perdant en 2009/2010 quatre places pour se positionner au 130e rang mondial. Un classement d'ailleurs qui peut être expliqué, entre autres, par une forte exclusion de la femme de l'éducation, par des taux de mortalité élevés dont elles souffrent, notamment en phase d'accouchement, et enfin par le manque à gagner en termes économiques, suite à la faible participation de la femme au processus économique.

C'est dans ce contexte d'inégalité par le genre et de retard accumulé en termes de développement humain que s'inscrit la problématique de ce papier. Il s'agit de mettre en évidence les répercussions néfastes d'inégalité d'accès aux droits de citoyenneté par la femme sur le niveau du développement humain au Maroc. De cette problématique centrale découlent deux principales questions de recherche : Quelles sont les différentes formes d'inégalités ou d'exclusion dont souffre la femme marocaine? Comment affectent-elles la citoyenneté et le processus du développement humain au Maroc ?

Citoyenneté, genre et développement : quels liens théoriques

Jusqu'à la fin des années quatre-vingt, les sociologues et politologues n'envisageaient pas la citoyenneté dans le cadre de la problématique des rapports de genre (Bourque et Grossholtz 1974; Githens 1983; Kathleen 1990; Vicky 1991). L'analyse de la citoyenneté en termes d'individu abstrait et d'égalité de sexe explique cette neutralité de la citoyenneté. Les recherches récentes aussi bien théoriques qu'empiriques mettent en évidence la sensibilité extrême de la question de la citoyenneté au genre (Pateman 1988 ; Phillips 1991, 1993 ; Yuval-Davis 1993, 1997 ; Lister 1997a ; Voet 1998). Elles cherchent, par ailleurs, à dépasser les tensions entre, d'une part, égalité et différence et, d'autre part, universalisme et particularisme. Cette nouvelle problématique explore l'impact des systèmes liés au genre et des systèmes culturels sur la production des relations inégales qu'ont les femmes et les hommes face aux lois et pratiques régissant la citoyenneté.

L'idéologie traditionnelle dominante postule une subordination des femmes allant souvent de pair avec l'exclusion de la sphère publique et plus particulièrement de la sphère politique réservée aux hommes. Bien que les constitutions reconnaissent les mêmes droits aux hommes et aux femmes, les systèmes législatifs n'ont cependant pas toujours facilité l'exercice des droits politiques et économiques (Coquery-Vidrovitch 1994; H. Dagenais 1994; Dalloz 1991) Cette exclusion s'explique aussi par le désintérêt qu'elles manifestent pour la chose publique et la difficulté de s'y investir (Naciri 2005 ; Meer et Sever 2004). Mais ce désintéressement et cette difficulté résultent de la nature des régimes politiques régnant caractérisés par la violence qui entoure les pratiques d'accès aux droits politiques, notamment lors des élections présidentielles, législatives ou communales.

Cette exclusion de la sphère publique peut aussi trouver ses origines dans des contraintes classiques inhérentes aux femmes. Elles n'ont pas le temps, elles n'ont pas la formation suffisante et pas assez d'expérience politique relativement aux hommes. Ce constat s'explique par la distribution des rôles qui prédominent dans les rapports sociaux, c'est-à-dire de la place qui leur est assignée historiquement. Alami Machichi (2001) évoque dans ce cadre le *paradoxe de la doxa*, c'est-à-dire l'ensemble des croyances qu'on ne cherche plus à comprendre, qui sont considérées comme des vérités qu'on ne peut remettre en question. Or, ces croyances accréditent l'idée que la répartition des tâches entre sphère publique, domaine des hommes, et sphère privée, domaine des femmes, est incontournable. L'insertion des femmes dans l'univers public apparaît dès lors complexe. Les femmes se trouvent ainsi cantonnées dans des obligations familiales et manquent de temps pour pratiquer des activités politiques.

En conséquence, les données révèlent une présence marginale des femmes dans les rouages institutionnels de la vie politique (Banque Mondiale 2004 ; PNUD 1995). La faible représentation est surtout accentuée au sein de l'exécutif. Lorsqu'elles y sont, elles se voient confier des portefeuilles ne traitant pas de questions liées à l'exercice de la souveraineté et de moyens si dérisoires. Elles se chargent généralement de portefeuilles ministériels des affaires sociales, de la promotion féminine et rarement de la santé et de l'éducation.

En plus de l'exclusion politique, les femmes souffrent d'autres formes d'inégalité. La liaison homme/père-Etat renforce la création des hiérarchies liées au sexe et facilite l'institutionnalisation d'une citoyenneté discriminatoire dans les projets de construction de l'Etat. Cette liaison est présente dans la majorité des pays en développement, notamment africains (Papaneck 1994; Dalaney 1995; Ruddick 1997). Cette liaison privilégie le droit du sang dans la réglementation de la citoyenneté, ce qui va de pair avec la masculinisation de la descendance et la valorisation de la patrilinéarité au détriment de la matrilinéarité. En outre, Le droit familial a soutenu l'appropriation des enfants par les hommes. Les enfants sont nés sujets de leur père. En cas de divorce, la possession des enfants revient au père et la famille paternelle a la priorité sur la mère.[1] Les mouvements féministes considèrent les pouvoirs publics comme l'acteur le plus critiqué dans cette question de citoyenneté discriminatoire. Ils affirment que c'est l'Etat qui régit les règles par lesquelles on devient citoyen et par lesquelles se fait la transmission de la citoyenneté aux enfants et aux conjoints.

Enfin, signalons que parfois les femmes sont privées des droits les plus rudimentaires. Le vote féminin demeure encore contrôlé ou même exercé par les hommes, surtout dans les milieux ruraux (Sassi 1995). Par ailleurs, on exige des femmes dans certains Etats d'obtenir la permission de leurs pères, frères ou autres tuteurs mâles pour se marier, voyager ou créer une entreprise commerciale (Lazreg 2000). De fait aussi, parfois des restrictions même d'ordre vestimentaire s'imposent.

Ces diverses pratiques inégalitaires confinent les femmes à la sphère domestique et illustrent ces mentalités et cultures vivaces selon lesquelles les femmes ne peuvent prétendre participer à des décisions engageant la vie de la nation. Ces diverses exclusions contribuent au sous-développement et entravent l'émergence d'un développement socioéconomique équilibré (Sever 2004). L'exclusion politique et socioéconomique des femmes réduit le bien-être collectif. A titre illustratif, le fait que le Moyen-Orient[2] se caractérise par les taux les plus faibles de participation et de représentation des femmes dans les structures politiques a eu des répercussions sur le développement de la région et sa capacité de relever les défis de la mondialisation (Karshenas et Moghadam 2006).

Par ailleurs, plusieurs auteurs mettent en évidence la relation entre la citoyenneté des femmes, la démocratisation et le développement. Selon Moghadam (2007:7), si l'inégalité d'accès des femmes aux entités juridiques et aux structures de gouvernance est « le résultat logique découlant d'un système étatique autoritaire et néopatriarcal, les luttes des femmes pour devenir des citoyennes à part entière contribuent à changer les relations entre l'État et le citoyen, à élargir l'espace politique et à faire progresser la démocratisation de la région ». Elle affirme aussi que la participation des femmes à de nombreux domaines, pierre angulaire de la citoyenneté, contribue également à la croissance et au développement économique et social. La participation des femmes dans les processus économique et politique est essentielle à la gouvernance démocratique et au développement (Ahern, Nuti et Masteron 2000).

Cette participation peut permettre aux femmes de développer de nouvelles compétences et d'accéder à de nouveaux droits. A contrario, l'exclusion de la femme affecte le bien-être et le développement du fait que les responsabilités citoyennes des femmes (travail domestique, maternité, éducation des enfants,...) sont souvent non rémunérées et par là même ignorées des systèmes de gestion économique (Mukhopadhyay 2003). Cela permet au gouvernement de n'avoir aucun compte à rendre en matière de besoins des femmes. Une institutionnalisation de la participation citoyenne permettrait la protection et l'inclusion de la femme et surtout son émancipation pour une contribution plus efficace au développement.

Selon la Conférence de Beijing de 1995, l'intégration de l'approche genre est une condition *sine qua non* de la réalisation du développement. Elle annonce que

> La participation des femmes au développement économique et social, l'égalité des chances et la pleine participation, sur un pied d'égalité, des femmes et des hommes, en tant qu'agents et bénéficiaires d'un développement durable *au service de l'individu* sont des conditions essentielles à l'élimination de la pauvreté au moyen d'une croissance économique soutenue, du développement social, de la protection de l'environnement et de la justice sociale.

La notion de l'intégration du genre *(gender mainstreaming)* a été définie, par la suite, par le Conseil Economique et Social de l'ONU en 1997 comme

> Une stratégie visant à faire des préoccupations et des expériences des femmes et des hommes une dimension intégrale de la conception, de la mise en œuvre, du suivi et de l'évaluation des politiques et des programmes dans toutes les sphères politique, économique et sociétale, de façon à ce que femmes et hommes en bénéficient à égalité, et que l'inégalité entre les sexes ne soit pas perpétuée.

L'intégration du genre implique, entre autres, d'identifier les écarts entre les femmes et les hommes à travers l'utilisation de données désagrégées par sexe, de développer des stratégies pour éliminer ces écarts, de mobiliser des ressources pour mettre en œuvre ces stratégies, d'assurer le suivi de la mise en œuvre de ces stratégies et de responsabiliser les individus et les institutions pour une transparence des résultats obtenus (Rapport genre 2007).

Par ailleurs, la redéfinition du concept de la citoyenneté en élargissant son socle d'origine, basé sur les droits civiques et politiques, aux droits économiques et sociaux prend toute son importance dans le cadre du travail en développement (Sweetman 2003). Elle recherche avant tout de meilleures stratégies pour réduire la pauvreté et renforcer la participation de la femme au développement socioéconomique. Le faible nombre de femmes occupant des fonctions politiques est lié au grand nombre de femmes en situation de pauvreté (PNUD 2000).

La réalisation d'une participation active de la femme au développement passe, impérativement, par un changement de mentalité et de culture instituant la discrimination sexuelle (Sinha 2003). L'accroissement de sa participation aux prises de décisions locales peut aussi constituer une bonne formation à l'exercice d'une influence politique à des échelons supérieurs. Le PNUD (2000) recommande même des formations formelles et informelles des femmes en matière de savoir-faire politique afin de les encourager et de valoriser leur accès aux responsabilités dirigeantes. Il propose même des réformes des systèmes électoraux et des partis sur une base de discrimination positive afin de prescrire la présence d'un pourcentage de femmes dans les législatifs et les exécutifs (principe des quotas).

Les différentes formes d'inégalité par le genre au Maroc

La citoyenneté moderne et le développement humain reposent sur la notion des droits et des obligations de l'individu vis-à-vis de la collectivité, sans occulter les droits de la collectivité vis-à-vis de l'individu. Ni la citoyenneté ni le développement humain ne sont concevables en l'absence de l'égalité de tous les citoyens en droits et en devoirs. Or, au Maroc, les femmes et les hommes n'ont pas eu accès aux mêmes droits en même temps. En effet, une analyse quantitative et qualitative des statistiques montre que les femmes, qui représentent la moitié de la population, ont souvent fait l'objet de discrimination et d'exclusion.

Les dissymétries dans l'accès à l'éducation et aux services de santé

La promotion de la participation des femmes au développement requiert une valorisation et une implication des forces féminines dans le processus productif de l'économie nationale. Afin de renforcer cette participation dans les projets de développement, il est indispensable de surmonter toutes les difficultés qui entravent le renforcement des capacités féminines et la promotion de l'égalité et de l'équité.

Analphabétisme et inégalité d'accès à l'éducation

Le droit à l'enseignement est inscrit dans la Constitution. Il a été promulgué par Dahir le 13 novembre 1963. Ce dernier a rendu pour la première fois l'enseignement obligatoire pour les enfants de 7 à 13 ans. Pour comprendre les évolutions survenues dans ce domaine, certaines données quantitatives sont particulièrement édifiantes. A l'aube de l'indépendance, la scolarisation ne touchait que 15 pour cent de la population et environ neuf personnes sur dix ne savaient ni lire ni écrire, pour une proportion de 96 pour cent de femmes. Certes, des efforts colossaux[3] ont été aménagés pour généraliser l'enseignement et lutter contre l'analphabétisme, mais la situation demeure encore préoccupante, notamment en termes de genre.

Le tableau 1 confirme le déficit qu'a accumulé le Maroc en termes d'alphabétisation et la discrimination dont a fait l'objet le sexe féminin durant toute cette période. En effet, les différents recensements mettent en évidence la gravité de l'analphabétisation et son caractère sexo-spécifique. Ce résultat est confirmé par les résultats de l'enquête nationale sur l'analphabétisme, la non scolarisation et l'abandon scolaire, le taux d'analphabétisme en 2007 est estimé à 38,45 pour cent pour la population âgée de 10 ans et plus, soit 31,38 pour cent chez les hommes, contre 46,8 pour cent chez les femmes. En valeur absolue, ce taux se traduit par près de 9 millions de personnes analphabètes. Par ailleurs, les taux d'analphabétisme par milieu sont de 27,2 pour cent en milieu urbain et de 54,4 pour cent en milieu rural. Le taux des enfants non scolarisés, âgés entre 10 et 14 ans, est de 13,3 pour cent, dont 87 pour cent dans le milieu rural et 64 pour cent chez les filles.

Tableau 1 : Taux d'analphabétisme par sexe (en %)

	1960	1971	1982	1994	2004	2007
Masculin	78	63	51	41	30,8	31,38
Féminin	96	87	78	67	54,7	46,8
Ensemble	87	75	65	55	43	38,45

Source : Direction de la statistique

Ces statistiques révèlent le caractère préoccupant de l'analphabétisme des femmes au Maroc. A en croire les chiffres officiels, l'analphabétisme touche encore environ 50 pour cent des femmes. L'écart entre femmes et hommes analphabètes est estimé à trois millions, dont le plus grand nombre est en milieu rural. Selon certaines associations oeuvrant dans le domaine de la lutte contre l'analphabétisme, les taux sont plus élevés que ce qui est présenté officiellement et dépassent dans certaines régions rurales, notamment celles les plus touchées par la pauvreté, le seuil de

80 pour cent. Selon le Rapport de Développement Humain (2005), le taux d'analphabétisme s'approche de 70 pour cent pour les femmes au-dessus de 35 ans. Les zones rurales sont les plus affectées, puisque l'on y compte une proportion de femmes analphabètes de 74,5 pour cent. Pour la Banque Mondiale (2007), en milieu rural, 83 pour cent des femmes sont toujours analphabètes.

Partant de ces chiffres et suite à l'échec de la réalisation de l'objectif de la généralisation de la scolarisation, on peut facilement prévoir que l'analphabétisme sera encore un problème réel au Maroc pendant plusieurs décennies. Sa dimension féminine demeurera encore du fait que les non scolarisés âgés entre 10 et 14 ans sont des filles à concurrence de 64 pour cent.

Pour éradiquer ce fléau d'analphabétisme, les efforts de scolarisation de la fille ont été multipliés et le constat de la scolarisation des filles restée pour longtemps un phénomène citadin a été écarté. En effet, selon le Rapport genre (2008), le taux de scolarisation des filles de 6 à 11 ans a dépassé le cap de 90 pour cent, avec les taux de progression les plus significatifs enregistrés au niveau rural. En effet, le taux de scolarisation de la fille rurale est passé de 44 pour cent en 1997 à 83 pour cent en 2004 (RDH 2005) pour s'établir actuellement à 84,3 pour cent, contre 95,7 pour cent pour les filles urbaines.

Toutefois, malgré les efforts accomplis, des problèmes de scolarisation accompagnés de la discrimination demeurent. La charte nationale de l'éducation et de la formation s'est fixé des objectifs qui n'ont pas été réalisés. En effet, les statistiques ci-dessus révèlent la non généralisation de la scolarisation avec un déficit de plus de 15 pour cent pour la fille rurale et la non généralisation, même pour la fille citadine. La généralisation du préscolaire a été prévue pour 2004. Cet objectif est loin d'être atteint et même une régression a été enregistrée ; le taux de la pré-scolarisation a diminué, passant de 68,6 pour cent en 1999/2000 à 53,4 pour cent en 2003/2004 (Rapport genre 2008). A ce niveau aussi la discrimination sexo-spécifique apparaît et le déficit est alarmant pour la fille d'une manière globale et pour la rurale en particulier. Le rapport moyen des filles dans les effectifs d'élèves préscolarisés âgés de 4 à 5 ans avoisinait 36,5 pour cent au niveau national, 46 pour cent en milieu urbain et seulement 21,1 pour cent en milieu rural.

En avançant dans les niveaux supérieurs de scolarisation, ce phénomène de pénalisation des filles s'accentue. En 2004, 52 ,2 pour cent uniquement des filles arrivent à terminer leurs études collégiales et uniquement 8,9 pour cent d'entre elles accèdent à l'enseignement supérieur. Ces taux sont encore dérisoires pour la fille rurale du fait que 22 pour cent arrivent à achever leurs études collégiales et leur possibilité d'accès au supérieur est insignifiante, voire inexistante.

Cette exclusion de la fille rurale est surtout un signe tangible de la discrimination à l'égard de la femme. Plusieurs contraintes peuvent être énumérées pour expliquer une telle situation : la pauvreté, l'éloignement géographique des lieux d'implantation des collèges et des lycées, l'accessibilité aux lieux d'enseignement, la priorité des garçons sur les filles, l'analphabétisme des mères, le mariage précoce des filles, l'absence de conditions appropriées dans les agglomérations où sont situés les collèges, le contrôle social des filles et la limitation des déplacements en dehors du foyer familial (Zirari 2005:175).

En général, on peut dire que malgré les efforts considérables qui ont été consentis durant les cinq dernières décennies, à travers les programmes de scolarisation et d'éducation non formelle, on n'a pas pu réduire significativement les écarts persistants entre hommes et femmes, surtout en milieu rural. La raison principale, selon les organisations féministes, ayant fait de cette affaire de lutte contre l'analphabétisme féminin leur principale cause est que les efforts publics insuffisants se trouvent en plus bloqués par certains comportements sociaux. Plusieurs recherches ont pu démontrer

> l'existence de stéréotypes sexistes, d'images négatives, réduisant les femmes au rôle de reproductrices, limitant ainsi leur champs de développement et de compétence… La masculinité, quant à elle, est érigée en modèle d'intelligence, de courage et d'aventure. La valorisation de ces capacités intellectuelles et sociales tend à légitimer l'autorité des hommes et leur supériorité (Zirari 2005:75).

Ces difficultés d'accès à l'éducation limitent les potentialités d'épanouissement des femmes. Cet effet négatif apparaît en premier lieu au niveau sanitaire, mettant en évidence une corrélation nette entre le niveau de l'éducation et les indicateurs sanitaires.

Difficultés d'accès aux soins médicaux

Acquérir le droit du contrôle de son propre corps constitue le premier pas vers l'autonomisation et l'émancipation de la femme. Dans le cadre de l'amélioration quantitative et qualitative des soins de santé, particulièrement à destination des populations démunies et de la garantie d'un accès à la santé à tous les citoyens, un intérêt particulier est accordé à la santé de la femme qui, du fait de son rôle de reproduction, est exposée à certains risques affectant sa santé. Néanmoins, malgré les efforts déployés, les avancées réalisées restent en deçà des attentes.

L'espérance de vie est un premier indicateur pertinent pour évaluer les efforts entrepris en matière de santé. Cet indicateur a évolué positivement au Maroc, passant de 47 ans en 1960[4] à 70,4 en 2004, ce qui traduit une amélioration générale de l'état de santé de la population marocaine. Comme dans la plupart des autres sociétés, on constate une longévité féminine supérieure à celle des hommes. Ces constats dissimulent cependant des disparités importantes. On vit, en effet, moins longtemps en milieu rural que dans les villes: 4,8 ans de moins pour les hommes (66,2 contre 71 ans en 2002) et 7,3 ans de moins pour les femmes (68,1 contre 75,4 ans). Ces écarts mettent en évidence la situation particulièrement défavorisée des femmes rurales, à la fois par rapport à leurs consoeurs des villes et par rapport aux hommes ruraux, beaucoup plus proches qu'elles de l'état sanitaire des populations urbaines des femmes.

En plus de l'espérance de vie à la naissance, le deuxième indicateur permettant d'évaluer les performances en matière de santé et sa sensibilité au genre est le *taux de mortalité maternelle*. C'est certainement l'aspect le plus inquiétant de la situation sanitaire des femmes au Maroc. Se situant à hauteur de 227 pour 100 000, le taux reste élevé comparativement à d'autres pays ayant un niveau de développement similaire. En effet, le risque de décéder à la suite d'un accouchement est deux fois plus élevé qu'en Tunisie et en Egypte et presque six fois plus qu'en Jordanie. En outre, ce taux est doublement inquiétant et cache des disparités. C'est préoccupant, en premier lieu, vu l'évolution de ce taux dans le temps. Malgré les efforts consentis ces dernières années en la matière, ce taux n'a pas évolué par rapport à 1997 où il a été estimé à 228 pour 100 000 naissances, avec même une aggravation curieuse de la situation urbaine. En deuxième lieu, la situation est aggravée par les disparités villes-campagnes. Ainsi, pour 100 000 naissances vivantes, on compte 267 décès maternels dans les campagnes, contre 187 dans les villes. Cet écart est surtout imputable à la faible couverture médicale, au manque d'infrastructures sanitaires, à l'éloignement des structures de santé, à l'enclavement et à l'absence de moyens de transport, à la pauvreté de la plupart des ruraux.

Tableau 2 : Évolution par milieu de résidence du taux de mortalité maternelle (décès maternels pour 100 000 naissances vivantes)

	1978-1984	1985-1991	1992-1997	2003-2004
Urbain	249	284	125	187
Rural	423	362	307	267
Ensemble	359	332	228	227

Source : ENPSII (1992), PAPCHILD (1997) et RGPH (2004)

Ce taux de mortalité maternelle élevé met en évidence l'un des principaux problèmes du système de santé au Maroc, en l'occurrence la prise en charge de la grossesse et de l'accouchement. Selon CEDAW[5] (2006), au cours de la période 1999-2003, seules 68 pour cent des femmes enceintes ont eu recours à une consultation prénatale, dont les femmes rurales ne représentent que 48 pour cent par rapport au milieu urbain où cette proportion est de 85 pour cent. Les disparités se creusent davantage pour les femmes analphabètes dont seulement 56 pour cent ont effectué une consultation prénatale, contre 94 pour cent pour les femmes ayant atteint le niveau d'éducation secondaire ou plus.

En outre, les accouchements en milieu surveillé demeurent insuffisants et empreints par la disparité qui caractérise les milieux urbain et rural ainsi que le niveau d'éducation des femmes. En milieu rural, la proportion des accouchements assistés n'est que de 40 pour cent, contre 63 pour cent en milieu urbain. La part des femmes qui bénéficient d'une assistance lors de l'accouchement est de seulement 49 pour cent pour les femmes analphabètes, alors qu'elle est de 94 pour cent pour les femmes ayant atteint un niveau d'études secondaires ou plus.

Outre l'analphabétisme, ces résultats s'expliquent par des raisons d'ordre économique, ou des difficulté d'accès aux services de santé en raison de l'éloignement et la dispersion de l'habitat rural, ainsi que l'insuffisance des campagnes de sensibilisation particulièrement au niveau des risques de mortalité maternelle. Par ailleurs, la persistance de barrières culturelles est en grande partie à l'origine de la faible efficacité des programmes de santé maternelle. De nombreuses femmes ne peuvent accoucher en milieu surveillé du fait du refus de leur mari. Cela est révélateur des rapports de pouvoir des hommes sur les femmes en matière de santé reproductive et sexuelle. Les résultats de l'Enquête sur la Population et la Santé Familiale 2003-2004 sont révélateurs. L'insuffisance des moyens financiers demeure l'obstacle majeur qui empêche les femmes d'accéder aux soins (74% des femmes enquêtées) et se pose avec plus d'acuité en milieu rural (85% contre 66% en milieu urbain), suivie de la longueur de la distance à parcourir pour atteindre le centre de soins (60%) ; la méconnaissance du lieu où se trouve le centre de soins (52%), le souhait de ne pas vouloir aller seules (49%) et le fait d'avoir à demander la permission d'aller se soigner (47%).

Enfin, une dernière forme de la discrimination contre les femmes apparaît explicitement s'agissant de la surmortalité des petites filles de 1 à 5 ans (11 pour mille pour les filles, contre 8 pour mille pour les garçons). Selon HCP, cette surmortalité s'est aggravée dans le temps, passant de 20 pour cent entre 1982 et 1991 à 37 pour cent entre 1994 et 2003, et sévit particulièrement en milieu rural. Ce phénomène, à l'opposé de l'évidence biologique universelle, pourrait s'expliquer, outre par la persistance des maladies infectieuses et nutritionnelles, par des acteurs socioculturels en faveur des garçons. Les parents se rendent plus volontiers aux centres de soins éloignés quand un petit garçon est malade que lorsqu'il s'agit d'une petite fille.

La discrimination en matière d'accès à l'activité économique et politique

L'exercice d'une véritable citoyenneté et la réalisation du développement humain requièrent une participation active des femmes à l'activité économique et aux rouages politiques et décisionnelles. La Constitution et différentes lois garantissent l'égalité des deux sexes en matière de participation à la chose publique. Toutefois, la réalité révèle des discriminations à l'égard des femmes aussi bien dans le domaine de l'activité économique que politique.

Inégalités de participation à l'activité économique

La législation du travail consacre expressément la liberté et l'égalité entre les femmes et les hommes en matière d'accès au travail. C'est dans ce sens que l'article 9 interdit toute discrimination fondée sur le sexe ayant pour effet de violer ou d'altérer le principe d'égalité des chances ou de traitement, sur un pied d'égalité, en matière d'emploi ou d'exercice d'une profession, notamment en ce qui concerne l'embauche, la conduite et la répartition du travail, la formation professionnelle, le salaire, l'avancement, l'octroi des avantages sociaux, les mesures disciplinaires et le licenciement. Il résulte de ce qui précède le droit de la femme de conclure un contrat de travail, l'interdiction de toute mesure discriminatoire fondée sur l'affiliation syndicale des salariés et le droit de la femme, mariée ou non, d'adhérer à un syndicat professionnel et de participer à son administration et à sa gestion.

Néanmoins, les avancées de cet article 9 sont loin d'être réelles et réalisables dans une société pensant masculin et poussant à la persistance des gaps importants. En effet, le marché du travail est caractérisé par la faible participation des femmes et leur souffrance d'inégalités multiples. Ces inégalités hommes-femmes se déclinent en termes d'accès à l'emploi, de niveau des salaires, de responsabilité et de participation à la prise de décision dans la vie publique et économique qui demeure restreinte. Par ailleurs, les femmes exercent ce qu'on appelle le travail impayé, qui n'est pas comptabilisé et qui se décline dans le travail domestique et les soins en faveur de la famille et de la communauté.

Les statistiques révèlent diverses formes de discrimination à l'égard des femmes sur le marché du travail. L'implication des femmes dans l'activité économique reste encore limitée : le taux d'activité des femmes au niveau national est uniquement de 27,2 pour cent, contre 76,4 pour cent pour les hommes en 2006. En milieu urbain, ce taux n'est que 19,3 pour cent, contre 71,4 pour cent pour les hommes. Des disparités apparaissent aussi, en ce qui concerne le taux d'emploi. En milieu urbain, ce taux est évalué à 61,5 pour cent en 2006 pour les hommes, contre seulement 15,2 pour cent pour les femmes. Le taux de féminisation de l'emploi a subi un affaissement, soit 20,7 pour cent en 2006, contre 21,1 pour cent en 2005. En milieu rural, le taux d'emploi est de 37,7 pour cent pour les femmes, contre et 79,6 pour cent pour les hommes. Ainsi, la ventilation du taux d'emploi selon le sexe, montre qu'il y a un accès inégal de la femme à l'activité économique. Le taux d'emploi des femmes ne représente que 34 pour cent du taux d'emploi des hommes (Rapport genre 2008). La forte distorsion enregistrée entre l'emploi féminin et masculin traduit un rapport homme/femme inégalitaire dans l'emploi.

La population active féminine est à majorité peu qualifiée. 72 pour cent des travailleuses n'ont aucun diplôme et 11,2 pour cent ont des diplômes et certificats de l'enseignement fondamental. Le même constat se dégage par milieu où la part de la population active féminine sans diplôme est de l'ordre de 40,5 pour cent (urbain), contre 93,4 pour cent (rural). Cette situation démontre la précarité des emplois féminins. Cette précarité est davantage aggravée par plusieurs autres aspects liés au travail de la femme. Il est, généralement, occasionnel et également itératif et manuel, ce qui entrave la promotion institutionnelle, la stabilité et l'accumulation de l'expertise des femmes.

En effet, si sur 100 actifs occupés âgés de 15 ans et plus exerçant en tant qu'ouvriers et manœuvres agricoles 46 sont des femmes, cette proportion n'est que de 37 pour cent pour les cadres moyens, près de 30 pour cent pour les cadres supérieurs et les membres des professions libérales et de 11 pour cent pour les membres du corps législatif, les élus locaux, les responsables hiérarchiques de la fonction publique. En outre, il faut signaler que pour réduire leurs charges sociales, les entreprises pratiquent le licenciement des ouvrières à la fin de chaque année de sorte qu'elles restent des « temporaires permanentes ».

Il en résulte un décalage dans les salaires entre les femmes et les hommes. Selon le Rapport de Développement Humain (2006), les salaires des femmes sont largement discriminatoires. Les entreprises dans toutes les branches imposent une nette discrimination vis-à-vis des femmes. Cette discrimination va du simple au double dans le tapis et tourne autour de 50 pour cent dans la bonneterie et la confection. Cependant, il arrive que la situation s'inverse, comme dans le commerce et le bâtiment. Dans les autres branches, on relève une discrimination de 15 à 25 pour cent sur les salaires des femmes. Selon un rapport récent du ministère de l'Emploi en 2008, ce décalage est de 25 pour cent alors que d'autres études avancent des taux situant entre 30 et 40 pour cent pour certains secteurs, notamment la filière textile.

Tableau 3 : Salaire mensuel moyen en DH par sexe et secteur d'activité

Salaire	Transfor-mation	Bâtiment	Service	Commerce	Total
Homme	1266,81	1166,89	1653,21	1311,42	1380,21
Femme	1003,85	1250,00	1260,00	1490,00	1207,14
Moyenne	1233,94	1171,15	1593,64	1324,17	1361,28

Source : RDH 2006

La précarité s'explique aussi par le statut dans l'emploi exercé. Dans les villes comme dans les zones rurales, la majorité des hommes employés déclarent avoir un emploi rémunéré (93,4% et 60,7%). Pour les femmes, si la proportion des citadines actives occupées exerçant un emploi rémunéré est égale à celle des hommes, elle n'est que de 15 pour cent dans les zones rurales. Autrement dit, le travail de la femme rurale entre dans 85 pour cent des cas dans le cadre de l'aide familiale (RDH, 2006). En outre, en matière d'emploi, les femmes sont confrontées à des problématiques spécifiques liées notamment à :

- la difficulté d'estimation de leur travail invisible et non rémunéré (la corvée d'eau, le ramassage du bois de chauffe, le soin aux malades aux personnes âgées ou aux enfants, le transport, la préparation des repas …,) qui n'apparaît pas dans les statistiques officielles et ce, malgré l'importance de leur contribution à l'économie nationale ;

- la difficulté de mesurer leur participation à l'économie, notamment dans le milieu rural (agriculture) et dans le secteur informel (textile).

La discrimination à l'égard des femmes apparaît aussi dans les statistiques du chômage. En effet, le chômage touche les femmes plus que les hommes. En 2007, le taux de chômage des femmes dans les villes atteint 24,20 pour cent, contre 16,6 pour cent, pour les hommes. Les caractéristiques de ce chômage des femmes montrent les difficultés de leur accès au marché du travail. Selon le Rapport de Développement Humain de 2006, près de 70 pour cent des jeunes, hommes et femmes, de 15 à 24 ans, titulaires du baccalauréat, sont au chômage. En outre, et pour la même tranche d'âge, 75 pour cent des femmes diplômées des facultés sont au chômage (contre 69,4% pour les diplômés hommes). Pour le Rapport genre de 2007, l'analyse de la structure du chômage urbain féminin par tranche d'âge révèle que les catégories les plus touchées sont celles des actifs de 15 à 24 ans et de 25 à 44 ans, qui constituent respectivement 31 pour cent et 62,7 pour cent de la population active féminine au chômage en 2003, ce qui traduit les difficultés du premier emploi et l'importance du chômage de longue durée. Il faut en outre signaler que les femmes sont plus touchées par le chômage tributaire des fluctuations économiques. A titre illustratif, les difficultés du secteur du textile se sont répercutées négativement sur l'emploi de la femme, entraînant des licenciements et du chômage.

D'autres formes de discrimination et d'exclusion des femmes de l'activité économique subsistent encore. Le taux de l'auto-emploi est élevé chez les hommes (29,30 %) et très limité dans les rangs des femmes actives (9,30 %). 14 pour cent des entreprises sont gérées par des femmes, selon le rapport de la Banque Mondiale de 2007 sur l'évolution de la condition des femmes en Afrique du Nord et au Moyen-Orient. Les études ont montré que pour créer une entreprise familiale, les femmes en général et les rurales en particulier ne bénéficient que faiblement de l'assistance du réseau bancaire. Par ailleurs dans le milieu urbain, l'héritage de l'entreprise familiale va à l'homme dans 87,2 pour cent des cas et dans le milieu rural, l'homme hérite de l'avoir productif familial dans 87,4 pour cent des cas. En plus, les femmes ne gèrent elles-mêmes leurs avoirs productifs que dans 27,3 pour cent des cas (16,4% dans le rural). En ce qui concerne le régime de protection sociale des travailleurs du secteur privé, celui-ci exclut les catégories professionnelles qui sont constituées, dans leur écrasante majorité, par des actifs de sexe féminin (domestiques de maisons, travailleurs des entreprises artisanales, aides familiales et travailleurs temporaires et occasionnels).

En guise de conclusion, les différentes statistiques révèlent une grande difficulté d'accès des femmes à l'activité économique. Ces difficultés peuvent s'expliquer, en partie, par l'absence des femmes dans les rouages politiques et décisionnels et par l'impossibilité de défendre convenablement leurs intérêts.

Inégalité de participation au champ politique

La première Constitution du Maroc indépendant (1962) reconnaît l'égalité de tous les citoyens en matière de droits politiques que les Constitutions suivantes (1970, 1972, 1992 et 1996) ont confirmés : « L'homme et la femme jouissent de droits politiques égaux. Sont électeurs tous les citoyens majeurs des deux sexes jouissant de leurs droits civils et politiques ».

Bien que le discours politique et politicien tende à aller dans le même sens de la Constitution, la réalité de l'exercice politique et décisionnel atteste du décalage entre le texte et les faits. Ce constat s'explique par la persistance pesante de l'ordre patriarcal et l'absence d'une stratégie globale et intégrée, déclinée en actions positives en faveur de la promotion des femmes. En témoignent les résistances à l'entrée des femmes en politique par des mécanismes spécifiques et positifs tels que le système des quotas qui s'expliquent non pas par le fait que ce dernier est anti-démocratique, mais plus par la réaction opposante d'une élite politique masculine. Il faut attendre les législatives de 2002 pour que, suite à un débat intense impliquant l'ensemble des acteurs sociaux, la société civile, les ONG féminines et de défense des droits humains, les partis politiques, certaines personnalités politiques, les universitaires et le monde des médias, le principe d'un quota féminin minimum de 10 pour cent pour les élections de la Chambre des représentants soit accepté.

Il en a résulté, pendant longtemps, des inégalités politiques basées sur le genre et matérialisées par une faible participation des femmes aux rouages politiques et administratifs. Bien que depuis 1963, date des premières élections législatives de l'histoire du Maroc indépendant, la femme ait obtenu et ait exercé le droit de voter et celui de poser sa candidature aux élections législatives dans les mêmes conditions que l'homme, il fallut attendre l'année 1993 pour voir la première femme marocaine siéger au Parlement. La mentalité masculine de la société a entravé, pendant longtemps, l'accès aux pouvoirs législatifs malgré les candidatures qui se sont multipliées à chaque occasion.

Tableau 4 : Evolution des femmes candidates et élues aux élections législatives (Chambre des représentants)

Date des élections	Candidates		Elues	
	Nombre	%	Nombre	%
1963	16	2,3	0	0
1977	8	1,2	0	0
1984	15	1,1	0	0
1993	36	1,7	2	0,6
1997	87	2,6	2	0,6
2002	269 : Listes locales 697 : Listes nationales	0,05 -	5 30	10,7
2007	269 : Listes locales 697 : Listes nationales		4 30	10,4

Tableau 5 : Femmes dans les Chambres basses ou uniques après les renouvellements parlementaires de 2007

Pays	Nombre total de siéges	Nombre total de femmes	% total des femmes	Quotas
Finlande	200	84	42,0	Non
Argentine	255	102	40,0	Oui
Danemark	179	67	37,4	Non
France	577	107	18,5	Non
Sénégal	150	27	18,0	Oui
Cameroun	180	25	13,3	Oui
Maroc	325	34	10,5	Oui
Algérie	389	30	7,7	0ui
Qatar	35	0	0	Non
Monde	-	-	17,7	-
Pays nordiques	-	-	41,4	-
Europe	-	-	20,9	-
Afrique sub-saharienne	-	-	17,3	-
Etat arabe	-	-	9,6	-

Source : Union interparlementaire, 2007

Pour protéger les droits électoraux des femmes, le législateur a pris plusieurs mesures. À titre d'exemple, l'inscription pour chaque Marocain sur les listes électorales est devenue obligatoire en 1997. Cette mesure pourrait inciter la femme à prendre conscience de son droit de vote. Puisque le vote demeure personnel, l'homme ne peut pas voter à la place de la femme. Mais c'est surtout le quota adopté depuis les législatifs de 2002, en tant que mesure de discrimination positive, qui a montré son efficacité pour faciliter l'inclusion des femmes dans les fonctions électives. L'article 1 de la loi organique de la Chambre des représentants a introduit le principe de réserver 30 sièges, sur les 325 que compte la première Chambre du Parlement, pour les femmes à élire sur une liste nationale. Il en a résulté l'élection de 35 femmes à la Chambre des représentants, 30 élues sur la liste nationale et 5 sur les listes locales. Le pourcentage des femmes siégeant à la Chambre des représentants est ainsi passé de 0,66 pour cent lors des élections législatives de novembre 1997 à 10,77 pour cent pour les consultations de septembre 2002.

Certes, l'adoption du système de la liste nationale en 2002 a permis de promouvoir la participation des femmes au Parlement. Mais, malheureusement, il apparaît que les élections de 2007 n'ont pas réussi à consolider la participation des femmes dans la vie politique. En effet, cette discrimination positive visait à améliorer la participation des femmes, non pas uniquement par les quotas, mais aussi par les listes locales. Néanmoins, les législatives de 2007 montrent les difficultés de la femme à concurrencer l'homme du fait qu'une régression a été enregistrée sur les listes locales et seulement 4 femmes ont été élues, contre 5 pour les élections de 2002. Par ailleurs, il convient de signaler que malgré la discrimination positive permettant plus de participation politique, le classement mondial établi par l'Union interparlementaire montre une sous-représentativité des femmes au sein du Parlement. En termes de pourcentage, on remarque que la participation de la femme marocaine au Parlement demeure faible par rapport à la moyenne mondiale et même inférieure à celle africaine et très légèrement supérieure à celle des pays arabes.

Cette faible participation politique apparaît clairement dans les communes en l'absence d'une discrimination positive. Malgré la mobilisation du mouvement des femmes pour qu'une charte d'honneur soit signée par les partis politiques, le principe du quota n'a pas été officiellement adopté lors des élections communales de septembre 2003. Ainsi, les partis politiques ont présenté peu de femmes et les résultats obtenus sont à l'image des anciennes élections communales. Comme indiqué par le tableau ci-dessous, le nombre de femmes élues ne représente même pas le 1 pour cent du total, bien qu'elles représentent plus de 50 pour cent de la population. En outre, 2 femmes, uniquement, ont été élues dans les communes rurales, et 2 femmes ont été élues présidentes de communes sur 41 communes, 22 femmes vice-présidentes. Aucune femme n'est nommée à la tête d'un conseil régional et une seule région a connu l'élection d'une femme vice-présidente du conseil régional.

Tableau 6 : Évolution du nombre de candidates et du nombre de femmes élues aux élections communales

Année	Inscrits	Votants	Taux de partici-pation %	Candidats		Élus	
				Nombre total	Nombre de femmes	Nombre total	Nombre de femmes
1976	6 566 961	4 331 438	65,95	42 638	76 (0,17 %)	13 358	9 (0,067%)
1983	7 069 385	5 085 226	71,93	54 162	307 (0,57 %)	15 493	43 (0,28%)
1992	11 513 809	8 793 682	74,64	93 773	1 086 (1,16 %)	22 240	77 (0,35%)
1997	12 941 779	9 724 199	75,13	102 292	1 651 (1,61 %)	24 236	83 (0,34%)
2003	14 620 937	7 918 640	51,55	122 658	6 024 (4,91 %)	23 689	127 (0,54%)

Source : Enhaili (2007)

Ces chiffres relatifs aux élections communales et législatives témoignent certes d'une forte inégalité et de l'exclusion des femmes marocaines du champ de la participation politique, bien que les lois et les dispositions institutionnelles, prévoient l'égalité en la matière. Les hommes ont, pendant longtemps, su se réserver le champ politique ainsi que les centres de décisions économiques et sociales, reléguant les femmes à des rôles subalternes. Ces dernières, malgré leur investissement grandissant de l'espace public, sont souvent cantonnées à des postes d'exécution et rarement de décision.

Tableau 7 : Participation des femmes aux postes de responsabilité en 2003

Poste de responsabilité	Nombre total	Nombre de femmes
Secrétaire général d'un département	29	2
Directrices centrales	167	18
Inspecteur général	19	0
Ambassadrice	80	3
Directrices de cabinet		2
Consul général	25	2
Directrice adjointe	35	2
Chef de service	2230	366
Directrice régionale	69	0
Déléguée provinciale ou préfectorale	260	11
Procureur	74	1
Délégué (ministère de l'Education nationale)	69	5
Directrice de l'académie de l'éducation et de la formation	1	1
Directrice de conservatoire	18	0
Percepteur	39	5
Percepteur local	259	9
Secrétaire général de faculté	81	5

Source : Rapport CEDAW 2006

Cette inégalité politique s'explique en premier lieu par le fait que le processus démocratique est hypothéqué par des intérêts privés et par des groupes puissants, habitués à agir hors des règles démocratiques et à influencer ou à corrompre les électeurs dans le cadre des consultations. Il en ressort l'absence de consultations transparentes ou l'existence de modes de scrutin basés sur la représentation truquée. Ce faisant, ces pratiques participent au désenchantement des électeurs et à l'éloignement de la participation politique des femmes. De même, élues sans avoir réellement brigué le suffrage universel et grâce au système des sièges réservés, elles ne peuvent que difficilement exprimer leur désaccord sur les lois ou les politiques suivies.[6]

En outre, cette faible participation politique des femmes s'explique par leur présence peu significative dans les organes et les instances de décision des partis politiques, bien que l'article 22 de la loi sur les partis politiques impose aux partis de prévoir dans leur règlement la proportion réservée aux femmes. Les statistiques relatives aux élections 2007 montrent une fois encore que les partis politiques ne sont pas disposés à soutenir leurs candidates et à assurer l'égalité politique. Les femmes n'ont représenté, en effet, que trois pour cent du total des candidats têtes de liste et cinq pour cent de l'ensemble des candidatures présentées. Les femmes ne sont souvent intégrées que pour compléter les listes pour la majorité des partis politiques du fait que les femmes sont encore minoritaires dans les instances dirigeantes de leurs partis et n'ont pas, ainsi, le poids qui leur permettait d'imposer leur volonté.

Les résistances à l'entrée des femmes se retrouvent également dans la sphère publique qui, malgré les avancées, demeure associée au sexe masculin. Les femmes ne sont que 10 à 12 pour cent aux postes de direction et de chefs de division dans les secteurs gouvernementaux sociaux traditionnellement féminins. Le nombre des femmes ministres dans les différents cabinets qui se sont succédé au Maroc depuis 1997 – date d'entrée des premières femmes au gouvernement (4 ministres) – reste dérisoire. De plus, les porte-feuilles confiés aux femmes sont généralement des secrétariats d'État et/ou des ministères délégués dans les secteurs sociaux (famille, enfants, personnes handicapées, etc.) et manquent de mandats institutionnels forts et de moyens humains et financiers. Toutefois, une avancée remarquable a été enregistrée en 2007, suite à la désignation de 5 femmes en poste de ministre et 3 femmes en poste de secrétaire général.

En définitive, la femme marocaine a fait l'objet de diverses formes d'inégalité. Une majorité des femmes est restée pour longtemps privée de ses droits les plus absolus, à savoir l'éducation, l'emploi, et la participation aux rouages de décision. Elle fait l'objet de diverses discriminations sur le marché du travail et subit diverses formes de pressions et de violence. Il en résulte une atteinte à la citoyenneté de la femme et un affaiblissement de son apport au développement humain.

Cercle vicieux, inégalités du genre, crise de citoyenneté et sous-développement humain

La citoyenneté moderne repose sur la notion des droits et des obligations de l'individu vis-à-vis de la collectivité et représente *un ensemble de processus légaux par lesquels sont définis les sujets d'un État.* Si l'on se place sur le plan de la théorie libérale, la citoyenneté n'est pas concevable en l'absence de l'égalité de tous les citoyens en droits et en devoirs. Par ailleurs, par la notion, encore récente, de développement humain, on entend un accroissement des libertés et des potentialités des individus dans toutes ses composantes : économique, sociale, culturelle, ethnique et politique. Chaque jour, les êtres humains opèrent des choix, certains sont relatifs au domaine économique, d'autres relèvent de la sphère politique, sociale ou culturelle. Certains de ces choix sont essentiels à la vie humaine :

- celui de vivre le plus longtemps possible en bonne santé ;
- celui d'être instruit ;
- celui de vivre dans des conditions décentes.

Si ces trois choix sont fondamentaux pour les êtres humains, ceux qui sont relatifs à la participation au jeu politique, à la diversité culturelle, aux droits de l'homme et à la liberté sont des aspects tout aussi importants de la vie humaine.

De ces deux notions découlent des droits divers dont la non appropriation entraîne une forme ou une autre de l'exclusion provoquant une crise de citoyenneté et un sous-développement humain. Or, au Maroc, les femmes n'ont pas eu accès à l'ensemble de ces droits ou n'ont pas accès aux mêmes droits en même temps que les hommes. Il en résulte une détérioration du niveau du développement humain en général et celui des femmes en particulier, et en plus une atteinte à la citoyenneté des femmes.

Exclusion et pauvreté des femmes

C'est lorsque la population dispose des outils nécessaires pour participer à la croissance et en recueillir les fruits que l'économie d'un pays prospère et se développe le plus (Wolfensohn et Bourguignon 2004). Il est ainsi évident que les différentes formes d'inégalité ayant touché et touchant encore la femme marocaine entravent le développement humain du pays. Les différentes formes d'exclusion des femmes au Maroc et la propagation de la pauvreté féminine qui en a résulté entraînent un manque à gagner de croissance et de développement humain.

D'ailleurs, le développement humain est intimement lié au concept de la pauvreté tel qu'il a été élargi par Sen (1999) pour prendre plusieurs dimensions :

> Le pauvre est celui qui n'a pas la liberté fondamentale de choisir le mode de vie qu'il souhaite mener. C'est donc celui qui n'a pas souvent les moyens de se nourrir, de se loger, et de se soigner convenablement. C'est aussi celui qui est totalement désarmé face à la maladie, à la violence, aux perturbations économiques et aux catastrophes naturelles. C'est enfin celui qui est mal servi par les institutions de l'Etat et de la société et qui n'a aucun moyen de peser sur les décisions qui influencent sa vie.

Les inégalités dont souffrent les femmes dans la distribution des revenus et de la richesse, leur accès limité aux ressources économiques, au marché du travail et autres institutions économiques, y compris financières, et le poids des responsabilités familiales ainsi que celles qui leur incombent pour approvisionner en eau et en énergie leurs familles les rendent particulièrement vulnérables à la pauvreté, qu'elle soit structurelle ou conjoncturelle, personnelle ou liée à l'économie nationale. En effet, selon le RGPH[7] (2004, et en matière de pauvreté, 14,2 pour cent de la population vivent en dessous du seuil de pauvreté et la ventilation de ce taux selon le genre montre que les femmes sont les plus touchées aussi bien en milieu urbain que rural : 11,9 pour cent pour les hommes contre 12,8 pour cent pour les femmes en milieu urbain et 27,2 pour cent pour les hommes contre 28 pour cent pour les femmes en milieu rural.

Ces chiffres cachent d'autres disparités. Les femmes veuves et divorcées sont les plus touchées par la pauvreté et les plus exposées à ces risques. Selon les Enquêtes Nationales sur le Niveau de Vie des Ménages, en milieu urbain, le taux de pauvreté des femmes veuves est deux fois plus élevé que celui des hommes; mais ce sont surtout les femmes divorcées qui en souffrent le plus, d'où un taux de pauvreté très élevé. De plus, ces deux catégories sont d'autant plus vulnérables à la pauvreté vu qu'aucune disposition sociale particulière n'est prévue pour les soutenir. Au Maroc, les femmes divorcées et abandonnées ayant des enfants à charge se trouvent très souvent complètement démunies, financièrement et socialement.

Il est évident que cette pauvreté monétaire des femmes conjuguée aux différentes formes d'exclusion présentées dans la section précédente contribue au déficit flagrant en matière de développement humain. Le Maroc ne cesse de régresser dans le classement mondial pour se situer actuellement à la 126e, rang selon l'Indicateur de Développement Humain (PNUD 2008), perdant une autre fois trois places en une seule année et pour occuper une position reculée par rapport au pays à niveau de développement moyen. La contribution de la condition féminine malsaine à cette détérioration du niveau de développement humain apparaît dans l'analyse différenciée de l'IDH et le retard cumulé en la matière pour les femmes.

L'analyse au niveau infra-national montre que le développement humain atteint par le Maroc en 2004 (0,642) recouvre, en fait, d'importantes disparités selon le milieu et le sexe. Selon le Rapport de Développement Humain (2006), les hommes ont un IDH (0,665) qui dépasse de 7,1 pour cent celui des femmes (0,621). Lorsque l'on combine le sexe et le milieu de résidence, on constate que les citadins (0,739) suivis des citadines (0,704) ont un IDH supérieur à la moyenne nationale, à celle des pays arabes (0,679 en 2003) et à celle des pays en développement (0,694 en 2003). En revanche, on constate que les retards se sont accumulés chez les hommes ruraux (0,566) et chez les femmes rurales (0,509). Ces données placent les femmes rurales marocaines dans la tranche de classement des pays les moins avancés (IDH inférieur à 0,518 en 2003). Ces pays n'ont pas encore atteint le niveau de développement humain réalisé par le Maroc il y a vingt ans (0,515 en 1985). Cette inégale répartition du développement humain est principalement imputable à l'accès inégal à l'éducation, aux limites de la capacité productive et à la faiblesse des revenus des femmes.

L'approche du développement humain a aussi mis en évidence l'impact des inégalités dont souffrent les femmes sur la pauvreté en général, y compris sur le bien-être des hommes et des enfants. La population, l'éducation des filles, le travail des enfants, la sécurité alimentaire, et l'environnement sont des variables qui sont directement liées à la pauvreté des femmes. Autrement, des corrélations multidirectionnelles peuvent être soulevées entre les différentes formes d'exclusion, la pauvreté et le niveau de développement humain et ainsi le risque de se situer dans un cercle vicieux de sous-développement humain et d'exclusion des femmes est élevé.

A cet égard, il est important de souligner que la pauvreté humaine des femmes se transmet de génération en génération. Par exemple, les femmes souffrant de malnutrition sont plus susceptibles de donner naissance à des enfants souffrant d'insuffisance pondérale à la naissance ; les mères analphabètes sont aussi moins capables de favoriser et de contribuer à l'éducation de leurs enfants ; en outre, elles présentent des niveaux de fertilité et de mortalité infantile et juvénile plus élevés. La pauvreté des mères se transmet de manière directe à leurs filles, car ces dernières permettent aux mères d'ajuster leurs stratégies de survie, à travers une participation accrue aux activités de reproduction et/ou de production ou bien à travers des mariages précoces. Ce qui ne fait que perpétuer le cycle de la pauvreté, de l'exclusion et du retard de développement humain.

Une trappe de pauvreté et de sous-développement humain peut d'ailleurs résulter des différentes inégalités basées sur le genre soulevées précédemment. Les effets de la difficulté d'accès de la femme, surtout rurale, aux soins médicaux peuvent être facilement attribués à ses conséquences sociales – sentiments de risque, d'impuissance, de vulnérabilité ou de faible estime de soi – ainsi qu'à l'incidence absolue de la privation matérielle. De cette privation peut découler une détérioration de son état de santé et de son état nutritionnel et une vulnérabilité à d'autres maladies. La privation matérielle signifie aussi une diminution de la somme de travail, mais aussi une réduction de la capacité à participer au marché de l'emploi et à la production. Ainsi, la difficulté d'accès de la femme marocaine aux soins médicaux présente un manque à gagner de production, de bien-être, de développement et constitue une forme d'auto-exclusion ou de trappe de la pauvreté. Cette situation est surtout préoccupante dans les zones rurales privées d'infrastructure de base suffisante en matière d'hôpitaux et de dispensaires privés, ainsi que de médecins spécialistes et d'équipes médicales suffisantes. L'enclavement de ces zones et les difficultés de déplacement rendent encore l'effet de l'exclusion des femmes en termes de santé plus percutant, étant donné la difficulté d'accès aux soins médicaux dans les villes.

Par ailleurs, Le développement humain est intimement lié au capital humain. Un enseignement de qualité est une condition nécessaire pour le développement d'un capital humain de qualité. Parmi les facettes de l'exclusion des femmes au Maroc, la propagation de l'analphabétisme touchant plus de la moitié de la population âgée de 15 ans et plus. Il s'ensuit un faible capital humain et une contribution limitée au développement socioéconomique. La difficulté d'accès à l'enseignement s'explique en premier lieu par la pauvreté. Les pauvres peuvent être contraints d'envoyer leurs filles au travail (travail dans les champs ou comme domestiques ou comme aides familiales), si bien qu'ils ne sont pas éduqués, et dès lors l'héritage de faible niveau de capital humain est transmis à la génération suivante et de là se forme un cercle vicieux de sous-développement. L'analphabétisme et la scolarité insuffisante empêchent le plein développement du potentiel d'un individu et réduisent ses possibilités de contribution à l'amélioration du bien-être.

En relation avec le capital humain, les différentes inégalités touchant les femmes ont provoqué une fuite intense de cerveaux, notamment les enseignantes universitaires, les médecins, les cadres, les informaticiennes, infirmières, les ingénieurs... Il en résulte une double perte, d'une part l'Etat a dépensé énormément dans leur formation et, d'autre part, l'économie ne bénéficie absolument pas de leurs compétences. Le manque à gagner en matière de développement est non négligeable. Les pertes humaines causées par l'émigration clandestine, touchant de plus en plus les femmes, constituent aussi un potentiel de développement si les émigrés clandestins ont eu la chance de participer au développement du pays.

En guise de conclusion, les différentes formes d'exclusion des femmes touchant au nutritionnel, à l'éducation, à la santé, à l'emploi, à la participation politique... contribuent significativement au retard cumulé en matière de développement humain. Ces exclusions entravent le développement indispensable pour l'inclusion de la femme et une trappe d'exclusion émerge. Lorsque ces exclusions touchent aux besoins les plus rudimentaires des citoyennes, il est évident que différentes formes de crise de citoyenneté s'installent.

La crise de citoyenneté au Maroc

Certes, la citoyenneté revêt principalement un sens juridique et se définit comme la jouissance des droits civiques attachés à la nationalité. Concrètement, le détenteur de la nationalité dispose des droits civils (l'ensemble des libertés individuelles) et politiques (droit de vote, d'éligibilité, d'accès à la fonction publique...). Mais il est également soumis à des devoirs (obligation militaire, obligation de respecter la loi, respect des droits et des libertés des autres, exercice de son droit de vote, participation aux dépenses collectives...). Néanmoins, en plus de son aspect juridique, la citoyenneté revêt d'autres dimensions, notamment sociales et économiques. Sur le plan social, la citoyenneté peut signifier l'implication dans son environnement pour assurer à chacun un minimum de bien-être en accord avec les standards établis par la société. Autrement, est considéré comme citoyen celui qui participe à la vie des institutions politiques et au façonnement du bien commun. La citoyenneté est également une série de pratiques économiques et culturelles. Elle permet l'accès à des besoins économiques comme le travail, l'infrastructure, le bien public et la sécurité sociale tout en préservant les spécificités culturelles, notamment le choix de la langue. Elle revêt aussi un pôle identitaire du fait qu'elle est pleinement réalisée lorsque le statut du citoyen a une importance subjective pour l'individu.

Sur le plan juridique, la citoyenneté est souvent liée à la participation à la chose publique. La domination de l'activité politique par les hommes constitue une atteinte à la citoyenneté des femmes dans un contexte de partage inégal du pouvoir. Les droits politiques acquis récemment dans le cadre de la discrimination positive restent à traduire et à concrétiser dans la réalité afin de favoriser l'élargissement de la participation citoyenne des femmes et le renouvellement des élites politiques et de permettre ainsi l'émergence d'une véritable citoyenneté.

Par ailleurs, et toujours sur le plan juridique, pendant plusieurs années, les femmes sont restées reléguées à un second plan social sans véritable protection juridique, ce qui a participé à augmenter la vulnérabilité de plusieurs catégories d'entre elles :

- Les mères célibataires et leurs enfants sont les principales victimes de lois souvent jugées discriminatoires. Ce sont généralement des jeunes filles issues des milieux les plus défavorisés qui n'ont pas de possibilité de recours à des méthodes contraceptives ou à l'avortement clandestin (très coûteux) qui se trouvent généralement victimes de telles situations. Les lois sont à cet égard discriminatoires à l'égard des femmes. Ainsi, et bien que le Code pénal sanctionne les relations sexuelles hors mariage pour les deux sexes, dans la pratique, quand elle est enceinte, la mère célibataire peut être condamnée d'office, alors que la preuve contre l'homme est plus difficile, même en cas de dénonciation par la mère.

- Les femmes vivent aussi mal leur citoyenneté, car il y a une catégorie de femmes victimes de violences conjugales et d'harcèlement sexuel, que ce soit sur les lieux de travail ou dans les rues. Une enquête réalisée en juin 2000 par l'Association démocratique des femmes du Maroc (ADFM) montre que la violence à l'égard des femmes est une pratique courante dans le pays. 55,3 pour cent des personnes interrogées ont reconnu connaître dans leur entourage une femme battue par son époux. Celles qui souhaitent s'adresser à la justice sont rapidement découragées par les procédures longues et compliquées. La loi marocaine exige que douze témoins appuient la déclaration de la femme battue. Or, les violences se déroulent généralement au foyer familial, en privé. Même avec le nouveau Code de la famille, les dispositions légales à l'égard de ces pratiques restent insuffisantes.

- La situation des femmes domestiques, et surtout les mineurs d'entre elles, reste très préoccupante. Ces citoyennes de « troisième catégorie » souffrent de beaucoup de maux, à commencer par l'absence d'une réglementation de leurs conditions de travail. Les parents poussent leurs fillettes à travailler dès leur jeune âge en tant que domestiques, pour des salaires de misère et dans des conditions souvent difficiles. La réglementation du travail au Maroc exclut le travail domestique et dans le secteur de l'artisanat. Ce code renvoie à une loi spéciale, qui régira les relations entre les domestiques et les maîtres de maison, une loi qui n'a pas encore vu le jour.

- En plus du mariage précoce handicapant la femme surtout rurale sur plusieurs plans, les filles rurales souffrent aussi de l'entrée précoce en activité précoce. Selon l'enquête nationale sur l'emploi réalisée en 2004, cette activité précoce des filles est une caractéristique essentiellement rurale puisqu'elle concerne 7,7 pour cent des femmes rurales effectivement en activité (0,7 pour cent des actives dans les villes). La petite fille rurale est ainsi nettement handicapée dans sa vie future puisqu'elle est, du fait de l'activité précoce, privée de scolarisation et donc de toute possibilité d'améliorer ses capacités productives et sociales futures.

Enfin, l'ignorance et la mauvaise application des lois dans un contexte déjà patriarcal expliquent la position subalterne des femmes dans la société. Selon l'enquête réalisée par le ministère de la Prévision Economique et du Plan sur les conditions socioéconomiques de la femme au Maroc en 1999, l'autorisation du mari ou du tuteur est indispensable pour que 85,3 pour cent des femmes rurales enquêtées et 61,2 pour cent des citadines puissent sortir de chez elles. Les parents ou la famille ont décidé du premier mariage de 85,1 pour cent des femmes rurales enquêtées et de 73,3 pour cent des citadines. 53,8 pour cent des femmes rurales doivent être accompagnées quand elles sortent, mais seulement 16,4 pour cent des citadines.

Du fait que la citoyenneté est également une série de pratiques socioéconomiques et permet l'accès à des besoins économiques comme le travail, l'infrastructure, le bien public et la sécurité sociale, il est évident que le sous-développement et la répartition inéquitable des richesses provoquent une crise de citoyenneté et même d'identité. Cette crise de citoyenneté a atteint des niveaux alarmants lorsque la femme est privée de ses droits les plus élémentaires, tels que les soins médicaux, l'eau potable, l'éducation… Et de toute évidence, il est complètement absurde de parler des droits politiques et civiques alors que la femme, surtout pauvre ou encore veuve ou divorcée, est privée de son droit le plus rudimentaire tel que la nourriture. Cette forme indigne d'exclusion entrave tout processus de démocratisation du fait que les voix seront achetées facilement lors des élections contre la nourriture. De même, le taux d'analphabétisation des femmes élevé au Maroc rend le choix des électrices arbitraire et souvent basé sur la corruption, le clientélisme, les relations familiales et non sur la base du programme présenté.

La crise de citoyenneté, résultant de l'exclusion socioéconomique, est manifestée par la femme de diverses formes. L'exclusion sociale touchant les diplômées suite aux difficultés et même l'impossibilité d'accès au marché du travail sont à l'origine de leurs manifestations d'une manière continue et d'une façon très significative à coté des diplômés-hommes devant le Parlement et les locaux des ministères. Les femmes participent aussi activement aux grèves touchant les différents secteurs (santé, enseignement, collectivités locales…) et même aux grèves globales proposées par les syndicats et suivies par les citoyens. Ces manifestations jugeant de la gravité de la crise de citoyenneté prennent parfois des formes régionales; c'est le cas notamment au nord et à l'est. La marginalisation de ces régions et l'exclusion des femmes qui en a résulté provoquent même le sentiment d'une crise d'identité. Enfin, la crise de citoyenneté et la colère de la population, notamment celle des femmes, se sont matérialisées par des émeutes, notamment suite à l'application du Programme d'Ajustement Structurel et de l'exclusion sociale qui en a découlé.

Enfin, les diverses formes d'exclusion des femmes sont à l'origine des problèmes de prostitution, de contrebande, de délinquance, de violence, de drogue … Il s'agit là d'une autre forme de crise de citoyenneté à effet néfaste sur le bien-être global. Cette crise de citoyenneté et même d'identité prend une dimension plus préoccupante et plus grave lorsqu'elle se concrétise par une perte de vie humaine. C'est le cas des victimes de l'émigration clandestine, attirant de plus en plus de femmes, qui se chiffrent annuellement par centaines et même par milliers. Les différentes formes d'exclusion sociale des femmes provoquent, en effet, un désir massif de rejoindre le vieux continent pour une amélioration de leur condition de vie et à la recherche d'une meilleure citoyenneté ou d'un véritable statut du citoyen. Forcées par leurs conditions difficiles, elles acceptent même de rejoindre de nouvelles destinations, soit en se mariant avec des étrangers (européens ou autres), soit en acceptant de travailler dans des conditions très difficiles à l'étranger (travailleuses de sexe, domestiques, activités de drogue …).

Conclusions et implications

En dépit du cadre normatif s'inscrivant davantage dans la consécration de l'égalité entre les femmes et les hommes, de grandes différences sont encore à relever entre les proportions des femmes et des hommes, quant à la jouissance de certains droits, tels que le bénéfice des prestations de sécurité sociale; les emplois occupés par les femmes par rapport à ceux des hommes, le niveau des salaires, le risque d'exclusion, la proportion des femmes pauvres, les prédispositions à la précarité, l'analphabétisme, etc. Ces différences s'expliquent par des situations de fait où interfèrent aussi bien des éléments sociologiques, culturels que la situation économique et sociale de la femme. Quoi qu'il en soit, le manque d'accès aux opportunités et services peut, en fin de compte, affecter l'activité économique, politique et sociale des femmes et son émancipation par la suite. En outre, les différentes formes d'exclusion ayant touché les femmes ont contribué largement au déficit flagrant en matière de développement humain enregistré au Maroc. Elles entravent aussi l'épanouissement de la femme, provoquant un sentiment de marginalisation et une atteinte à sa citoyenneté et parfois même à son identité.

Conscient de la gravité du recul enregistré dans son développement humain et de la contribution de l'exclusion des femmes à ce déficit, le Maroc intègre de plus en plus l'approche genre dans ses politiques de développement. Cette intégration, exigée d'ailleurs par les Objectifs du Millénaire pour le Développement (OMD), dont l'objet consiste à relever les défis de la réduction de la pauvreté et des disparités basées sur le genre, pourrait ouvrir la voie à un accès égal aux ressources, aux opportunités et aux droits économiques et sociaux et à une reconsidération des femmes en tant qu'actrices à part entière dans le développement. Dans ce sens, des efforts ont été déployés, et dans divers domaines. D'importantes réformes législatives ont été engagées en vue d'éliminer la discrimination à l'égard des femmes, notamment l'adoption du Code de la famille, de la loi régissant la nationalité, de la loi régissant l'Etat civil, du Code du travail et du Code de procédure pénale et la modification du Code pénal. En outre, des stratégies nationales ont été adoptées pour l'équité et l'égalité entre les sexes sur les migrations, pour la généralisation de l'éducation de base et de la lutte contre la violence à l'égard des femmes. Par ailleurs, l'option pour la discrimination positive a permis une contribution significative des femmes au Parlement. Sur le plan du développement humain, l'initiative nationale (INDH),[8] visant à exclure l'exclusion, a introduit comme un de ses trois piliers solides l'approche genre, notamment dans les activités génératrices de revenus et d'emploi (AGRE). Toutes ces avancées ont été corroborées récemment par la désignation d'un nouveau gouvernement, avec une participation pesante des femmes qui se sont vu attribuer 8 portefeuilles.

Toutefois, les détériorations enregistrées, encore récemment, en matière de développement humain exigent de multiplier les efforts afin de mieux intégrer l'approche genre, de réduire les inégalités en termes de sexe et d'assurer ainsi l'épanouissement de la femme dans le cadre d'une véritable citoyenneté. Ces efforts passent, en premier lieu, par une activation des différentes lois permettant de lutter contre la discrimination des femmes. En effet, les lois qui protègent les droits des femmes existent bien, mais elles restent sans effet par manque de mise en pratique. A titre d'exemple, les nouveaux textes législatifs adoptés, comme le Code de la famille, sont encore méconnus, surtout des membres du pouvoir judiciaire, et ne sont pas appliqués dans toutes les régions du pays.

Un autre problème provient du fait que le public méconnaît les lois et ne fait pas la différence entre les lois et les attitudes et pratiques sociales. Dans ce cadre, des campagnes de sensibilisation du public, mettant en évidence les effets négatifs de discrimination dont la femme victime fait sur le développement de toute la société, doivent être envisagées dans une grande envergure. Il est aussi recommandé de mieux faire connaître leurs droits aux femmes en mettant en place des programmes de vulgarisation et une assistance juridique.

En plus de l'activation des lois, il convient de préciser que le Maroc est appelé à renforcer davantage son arsenal juridique afin de garantir l'égalité d'accès aux ressources et aux opportunités pour les deux sexes. En effet, tout en garantissant l'égalité devant la loi, la Constitution ne consacre pas le principe de l'égalité entre les femmes et les hommes dans tous les domaines et la législation ne contient pas de définition explicite du principe d'égalité entre les femmes et les hommes ni de la discrimination sexiste. Ainsi, il est préconisé de promulguer et de faire appliquer une loi générale relative à l'égalité des sexes, qui aurait une valeur contraignante dans le secteur public comme privé, et de faire connaître aux femmes les droits qui sont les leurs en vertu de ces textes. En outre, il faut signaler l'absence de lois visant expressément la violence à l'égard des femmes et des filles, notamment la violence dans la famille et la violence à l'égard des employées de maison.

Par ailleurs, certes l'épanouissement de la femme, sa citoyenneté et la réalisation du développement humain exigent une forte participation des femmes aux activités socioéconomiques et politiques. On déplore encore la très faible proportion de femmes occupant des postes de responsabilité dans tous les domaines, notamment à la Chambre des conseillers (1,1 %), dans les municipalités (0,53 %), dans les secteurs public et privé, dans l'appareil judiciaire, au ministère des Affaires étrangères et dans les milieux universitaires. En attendant que les femmes investissent délibérément ces champs, l'option pour la discrimination positive et son institutionnalisation afin d'intégrer les femmes aux rouages politiques et décisionnels sont très souhaitables. Cette discrimination positive est aussi indispensable pour encourager la femme à participer aux instances partisanes et à la politique en général.

Sur le plan social, les taux d'analphabétisme élevés chez les femmes et les filles, notamment en milieu rural, le taux élevé d'abandon scolaire parmi les filles ainsi que les difficultés de scolarisation auxquelles se heurtent celles qui sont employées de maison constituent un net indice de discrimination indirecte et un obstacle au développement humain et à l'exercice d'une véritable citoyenneté. Il convient, alors, de sensibiliser l'opinion à l'importance de l'éducation en tant que droit fondamental et condition de l'autonomisation des femmes et de prendre des mesures pour modifier les attitudes traditionnelles qui tendent à perpétuer la discrimination. En outre, et toujours sur le plan social, le taux élevé de mortalité infantile et maternelle, l'accès limité aux services de santé et de planification familiale et la fréquence des avortements clandestins qui mettent en danger la santé des femmes demeurent encore préoccupants. Des efforts sont à accomplir en vue d'améliorer l'accès des femmes aux soins de santé primaires, notamment pour ce qui est de la santé procréative et des moyens de planification de la famille.

Sur le plan socioéconomique, on regrette encore les possibilités limitées qui s'offrent aux femmes sur le marché de l'emploi, le très grand nombre parmi elles qui occupent des emplois peu qualifiés et faiblement payés, les mauvaises conditions de travail, la ségrégation par profession, l'écart persistant entre les salaires aussi bien dans le secteur public que privé et le nombre élevé de femmes travaillant dans le secteur informel où elles n'ont aucune protection sociale. Autrement, le Code du travail n'est pas bien appliqué, ce qui favorise la discrimination à l'égard des femmes. Des mesures d'inspection doivent être envisagées pour assurer une meilleure application de la législation du travail. En outre, il convient de concevoir des lois pour réglementer l'emploi des travailleuses domestiques et d'adopter une politique d'emploi soucieuse de l'égalité entre les sexes pour réglementer le travail des femmes dans le secteur informel et améliorer leur accès aux emplois dans le secteur formel. En guise de conclusion, des efforts sont à déployer pour lutter contre l'exclusion des femmes et contribuer ainsi à asseoir une véritable citoyenneté et des bases solides de développement humain. Néanmoins, la responsabilité n'incombe pas uniquement aux autorités, mais à l'ensemble des parties prenantes, en l'occurrence la femme elle-même, la société civile, le citoyen, les partis politiques, les intellectuels, les médias…

Notes

1. Ce jugement est à nuancer surtout pour certains pays musulmans dont les codes de familles s'inspirent de la religion, où la garde des enfants est accordée à la mère ou à sa famille à condition qu'elle ne se remarie pas.
2. Selon l'Union Inter-Parlementaire (UIP), en 2010, les femmes élues dans les Etats arabes aux Chambres basses représentent un pourcentage de 9 pour cent, contre une moyenne mondiale de 19 pour cent. Pour certains pays arabes, cette participation est inexistante, notamment en Arabie Saoudite, au Qatar ou encore à Oman.
3. L'éducation nationale accapare 25 pour cent du budget général, soit la part la plus élevée en comparant aux autres départements ministériels.
4. Les données statistiques sont tirées de diverses sources officielles : ministère de la Santé, ministère des Finances (Rapport genre), ministère du Développement Social et de la Famille, CEDAW, Banque mondiale...
5. Voir CEDAW : *Committee on the Elimination of Discrimination against Women.*
6. Certes, ce principe de discrimination positive a assuré une participation significative de la femme aux rouages décisionnels en l'absence d'un accès légitime et démocratique. Bien que cette discrimination soit sujette à controverse, elle demeure justifiée à l'état actuel où le suffrage universel ne peut pas contribuer à l'élection de la femme dans une société encore masculine.
7. RGPH : Recensement Général de la Population et de l'Habitat.
8. INDH : Initiative Nationale de Développement Humain.

Bibliographie

Ahern, P., Nuti, P. et Masteron, J., 2000, « Promoting gender equity in the democratic process: Womens path to political participation and decision-making », *PROWID Synthesis Paper*, Washington: CEDPA.

Alami Mchichi, H., 2001, « Inégalités d'accès à la citoyenneté : les discours politiques et la participation des femmes au champ politique au Maroc », Communication au colloque international sur « Genre, population et développement en Afrique », Abidjan 16-21 juillet.

Banque Mondiale, 2004, *Genre et développement au Moyen-Orient et Afrique du Nord : les femmes dans la sphère publique*, Washington, DC: Banque Mondiale.

Bourque, S. etGrossholtz, J., 1974, « Politis an unnatural practice: political science looks at female participation », *Politics and society*, n°4.

CEDAW, 2006, Rapport du Comité pour l'élimination de la discrimination à l'égard des femmes sur le Maroc.

CEDAW, 2008, Rapport du Comité pour l'élimination de la discrimination à l'égard des femmes sur le Maroc.

Chraibi, S., 2006, « La place des femmes marocaines dans la vie publique et dans la prise de décision », in *50 ans de développement humain au Maroc*, Publication collective.

Coquery-Vidrovitch, C., 1994, *Les Africaines: histoire des femmes d'Afrique noire du 19ème siècle*, Paris : Des jonquères.

Dagenais, H., 1994, *Femmes, féminisme et développement*. Montréal: McGill Univerity Press.

Dalloz, J.-P., 1991, « L'émergence des femmes politiques au Nigeria », *Politique africaine*, no 42.

Enhaili, A., 2006, « Femmes, Développement Humain et participation politique au Maroc », *Journal d'étude des relations internationales au Moyen-Orient*, Vol 1 n°1, juillet.

Githens, M., 1983, *The elusive paradigm: Gender, Politics and political behaviour: the state of arts*, Finiter Ed.

Karshenas, M. et Valentine M. Moghadam, 2006, « Social Policy in the Middle East: Introduction and Overview », dans Karshenas and Moghadam (dir.), *Social Policy in the Middle East: Economic, Political, and Gender Dynamics*, Londres: Palgrave Macmillan,.

Kathleen, J., 1990, « Citizenship in a women friendly-polity », *Signs Review*, n°4.

Kuznets, S., 1955, « Economic Growth and Income Inequality », *American Economic Review*, 45 (1) : 1-28.

Lazreg, 2000, *Citizenship, et gender in Algeria*. in Suad Joseph (ed.), "Gender et citizenship in the middle East" Syrasuse: Syracuse University Press.

Lister, R., 1997, *Citizenship : feminist perspectives*, New York: New York University Press.

Meer, S., et Sever, C., 2004, *Genre et citoyenneté : panorma*, Agence intergouvernementale de la francophonie.

Moghadam, Valentine M., 2007, « Gouvernance et participation citoyenne des femmes au Moyen-Orient et en Afrique du Nord », in La consultation régionale de la région MENA du CRDI intitulée *Droits des femmes et participation citoyenne*, Le Caire (Égypte): 9-11 décembre.

Mukhopadhyay, M., 2003, *Governing for equity, gender, citizenship and governance*, Amsterdam: Royal topical Institute.

Naciri, R., 2006, « Les droits des femmes », in *50 ans de développement humain au Maroc*, Publication collective, www.rdh50.ma

Papaneck, H., 1994, "The ideal women et the ideal society: control et autonomy in the construction of identity", Valentine M. Moghadam (editor) in *Identity Politics et Women. Culturel Reassertions et feminisms in International perspectives* Boulder, CO: Westview Press.

Patenam, C., 1988, The sexual contact, Cambridge: Polity Press.

Phillips, A., 1991, *Engendering democracy*, Cambridge: Polity Press.

Phillips, A., 1993, *Democracy et difference*, Cambridge: Polity Press.

PNUD, 1995, *Rapport mondial pour le développement humain*. Paris: Economica.

PNUD, 2000, *Women's political participation and good governance*, New York: 21st Century Challenges.

Rapport de Développement Humain, 2005, *Femmes et dynamiques de développement*. Rapport piloté par le Haut Commissariat au Plan en collaboration avec le PNUD.

Rapport sur le budget genre, 2007, ministère de l'Economie et des finances, www.finances.gov.ma

Ministère de l'Economie et des finances, 2008, *Rapport sur le budget genre* www.finances.gov.ma

Ministère de la Santé, 1993, Enquête Nationale sur la Population et la Santé (ENPS-II) 1992, DHS, Service des Etudes et de l'Information Sanitaire, 279 p.

Ministère de la Santé, 1999, *Enquête Nationale sur la Santé de la Mère et de l'Enfant* (ENSME) 1997, PAPCHILD, Service des Etudes et de l'Information Sanitaire.

Ruddick, S., 1997, "The idea of fatherhood" In Hidle lindemman Nelson (edited by), *Feminisme et families*, New York: Routledge.

Sassi, N., 1995, « Les femmes algériennes aujourd'hui, quels choix politiques ? » in Ephesia (collectif), *La place des femmes, les enjeux de l'égalité et de l'identité au regard des sciences sociales*, Paris: La Découverte.

Secrétariat d'Etat Chargé de l'Alphabétisation et de l'Education non formelle, 2007; Enquête Nationale sur l'Analphabétisme, la Non Scolarisation et la Déscolarisation au Maroc.

Sen, A., 1992, *Poverty re-examined*, Cambridge: Havard University Press.

Sen, A., 1999, *Development as Freedom*, Oxford: Oxford University Press, UK.

Sever, 2004, *Genre et citoyenneté: boîte à outils*, Agence intergouvernementale de la francophonie.

Sinha, K., 2003, « Citizenship degraded: Indian women in a modern state and a pre-modern society », *Gender and development*, Vol. 11, No 3.

Sweetman, C., 2003, « Gender and citizenship », *Editorial Gender and development*, Vol. 11, No 3.

Union interparlementaire, 2007, Les femmes au Parlement, Rapport annuel.

Vicky, R., 1991, « Feminism and political analysis », *Political Studies,* Vol 34.

Voet, R., 1998, Feminism et Citizenship, London: Sage publications.

Wolfensolin, J. D. et Bourguignon F., 2004, *Développement et réduction de la pauvreté : revoir le passé, penser l'avenir* ; document préparé pour les assemblées annuelles de la Banque mondiale et le Fonds monétaire internationale, octobre, Washington.

Yuval-Davis, N., 1993, « Gender et Nation », *Ethnic et racial studies*, Vol. 16, N° 4.

Yuval-Davis, N., 1997, « Women, citizenship et difference », *Feminist Review* N° 57.

Ziky, M. et Rigar, M., 2006, *Citoyenneté et Développement au Maroc Face aux Différentes Formes d'Exclusion : Rétrospectives et Enjeux Futurs*, GMT, CODESRIA.

Zirari, H., 2006, *Évolution des conditions de vie des femmes au Maroc*, in « 50 ans de développement humain au Maroc », Publication collective www.rdh50.ma

9

Uganda's Gendered Polity Since 1995: Reconstitution of the Public Sphere to Enhance the Presence and Participation of Women

Sabastiano Rwengabo

Introduction

The 1995 Constitution of Uganda signified the reconstitution of the public sphere to enhance the presence and participation of women in governance. Two global forces coincided with, and have aided, this development: third wave democratisation, and the campaign for the emancipation of women. These forces lay on a fertile ground in Uganda. The National Resistance Movement (NRM) government, having acquired power through a civil war (1981-86), tried to reconstitute the politics of the country by shifting, so to speak, from the bullet to the ballot in determining the country's political destiny. The government also sought to promote the emancipation of women, partly to reward them for their role in the bush war, and partly as a response to the demands for women's emancipation. These considerations precipitated relevant constitutional provisions, hence the subsequent institutional and structural changes in governance that followed these provisions. Bullet-to-ballot change and women's involvement would provide a 'reputational shield' (Ivarsflaten 2007) to the NRM (known as the Movement), a former rebel force that had claimed to be fighting to liberate Uganda. The rebel movement had got support from the *wananchi* (citizens). It now sought to 'transform' itself from a military to an elected government. This would help secure international legitimacy in a world experiencing a wave of democratisation and advances in the emancipation of women.

Writers on post-1995 governance and democratisation in Uganda have stressed the democratic ethos promised (and practised?) by the government, as observed in regular, free and fair elections, as well as in allowing women to participate in running government at all levels (Makara *et al.* 2003; Republic of Uganda 1995, 2005; Ssali and Atoo 2008). These and other works have shown a shift from a 'revolution' to a 'democracy'; from a military to an elected government; as well as the opening of the public sphere to women. Evidence of women's participation in all levels of government, as provided for under the law, has been reflected in affirmative action to enhance the presence and upgrade the position of women. Less recognised in the literature, however, is the influence of two global forces – democratisation and the campaign for the emancipation of women – in catalysing the Ugandan government's intention to reward women for their role in the armed struggle (Museveni 1997.) This paper attempts to fill the gap.

The two global processes of democratisation[1] and the campaign for women's emancipation coincided with the entry of women into Uganda's public sphere. First, this was part of a longstanding struggle by women; secondly, their entry was a reward from the government for their contribution to the liberation struggle. There were also feminist demands from women leaders for inclusion in governance of society, especially through increased political participation at local and national levels. The campaign for women's political empowerment thrived on the knowledge that women had assisted the National Resistance Movement/Army (NRM/A) to evolve, metamorphose and succeed in taking state power in 1986. Women had taken part as rebels and rebel commanders; others worked as spies; some shielded and hid rebels and provided them with food; while others still, such as Edith Nyugunyu, who typed the original Ten-Point Programme of the NRM/A, had rendered technical services in the 1981-1986 war effort (Museveni 1997). NRM policies have been centred on this Ten-Point Programme, which has since 2003 been expanded to fifteen. It was very logical for such women – mothers, daughters and sisters of Ugandans who sacrificed for the struggle – to be brought into governance of the society.

In addition, global forces pushed countries of the South to democratise. Political elites in the South utilised democratisation processes to further entrench themselves. '[T]he local habitat will still determine concrete responses to globalisation processes, thereby moulding, to some extent, the shape and strength (and also influence) of globalisation' (Tranvik and Selle 2007). Thus, global waves of democratisation that swept across the African continent influenced certain ways of organising social relationships in various local contexts. The local actor was striving for a niche in these new establishments (Gloppen and Rakner 2007:195).

Against this background, the inclusion of women in state structures was constitutionalised and institutionalised. The Constitution forms the benchmark of national legislation and governance. As a means by which leaders can legalise and legitimise their actions/policies, it allows citizens the right to take part in the 'Assembly' and to serve in its juries (Sabine and Thorson 1973: 105). Equal participation means equality of participants. With campaigns for gender equity already gaining momentum in 1990s, the entrenchment of this 'equity' was backed by subsequent legal provisions relating to local governance as well as elections during the post-1995 era in Uganda (Republic of Uganda 1995, 1997, 2000, 2005). Women have tried to use these legal and institutional mechanisms to secure meaningful and recognised participation in all structures of government.

The post-1995 period in Uganda may be characterised as one of political stability, a Constitution in place, and regular elections.[2] It is the longest period of political stability in post-colonial Uganda. During the same period, women began to feature significantly in the public realm. It was also a time when, through constitutionally established state structures, citizenship was expressed and exercised on a regular basis, both in terms of ideas (through debates) and practically (through such actions as elections). Such a period is vital for a gendered analysis of developments in the country, particularly those regarding women in public sphere. The idea of citizenship is useful in the analysis of such a period in the history and development of a country that has, since independence, been bedevilled by political instability, state malfunctioning, civil wars and interruptions of democracy.

Citizenship in Theory and Practice: Positioning Women

Citizenship is complex, multi-level and multidimensional. There may be citizenship as defined by the state, local communities, groups, ethnic groups and residents in a locality. In this usage, it implies the legal recognition of a person as a resident and national of a state/country. The 1991 Citizenship Charter spells out the rights of citizens, such as the right to redress where a public service fails to meet certain standards (Pearsall 2002:260). By implication, the state has responsibility for its citizens. National constitutions spell out this responsibility (Republic of Uganda 1995). Citizenship then is a state construction of a political status assigned to individuals in relation to belonging to certain communities, or as a set of social practices that define the relationship between people and the state; and among peoples within communities, particularly with regard to institutions and legal rules established by the state (Canning and Rose 2001).[3] This idea relates to responsible and responsive leadership and, in developing country context, the transformational leadership (Aseka 2005) needed to spark off socio economic transformation. Such definitions and explanations conceptualise a modern citizen, but then leave out the idea of dual citizenship common in scholarly debates and legal decisions today (Bloemraad 2004; Republic of Uganda 2005; Waters 2003).[4] Citizenship, in a modern sense (and probably in Ancient Greek terms), carries with it civil, political and social rights (Canning and Rose 2001).

In the pre-colonial Africa, a citizen implied *omutuuragye, mukaagi* (a resident) – as opposed to *omwiziizi/enshangaangi* (a newcomer/wanderer), or *omunya-mahaanga* (a foreigner/alien from the other land/country). Migrants satisfied certain conditions before being recognised as citizens. These conditions related to conduct, sociability and longevity of residence. In a Greek city-state, where the idea of democracy (*demos kratos*) started, a citizen was considered an adult male who could be allowed to take part in decisions affecting the polity, mainly in an *ekklesia* (General Assembly). Citizens who were members of an *ekklesia* were entitled to take part in its political life. This was a privilege obtained by birth, for a Greek remained a citizen of the city to which his parents belonged (Sabine and Thorson 1973:21-73). And in Plato and Aristotle's view, every adult man shared in the duties and privileges of government, while governments derived their just powers from the consent of the governed (*ibid*:105,142). It implied equality, since all citizens had equal participation. Hence the ancient and traditional understanding of citizenship excluded foreigners, women and children, some of whom (in some societies) were regarded as secondary citizens. Citizens were defined by households, with a man representing the totality of his family as the head. This has since changed. Now, one can become a citizen by descent, origin, birth, registration or naturalisation (Republic of Uganda 1995), and one can have dual citizenship (Republic of Uganda 2005; Waters 2003).

Citizenship is an important basis of identity and state responsibility for the well-being of the people. All persons under the jurisdiction of the state, and who pay allegiance to the said state, are its citizens. These may be resident in, or outside, its territorial boundaries. This excludes migrant part-time labourers, refugees and visitors who may be dependent on the state (in whose territorial boundaries they are presently resident) for certain services but are not recognised by law as citizens. Equality of citizens is promised and premised on the understanding that there should be non-discrimination by the state in rendering services, and there should (paradoxically?) be considerate treatment for disadvantaged groups. The idea of equality before the law derives from this liberal notion of modern citizenship, which includes women.

Paradoxically, the definition of some aspects of citizenship remains elusive. It implies something one can have as a whole and not in part, which everyone has (or may not have) in the same degree. It encompasses citizen rights and the status of nationality (Ruth 1937; Studer 2001).[5] Citizen rights implies that one has been integrated into the sociopolitical and judicial space that carries with it universal rights and obligations; while nationality implies inclusion in the *national* community. Therefore, citizenship in this analysis will be used in the context of nationality. This is because married women today are not forced to renounce their (other, if any) nationality *(ibid)*. So, equality of gender and persons comes in here, in contrast to what obtained in Greek democracy.

We may talk of multilevel citizenship (based on the idea of the nation-state, transnational and global citizenships). One may talk of heterogeneous citizenship in developed countries, where the compatibility of many forms of citizenship is possible; or differential citizenship involving the exercise of civic powers and capacities, hence the multiplicity and irreducibility of the concept, as opposed to uniformitarian citizenship. By implication, at different times and in different spaces, citizenship differs. Exercise of multiple civic capabilities does not limit one to single citizenship; hence not all citizenships can be constituted in nation-state citizenships (Hudson 2003).

Similarly, gender equality does not take place in the void; there must be a state to allow for its possibility. In patriarchal societies, which most African societies still are, gender equality is a struggle for the emancipation of women, so that both sexes are seen as equal citizens and participants in political affairs.

Gender-sensitive political participation implies 'free politics' and equality without discrimination on the basis of sex differences. While free politics historically predates democracy (Crick 2007), the campaign for gender equality is a modern attempt at ensuring freer politics, social relations and cultural practices that avail both sexes equal opportunities. On the basis of this thinking, democratic practices, which had taken root in the West/North and were spreading to the South, were accompanied by struggles for the emancipation of women.

Two Global Processes: Democratisation in Africa or Globalisation of 'Democracy'?

The third wave of democratisation, in the African context, is seen in post-colonial elections of governments and the reforms of the 1980s (Huntington 1991; Kiiza *et al.* 2008). Democracy itself remains an elusive term, but may be defined, for the purpose of this contextual analysis, as a mechanism for sociopolitical and governance practices and values that allow citizens control over their own destinies, and ensures equality for all within the polity (Dahl 1998). This equality and control over the political agenda can be expressed, in part, through regular, free and fair elections (Bwengye 1985; Bratton and van de Walle 1997), participation in public management, as well as other practices that ensure that *the people* are in charge. It is these experiments that were prescribed for, and the swept across, Africa, in what Huntington calls 'third wave democratisation'. The first wave had swept across Europe with the constitutionalisation of monarchies in Western and Central Europe (characterised by revolutions, such as the one in France in 1789; see Nabudere 1983); establishment of constitutional governments in the USA; and the rights campaign. The second had occurred in Eastern Europe when the triumph of capitalism led to the decline of socialism and the establishment of elected governments in former socialist states (Huntington 1991). Then came Africa – having decolonised, it was now the epicentre of democratisation. It is not the purpose of this paper to debate the Huntington waves, or delve into issues of whether or not Africa has democratised or is still entangled in a democratic crisis, but to examine the reconstitution of the public sphere to enhance the presence and participation of women when Uganda/ Africa was 'democratising', and the source of these forces.

Contemporary democratisation in Africa was a Western construct, involving notions foreign to Africa, such as election of leaders (Bwengye 1985) and subsequent disempowerment and dethronement of traditional leaders (Kabwegyere 1995). This is not to say that there was no democracy in Africa, but that post-colonial Africa experimented with Western notions of democracy. Moreover, new states had been established over geographical entities, with some kingdoms and empires killed and others split. By implication, the new states – colonial and later post-colonial – were the ones 'democratising'. Because [electoral] democracy had become a catchword in the West, it was prescribed for Africa by the West. Countries and governments had to cope with this demand by appearing to be democratising. Rebel movements such as the NRA promised democratic governance (Museveni 1997). This would allow the rebels to appear as liberators and legitimise their fight. New practices and ideas then being prescribed and popularised, such as gender equality, were incorporated into the new governance. It may also be added that the link between globalisation and local politics was that political globalisation led to a uniform system of governance all over the world, in the form of democracy. This uniform governance involved steps towards gender equality in the political/public realms.

The Campaign for the Emancipation of Women

In the 1980s, cries for gender equality were intensified by feminists who decried the untold misdeeds of men towards women. Democratisation itself was meaningless if it did not bring women in the public realm and ensure equality of persons, irrespective of gender. This necessitated political empowerment of women – as voters, electoral candidates and political leaders.

Empowerment of women derived from the understanding that men dominated most spheres of life and women were marginalised. No social institution allowed equality of gender. Religion itself favoured men over women. In fact, women's position in society was regulated by religious institutions at family and community levels. Custom and tradition, usually justified on religious grounds, ensured women's conformity to conventional gender roles, which led to powerlessness, pain and exploitation (Sweetman 1998:2). Women were thus relegated to the private realm and restricted to their roles as wives, mothers and transmitters of cultural and religious beliefs (Mukhopadhayay 1995). This made it important for their behaviour to be regulated (by men) (Sweetman 1998; Ruether 1990). Women's political and economic power was minimal globally. In other words, women suffered injustices both in the public and private realms. Emancipationists sought to challenge the above injustices against women.

One of the arguments advanced for the struggle for the empowerment of women was that the problem of women had been men. In the South, it was argued that , cultural relativity is patronising, and potentially allows for violations of women's rights. Men in the South tend to argue that gender equality is a Western construct, thereby justifying their continued subjugation of women (Sweetman 1998:3). Feminists challenged this. They revealed how women's marginalisation was inherent in colonialism, in traditional African societies, and was entrenched in social systems. They showed how gender has been a social construct that 'describes the traits and behaviour that are regarded by the culture as appropriate to men and women' (Brannon 2005:15); hence a social label, not a description of biology. Feminist arguments led to the emergence and development of political and cultural movements bidding for political power, legal and constitutional reforms, and social reconstitution that would allow women's voices to be heard. These movements base their claims on notions of religious, ethnic and national identity. There have been recently developed attitudes toward women and attempts to curtail female freedom and sexuality by invoking woman as a cultural symbol. Women have responded; some were subdued, some resisted (Mahgadam 1994). There has been repeated advice to women to 'challenge the oppressive structures in the global community, their country and their church' (Musimbi-Kanyoro and Robbins 1992). For this trend of marginalisation and subjugation to be reversed, women's participation in the politics of their countries – as candidates, voters and public servants – and in making decisions affecting their lives, had to be secured. This entails 'destroying' a men-only public sphere and establishing a gender-sensitive one.

The Idea of Participation

Campaigners for the emancipation of women have demanded, *inter alia*, gender equality in political participation. Participation goes hand-in-hand with empowerment. It involves taking part in the socioeconomic, political, administrative and cultural spheres of one's life. This can be direct (for instance, through meetings); representational (by electing representatives of a group, constituency, club or association); political (through elected and appointed local and central government legislators, advocates and other lobbyists) or information-based (through collection and channelling of important information to the decision points, mainly to influence policy) (Sidorenko 2006). Participation empowers one to develop confidence and willingness to take part in decisions affecting one's life at the micro (community) and macro (national) levels. Yet participation has its own challenges.

Oakley and Mardsen (1984) observe that only a few countries have achieved meaningful women participation in all development programmes and formal organisation structures. Women, the literature echoes, have been relegated when it comes to participation in decision making, especially at the policy level. Participation challenges the hegemonic position of dominant forces and groups; hence, it is counter-hegemonic and antithetic to that domination. It therefore meets resistance and the channels through which it can be attained are deliberately blocked by the relevant dominant forces.

Limited participation by women in elections and other political activities has been exploited. Not only are they deprecated in oral and written speech, they are also confronted with traditional values which further limit their involvement. Those who have gotten a chance have used fellow women as stepping-stones to achieve their interests. Lack of information further complicates women's role as active political participants. Their multiple roles as housewives, mothers and breadwinners tend to keep them away from the public realm. Even when their situation has been considered, politicians have used their plight to win electoral success for themselves. Where women have played a meaningful role, they have remained only in the vicinity of recognition. Tripp (2000), for instance, shows how Ugandan women were marginalised during colonial and post-colonial periods in the public sphere, until they were mainstreamede by the Movement government:

> No women held seats in Parliament from 1962 until the NRM came to power in 1986, apart from Visram and Lubega whom the Buganda *Lukiiko* delegation sent to the National Assembly in 1962, and the brief presence of Rhoda Kalema and Geraldine Bitamazire in 1979-80 and Theresa Odongo-Oduka in 1980-85. Women fared no better in local and urban councils, in which they (the women) made up only 2 per cent of all delegates' (White 1973:223; Tripp 2000:39).

Women in the NRA/M Struggle, and later in Uganda's Public Sphere

Constitutional and Institutional Reconstitution since 1995

Women took part as rebels and rebel commanders in the earlier struggles of the National Resistance Army/Movement (NRA/M). Some former women rebels, such as Brigadier Proscovia Nalweyiso, maintain their professional military role in the Uganda People's Defence Forces (UPDF). Some represent the UPDF in Parliament as provided for in the Constitution. Others worked as spies; some shielded and hid rebels and provided them with food. During the war in the area that came to be termed as the 'Luwero Triangle',[6] NRA rebels depended on the gardens and livestock of local people for food, mainly grown by women.

Tripp (2000) reveals the earlier position of women in the political structures of Uganda. While they were actively involved in the struggle to reconstruct the state, they secured for themselves some influence on the politics of the country because of their role in the rebellion. 'Women had earned considerable respect through their participation in the 1980-85 guerrilla struggle against Obote's forces, which had helped them establish themselves as a force to reckon with' (*ibid.*61). Indeed the NRM saw 'women's endorsement as critical to the regime's success'. So they encouraged them to form clubs at Local Council One (LC I) level; supported their leadership in the LC system, and reserved one seat for a woman secretary at all council levels. This was already the practice during the guerrilla war in areas which the NRA controlled, such as Luwero and later Western Uganda (*ibid*:69-70). The immediate period following the 1986 NRA/M takeover witnessed women's continued struggle for inclusion in the governance of Uganda, and government. Although the president was at first reluctant (Tripp 2000), he had no choice but to open up political space for them. Fortunately, women had enough connections in the government from their guerrilla war period to remind the government firmly that they had been lobbying for women's participation even before the NRM came to power.

The president asked women lobbyists, led by the National Council of Women (NCW) and Action for Women in Development (ACFODE) to identify potential women leaders. Their recommendations were accepted. By 1989, 8 out of 75 ministers were women. By 1995, women constituted 17 per cent of all ministers, 21 per cent of all permanent secretaries and 35 per cent of all Under-Secretaries. Sixteen per cent of all district administrators by 1995 were women. By 1994, there were four women judges (17 %) and five chief magistrates (23 %). The women had also taken on various positions in government.[7] These positions were secured not only because women had the requisite qualifications (even though men had had more chances of education than women in the colonial and post-colonial period), but also because of their varied contributions to the bush war.

In 1989, the National Resistance Council (NRC, Parliament of the time) was constituted with collegially elected representatives, and only two women (Rhoda Kalema and Victoria Ssekitoleko) won seats in open contest against male candidates. In any case, 34 seats had been reserved for women. Three women were appointed to the NRC by the president, two of whom '*were historical members of the NRM appointed because of their participation in the guerrilla war ...*' (Tripp 2000:71, emphasis added). It was logical for such women – mothers, daughters and sisters of Ugandans who sacrificed for the struggle, and who themselves risked their lives for the liberation of the country – to be brought into the mainstream of governance, and to have a share of the resources and power now controlled by their government.

The NRM government adopted an affirmative action strategy to make place for women in parliament. This 'ring-fencing' ensured that women had guaranteed access to Parliament and Local Councils, through provisions for women-only electoral districts and electoral areas. Every district must, by law, be represented by a woman in Parliament – locally known as District Women

Members of Parliament. At district and sub-county levels, at least one-third of the council positions must be reserved for women, and there are legal provisions for the demarcation of these electoral areas (Republic of Uganda 1997; Local Governments Act Cap 142, as amended; Sections 108-110).

The impact these provisions have had on women's citizenship is double pronged: first, women have had uninterrupted access to legislative organs; secondly, they are free to contest as directly elected legislators at parliamentary and local government levels; thirdly, Ugandans are now used to voting for women as representatives, with some women performing better than men in these institutions of governance. It should be noted that the affirmative action strategy and reserved seats for women has long been a demand of the international women's movement, which realised that it is not easy to have an equal contest between men and women in patriarchal societies. This was carried through by the Ugandan women's movement, thereby linking democratic developments in Uganda with global processes through networking.

To some extent, the campaign for the emancipation of women and democratisation processes worldwide instituted public recognition of the importance of women as social and political actors and citizens. It was clear to the political leadership in Uganda after 1986 that had it not been for the contribution of women, the struggle would have taken a different turn. Moreover, the restoration of law and order, reconstruction of the then dilapidated economy and state (Kabwegyere 1995; Aseka 2005), enhancement of local productivity and improvement of social harmony could not be accomplished by men alone. Still, the emancipation of women could not be achieved by merely saying they were free to participate in all spheres of public life, including elective politics. It was well known that the patriarchal society and traditional values around them would act as obstacles. Therefore, deliberate legal and institutional provisions had to be put in place to aid the advancement of women.

Constitutional (Legal) and Institutional Reconstitution of the Public Sphere

Bringing Women into the Public Realm

One of the most important instruments for reconstituting Uganda's public sphere was the promulgation of the 1995 Constitution.[8] The Constitution provided for equality of all citizens and for non-discrimination on the basis of gender and other sectarian grounds. It provided for special positions in government that would be filled by women (Republic of Uganda 1995). Operational laws made in accordance with the Constitution made provision for bringing women into the public realm. The 1997 Local Governments Act (LGA) cap. 243, for instance, provided that at least one third of the members of district and sub-county councils shall be women [(LGA, 10(e)]. It provided for two youth councillors and two councillors for people with disabilities (PWDs) in each of the district and sub-county councils. One of each of these must be a female (Sections: 10, 23). This provision in local governments was extended to national level.

Parliamentary Elections Acts (1996, 2000, and 2005) provided for the same, with women forming at least one-third of the Members of Parliament. While districts are divisible into various constituencies, each district has a woman representative in Parliament. Women are also allowed to contest as directly elected Members of Parliament (MPs) representing constituencies. Some, such as Eng. Winnie Byanyima, Cecilia Ogwal and Janet Mukwaya, trounced men in constituency elections. Following the 2006 elections, Uganda had 14 women as directly elected MPs (Ssali and Atoo 2008).[9]

It may even appear to some that women now have more opportunity to contest for positions than men. Uganda's Parliament is composed of directly elected constituency MPs; district women MPs; five MPs representing people with disabilities (at least one of whom must be a woman); ten representatives of the Uganda People's Defence Forces (two of whom must be women); five workers' MPs (one of whom must be a woman); five youth MPs (one of whom must be a woman) (Parliamentary Elections Act No. 17, 2005, 8 (1)-(5)); and *ex-officio* MPs, mainly cabinet ministers not appointed from among the MPs.

Thus, women's representation was systematised at all levels of national and local governance and public life, with women enabled to venture into previously men-only spaces, and men excluded from venturing in some women's political spaces. Legally and institutionally, women's presence and participation in politics and governance of society was enhanced and entrenched. The quality and effect of this participation is outside the scope of this analysis, but women have certainly contributed meaningfully as legislators, civil servants, academics, and as advocates of important values and policies.

Women's participation has not been limited to these constitutional and political arrangements. Cabinet appointments have recognised women as important partners in the governance of society. There are remarkable public figures in Uganda's governance structures. Examples of the former Vice-President, Dr. Specioza Wandera Kazibwe, appointed in 1996 until 2001;

and current women cabinet ministers and MPs. The Inspector-General of Government, Justice Faith Mwondha; Chairperson of the Uganda Human Rights Commission (UHRC), Mrs. Margaret Ssekajja; Deputy Speaker of Parliament, Rt. Hon. Rebecca Kadaga; Justice Leticia Kikonyogo (Supreme Court); Colonel Namakula and Brig. Proscovia Nalweyiso (UPDF); Justice Juliet Ssebutinde (former head of commissions of inquiry into corruption in Uganda's public institutions, who now heads the UN Tribunal trying crimes in Liberia-Sierra Leone); Allen Kagina (Commissioner-General, Uganda Revenue Authority); women in the political opposition; academics (such as Joy Kwesiga, and Sylvia Tamale); as well as women active in civil society, all speak for themselves.[10]

It is, however, arguable that the government has used these processes to legitimise its policies and win public support and sympathy from female voters. The fact that females, especially in rural Uganda, voted for Museveni, is well known. Hence while these processes were doing their part, 'the local habitat' was still determining 'concrete response to globalisation processes, thereby moulding, to some extent, the shape and strength of globalisation' to his local condition and survival (Tranvik and Selle 2007). The politicisation of global processes signifies that those processes themselves were political. There was an objective behind their popularisation and internationalisationwhich led to their failure to attain their promised objectives, although, perhaps, a lot still needs to be done to reach the desired end. Something is still missing in the emancipation of women.

Women in the Public Sphere: The Missing Link in the Political Empowerment of Women

The difficulties women experience in undertaking activities outside the home result from the behaviour of dominant groups, mainly men and some adamant women, who want to maintain unequal relations between men and women (Peleman 2003). Policy measures to reduce situations that obstruct women's presence and participation in the public sphere seldom have the anticipated success, partly because all components of the restrictive circumstances and the power relations at stake are not known (*ibid.*). This means that the failure of citizens to participate in politics is a deficit – a 'citizenship deficit' (Chesterman 2001; Rouban 1999; Hudson and Kene 2000; Siim 2000).

In Uganda, there is a feeling that the government is reaping electoral gains from the public advancement of women. The merits of reserving seats for women ('ring-fencing') at all levels of government are debatable. Some commentators argue that this measure is politically motivated. It is aimed at winning women's votes and censures a women's bloc vote for President Museveni and his government, and a solid vote for female NRM candidates in Parliament. Others argue that the measure is positive. It is aimed at encouraging women to enter political life (and strengthen their acceptance in the rest of the public realm), and become politically visible so that the electorate gets used to voting for women as leaders and representatives (such as legislators – Members of Parliament – and councillors) (Tripp 2000:71). This idea has been incorporated into schools and institutions of higher learning, through the elections of prefects and members of student councils. Yet the debate continues on the merits and demerits of reserving seats for women.

A meaningful emancipation campaign ought to address issues of perception so that no sex presents the other as exclusively favoured, and no sex should allow itself to be so used. There is a feeling in some quarters that gender equality is coming to mean the marginalisation of men (Olai 2008). For Olai, 'we can't fight gender inequality when we only redirect it towards men'.[11] Hence the fight for gender equality may be misconstrued as being misdirected against men. Nevertheless, there should not be total disregard of women who may be marginalising and mistreating men and fellow women; secondly, one must not assume that women do not exploit men at all. The need to balance gender emancipation and women's responsibilities, and the need to enlighten both men and women about the importance of a gender equitable society, is still missing in the emancipationists' 'information brochure'.

The Museveni government has endorsed the emancipation of women, but has at the same time exploited the rhetoric of women's mobilisation to win women's endorsement and votes (Tripp 2000:102). It has done so by presenting a few women public figures to win the hearts of the majority rural poor and unsuspecting urban women. Women who have come up, then, become agents of the government for mobilisation of further support, instead of assisting fellow women through meaningful mobilisation and project establishments. This has made the presence and participation of women in the public sphere an exclusive opportunity for women elites.

Otto (2008) has documented the various constraints to the emancipation of women. She reveals that while government policies such as democratisation, decentralisation and affirmative action have enhanced women's contribution in local governance, several things continue to limit women. Low levels of education, low self-esteem, lack of confidence, gender stereotypes, cultural rigidities, low economic status, lack of exposure, and insecurity, still constrain women's presence and participation in the politics of their societies (Otto 2008:iii). This is echoed in Ssali and Atoo (2008), who reveal that although women's participation in the 2006 elections showed some improvements, they are still limited to reserved seats in the legislative system (Parliament and Local Councils). This is shown in the fact that of the 208 directly elected parliamentary constituencies, only fourteen are represented by women in Parliament. So, only fourteen women were able to defeat men in open electoral contests for parliamentary seats. Moreover, fewer women than men had contested these seats.

Conclusion

The globalisation of democratic values and the campaign for the emancipation of women were global processes. They influenced the reconstitution of the public sphere to enhance the presence and participation of women. However, these were not enough in themselves to cause significant change in Uganda. There are countries that have witnessed the waves of democratisation and the emancipation campaign yet increased participation by women in the public sphere has not taken place. Thus, there are country-specific experiences that, as in the Ugandan case, make it more worthwhile and rewarding to reconstitute the public sphere and engender participation in public, especially political affairs.

Women have been struggling to take advantage of a deliberate government policy to empower them. They have been involved in the general struggle for the socioeconomic and political transformation of Uganda, and could not be relegated by the new government that assumed power through a civil war in which they had actively been involved. For this reconstitution to be effected and women's reward sustained, there had to be constitutional and institutional mechanisms in place to allow for an equal presence and participation of men and women in the political sphere. That some women have not fully utilised this opportunity is a result of the socio-cultural and economic impediments that have for long favoured the subjugation of women by men. As equal citizens, men and women are exposed to equal opportunities; as a hitherto marginalised group, women have been accorded deliberate affirmative action. Some have, but some have not, benefited from this emancipation. As this struggle continues, an attempt at alleviating the socio-cultural, economic, environmental, educational, political and other gendered constraints to increased women's participation is worth undertaking.

This involves seeking to balance the roles of both sexes with new public roles, and ensuring the continuity of the family institution as a basic unit of the community. The role of men in sustainable women's emancipation is central. Thus while globalisation of democracy and the emancipation of women were necessary but not sufficient forces behind the reconstitution of the public sphere to increase the presence and participation of women in Uganda, they catalysed the already existing 'project' by contributing to the takeover of power by the Movement. It is the maintenance and sustenance of this 'women's liberation' that needs to be guarded jealously, by both men and women, public and non-public actors, from the family to the societal level, because women played a vital role in realising this reconstitution. The analysis of women's presence and participation in the public sphere in Africa, therefore, must take into account women's struggles for this attainment. It has not been achieved on a silver platter. And the struggle continues.

In Uganda's particular context, it is not enough to say that women have surfaced in the public sphere, that they have increased and improved their participation in politics at all levels, when some sections of society consider the development a creation of the Museveni government; a process of marginalisation of men; discrimination against the boy-child; and/or Western stereotypes. Sensitisation of men about the partnership they have with their spouses; the benefits accruing from equal treatment of both men and women; and women's role in socioeconomic transformation of society, is still lacking.

Since the 1995 Constitution was promulgated, a process of democratisation has been on-going in Uganda. Men and women have featured as equal citizens in all spheres of life. If democratisation implies the emancipation of women, then Uganda is treading the right path. Advocates of women's emancipation have reason to smile, considering the challenges women have faced in Uganda. However, the marginalisation of women still remains evident in some areas – both deliberately and inadvertently caused by members of the public and the government. More needs to be done to improve women's participation in Uganda's politics and their political citizenship.

Notes

1. This may be seen in Samuel Huntington's 'Third Wave Democratisation', which, he argues, swept across the developing world in the late 20th century. See Huntington, S.P., 1968, *Political Order in Changing Societies*, New Haven: Yale University Press; and Huntington, S.P., 1991, *The Third Wave: Democratisation in the Late Twentieth*

Century, Norman: University of Oklahoma Press; or Przeworski, A. and F. Limongi, 1997, 'Modernisation: Theories and Facts', *World Politics,* 49:2 (1997), pp. 155-83.

2. Political stability is used here to imply the continued hold over state power by the same government (under the same President) without being interrupted by a coup, military/revolutionary overthrow or electoral defeat. Following the 1995 Constitution, elections were held in 1996 and 1997; 2001 and 2002; and 2006. Whether these elections have been free and fair, met international standards or were acceptable to stakeholders, is outside the scope of this analysis. For an analysis of the 1996/7, 2001/2, and the 2006 elections in Uganda, see Makara *et al.* 2003; Tumwine-Mukubwa 2004; Aseka 2005; Rwengabo 2008; and Kiiza *et al.* 2008.

3. Canning, Kathleen and Rose, Sonya O., 2001, 'Gender Citizenship and Subjectivity: Some Historical and Theoretical Considerations', *Gender and History,* 13(3):427-443.

4. Bloemraad, I., 2004, 'Who claims dual citizenship? The limits of postnationalism, the possibilities of transnationalism, and the persistence of traditional citizenship', *International Migration Review* 38 (2):389-426.; Waters, Johanna, 2003, 'Flexible citizens? Transnationalism and citizenship amongst economic immigrants in Vancouver', *The Canadian Geographer,* 47(3):219-234

5. Studer, Brigitte, 2001, 'Citizenship as Contingent National Belonging: Married Women and Foreigners in Twentieth-Century Switzerland', *Gender and History,* 13(3): 622-654; Sir Bernard Crick, 2007, 'Citizenship: The Political and the Democratic', *British Journal of Educational Studies,* 55(3): 235-248.

6. The term 'Luwero Triangle' implies the area around and near the capital, Kampala, where the NRA centred its rebel activities in the 1981-6 bush war. It comprised the three districts of Mpigi, Luwero and Mukono, all of which form a triangle to the west (Mpigi), north (Luwero) and east (Mukono) of Kampala, which was later to be besieged, and the government overrun. The core of rebel activities was centred on Luwero, a few kilometres north of Kampala. After the 1980 elections, the NRA started a 'protracted people's struggle' in 1981. In 1986, the NRA/NRM took over power as the first rebel movement in Africa to capture state power, from a constituted postcolonial government, using the gun but with limited external support. Its Ten-Point Programme, developed during the bush war, was a programmatic representation of the policies the new government was to pursue, though some of its policies were influenced and affected by globalisation and neoliberalism. One such policy was good, democratic governance. Such governance coincided with neoliberal prescriptions, which called for, *inter alia,* gender equality. Women's support for the NRM government has been overwhelming, both in speech and in election choices. The local council system developed and prescribed during the bush war in 'liberated areas' was based on Ten-Households (Mayumba Kumi) forming a village. Each village had a nine-member Resistance Committee (RC), wth a secretary for women affairs. Several villages formed a Parish (RC II) and several parishes formed a

Sub-county (RC III), sub-counties formed a County (RC IV) and counties formed a District (RC V). This local government system was maintained during the post-1995 Uganda (constitutional period) but renamed Local Councils under the 1995 Constitution and the 1997 Local Government Act.

7. Miria Matembe and Mary Maitum were members of the Constitutional Committee that drafted the national Constitution. One woman was a member of the six-member Human Rights Commission. Two women were members of the nine-member Public Service Reorganisation Commission.

8. This followed recommendations of the Constitutional Commission (led by Justice Benjamin Odoki, later, Uganda's Chief Justice), established in 1989, to gather views countrywide on the making of the Constitution. The Commission produced a draft Constitution, and recommended the holding of elections of the Constituent Assembly (CA), which would debate the draft Constitution. On 28 March 1994, CA elections were held countrywide, with women representing districts (forming one-third of the CA). The Constitution was promulgated in October 1995.

9. These women include the First Lady, Janet Kataaha Museveni.

10. The deliberate effort to increase the presence and participation of women extends to the affirmative action taken by government institutions. In public universities, girls have an added 1.5 points to government sponsorship, which boys do not get. In Makerere University, for instance, a Gender Mainstreaming Division in the Academic Registry was established to look after the interests of female students and members of staff. The division gets scholarships from the Carnegie Foundation (the Carnegie Female Scholarships Initiative - FSI) for female students from poor families seeking admission to Makerere. While the last a female student (Sarah Kagingo) had contested the Presidency of the Students' Guild was in the 1990s, in 2007. Susan Abbo emerged and trounced male counterparts. This was after encouragement by women public figures, especially politicians, and the affirmative action that has increased female enrolment in university, and the changing perceptions among male students of female abilities.

11. Olai reveals that for the 2008/2009 academic year, sixty-six female students, compared to nine males, were admitted to Makerere University to pursue the Bachelor of Law programme with government sponsorship, because of the affirmative action policy of adding 1.5 points to females applying to public universities. The weighing system used and the cut-off points for law (54.3) hinder males from qualifying, even when males score a whopping AAAA1 at A'Level! By implication, males are at a disadvantage even when they have the otherwise requisite qualification, and women are advantaged, even when, they would not have met the requisite requirements without the 1.5 points. There are similar issues of marginalisation of men in other sectors and in terms of preferential treatment at social and public functions; this make the need for further emancipation of women appear an exaggeration.

References

Amal, C., 2008, *A Gender Perspective of Urban Poverty: A Case of Tororo Municipality*, MA Dissertation, Kampala: Makerere University.

Aseka, E.M., 2005, T*ransformational Leadership in East Africa: Politics, Ideology and Community*, Kampala: Fountain Publishers.

Brannon, L., 2005, *Gender: Psychological Perspectives*, Boston: Pearson Education Inc.

Bratton M. and van *de* Walle, N., 1997, *Democratic Experiments in Africa: Regime Transitions in Comparative Perspective*, Cambridge: Cambridge University Press.

Bronstein, K., 1998, My Gender Workbook, London: Routledge.

Bwengye, F.A.W., 1985, *The Agony of Uganda: From Idi Amin to Obote – An Analysis of the 1980 Controversial General Election and its Aftermath. Regressive Rule and Bloodshed: Causes, Effects and the Cure,* London: Regency Press.

Canning, K. and Rose, S.O., 2001, 'Gender Citizenship and Subjectivity: Some Historical and Theoretical Considerations', *Gender and History*, Vol. 13, No. 3, pp. 427-443.

Chesterman, J., 2001, 'The State of Citizenship', *Australian Journal of Public Administration*, Vol. 60, No. 2,   pp. 115-118..

Crick, B., 2007, 'Citizenship: The Political and the Democratic', *British Journal of Educational Studies,* Vol. 55, No. 3, pp. 235-248.

Dahl, R., 1998, *On Democracy*, New Haven: Yale University Press.

Hudson, W., 2003, 'Religious Citizenship', *Australian Journal of Politics and History*, 49(3): 425-429.

Hudson, W. and Kene, J., eds., 2000, *Rethinking Australian Citizenship*, Cambridge: Cambridge University Press Vol. 49, No. 3, pp. 425-429.

Huntington, S. P., 1996, *The Clash of Civilisations and the Remaking of World Order*, New York: Simon and Schuster.

Huntington, S.P., 1991, *The Third Wave: Democratisation in the Late Twentieth Century,* Norman: University of Oklahoma Press.

Huntington, S. P., 1968, *Political Order in Changing Societies*, New Haven: Yale University Press.

Kabwegyere, T.B., 1995, *The Politics of State Formation and Destruction in Uganda,* Kampala: Fountain Publishers.

Katleen P.K., 2003, 'Power and Territoriality: A Study of Moroccan Women in Antwerp', *Tijdschrift Voor Economische en Sociale Geografi*e , Vol. 94, No. 2, pp. 151-163.

Kiiza, J., Sabiti Makara and Lise Rakner, eds., 2008, *Electoral Democracy in Uganda: Understanding the Institutional Processes and Outcomes of the 2006 Multiparty Elections,* Kampala: Fountain Publishers.

Madison, J., 1966, 'The Federalist No. 7', in Roy P. Fairfield, ed., *The Federalist Papers*, New York: Doubleday.

Moghadam, V., ed., 1994, *Identity Politics and Women: Reassertions and Feminism in Perspective*, Boulder: Westview Press.

Makara, S. *et al.*, 2003, *Voting for Democracy in Uganda: Issues in Recent Elections*, Kampala: LDC Publishers.

Musimbi-Kanyoro and Wendy R.S. Robins, eds., 1992, *The Power We Celebrate: Women's Stories of Faith and Power*, Geneva: WCC Publications.

Nabudere, D., 1983, *The Political Economy of Imperialism*, London: Zed Books.

Neysmith, S. and C. Xiaobei, 2002, 'Understanding how Globalisation and Restructuring Affect Women's Lives: Implications for Comparative Policy Analysis', *International Journal of Social Welfare*, No. 11, pp. 243-253.

Olai, E., 2008, 'Gender Equality Becoming Marginalisation of Men', *The New Vision*, Thursday, 12 June, Kampala.

Otto, L., 2008, 'The Contribution of Decentralisation toward Enhancing Women Participation in LCs in Kitgum District', MA Dissertation, Kampala: Makerere University.

Przeworski, A. and F. Limongi, 1997, 'Modernisation: Theories and Facts', *World Politics*, Vol. 49, No. 2, pp. 155–83.

Republic of Uganda, 1997, *Electoral Commission Act, Cap 140*, Kampala: LDC Publishers.

Republic of Uganda, 1995, *Constitution of the Republic of Uganda*, Kampala: LDC Publishers.

Republic of Uganda, 1996, *Parliamentary Elections Act, 1996*, Entebbe: UPPC.

Republic of Uganda, 1996, 2000, *Parliamentary and Presidential Elections Acts, 1996, 2000*, Kampala: LDC Publishers.

Republic of Uganda, 1997, *Local Governments Act, 1997*, Entebbe: UPPC.

Republic of Uganda, 1997, *Local Governments Act, Cap 243 (amended 2005)*, Kampala: LDC Publishers.

Republic of Uganda, 2000, *Parliamentary Elections Act, 2000*, Entebbe, UPPC.

Republic of Uganda, 2000, *Presidential Elections Act, 2000*, Entebbe: UPPC.

Republic of Uganda, 2000, *Uganda Participatory Poverty Assessment*, Kampala: Ministry of Finance, Planning and Economic Development.

Republic of Uganda, 2005, *Parliamentary Elections Act No. 17*, Kampala: LDC Publishers.

Republic of Uganda, 2005, *Political Parties and Organisations Act, No. 18*, Kampala, LDC Publishers.

Republic of Uganda, 2005, *Presidential and Parliamentary Elections Act, No. 15*, Kampala, LDC Publishers.

Republic of Uganda, 2005, *Presidential Elections Act, No. 16*, Kampala: LDC Publishers; Amsterdam: IOS Press.

Rwengabo, S., 2008, *Uganda's Electoral Commission and the Management of the 2006 Presidential Elections*, MA (Public Administration and Management) Dissertation, Kampala: Makerere University.

Sabine, G.H. and T.L. Thorson, 1973, *A History of Political Theory*, fourth edition (New Delhi, Calcutta: Oxford & IBH Publishing.

Sheriff, C.W., 1982, 'Needed Concepts in the Study of Gender Identity', Psychology of Women Quarterly, 6, 375-98.

Sidorenko, A., 2006, 'Empowerment & Participation in Policy Action on Ageing', UN Programme on Ageing, International Design for All Conference 2006, Rovaniemi, Finland - Full papers Keynotes accessed from: http://dfasuomi.stakes.fi/ NR/ rdonlyres/ABF1AF26-5D33-458A-ABAD-3E4E284FD85D/0/Sidorenko.pdf, Accessed on 15 May 2008.

Siim, B., 2000, *Gender and Citizenship: Politics and Agency in France, Britain and Denmark*, Cambridge: Cambridge University Press.

Ssali, S. and Clare Pamella Atoo, 2008, 'Women Participation in the 2006 Multiparty Elections in Uganda', in Kiiza, J., Sabiti Makara and Lise Rakner, eds., *Electoral Democracy in Uganda: Understanding the Institutional Processes and Outcomes of the 2006 Multiparty Election,* Kampala: Fountain Publishers.

Studer, B., 2001, 'Citizenship as Contingent National Belonging: Married Women and Foreigners in Twentieth-Century Switzerland', *Gender and History,* 13(3): 622-654.

Sweetmen, C., ed., 1998, *Gender, Religion and Spirituality*, Oxford: Oxfam GB.

Tripp, A.M., 2000, *Women and Politics in Uganda*, Kampala: Fountain Publishers.

Tumwine-Mukubwa, G.P., 2004, *Free and Fair Democratic Elections. A Commentary on the Uganda Case of (Rtd.) Col. Dr. Kiiza Besigye Versus Lt. Gen. Yoweri Kaguta Museveni and Another*, Kampala: Makerere University Printers.

Unger, R. K., 1995, 'Conclusion: Cultural Diversity and the Future of Feminist Psychology', in L. Hope, ed., Bringing *Cultural Diversity to Feminist Psychology,* Washington, D.C.: American Psychological Association.

Waters, J., 2003, 'Flexible Citizens? Transnationalism and Citizenship amongst Economic Immigrants in Vancouver', *The Canadian Geographer*, 47(3): 219-234.

10

Globalisation and the Gender Question: The Role of CEDAW in Enhancing Women's Experience of Citizenship in Kenya

Samwel Ong'wen Okuro

Introduction

The term globalisation has become very current in the domains of economics, politics, sociology, and in the mass media, particularly during the 1990s. While there are widely differing definitions of globalisation (Giddens 1990: 64; Clark 1997:1), it generally refers to the process by which the economic and social relations between human beings have tended to extend to cover the territorial and demographic space of the entire planet. As for the more recent developments of globalisation, it is generally felt that they have taken on particular importance in the last three decades of the twentieth century. In this more specific sense, the term globalization has been used to indicate the social process, highly influenced by technological developments, rapid means of transport, and the information revolution, which has created a truly worldwide web of spatial connections and functional interdependence. This network brings into contact an ever greater number of social actors at economic, political, cultural and communication events which previously existed in isolation, separated by geographic remoteness or various kinds of cultural and social barriers. In this sense, the contraction of spatial and temporal dimensions is seen as being one of the most intensively perceived human consequences of globalisation (Bauman 1998).

The process of globalisation affects a wide range of spheres: political ideas and practices – the geography of social interaction, the integration of economic activities, the delocalisation of work, the diffusion of technologies – which are able to overcome the traditional construction of space, and the dissemination of cultural symbols and messages. In spite of widespread conviction to the contrary, globalisation is not an irreversible phenomenon, imposed by the inexorable logic of technological development and market forces and immune to political control (Clark 1997:1). It is also not an exclusively international phenomenon: it concerns individual countries directly, producing domestic consequences that can be fostered or countered by governments. The governments of superpowers are not passive onlookers of globalisation; on the contrary, they promote and shape it, with recourse to the use of force should this prove necessary in their judgement.

For women and other marginalised groups, inequality and exclusion has, on the whole, increased over the past decades of increasing globalisation. Economic models have been faulted for not bringing about real positive change to vulnerable groups such as women. This has necessitated a search for approaches and programmes that look beyond economics and into the political, social, and cultural world (Meer and Sever 2004:2). Globalisation has not only seen greater attention paid to human rights discourse but also concerted efforts towards addressing discrimination and exclusion alongside economic and technical development. These have had considerable consequences on the established concept of citizenship as traditionally constituted.

Thus, the process of globalisation has more than ever before put the concept of citizenship at the centre of political debates within and across national borders. At the centre of this debate is the issue of the shifting relationship between the rights and obligations of citizenship and the questions of membership of the national communities in an era characterised by economic globalisation, migration, and an increasingly multi-ethnic population (Hobson and Lister 2001). The academic works emanating from these debates focus on two broad but related issues. On the one hand, there are works that acknowledge the contested nature of the concept of citizenship, arguing that the concept has roots in two very different, and at times antagonistic political traditions: liberalism and civic republicanism.

Liberalism casts citizenship as a status involving primary rights accorded to individuals (Heater 1990; Oldfield 1990). In the classical liberal tradition, civil and political rights are the essence of citizenship; they are the guarantee of the freedom and formal equality of the individual who is sovereign. Social liberalism extends the scope of rights to the social in recognition of the ways in which substantive inequalities can undermine the formal equality derived from civil and political rights alone (Hobson and Lister 2001). It is important to note that the liberal conception of citizenship was highly influenced by Marshall's *Citizenship and Social Class* (1950). Marshall's work provides an account of the evolution of the citizenship rights of men; women are largely invisible. Civic republicanism casts citizenship as a practice involving responsibilities to the wider society (Heater 1990; Oldfield 1990). Within civic republicanism, the citizen is primarily a political actor, exercising 'his' civic duty within the public sphere. Thus, the androcentric bias is evident in the theory and practice of liberalism and the civic republican conceptualisation of citizenship.

On the other hand, we have works that strive to re-gender citizenship. The majority of these works have been written within feminist scholarship, whose preoccupation has been to reclaim concepts that have been hijacked in the interests of men. As a consequence, works such as Walby (1994), Lister (1997), Pateman (1989), and Voet (1998) have demonstrated ways in which citizenship, in both its civic republican and liberal forms, developed as a quintessentially male practice and ideal. They locate gender within a broader analysis of diversity and social divisions, in developing an understanding of both the nature of citizenship as membership of a community and of the patterns of inclusion and exclusion, which shape that membership. These works identify citizenship as more than simply the formal relationship between an individual and the state as presented by earlier liberal and political science literature. Instead they conceptualise citizenship as a more total relationship, inflected by identity, social positioning, cultural assumptions, institutional practices and a sense of belonging (Webner and Yuval-Davis 1999).

The contemporary discourse on re-gendering citizenship has been centred on rights, political participation, and responsibilities. The discourse on rights has been anchored on women's claim to basic rights to education, property, to custody of children and to suffrage so as to achieve equal rights with men and enjoy full citizenship. Political participation has emerged out of dissatisfaction with rights discourse. Its major preposition is made explicit by Voet when she argues that 'instead of seeing citizenship as the means to realise rights, we should see rights as one of the means to realise equal citizenship. This implies that feminism ought to be more than a movement for women's rights; it ought to be a movement for women's participation' (Voet 1998:73). It is the exercise of those rights, especially in the political sphere, which is crucial to the full development of women's citizenship. It is important to pay attention to the unpaid care and work that many women still undertake in the home and which needs to be recognised just as paid work is. This paper will, however, lay emphasis on the legal dimensions of citizenship, especially how Kenyan women have appropriated the Convention on the Elimination of All Forms of Discrimination against Women (CEDAW), not only to consolidate their legal rights in Kenya but also expand their political participation.

This chapter is divided into three parts. The first part examines the nexus between globalisation and the emergence of international instruments concerning women's rights and freedoms. The second part examines the development of CEDAW and the extent to which the government and civil society organisations have appropriated this international instrument to agitate for gender-friendly legislation. The last part of the paper looks at the challenges and opportunities in the application of CEDAW instrument to consolidate and expand women's legal rights.

Globalisation and Citizenship

Notions about citizenship have been significantly mediated by globalisation in several interrelated global shifts. First, experience has shown that national laws and policies in many countries cannot sufficiently guarantee the rights and obligations of the subjects residing within the jurisdiction of a particular state. Secondly, national agendas are increasingly framed by the policies of international organisations such as the World Bank, International Monetary Fund (IMF) and World Trade Organisation (WTO), which national citizens cannot hold accountable. Thirdly, the acceptance of neo-liberal economic policies as the only approach has limited the role of the nation-state in addressing the needs of the poor and the marginalised. Fourthly, increased international migration and tensions around ethnic and cultural differences within countries have fractured relationships among citizens and states. Fifthly, globalisation has seen the ascendance of human rights discourse and the development of international instruments with which to claim rights on the basis of membership of the global community (Sen 2003; Gouws 2006). These have increased the possibility of addressing discrimination against women, gender inequality, exclusion, poverty and other social evils facing humanity. More recently, a sense of 'global citizenship' has emerged in which people from all over the world come together as members of the global community in international movements and protests against injustices.

Women globally have had an ambivalent experience of globalisation at the national and international level. Globalisation has fragmented the centralisation of power within the sovereign state – the state that has traditionally been unsupportive of gender equality and equity. The power structures of the nation-state have been organised around patriarchal assumptions that have accorded to men a monopoly over power, authority and wealth. A number of structures have been erected to achieve these imbalances and to disguise inequality by making it appear as natural and universal. The opening up of new spaces by the apparent weakening of the nation-state holds open the possibility of undermining the traditional gender hierarchies and devising new bases for gender relations. Similarly, the rise of non-democratic forces and increased migration have also enhanced women's freedom of movement and opened up more choices for women

While these may be heralded as some of the areas where women have benefited as far as the process of globalisation is concerned, in reality there are challenges and contradictory outcomes. Where governments are unwilling to uphold the rights of workers so as not to discourage investment, there can greater incidence of social exclusion, unemployment, low wages and limited activity by trade unions, all of which have serious gender dimensions. Women are seen as a passive, compliant, temporary workforce that will accept low wages without demanding labour and human rights. These new labour arrangements have seen increased violation of women's human rights and the feminisation of poverty (Okuro 2002). These arrangements may be exploitative for women, but they have nonetheless facilitated a new degree of economic independence for many women and lessened their subordination within the family by freeing them from early marriage or pregnancy. In addition, this has provided the public space for women to assert their own agency and self-esteem that comes with independence..

The Convention on the Elimination of All Forms of Discrimination Against Women (CEDAW)

One of the remarkable outcomes of globalisation is the rise and consolidation of supranational bodies, global social movements on human rights, and the agitation around the provisions of international law. The most relevant body in this context is the United Nations (UN). The adoption of the UN Charter in 1945 marked a watershed as far as human rights are concerned. The Charter declared that the UN would promote and encourage respect for human rights. The Universal Declaration of Human Rights (UDHR), followed the Charter in 1948 and can be described as the first and one of the most significant instruments of international human rights. The UDHR arose directly in consideration of the atrocities and human rights violations perpetrated by the Nazi regime during the Second World War. The declaration established noble provisions for the achievement of world peace and set the framework for the recognition and protection of human rights without sexual distinction (Thogori 2005:61).

The UDHR set out the basic rights and freedoms to which all women and men are entitled – among them the right to life, liberty and nationality; freedom of thought, conscience and religion; the right to work and to education; the right to food and housing; and the right to take part in government. Despite its lack of binding effect, the UDHR set the framework for the adoption of two fundamental documents for the protection of both men and women, namely: the International Covenant on Civil and Political Rights 1966, and the International Covenant on Economic, Social and Cultural Rights, 1966. These two documents, together with the UDHR, have come to be called the international bill of rights owing to their substantial contributions towards the rights of both men and women. They also set the framework for the adoption of more than 80 conventions and declarations on human rights (Thogori 2005:61).

While the UDHR addressed many facets of human rights discourse, it appeared not to have a specific focus on women's concerns or was not developed from the perspective of women. As Bunch rightly observed, 'the dominant definition of human rights and the mechanisms to enforce them pertain primarily to the types of violation which the men who articulated the concept most feared' (Bunch 1995:13). Therefore, in addition to the UDHR, women around the world needed an international instrument that could address gender inequality, social injustice and other forms of discrimination against them in every aspect of their lives. Such an instrument would be based on the understanding that the distinctive characteristics of women and their vulnerability to discrimination merited a specific legal response both nationally and internationally.

During the 1970s and 1980s, there was an increasing need to consolidate the global women's human rights concerns into an international human rights framework (Friedman 1995). This was particularly so in reference to the many forms of discrimination against women which exposed in the series of international conferences, workshops and seminars that the UN organised to monitor the status of women; to suggest initiatives against a host of persistent problems; and to encourage the implementation of platforms agreed upon by participating nations (Pearce 2000). Globally, there were also concerns and outrage, particularly over the prevalence, magnitude and impact of violence against women (hereafter VAW), to the point that VAW was recognised as a global human rights issue that required a comprehensive and coordinated response from civil society, the state and the international community.

VAW was thus conceptualised into a violation of several human rights as enshrined in the UDHR and other subsequent covenants. VAW violated the rights to life, the right to liberty and security of person, the right to equal protection under the law, the right not to be subjected to torture or other cruel, inhuman or degrading treatment, the right to the highest attainable standards of physical and mental health, the right to equality, the right to be free from all forms of discrimination and the right to just and favourable conditions of work.

With a lot of advocacy and lobbying by a host of international civil society organisations and the Commission on the Status of Women, in 1979, the UN adopted CEDAW (Convention on the Elimination of All Forms of Discrimination against Women). This convention was referred to as a woman's convention particularly because it was the first international human rights instrument to exclusively and explicitly address the issue of violence against women. CEDAW was first adopted as UN General Assembly Resolution 34/180 in December 1979 and became a treaty in 1980 having acquired the necessary number of adoptions by states. It entered into force on 3 September 1981, in accordance with Article 27(1). CEDAW defined discrimination against women under its Article 1 as: any distinction, exclusion or restriction made on the basis of sex which has the effect or purpose of impairing or nullifying the recognition, enjoyment or exercise by women, irrespective of their marital status, on the basis of equality of men and women, of human rights and fundamental freedoms in the political, economic, social, cultural, civil, or other fields.

In the eyes of human rights activists, this convention was more comprehensive than previous international conventions that paid little attention to gender equality and the advancement of women's legal rights. CEDAW explicitly called for equality in civil, economic, political and social rights and encompassed rights that were guaranteed under different conventions such as the Convention on the Nationality of Married Woman, 1957; the Convention on Consent to Marriage; Minimum Age for Marriage and Registration of Marriages, 1962; and the Recommendation on Consent to Marriage; Minimum Age for Marriage and Registration of Marriages, 1965.

The progress of CEDAW got a boost in 1992 when the issue of violence against women was brought to international attention at the World Conference on Human Rights in Vienna in 1993. Under Article 18, the Vienna Declaration and Programme of Action recognised that the human rights of women and girl-children were inalienable, and an integral and indivisible part of universal human rights. It condemned gender-based violence and all forms of sexual harassment and exploitation, including that resulting from cultural prejudice as well as international trafficking, as incompatible with the dignity and worth of the human person and thus must be eliminated. The Vienna Conference marked a further milestone in the history of the recognition of women's specific interests in international human rights discourse. The Vienna Declaration and Programme of Action clearly pointed out that women's rights are to be recognised and protected as human rights.

In response to the Vienna conference, the UN General Assembly on 20 December 1993 unanimously adopted the declaration on VAW. This was another major landmark declaration at the international level for the advancement of gender equality and equity. Article 1 of the Declaration on VAW defined violence as any act of gender-based violence that results in, or is likely to result in physical, sexual or psychological harm or suffering to women, including threats of such acts, coercion or arbitrary deprivation of liberty, whether occurring in public or in the private. It was also resolved that VAW constitutes a violation of the rights and freedoms of women, that VAW is a manifestation of historically unequal power relations between men and women and that VAW is one of the crucial social mechanisms by which women are forced into a subordinate position compared with men. It was also stated that opportunities for women to achieve legal, social, political, and economic equality in society are limited, inter alia, by continuing and endemic violence.

As it exists today, CEDAW has all the necessary instruments towards the elimination of various forms of discrimination against women. CEDAW has defined women's rights and specified the obligations on all states parties to ensure equal treatment of women. It has been ratified by about 185 states, though in many cases with substantial reservations. It defines the term discrimination, VAW (General Assembly Recommendation No. 12-19, 1992) and comes out as a single international instrument that aims to protect women against discrimination. It specifies in detail the obligations that states enter into upon ratification, which include:

- the principle of gender equality in their national constitutions or similar legislation, and to ensure through law and other appropriate means, the practical realisation of this principle (Article 2 (a);
- to take all appropriate measures to eliminate discrimination against women by persons, organisations, and enterprises;

- to take appropriate measures to guarantee women the exercise and enjoyment of human rights and fundamental freedoms on the basis of equality with men (Article 3);
- to modify the social and cultural patterns of conduct of men and women, with a view to achieving the elimination of prejudices and customary and all other practices which are based on the idea of the inferiority or the superiority of either of the sexes or on stereotyped roles for men and women (Article 5).

It also specifies the obligations on states parties to implement the prohibitions of discrimination against women in various areas of public and private life.

CEDAW became fully operational by the adoption on 6 October 1999 of an Optional Protocol (containing 21 articles), which calls on all states-parties to the Convention to become party to the new instrument. This Optional Protocol recognises the Committee on the Elimination of Discrimination Against Women. Also known as CEDAW, this is an expert body that monitors states-parties' compliance with the convention. The protocol contains two key procedures: first, the communication procedure, which allows individual women or groups of women to submit to the committee claims of violation of rights protected under the Convention; and secondly, the protocol that creates an inquiry procedure enabling the committee to initiate inquiries into situations of grave or systematic violations of women's rights. The entry into force of the Optional Protocol on 22 December 2000 put CEDAW on an equal footing with the International Covenant on Civil and Political Rights, CEDAW and the Convention against Torture and Other Forms of Cruel, Inhuman, or Degrading Treatment or Punishment, which also have communication procedures.

The state duties and obligations under CEDAW are further elaborated, concretised and complemented by the Beijing Declaration and Platform of Action 1995. In the African context, there is the Southern African Development Community Declaration on Gender and Development, the African Charter on Human and People's Rights, and the African Union Protocol on the Rights of Women in Africa. All these declarations and protocols acknowledge that women's rights have been marginalised. They thus provide broad and specific protection for women's human rights, including their sexual and reproductive rights, in individual countries. In addition, the Beijing Declaration calls on governments to implement measures to eliminate discrimination and violence against women and girls, and to recognise women's rights as human rights and allow women the right to control all aspects of their health.

CEDAW thus provides the basis for the realisation of equality between women and men through ensuring women's rights to equal access and equal opportunity in political and public life – including the right to vote and stand in elections – as well as in education, health and employment. States-parties agree to take all appropriate measures including legislation and temporary special measures, so that women can enjoy all their human rights and fundamental freedoms. In the whole debate of re-gendering citizenship, CEDAW sets out a host of legal instruments that, when implemented, can establish the full range of women's equal rights in the civil, political, economic and social spheres. It also sets out to dismantle a host of socio-cultural and domestic constraints that hinder women's active role in defining their own destiny.

Kenya and CEDAW

As an independent country, Kenya is a member of the UN and is party to the UN Charter of 1945 and the UDHR of 1948. This means that Kenya, in terms of international law, has accepted to protect and promote a number of human, civil, economic and social rights and has in addition asserted these rights as part of the foundation of freedom, justice and peace. As part of the UN family, Kenya has ratified six of the UN treaties, one Optional Protocol, and one protocol. These are the:

- International Covenant on Economic Social and Cultural Rights ratified on 3 January 1976;
- International Covenant on Civil and Political Rights, ratified on 23 March 1976;
- International Covenant on the Elimination of All Forms of Racial Discrimination, ratified on 13 October 2001;
- International Covenant on the Elimination of All Forms of Discrimination against Women, ratified on 8 April 1984;
- Convention against Torture and other Cruel, Inhuman or Degrading Treatment or Punishment, ratified on 23 March 1997;
- Convention on the Rights Child, ratified on 22 September 1990;
- Optional Protocol to the Convention on the Rights of the Child on the Involvement of Children in Armed Conflict, ratified on 12 February 2002;
- Optional Protocol to the Convention on the Rights of the Child on the Sale of Children, Child Prostitution and Child Pornography, signed on 8 September 2000.

All these international instruments implicitly prohibit VAW. At regional level, Kenya is party to the African Charter on Human and Peoples' Rights of which Article 3 provides that 'each person is equal before the law and must be protected equally by the law'. Article 5 guarantees to every individual the right to the respect of the dignity inherent in a human being and prohibits torture, cruel, inhuman or degrading punishment or treatment.

Kenya became party to CEDAW on 9 March 1984. However, as last reported to the CEDAW Committee, Kenya had not ratified the CEDAW Optional Protocol that provides a communication procedure that allows either individuals or groups of individuals to submit complaints to the CEDAW Committee. Thus in the Kenyan context, the individual complaint mechanism is not available. It is important to note that while becoming party to this convention, Kenya made no reservations. Therefore, Kenya is required and bound to put CEDAW provisions into practice. This means it is obligated to submit national reports at least every four years on measures that it has taken to comply with CEDAW treaty as set out under Article 18. Other than compliance with reporting guidelines, the national reports also assess the implementation record, taking into account the policy, legal, judicial, and administrative measures to meet the obligations under the convention.

CEDAW and Women's Citizenship in Kenya

While women form a majority of the population (52 %) and play an active role in the development of the society, Kenya remains a very patriarchal society, and the status of women remains relatively low with a broad range of inequalities and inequities. Women continue to be marginalised and discriminated against in almost all aspects of their lives, a situation that is reinforced by existing laws and policies, as well as socio-cultural factors. As 2003, the female literacy rate stood at 79 per cent compared to 90 per cent for men. Similarly, about 83 per cent of the females were working in the informal sector compared to 59 per cent of men.

The current Parliament has fifteen elected and six nominated women out of a total of 222 members. Apart from cultural attitudes that obstruct women from vying for political leadership, and people from voting for them, there are several factors that have prevented women from making their numeric presence felt. The pre-election period is usually characterised by violence, but disproportionately directed against women candidates. Political campaigns also cost a lot of money, and many women are not able to raise the money needed to conduct a campaign.

Women are also underrepresented in the executive and judiciary. There are very few women appointed to ministerial posts in the government or to top posts in the parastatals. Although in the lower courts, women are relatively better represented at between 38 and 44 per cent of magistrates, in the higher courts, the percentage falls to 20 per cent. The same is evident in the local authorities. There is, therefore, an unacceptable degree of exclusion of women from leadership positions, in particular, national leadership. This means that the participation of women in political as well as public decision making is still low for the actual realisation of full citizenship.

Discrimination against women has been a concern for the government, civil society, and development partners. Partly as a result of the intensified lobbying, advocacy, and negotiations with human rights non-governmental organiszations and the need to fulfil its obligations under CEDAW, the government of Kenya has established national policies, programmes and legislation that promote gender equality. While the success of these initiatives remains minimal as will be discussed later, they nonetheless indicate a firm commitment on the part of the government to comply with CEDAW provisions.

The drive to achieve equal rights and equitable social, economic and legal conditions for Kenyan women has a very long history far beyond the scope of this paper. However, in the period after independence, initial credit goes to *Maendeleo Ya Wanawake*. This is a woman's organisation dealing with issues such as women's rights and gender equality. It was founded in 1952 and has approximately 600,000 groups contributing to a total membership of about 2 million women. The organisation is involved in a variety of areas such as maternal child health, family planning, advocacy for the elimination of female genital mutilation (FGM), girl-child education, civic education, engendering political space. Its intervention strategies address the core problems concerning the poor socio-economic status of women in Kenya.

In 1976, the government, in reaction to the increased awareness of women's contribution to development process occasioned by the UN Women's Decade for the Advancement of Women (1975), established Women's Bureaus. Their main mandate was to ensure the full participation of women in the social, economic and cultural fields. For example, there is a Women's Bureau in the Ministry of Gender, Sports, Culture, and Social Services. It is a department mandated to formulate and review policies across all sectors, facilitating domestication and implementation of international instruments affecting women, coordinating and harmonising the implementation of the National Policy on Gender as well as promoting the generation of gender disaggregated data. The Bureaus also strive to ensure that government policies diminish gender disparities in Kenya.

In 2000, the government (with advice from Women's Bureaus) recognised that national and sectoral policies have had different impacts on women and, more often than not they have overlooked gender concerns. The government, therefore, developed the National Policy on Gender and Development (NPGD) as a demonstration of its commitment to advancing the status of women in Kenya. This policy arose from the government's recognition that development policies do not affect people uniformly. The NPGD was thus consistent with government efforts to spur economic growth and reduce poverty and unemployment by considering the needs of all Kenyan women, men, and children across economic, social, and cultural lines. The policy was also consistent with government commitments to implementing the Beijing National Platform of Action, and other commitments to the various international conventions such as CEDAW and the Nairobi Forward-looking Strategies for the Advancement of Women. Overall, the policy was put in place to facilitate the mainstreaming of the needs and concerns of women and men in all areas of the development process in Kenya.

The change of government in 2002 was instrumental as far as the fight for gender equality and respect for human rights was concerned. This is because a significant number of gender and human rights activists entered the government. The new government thus made it its priority to eliminate all the obstacles that have made it difficult for the majority of Kenyans to enjoy their rights and fundamental freedoms. In 2003, the government introduced Free Primary Education (FPE), a demonstration of its commitment to eliminating the social and cultural discrimination in relation to access to education that had hindered many women from actively participating in the public sphere.

During the same year, the government established the National Commission on Gender and Development (NCGD), under the Act of Parliament No. 13 of 2003. The NCGD was formally launched in November 2004 as a parastatal within the Ministry of Gender, Sports, Culture and Social Services. The purpose of the NCGD was to coordinate, implement and facilitate gender mainstreaming in national development and to advise the government on all relevant issues. The Commission works with men, women, boys, girls, women's organisations, NGOs, ministries, donors, and community organisations.

At formation, it had the following mandates:

- participate in the formulation of national development policies;

- exercise supervision over the implementation of the National Policy on Gender and Development;
- initiate, lobby and conduct advocacy for legal reform affecting women, and formulate laws, practices, and policies that eliminate all forms of discrimination against women and all institutions, practices, and customs that are detrimental to their dignity;
- initiate proposals and advice on the strengthening of institutional mechanisms which promote gender equity and equality in all spheres of life and in particular, access to and benefit from education and healthcare, nutrition, shelter, employment and control of economic and natural resources;
- determine strategic priorities in all the socio-economic, political and development policies of the government and advise on their implementation;
- plan, supervise and coordinate education programmes to create public awareness and support for gender issues;
- evaluate aid policies to determine their impact on women in Kenya;
- conduct and coordinate research activities on gender issues;
- carry out investigations on gender-based rights violations and forward them to relevant authorities;
- receive and evaluate reports by government ministers and other sectors on gender mainstreaming and women's empowerment.

The NCGD received a major boost in 2006 when the government developed and passed Sessional Paper No. 2 of 2006 on Gender Equality and Development. This paper had the overall objective of ensuring women's empowerment and the mainstreaming of gender needs and concerns in all sectors of development. In addition, the paper recognised that it is the right of women, men, girls and boys to participate and benefit equally from development initiatives.

The clamour for constitutional reforms has been in the heart of many Kenyans since the early 1980s and 1990s. The reasons for constitutional reforms are obvious and include: the idea of law reform, which dictates that the law be reviewed regularly to keep it in conformity with real life as expressed in changing social, economic, political and cultural trends. With time, the socio-economic order is changing, and so are political and cultural trends, requiring the reform of the Constitution. Thus, it has remained important to take account of the continued existence of laws, customs, practices, and cultures that tend to impair the exercise of rights to equal protection of the law. It is also necessary to eliminate subjective , and discriminatory interpretation and implementation of the law. This has meant keeping abreast of developments in case law as well as international law, human rights and the broader global agreements recommended for incorporation in national legislation (Aluoch 2008). These efforts led to the establishment of the Constitution of Kenya Review Commission and the holding of Kenya's National Constitutional Conference which culminated in a Draft Bill of the Constitution of Kenya published by the Attorney-General in the Special Issue Kenya Gazette Supplement No. 63, 2005. The Draft Constitution was put to a national referendum in November 2005 but was overwhelmingly rejected, putting the clamour for constitutional reforms into disarray.

The provisions concerning women in the rejected Draft Constitution were lauded by constitutional experts and gender activists as representing major gains towards gender equality and equity and in essence delivering on many issues at the heart of the concerns of pro-women movements in Kenya since the 1980s (Nzomo and Kameri-Mbote 2003). The rejected draft constitution (RDC,) did away with sections of the law that encouraged discrimination against women. These included Article 82(4), which permitted discrimination with respect to adoption, marriage, divorce, burial, devolution of property on death or other matters of personal law. In addition to deleting the discriminatory sections, the RDC, provided a relatively good basis for the realisation of women's rights in Kenya.

For example, the RDC included international law as one of the classes of law applicable in Kenya. It explicitly spelt out that one-third of members of all elective and appointive positions should be women. It also offered equal protection before the law, which includes the full and equal enjoyment of all rights and freedoms. The RDC offered protection against discrimination by the state or any other person on the grounds of sex, pregnancy and marital status; gave provisions for affirmative action allowing the state to take legislative and other measures designed to benefit individuals or groups who are disadvantaged; gave women equal opportunity in political, economic, and social matters, including equal right to inherit, have access to and control property; prohibited any law, culture, customs, or traditions that undermined the dignity, welfare, interest or status of women; and offered marriage partners equal rights in marriage, during marriage and dissolution of marriage.

The RDC moved closer to bringing Kenya into compliance with all its international human rights obligations, including the right to non-discrimination and equality before the law and others relating to women's equal property rights as spelt out in CEDAW and other international covenants of which Kenya is a signatory.

The disillusionment that followed the rejection of the draft constitution did not stop Kenyan women and members of civil society from lobbying the government to advance their concerns both at policy and at legislative levels. In 2006, civil society groups and a few members of parliament mounted a spirited fight through a private member's motion for legislation against sexual violence, which had reached alarming rates in Kenyan society (FIDA-K 2007: 30). The need for the enactment of the Sexual Offences Act (SOA), No. 3 of 2006 was also prompted by other reasons including: the slow and inefficient manner in which the existing provisions addressed sexual violence; the unique characteristics of sexual violence; the scattered nature of laws relating to sexual violence in the Penal Code, Criminal Procedure Code and Criminal Amendment Act; the poor prosecution and shoddy investigations of sexual offences; and the unfriendliness to sexual victims in court rooms (Aluoch 2008).

The passage of the SOA into law was met with spirited resistance from some male parliamentarians. During the months of April and May 2006, the Kenyan parliament, mainstream media and political debates focused on the bill, particularly its weaknesses. In Parliament, some members argued that provisions of the bill criminalized African culture and that the bill was not alive to the diversity of cultural practices of the different Kenyan tribes. In addition the bill could easily ban African modes of courtship and also make it almost impossible for doctors to operate on their patients to save lives (*Daily Nation* 2006:19). During the acrimonious debate in Parliament, various male members gave conflicting and trivial reasons for rejecting the bill.

Hon. Kajwang for instance, argued that the bill failed to define genital organs to avoid confusion. He also argued that the bill put the burden of proof on the accused and hence contradicted the Constitution; to Hon. Keter, the bill could easily allow homosexuality and lesbianism, criminalise wooing, and had the potential to break up marriages. Referring to circumcision of girls, some members of parliament felt that the Sexual Offences Bill was an affront to people's culture. Hon. Angwenyi, in particular, argued that 'in Kisii culture, girls were not supposed to say yes to sexual advances lest they are branded prostitutes. A girl must resist by saying no, even if she means yes, in order to retain her honour. This is the culture that is being criminalised. We want to give our society that which God gave us and we are not ready to allow sex to be re-defined… this bill must respect our traditional African marriage before we support it' (*Daily Nation* 2006:19). This view was supported by several male members of parliament. In fact, Hon. Ahenda even became 'famous' for his remarks in parliament when he said that, 'African women always say no when they mean yes'. Similarly, most members felt that the bill adopted a more liberal definition of sexual harassment, particularly Article 23 which stated that 'a person who undertakes any unlawful, unsolicited and unwelcome sexual advance or request for sexual favours is guilty of the offence of sexual harassment (*Sunday Nation* 2006). They accused certain non-governmental organisations of sponsoring a bill that did not respect African values and sexuality.

At the end of the parliamentary debate, the mover of the motion Hon. Njoki Ndungu accepted to make certain amendments to the bill and particularly to do away with the provisions that the members of parliament frowned on such as marital rape and female circumcision.

When the diluted bill was finally passed as the Sexual Offences Act, it introduced new offences such as gang rape, child pornography, child prostitution, deliberate transmission of HIV/AIDS or any other life threatening disease, prostitution of persons with disabilities, child sex tourism, and sexual harassment. The Act also introduced new concepts such as vulnerable witnesses, and consolidated sexual offences under one statute. It provided minimum sentences and took away the magistrate's discretion in sentencing sexual offenders. The Act further gave special protection to child victims, persons with disabilities and elderly persons. And for the first time, the Act provided that upon conviction of an offender for sexual violence, the court shall order that a sample(s) taken from the accused to be tested for HIV and any other life threatening, sexually transmitted diseases.

To underscore the significance of this Act, the government through the Attorney-General set up a task force in March 2007 (Gazette Notice 2115), with a mandate to prepare and recommend a National Policy Framework and Guidelines for the Act, to review all existing policies, laws and regulations, practices, and customs relating to sexual offences and make amendments, and to carry out public education, awareness and sensitisation campaigns so that people can adhere to and promote the objectives of the Act. The task force was also mandated to undertake the training of judicial officers, police investigators, and prosecutors. As at 2008, the taskforce had managed to develop a manual for training police investigators (*Sunday Nation* 2008).

The discussion on how the government has attempted to domesticate the provisions of CEDAW would be in complete without mentioning the critical role played by civil society (Krut 1997). Organised civil society activities in

Kenya have experienced tremendous growth and visibility following the end of one-party rule in 1991. Since then, civil society organisations have continued to agitate for legal reforms to repeal repressive laws, respect for universally recognised human rights and fundamental freedoms, and an end to gender-based discrimination. Civil society organisations have been at the forefront of constitutional reform processes and nationwide civic education campaigns in Kenya. They have also been very instrumental in lobbying and negotiations with every strategically placed individual, legislators, ministers, and the donor community to ensure that constitutional provisions favourable to women are enacted without any delay.

Civil society organisations have also made remarkable contributions to government policy documents and Sessional Papers focusing on women and other vulnerable groups. This is understandable because the laws, policies, and government programmes operate in a social, economic and political context that has not been very supportive of gender equality and equity. In addition, certain norms and customary laws are so ingrained in people's minds that to deal with them necessitates a robust strategy that exists only within civil society. The many submissions, memoranda, reports, and critiques that civil society organisations made during the constitutional review process demonstrated their dedication towards the eradication of discrimination against women. Without them, Kenyan women would have not made any remarkable progress towards fighting for their social, economic, and cultural rights.

Since 1984, the government, acting under pressure from civil society and also to meet part of its obligations after ratification of CEDAW provisions, has enacted a number of policies and legal instruments aimed at addressing women's exclusion from the full enjoyment of citizenship. The National Policy on Gender and Development and the subsequent National Commission on Gender and Development were basically instituted to isolate and deal with the reality that some state policies are gender blind and perpetuate the exclusion of women from the public sphere. The RDC also had relatively good provisions.

For example, the requirement that one third of all elective posts be held by women promoted women's full and equal participation in formal politics. This was buttressed with the Sexual Offences Act, which particularly addressed the all forms of sexual violence against women which had contributed to reducing the number of women willing to stand in national and local elections. Similarly, the RDC also ensured that women have equal rights to property, particularly access to and ownership of land. In fact, the opposition to the draft constitution during the national referendum was partly in connection with the provision for women to be able to own land, which most men saw as an affront to established customs that denied women land ownership.

Challenges

It may appear that Kenya has made remarkable attempts towards implementation of CEDAW both at policy and at legislative levels. However, CEDAW Committee Annual Reports, Shadow CEDAW Reports and other research findings reveal serious flaws and limitations as far as the implementation of CEDAW provisions are concerned. These are due to several factors. First, there are weaknesses and conflicts in certain provisions of legislation that are supposed to safeguard against discrimination of women. Secondly, there is a persistence of harmful cultural practices, which have made it easy for women and girls to be discriminated against. Thirdly, a huge amount of resources is required to comply fully with CEDAW provisions. And finally, the level of illiteracy among women remains high. This is compounded by the limited campaigns to raise awareness on CEDAW and other woman-friendly structures and laws that are supposed to fully eliminate discrimination against women in Kenya.

The government is aware that discrimination against women remains rampant and continues to report that prohibitions against discrimination are contained in Article 82(4) of the Constitution. However, this prohibition against discrimination is subject to various limitations, exceptions and qualifications and is also subject to Kenya's patriarchal context. After the RDC, there is still an urgent need to repeal certain sections of the Constitution to make them gender friendly. These sections include: Article 82(1&2), Citizenship Act, Domicile Act, Laws of Succession Act, Kenya Labour Laws, and the Marriage Act. This legislation does not guarantee women equal protection under the law as stipulated in CEDAW. In addition to repealing these sections of the Constitution, the government needs to speedily enact the several pending gender-friendly bills such as the Equity Bill, Marriage Bill, Affirmative Action Bill, Family Protection Bill, and any other piece of legislation that gives effect to the provisions of the RDC that promote gender equality and equity.

While the Kenyan government enacted the Sexual Offences Act (SOA) in 2006 to curb the spread of heinous crimes of sexual violence against women and children, current statistics indicate that a woman is raped in Kenya roughly every thirty minutes (FIDA-K 2007). This means that almost two years since the Act was operational, it is still experiencing implementation problems.

Some of its provisions have even been interpreted as contrary to the principle of natural justice. For example, section 38 of the Act provides that any person who makes false allegations against another person to the effect that the second person has committed an offence, shall be liable to punishment equal to that for the offence complained of. This provision alone can persuade a survivor of sexual assault not to report to the police for fear of being punished if the case fails. Moreover, many victims of sexual violence have been subjected to harrowing interrogations by investigators and legal officers to prove their case even when there is glaring supporting evidence, raising fundamental ethical and moral questions (Wafula 2008:14). In addition, the new legislation is yet to be disseminated countrywide, and some members of the judiciary are still using the repealed provisions of the penal code to adjudicate offences of sexual violence (FIDA-K 2007).

Even the government's deliberate attempts to prohibit discrimination against women and girls through administrative decrees have not been very successful. For example, the administrative decree which instructed the Land Control Boards to take family interest into account on land issues is not always applied. Although Land Control Boards encourage men to get their wives' consent before selling land, some have reportedly sold land without their wives consent and no action is taken against them (Okuro, 2007). The same can be said of the administrative requirement seeking one-third representation for women in Land Tribunals. Available evidence shows that the prevailing patriarchal norms have made it difficult for women to have an appropriate impact in these tribunals during land dispute arbitration (Okuro 2008).

CEDAW also requires governments to prohibit any law, customs, or traditions that undermine women's dignity, welfare, interests or status and guarantees every person the right to acquire property. The government, however, has not been committed to modifying cultural and social practices that entrench discrimination against women and those that perpetuate gender stereotypes. Currently, areas such as marriage (particularly early marriage), wife inheritance, exchange of bride wealth, polygamy, FGM, and gender-based violence need to be addressed. These constraints and harmful practices have been responsible for the limited number of women and girls in political and public life and in educational institutions, and also for the increased violation of women's property rights. It seems the government has acquiesced to the prevailing social and cultural patterns of conduct that limit women's property rights. This violates the provisions of CEDAW.

The majority of communities in Kenya practice FGM (Female Genital Mutilation), a practice grounded in old customs. However, FGM exposes the girl-child to violence and discrimination and poses a potentially great risk to the health and wellbeing of the women/girls subjected to it. Of course, it is also in violation of CEDAW. Gains in campaigns against FGM in Kenya have included the Presidential Decree of 1999 and the National Plan of Action for the Elimination of Female Genital Mutilation in Kenya, 1999-2019. However, despite FGM being expressly outlawed, it is still rampant. Consequently, it may be time to rethink the methods with which the problem of gender-based violence is being tackled. More effort is needed to tackle the root causes of gender-based violence rather than addressing symptoms. Generally, campaigns for the prevention of gender-based violence are mainly targeted towards women; now men should also be targeted to create awareness of the issues and also to involve them in NGOs that deal with gender-based violence.

While it is important to commend the government for putting in place several policies, programmes and Sessional Papers that recognise and seek to address gender-based discrimination in the country, its failure to champion the Sexual Offences Bill raised questions about its commitment to the eradication of sexual offences. In addition, the implementation of some of these policies and programmes is yet to commence and there is no indication of what the government is doing to harness public and NGO efforts to raise awareness among both urban and rural populations and to ensure that all judicial officers understand the provisions of the gender-supportive policies.

For example the Women's Bureau whose mandate is to ensure the full participation of women in social, economic, and cultural areas remains seriously underfunded and, therefore, relatively ineffective. Similarly, the National Commission for Gender and Development is also facing problems with funding and how it should relate to other bodies such as the Ministry of Gender. These difficulties have left the Commission vulnerable and unable to meet the expectations and outputs of its operational plan. The Commission is notably missing from the list of constitutional commissions in the RDC thereby reducing its profile as the premier government body championing the rights of women. Furthermore, the work of the Task Force on Laws Affecting Women, which was completed in 1997, has not been implemented.

Substantial resources are required for implementation of the Sex Offenders Act (SOA). For example, the Act provides for the establishment of crisis centres and safe houses for victims of sexual abuse. There is also the need for training of all judicial officers and police investigators on the terms of the Act, and procurement of equipment for the preservation of forensic evidence by the police and for DNA and HIV testing. This is in addition to increasing the number of judicial officers and investigators. This situation may have led Muthien to conclude,

> 'If one looks at measures such as the allocation of resources, provision of services, evaluation of existing law and enactment of new legislative measures, it appears that a significant commitment in all spheres of government is required. From the perspective of those working to end gender-based violence, this is not asking too much; however, for governments in Africa, with failing infrastructures and economies in disarray, compliance with these standards may simply appear to be one more unrealistic demand on ever- dwindling resources (Muthien Forthcoming).

Article 10 of CEDAW recognises the importance of education in enabling women and men to participate equally in all aspects of life. Education is one of the inalienable rights and is a necessary precondition that enables women to gain confidence and to have access to other rights. CEDAW also recognises that special measures are necessary to ensure that these opportunities are available and taken, and to provide for the needs of women who have not had access to equal opportunities in the past. Towards the realisation of this obligation, the government introduced Free Primary Education (FPE). While FPE is laudable for addressing cultural and social issues that keep parents from sending their girl-children to school, girls' education in Kenya has continued to face multiple barriers as a result of poverty, early pregnancy, forced marriages and cultural and traditional practices. While at primary level there is near gender parity, the same does not apply to secondary and university education. An increasing impediment to girls' education is the HIV/AIDS pandemic which forces many of them to leave school to care for family members. Even girls who are educated often end up in lower paying jobs with fewer opportunities for professional development. The government and relevant NGOs needs to focus on increasing girl child enrolment and retention in schools in accordance with Article 4, paragraph 1 of CEDAW.

The high level of illiteracy has prevented many women from taking advantage of several temporary special measures that have been introduced by the government to ensure that women's interests are taken into account in the development process. These include the Women's Enterprise Fund, the Presidential Decree of October 2006 requiring 30 percent representation of women on decision-making boards and in government ministries, and lower entry criteria for female students applying to universities. Still, the situation is even more serious with rural women. A baseline survey conducted by FIDA-Kenya in 2006 on the level of awareness and impact of CEDAW on rural women found that the majority of them were not aware of the existence of CEDAW or of any report to the CEDAW by the government. They were also not aware of national policies and programmes to address the rights of rural women.

This shows that Kenya has excellent 'paper rights' for women and that the majority of women are yet to take advantage of CEDAW. There is a clear need for concerted efforts by the government, with support from civil society, to raise public awareness of legal reforms, effective law enforcement and legal literacy. Already organisations such as the Federation of Women Lawyers, *Kituo cha Sheria*, Kenya Human Rights Commission, Kenya National Commission on Human Rights, Political Caucus, League of Women Voters, and Kenya Women Political Alliance are already doing commendable work towards women's legal awareness. However, the government still needs to initiate deliberate approaches to make it easy for the most vulnerable to access justice on an equal basis with those who are better resourced.

While CEDAW has been grouped with a number of other declarations and conventions on human and women's rights in what has been referred to as an 'International Women's Rights Regime', it still faces several challenges at the local level, partly because of the following reasons. First, CEDAW is couched in a liberal, individual rights discourse. This discourse is quite critical of some aspects of tradition and culture, leading to one of the most serious areas of contestation against implementation (Ali 2002). Secondly, CEDAW is overly concerned with rule of law approaches and neglects the equally biased workings of traditional legal systems that have more relevance to the majority of women in developing countries such as Kenya (Haslegrave 1988). According to some analysts, the case of Kenya demonstrates that CEDAW is overtly blind to differences of power and resources and has succeeded in endorsing practices and policies that suit the privileged (O'Neill 2000). Despite the mobilisation of women and advocacy and increased political representation at national level, the normative gains are yet to translate into substantive changes in women's lives (Westhuizen 2005).

Conclusion

Kenya has ratified the required international instruments necessary to eliminate all forms of discrimination against women. In addition, Kenya has developed the required policies and programmes that correctly identify the sources of women's discrimination and propose bold steps towards reducing women's exclusion. However, Kenya is currently experiencing implementation challenges. These challenges are due to the huge resources required to fully comply with international instruments that seek to eliminate discrimination against women. Similarly, the prevailing norms and cultural practices still hinder the development of gender friendly legislation and programmes that can effectively guarantee women's legal rights and political participation. At the moment, Kenyan women and human rights campaigners need to ensure that the progressive provisions in the RDC remain intact and are even improved on when the final constitution is enacted. The government needs support from Kenyan people of goodwill and civil society organisations to increase awareness campaigns on harmful cultural practices and women's rights. The awareness will empower women to stand up for their rights and make informed choices that will result in leading better lives, free of discrimination.

References

Ali, S.S., 2002, 'Women's Rights, CEDAW, and International Human Rights Debates'. in J.L Parpart, S.M. Rai, and K. Staudt, eds., *Rethinking Empowerment: Gender and Development in a Global/Local World*, New York: Routledge.

Aluoch, J., 2008, 'Where Practice Meets Policy and the Law: The Implementation of Sexual Offences Act No. 3 of 2006', Paper presented to the International Association of Women Judges 9th Biennial International Conference, 25-28 March, 2008.

Bauman, Z., 1998, *Globalisation: The Human Consequences*, New York: Columbia University Press.

Bunch, C., 1995, 'Transforming Human Rights from a Feminist Perspective', in Julie Peters and Andrea Wolper, eds., *Women's Rights, Human Rights: International Feminist Perspectives*, New York and London: Routledge.

Clark, I., 1997, *Globalisation and Fragmentation*, Oxford: Oxford University Press.

FIDA-Kenya, 2007, Shadow Report to the 5th and 6th Combined Report of the Government of the Republic of Kenya, on the International Convention on the Elimination of All Forms of Discrimination Against Women, presented by FIDA-Kenya to the 39th Session of the United Nations Committee of CEDAW, 23 July-10 August 2007, New York.

Friedman, E., 1995, 'Women's Human Rights: The Emergence of A Movement', in Julie Peters and Andrea Wolper, eds., *Women's Rights, Human Rights: International Feminist Perspectives*, New York & London: Routledge, pp. 18-35.

Giddens, A., 1990, *The Consequences of Modernity*, Cambridge: Polity Press.

Gouws, A., 2006, 'Making Gains with Women's Rights: One Step Forward, Two or Three Steps Back, *CODESRIA Bulletin*, Nos 1 & 2, pp. 4-5.

Haslegrave, M., 1988, 'Women's Rights: The Road to the Millennium', in Peter Davies, ed., *Human Rights*, London: Routledge.

Heater, D., 1990, *Citizenship*, London: Longman.

Hobson, B. and Lister, R., 2001, 'Keyword: Citizenship', in J. Lewis, Hobson, B., and Siim, B., eds., Contested *Concepts: Gender and Social Politics*, Cheltenham: Edward Elgar.

Krut, R., 1997, 'Globalisation and Civil Society: NGO Influence in International Decision Making', UNRISD Discussion Paper No. 83, Geneva, United Nations Research Institute for Social Development.

Lister, R., 1997, *Citizenship: Feminist Perspectives*, Basingstoke: Macmillan.

Lister, R., 2001, 'Citizenship and Gender', in K. Nash and A. Scott, eds., *The Black Companion to Political Sociology*, Oxford: Blackwell.

Marshall, T.H., 1950, *Citizenship and Social Class*, Cambridge: Cambridge University Press.

Meer, S., and Sever, C., 2004, *Gender and Citizenship: Overview Report*, London: BRIDGE and Institute for Development Studies.

Muthien, B. and H. Combrinck, 2003, 'When Rights are Wronged: Gender Based Violence and Human Rights in Africa' in Kuumba, M. Bahati and Monica White, eds., *Transnational Transgressions: African Women, Struggle and Transformation in Global Perspective*, Trenton and Asmara: Africa World Press.

Nzomo, Maria and Patricia Kameri-Mbote, 2003, 'Gender Issues in the Draft Bill of the Constitution of Kenya: An Analysis', IELRC Working Paper, Nairobi: International Environmental Law Research Center.

O'Neill, O., 2000, 'Women's Rights, Whose Obligations?', in O. O'Neill, *Bounds of Justice*, Cambridge: Cambridge University Press

Okuro, O., 2007, 'Spoiling Property: The Impact of HIV/AIDS on Land Rights in Kombewa, Kenya 1983-2003, *African Sociological Review*, No. 2.

Okuro, O., 2008, 'HIV/AIDS Pandemic and its Impact on Land Rights in Kombewa Division - Kenya, 1983-2003. PhD Thesis: Maseno University - Kenya.

Okuro, S., 2002, 'The Impact of Globalisation on Smuggling: The Case of Women Smugglers Across the Kenya-Uganda Boundary', Paper presented during CODESRIA Gender Institute, Dakar-Senegal.

Oldfield, A., 1990, *Citizenship and Community, Civic Republicanism and the Modern World*, London: Routledge.

Pateman, C., 1989, *The Disorder of Women*, Cambridge: Polity Press.

Pearce, O. T., 2000, 'Gender and Governance in Africa: A Conceptual Framework for Research and Policy Analysis and Monitoring', Paper presented at the African Knowledge Networks Forum Preparatory Workshop, 17-18 August, Addis Ababa.

Sen, G., 2003, 'Feminist Politics in Fundamentalist World' in Mukhopadhyay M., ed., *Governing for Equity: Gender, Citizenship, and Governance*. Amsterdam: Royal Tropical Institute.

Thogori, J., 2005, 'Protocol to the African Charter on Human and Peoples Rights of Women in Africa - Kenya Case Study', in ICJ-K *International Human Rights Standards: Making a Case for Kenya's Ratification of Optional Protocols*, Nairobi: Kenya Section of International Commission of Jurists.

Voet, R., 1998, *Feminism and Citizenship*, London: Sage.

Wafula, C., 2008, 'War on Sexual Violence Stepped Up', *Daily Nation*, Wednesday, 13 August, Nairobi.

Walby, S., 1994, 'Is Citizenship Gendered?' in *Sociology*, 28(2), 379-95.

Werbner, P. and Yuval-Davis, N., 1999, 'Introduction: Women and the New Discourse of Citizenship', in Yuval-Davis, N. and Werbner, P., eds., *Women, Citizenship and Difference*, London and New York: Zed Books.

Westhuizen, Van der., 2005, *Gender Instruments in Africa: Critical Perspectives and Future Strategies*, Midrand: Institute for Global Dialogue.

11

Globalisation and Gendered Citizenship: The Mauritian Scenario[1]

Ramola Ramtohul

Introduction

This chapter examines the effects of globalisation on women's citizenship in Mauritius. Mauritius makes an interesting case study of the gender dimensions of globalisation, especially regarding citizenship. It is an island nation with an open economy, largely dependent on international trade for most of its food and export revenue. As such, globalisation has a direct impact on the lives of Mauritian citizens, and gender factors in prominently, given the differential access to resources and entitlements that men and women have in the country. Broadly speaking, globalisation denotes the process in which economic, financial, technical, and cultural transactions between different communities throughout the world become increasingly interconnected and embody common elements of experience, practice and understanding (Pearson 2000). With globalisation, time, place and space are all reconfigured and events, decisions and activities in one part of the world can have significant consequences for individuals and communities in other parts of the world (McGrew 1992).

Globalisation is occurring in a neoliberal era of free trade, free flow of capital, limited governmental regulation, and democratisation (Bayes *et al.* 2001). At the political level, globalisation leads to a decline in the power of the nation-state, causing it to lose crucial aspects of sovereignty, to the point where its role is transformed to that of acting local manager or facilitator for global capital (Pettman 1999). The nation-state also becomes subject to increasing influence from global and regional bodies, such as the United Nations and its associated agencies. The latter constitute a global forum within which states conduct aspects of their international relations. A number of international conventions and treaties prepared by these intergovernmental organisations have been ratified by most countries, legally binding the signatories to adhere to the conventions. Many of these pertain to human rights and also women's rights. In the case of the World Trade Organisation, trade liberalisation is a key concern.

Although globalisation creates new opportunities for people by increasing contacts across national boundaries, in the economy, in technology, in culture and in governance, it also fragments production processes, labour markets, political entities and societies, weakening their ability to resist the exploitative and, at times, destructive consequences of globalisation (UNDP 1999). Globalisation is indeed not a uniform and uni-linear process, and it has an uneven and differential impact on different regions, classes and people (Pettman 1999). As such, the impact of globalisation on gender relations and citizenship will be complex and contradictory, and largely determined by the level of development of a country, its culture and the literacy rate of women. Nevertheless, given that women were already differently positioned from men in relation to the state, citizenship and the labour market, the processes of globalisation and state transformation become highly gendered (Pettman 1999: 212). In order to analyse the gendered aspects of citizenship in the current era governed by the forces of globalisation, it becomes important to first examine the gender dimensions of citizenship.

Globalisation and gendered citizenship

Citizenship is a contested concept that has always been gendered since women and men have stood in a different relationship to it, largely to the disadvantage of women (Lister 2003). In fact, women have historically been denied the full and effective title of citizen in most countries of the world. Feminist authors[2] have argued that the exclusion of women from citizenship was an intrinsic feature of their seclusion and confinement to the private familial sphere, which then rendered their inclusion into the public sphere problematic. The public sphere was constructed as masculine, rational, responsible and respectable, and women became the 'property' that allowed married men, including the working classes, the right to be active citizens in this sphere (Werbner and Yuval-Davis, 1999).

Marshall (1950), the most prominent theorist of citizenship in Britain, defines citizenship as 'full membership in the community', while focussing on the relationship of class to social integration and omitting gender. Marshall's theory is nonetheless relevant for a gender analysis of citizenship in the current global era because it covers the focal areas of polity, economy and society. In fact, Mukhopadhyay (2004:19) contends that in feminist politics, the meaning of citizenship operates at four dimensions: the political level, the economic level, the cultural level of norms and values, and the personal level of family, home and relationships. Marshall's concept of citizenship also paves the way for an analysis of the degrees of citizenship obtained by different social groups at different times (Walby 1997).

Marshall (1950) posits that citizenship comprises three elements: civil, political and social. The civil element encompasses the rights necessary for individual freedom, such as liberty of the person, freedom of speech, thought and faith, the right to own property and to conclude valid contracts, as well as the right to justice. The primary institutions concerned with civil rights are the courts of justice. The political element involves the right to participate in the exercise of political power, either as a candidate standing for elections, or as a voter. The main institutions concerned are parliament and councils of local government. The social element covers the right to economic welfare and security, the right to social heritage and to a decent standard of living. The primary institutions concerned with social citizenship are the educational system and social services. Lister (1997) adds two further sets of rights to Marshall's formulation – reproductive rights and the right to participate in decision making. She views reproductive rights as an extension of an individual's civil, political and social rights. Moreover, the right to participate in decision making is currently a key tenet of modern feminism and has been given official recognition by global bodies, including the United Nations (Lister 1997). While the impact of globalisation on women's citizenship has been empowering at some levels, it has also been disempowering at other levels.

The opening up of new spaces driven by the weakening of the nation-state enables the undermining of traditional gender hierarchies, devising new bases of gender relations (Chinkin 2000; Bayes *et al.* 2001), thereby positively affecting women's social and economic citizenship. On the economic front for instance, with the New International Division of Labour (Frobel *et al.* 1980), globalisation entailed the relocation of factories and other transnational corporation activities to developing countries in search of cheap labour and lower costs of production for the world market. Free trade zones, also known as export processing zones, were set up in many developing countries in order to attract foreign capital with a package of incentives, including tax holidays, low interest loans and supple labour regulations. This was a major component of the export-oriented industrialisation (EOI) strategy adopted by a number of developing countries which had large reservoirs of cheap and available labour. The EOI model received the blessing of international agencies such as the International Monetary Fund (IMF) and the World Bank (Mitter 1986).

The economic forces of globalisation have strong gendered employment effects as women's labour was mainly absorbed in these industries in the low-skilled and low-paid jobs. Globalisation thus led to the rapid formation of a female, modern sector labour force in many countries, even those where women's participation in paid work was low and socially unacceptable.[3] Much of this increase was the result of a movement of female labour from the unpaid household and subsistence sectors to the paid economy where this labour was absorbed in labour-intensive assembly and manufacturing such as electronics, garments and sportswear, and data entry. Such employment has, however, also been exploitative. Sen (1997) notes, for instance, that a central feature of the current globalisation is the extent to which it draws upon and uses women's labour flexibility. Women have been considered to be a passive and compliant workforce, willing to accept low wages and a higher intensity of work than men without demanding labour and human rights (Frobel *et al*. 1980). This factor was attributed to the fact that women were given a secondary status in the labour market. It was generally assumed that women's employment provided a secondary rather than a primary family income and hence, because they were not expected to support dependents, they could be hired at relatively low wages (Mitter 1986).

Nevertheless, it cannot be denied that employment in free trade zones has provided some form of economic independence to women with low levels of literacy, thereby enhancing their social and economic citizenship. This has enabled many women to save for marriage or further education, delay marriage and childbearing and also to exercise personal choice of a marriage partner.[4] Such employment also enables women to enjoy a higher degree of personal freedom and more status within the household and society as a wage earner. However, globalisation is also fuelling the establishment of transnational enterprises in the fields of sex and pornography and human trafficking (Chinkin 2000), which exploit women and girls, depriving them of their basic rights as citizens.

Globalisation has weakened the decision-making and policy-making power of the nation-state and the consequences have been most visible in the domain of economic and labour policies – governments are slow or unwilling to implement policies to protect the rights of workers for fear of losing out on foreign direct investment. Moreover, structural adjustment policies (SAP), which were imposed on developing nations seeking loans from global monetary institutions (the World Bank and the IMF) have led to major reductions in government expenditure on the social sector, with disastrous consequences for women's citizenship. SAP affected women's earning capacity and right to social services including health and education, which jeopardised their citizenship at all levels.

The globalisation of governance and weakening of the nation-state has also impacted on women's citizenship in a positive manner, especially in areas concerning women's civil, political, social, reproductive and economic rights. In the last half of the twentieth century for instance, the global human rights movement has played a central role in legitimating the global demand for women's political citizenship (Bayes *et al.* 2001:7). The human rights agenda supports an undifferentiated juridical citizenship for all human beings regardless of sex or gender. At the 1994 United Nations World Conference on Human Rights, which was held in Vienna, delegates agreed that women's rights were human rights (Bayes *et al.* 2001). Furthermore, in the current global age, feminists have been organising transnationally for women's rights and peace such that a global gender regime now exists (Pettman 1999).

Globalisation has in fact facilitated the emergence of feminism as a goal in a wide variety of issue advocacy networks that are active at the transnational level (Ferree 2006). A number of international conferences organised under the patronage of the UN have brought together women's organisations and NGOs from all over the world to discuss and set a common agenda with regard to women's rights and women's citizenship, among other issues. Women's policy machineries have been set up in most countries of the world, nearly all of which have come into existence since the UN First World Conference on Women in Mexico City in 1975. These agencies have been charged with mainstreaming gender perspectives into policy and safeguarding women's political citizenship by ensuring that women receive a fair share of seats in elected and corporate bodies (Ferree 2006).

Women's constituencies have thus emerged as global citizens as they have lobbied at international forums for the right to development, freedom from domestic and sexual violence, sexual and reproductive rights, and the implementation of the Convention on the Elimination of All Forms of Discrimination against Women (CEDAW) as well as the Beijing Platform for Action (Mukhopadhyay 2004). On the African continent, many regional women's networks have been lobbying for the protection of women's rights in Africa. One important regional agreement concerned with women's rights and citizenship is the 1997 Southern African Development Community (SADC) Declaration on Gender and Development, which committed signatories to achieving at least 30 per cent representation of women in decision-making positions by 2005. In October 2000, African women's networks successfully lobbied for the adoption of UN Security Council Resolution 1325, which calls on states to increase the number of women in decision-making positions, incorporate women into peace negotiations, protect the human rights of women and girls, and integrate a gender perspective into peace processes (Adams 2006). Moreover, the African Union (AU), which was launched in 2003, has established a gender quota for national delegations to the Pan-African Parliament. In fact, Adams (2006:194) notes that African organisations were among the most active in the 50-50 gender equity campaigns that call for women to occupy at least half the seats in parliament. These examples highlight the positive impact of globalisation and regionalism on all aspects women's citizenship.

This overview of globalisation and gendered citizenship has highlighted some of the main aspects of women's citizenship that are affected by globalisation, in positive as well as negative ways. The next section briefly presents the demographic, economic and social dynamics of Mauritius, before discussing Mauritian women's citizenship in the global age. Data was collected from both primary and secondary sources, including semi-structured interviews of leaders of women's organisations and women politicians and documentary sources including press articles and parliamentary hansards of key time periods.

Mauritius: A Brief Introduction

Mauritius is a small island of 720 square miles, located in the south-western Indian Ocean with a population of approximately 1.2 million. It is one of the three small islands collectively called the Mascarene Islands. Mauritius lies on longitude 57 east of the Greenwich meridian and its latitude ranges from 19° 58' to 20° 32' in the southern hemisphere, just north of the Tropic of Capricorn. Mauritius has experienced successive waves of colonisers from the Dutch to the French and finally the British. The French played a highly significant role in the history and development of Mauritius, initially as colonisers and then as a local dominating group. Mauritian society is a plural one with the population presently made up of different groups.[5] Class and ethnic divisions in the population of Mauritius are very strong.

Mauritius gained political independence in 1968 and became a republic within the Commonwealth in 1992. Compared with most SADC countries, Mauritius combines a long tradition of democratic governance since independence with a relatively high ranking on the gender development index. Being a small and resource-poor country, Mauritius has tended to depend on imports for its supply of staple food while exports of sugar and textiles have been the main source of foreign currency. The island is far from its major markets and suppliers. During the colonial and immediate post-independence periods, Mauritius was essentially a sugar island, and the economy was totally dependent on the performance of the sugar industry and world price of sugar. This situation directly linked the fate of Mauritians to the vagaries of the weather and the world sugar price. Mauritius was a supplier of sugar to the British metropolis and remained a net importer of manufactured goods.

In the post-independence period to the early 1980s, the government sought to diversify sources of revenue by embarking on a path of industrialisation aimed at fostering economic development through export processing, agricultural diversification and tourism. The textile industry integrated in the Export Processing Zone provided significant employment opportunities for women and paved the way for many women to move out of the confines of the private sphere and step into the public sphere, thereby gaining some financial independence. Consequently, the economy experienced growth rates reaching a peak of 8 per cent (Alladin 1993). Mauritius now enjoys the status of a Newly Industrialising Country (NIC) and it is currently attempting to further diversify its economy by promoting investment in new sectors such as services, to develop the island as a regional financial centre and a 'cyber island'. The government is also trying to modernise the manufacturing sector by shifting to more capital-intensive, high-value commodities. With the erosion of preferential trade agreements, and in the face of globalisation, Mauritius is facing intense competition from larger textile producers such as India and China.

From the perspective of a small developing country endowed with limited resources, Mauritius has made commendable progress. It ranked 65th in the 2008 *Human Development Report* by the United Nations Development Programme (UNDP) with a Human Development Index (HDI) value of 0.802,[6] at 'high human development' level (UNDP 2008). However, the figure for the Gender Empowerment Measure[7] for Mauritius is relatively lower, at 0.509 in 2006,[8] indicating that Mauritian women still experience difficulties in acceding to positions of economic and political power. The post-independence government introduced a comprehensive welfare package that included free education and health services, and a subsidised food scheme. The country also resisted pressures from the IMF and World Bank to scale down welfare benefits, in order to maintain social cohesion in its plural society. The maintenance of the welfare state led to a rise in literacy rates for girls and the country has almost eradicated illiteracy.[9] Mauritius is known for its sustained political stability and its ability to preserve basic democratic rights for every citizen in a society consisting of different religions, ethnic backgrounds and languages. There has also been reference to the 'Mauritian Miracle' with Mauritius being considered as a model of development.[10]

Gendered Citizenship in Mauritius

The Mauritian state was modelled on the British colonial model, which is characterised by male hegemony at all levels of its structures. At independence, Mauritius thus inherited a structure ideology designed to systematically promote male privilege and power while consolidating women's subordination. The gendered quality of the state becomes clearly visible in its institutions, such as cabinet, parliament, the judiciary and the police force. Moreover, gender-based subordination has been and still is deeply ingrained in the consciousness of men and women in Mauritian society, and tends to be viewed as a natural corollary of the biological differences between them. Gender-based subordination is reinforced through religious beliefs, cultural practices, and educational systems that assign to women lesser status and power. The spheres of politics and religion, for instance, remain dominated by men. Moreover, a rigid sexual division of labour persists in the country, with domestic and reproductive work still considered to be 'women's work'. Men consider performing such work demeaning to them and their manhood..

Women have been unequal citizens in Mauritius since colonial times. The *Code Napoléon*[11] or 'Napoleon's Civil Code of 1804', adopted in 1808 in Mauritius, imposed the status of 'minor' on a married woman and was characterised by severe patriarchaly, restricting women to the private domestic sphere. Thus, for women from working class backgrounds, the nature of subordination primarily took the form of long hours of hard work coupled with sexual subordination. In the case of bourgeois women, it was amplified in terms of controls over physical mobility and sexuality. Women were legally and culturally ascribed second-class status in Mauritian society; marriage was considered to be the definitive fate of girls and any focus on women was limited to their reproductive roles. Moreover, women had little control over their own fertility and birth control depended on sexual abstinence, primitive forms of contraception, backstreet abortions and a high rate of infant mortality. There was also little concern for gender issues, except from the perspective of health, fertility and welfare (MAW/SARDC 1997).

Women's accession to civic, political and social citizenship was a gradual process, often hindered by religious and cultural patriarchal norms and beliefs. Male-dominated lobbies based on caste and communal identities attempted to block the proclamation of female suffrage in the late 1940s and hence opposed women's political citizenship (Ramtohul 2008b). Women's full civil citizenship has also been largely hindered by religious and communal lobbies that delayed the process. This necessitated strong lobbying from women's organisations, which was in the main driven by global factors, especially UN conventions and declarations and the international women's movement.

The response of Mauritian post-colonial leadership to cumulative gender inequalities that were historically embedded in the stratified and pluralistic society was primarily a policy of breaking down formal barriers to women's access to legal, political, educational and economic institutions. The assumption was that this would bring about significant changes in women's participatory roles. Wide-ranging opportunities became available to women. This included improved access to health services and reproductive health facilities, state provision of free education at all levels, employment opportunities and legal amendments to eliminate sex discrimination.

The Constitution of Mauritius, which is the supreme law of the country, currently enshrines the principle of equality such that all citizens irrespective of sex, ethnic background, religion and creed are equal before the law. Discriminatory clauses have been amended so that men and women are legally entitled to equal enjoyment of rights and freedoms, including opportunities and responsibilities in the social, economic, cultural and political spheres (Patten 2001). Mauritius is a signatory of a number of international conventions on women including CEDAW, the SADC Declaration on Gender and Development and the Commonwealth Plan of Action on Gender and Development.

Globalisation, Employment and the Emancipation of Mauritian Women

With regard to women's social and economic citizenship in Mauritius, globalisation has had a mixed impact. On one hand it has empowered a class of previously disadvantaged women. However, on the other hand, women have also had to face exploitation and the fact that globalisation requires a flexible labour force, which eventually jeopardises women's acquired rights and status as citizens. This sub-section discusses the impact of export-oriented industrialisation (EOI) and structural adjustment programmes (SAPs) on women's citizenship.

Mauritius has a comprehensive and well established welfare state which provides free education, health and universal pensions to the population. Mauritius is in fact a rare case study of a country that implemented SAPs and resisted the dictates of the IMF and the World Bank to scale down expenditure on its welfare state. Despite adverse economic conditions in the 1970s and early 1980s, the country maintained the welfare state with its comprehensive benefits and universal social provisions. The welfare state has largely cushioned the adverse effects of globalisation and unemployment in the industrial sector. The population has had access to free health facilities and education, which have had positive spin off effects on the working population. Hence, in Mauritius, global economic policy such as SAP did not have the severe effects on women's citizenship that occurred in much of the developing world.

Moreover, another aspect of SAPs in Mauritius involved the promotion of EOI, which required setting up the Mauritius Export Processing Zone (MEPZ), which eventually became the backbone of the country's export-led development (Frisen and Johansson 1993). From the early stages of the EPZ, women took up the new employment opportunities available. The setting up of the textile industry within the EPZ provided low-skill jobs for women, enabling them to obtain some degree of financial autonomy despite the precariousness of this form of employment. In his article on Mauritius, John McCarry (1993) spoke to a young woman who worked for a sweater factory in the EPZ. She had the following to say about the value of work for women:

> For a Mauritian woman, to work is to be free. Before, a girl could not leave home until her parents found a husband for her, and then she moved into her husband's family home and spent the rest of her life having babies.[12]

A major factor that contributed to the ready supply of women for factory work was the lack of employment opportunities for women in other parts of the Mauritian economy (Hein 1988). For women who did not graduate from secondary school, apart from work as an agricultural labourer or as a domestic servant, factory work was the only alternative available. This new economic status and freedom of women was in sharp contrast to their subservient position in the home, especially concerning marriage and parenthood (Dommen and Dommen 1999).

The fact that the Mauritian government created the EPZ in part to alleviate the unemployment problem, which was basically perceived as a male problem, highlights the male bias in economic policy and the odds that women faced. Yet, in spite of high unemployment among men, about 80 per cent of EPZ jobs went to women throughout the 1970s (Hein 1984). This situation caused an outcry among men, which even reached Parliament and is clearly visible in the statement of Opposition MP, Ivan Collendavelloo:

> ...Can we imagine the atmosphere in a house where the man is not working? We do not live in a matriarchal society; we live in a society, whether we like it or not, where the man has always been the head of the family ... So, let's not say that the increase in female employment, as compared with the decrease in male employment, is a problem to be set aside lightly...[13]

This statement highlights the strong patriarchal culture prevalent in Mauritian society and of the Mauritian state, since no specific policy had been set up to create employment opportunities for women. It was rather the nature of the industry, especially employers' preference for women, most of who already possessed sewing skills, which led to the preference for women workers in the textile and garment industry. By the late 1970s, women had also developed a reputation among employers as more reliable workers than men and as such, more productive. Women were considered to be more docile and easier to manage than men and consequently, involved lower supervisory costs.

Moreover, at that time, minimum wages for women were lower than for men, which may also explain why women were the preferred labour force for this industry. In December 1984, the government abolished the minimum wage for men in the EPZ with the aim of reducing the number of unemployed men and to try to correct the gender imbalance in EPZ employment. Wage liberalisation aligned men's fixed wages on those of women's and not the contrary. This measure led to greater male employment in the EPZ, although this industry has remained female dominated. Dommen and Dommen (1999) in fact contend that it was the opening up of the labour market to women that provided the impetus needed to modernise the role of women. Indeed, the increasing number of women working outside the home gradually undermined the stereotype that women's interests and capabilities were centred on the home. The creation of the EPZ thus enabled a general upgrading of the status and social and economic citizenship of Mauritian women, especially those with a low level of education, who make up the majority. With the availability of free education at primary, secondary and tertiary levels, Mauritian women have also found employment in the financial and service sectors of the economy (notably in tourism), with qualified women occupying high positions.

Accelerated globalisation and the removal of protectionism currently pose a tough challenge for the Mauritian textile industry, which is facing stiff competition from low-cost Asian producers. Many factories have closed down and women workers who make up the majority of the workforce of the industry have been laid off. Globalisation is, therefore, negatively affecting the citizenship of a class of women in Mauritius, those who are now older and have had a 'career' in the EPZ, and are now being laid off. Sustainability of the livelihoods of these women is thus in jeopardy at the moment. The industry is also increasingly hiring migrant workers, mostly single Chinese women. Chinese workers are forced into overtime because of an agreement with the Chinese government that their basic salaries be sent home in full. As such, overtime is their only legal means to make some money. Some of these workers are forcing into illegal trades such as sex work and illegal employment to earn an additional income. Most of the foreign workers are employed in the textile and garment sector (de Haan and Phillips 2002). Employers exhibit a strong preference for foreign workers since the latter are seen as more docile than their Mauritian counterparts and willing to work long hours without asking for sick leave and holidays. There are currently about 30,000 foreign workers in Mauritius of which more than half are women (Ackbarally 2006). These workers are cheaper to employ and more productive than Mauritian women who have family obligations and are unwilling to work long hours of overtime to meet delivery deadlines. The migrant workers are not citizens of Mauritius, and do not benefit from the rights and protection that Mauritians are entitled to, and as such, they face a greater risk of exploitation.

While economic globalisation has created employment opportunities for women, cultural and social attitudes have been slow to change. In fact, although increasing numbers of Mauritian women are now engaged in full-time employment, hardly any change has taken place at the level of the culture. The society still largely assigns reproductive and caregiver work to women. Thus, the majority of women continue to be burdened by triple roles with very little help from their spouses (MWRCDFW 2000). The growing burden of the triple load on women causes greater fatigue and stress among women, especially in cases where women are isolated in small nuclear families devoid of any form of kinship or neighbourhood support (MWRCDFW 1995). The need for quality and affordable support services for women is increasingly being felt.

Globalisation and Women's Rights in Mauritius

Prior to 1982, women's citizenship at the level of their civil rights was very low. Legislation governing marriage was discriminatory towards women and treated married women as minors. Men were abusing these laws and husbands often refused to contract civil marriages with their wives, leading to a large number of abandoned wives whose husbands had remarried.[14] Among Hindu families especially, the woman was under greater pressure to have a first-born male baby in order to 'deserve' civil marriage. Young girls were abused by their in-laws and this problem was more pronounced among Indo-Mauritian families.[15] Moreover, without a civil marriage, wives had no legal status within the marriage, children born to the union were not legitimate and husbands could refuse to acknowledge the children. Women had no rights within marriage, and the husband had the power to control whether his wife could work, open a bank account and even have access to her salary.

Mauritian women's fight for full citizenship benefited from the global attention on women's rights in the 1970s, with the proclamation of 1975 as International Women's Year and the decade 1975-1985 as the Decade for Women by the United Nations. This led to the creation of a feminist consciousness that was necessary for women to fight for equal civil rights. In fact, the global attention paid to women's soco-economic conditions facilitated the work of feminists. Shirin Aumeerudy Cziffra, who was a feminist activist and campaigner for equal rights for women and the first Minister of Women's Rights in 1982 explains:

> I was often considered to be an extremist in the days when feminism was looked down upon in Mauritius. I campaigned incessantly to forge a consciousness about women's rights which has gained momentum thanks to the internationalisation of the struggle by women in other countries, at the same period. The move for equal rights for women is at least irreversible – if not won. I also did everything in my power to forge solidarity amongst women and women's groups so that it was possible to lobby efficiently to bring change.[16]

Feminism and the struggle for women's rights have long been belittled in Mauritius as they were viewed as a threat to patriarchal authority and stability in the family. Such resistance reflected a fear and misunderstanding that feminism and the quest for equal rights for women would lead to a total transformation of the social order. A popular rendition of this anxiety is the notion that feminists are 'man haters' and that women would have to fight against men (Basu 1995). Feminism and the struggle for women's rights were also believed to alienate or divert women from their culture, religion and family responsibilities (Jayawardena 1986). This fear and misunderstanding led to reluctance on the part of many Mauritian women to be associated with feminist organisations, especially to avoid being alienated from their families.

The UN Declaration of 1975 as the Year of Women provided a much needed boost to the activities of women's organisations in the country, as explained by Shirin Aumeeruddy Cziffra:

> In 1975 the United Nations came out, all of a sudden declared the year of women and it was such a good opportunity for us … we used this year, UN year for women, to have exhibitions, to tell people about women's rights and it became OK because UN is giving us a sort of, you know, backing indirectly because this is the Year of Women.[17]

The support of the UN made the issue of women's rights politically acceptable and facilitated the organisation of seminars and discussions on this issue despite the conservative and patriarchal nature of Mauritian society. The UN Decade for Women was also instrumental in making space for leaders of women's organisations in Mauritius to interact with women activists from different countries. Twelve women were sent by the Mauritian government as delegates to the UN First World Conference on Women held in Mexico City in 1975.[18] The Mauritian delegation included the Minister of Women's Affairs and representatives of women's organisations. The issues discussed at the conference raised the awareness of these delegates on the problems women faced in Mauritius and possible strategies for action. Kokila Deepchand, a founder member of the Mauritius Alliance of Women, who attended the conference states:

> There, we realised the extent to which women were discriminated against.[19]

The participation of leaders of different women's organisations in international women's conferences encouraged women's organisations to group together and lobby for legal changes.

In 1976, the International Alliance of Women selected Mauritius as the venue for its international conference for women. International funding became available to women's organisations in Mauritius to initiate projects.[20] In 1977, amendments to the Immigration and Deportation Act were made so that all foreign men married to Mauritian women lost their right of residence in Mauritius. This discriminatory clause did not apply to foreign women married to Mauritian men. The aim of these amendments was essentially patriarchal; namely to protect the economic interests of the propertied class of Mauritian men. According to the *Muvman Liberasyon Fam* (MLF),[21] there was very strong pressure from the elite for nominations and appointments of Mauritian men in high-ranking jobs in government, parastatal bodies and private enterprises (MLF 1988). The interests of this group were threatened by foreign husbands of Mauritian women who were highly qualified and as such, competed with Mauritians for the high-ranking professions.

This blatant discrimination sparked indignation among women's organisations, which then grouped into a common front called *Front Commun Organisations Femmes* (FCOF).[22] The FCOF was specifically set up to fight against the Immigration and Deportation Act, which discriminated against women. It was the first women's front in Mauritius and initially, its actions were locally based, including petitions and demonstrations in front of Parliament. When these actions did not bring any change, the FCOF sought international action and took the case[23] to the United Nations Human Rights Committee on Sexual Discrimination in May 1978. This case set an international precedent and is still consulted by law students and jurists. It was in fact the first case on sexual discrimination was put before the Human Rights Committee. The women's front won the case and the government was asked to amend the law – which happened in 1982, after a change of government.

The utilisation of global governance instruments by the women's front to safeguard women's citizenship and civil liberties was successful and drew international attention to the plight of women in Mauritius, especially the dire state of affairs regarding women's rights. This was also an embarrassment to the Mauritian government, which was compelled to initiate action to redress the situation. Two other coalitions or alliances[24] between women's organisations were formed in 1978 to fight for women's rights in marriage and to pressure the government to amend the Code Napoléon. Many of these women leaders[25] had attended the 1975 First World Conference on Women in Mexico City and three years later, they were frustrated with the slow progress of the Ministry for Women's and Consumer Protection with regard to changes in the laws governing women's rights in marriage. The collective lobbying of the different women's groups was successful and led to a change in the civil code and an enhancement of women's rights and full citizenship.

Globalisation and Women's Political Citizenship

Women's representation in the Mauritian Parliament has been consistently marginal since women formally became political citizens in 1948. This state of affairs has not changed since independence in 1968 despite the prevalence of consolidated democratic governance and a distinct improvement in the status of women in Mauritius with regard to education, employment and rights. The report of the Task Force set up by the Ministry of Women's Rights, Child Development and Family Welfare to identify areas where discrimination against women prevailed, found that the gap between legal and actual equality in the area of power and decision making was extremely wide and that women's interests and concerns were not adequately represented at policy-making levels (Patten 2001). Consequently, women are largely unable to influence key decisions in social, economic and political areas that affect society as a whole (Sachs *et al.* 2002).

Following independence, Mauritius adhered to a number of international conventions which specifically promote women's empowerment and women's political citizenship. Mauritius has ratified the Convention on the Elimination of All Forms of Discrimination against Women (CEDAW) in 1984; the Beijing Declaration and Platform for Action in 1995; and the SADC Declaration on Gender and Development in 1997. CEDAW aims to bring an end to women's exclusion from a number of sectors, including politics. The Beijing Platform of Action requires a strong commitment from governments to promote women's advancement in twelve critical areas, one of which is politics. The signing the SADC Declaration on Gender and Development committed the governments of Mauritius and other SADC countries to reach the target of 30 per cent of MPs being women by 2005. These international conventions have acted as an external force exerting pressure on the Mauritian government to address the problem of women's marginal representation in Parliament and in general governance and initiate some form of action. Although very little concrete action has taken place, prior to the ratification of these international conventions and the subsequent rise in awareness of women's marginal presence in Mauritian politics, women's political citizenship as a political or even social issue was largely dormant.

Recommendations of these international conventions on the political citizenship of women encouraged some women's organisations to lobby for an increased presence of women in Parliament on the eve of the July 2005 general elections. Media Watch Organisation-GEMSA, a local women's organisation that has close links with the South African women's organisation Gender Links, has been lobbying for higher representation of women in Parliament and for the government to abide by its commitments to the 1997 SADC Gender Protocol. In February 2005, Media Watch Organisation-GEMSA organised a workshop on 'Gender, Media and Elections' in collaboration with Gender Links. Political leaders were invited to present the position of their parties on gender equality and making space for women in key political positions. Loga Virahsawmy explains:

> We got all the political leaders to sit together at one table. This was the first time
> in the history of Mauritius that political leaders sat down at the same table and we
> wanted them to make commitments – what they are going to do for the election,

how many women they were going to put as candidates and, their manifesto, their programme about gender.[26]

The impact of this workshop, which was given good coverage by the media, was a major contribution towards making women's marginal presence in the Mauritian Parliament a national issue that was for the first time openly discussed public.

Furthermore, in March 2005, the first women's party in Mauritius – the Majority Party – was set up with the aim of supporting women candidates of any political party and encouraging women to vote for women candidates. A women's platform called *FédèrAction* was also set up that same month. *FédèrAction* organised a demonstration on 28 March 2005 to express support for all political parties fielding at least one woman candidate per constituency. On this issue, Sheila Bunwaree, a founding member of *FédèrAction* states the following:

> We thought that the fact that Mauritius had the chair of SADC at that time ... it was an excellent opportunity to put pressure on this very male-dominated structure that are political parties and give them a kind of a lesson and tell them that hey, women want to make their voices heard and we want to claim for that political space ... we said that unless we protest openly and show up the politics of resistance to the way that they are handling things, the situation, they will not probably pay enough attention.[27]

Unfortunately, the march did not attract a large additional crowd,[28] particularly of women, but it brought a previously private issue to the public sphere, and contributed to raising nationwide awareness of women's marginalisation in politics. It was in fact the first public protest march that had been organised in favour of women's political citizenship in Mauritius. The international conventions governing women's rights and citizenship that had been ratified by the Mauritian state, especially the SADC Protocol on Gender and Development, contributed to the formation of new women's organisations that focused on women's political citizenship and initiated action to fight for women's right to political representation. Following the July 2005 elections, although the 30 per cent figure for women's representation in Parliament was not attained, women's parliamentary presence rose to 17 per cent, the highest figure ever attained. More recently, in May 2006, a new women's organisation called Women in Networking (WIN) was set up with the help of international organisations[29] and foreign funding. WIN and its sub-section Women in Politics (WIP) have been working towards doubling the number of women in Parliament in the future and to this end, they have been training potential women leaders. At this level, globalisation has indeed been a major support to the enhancement of women's political citizenship in Mauritius.

Conclusion

This chapter has highlighted a number of key areas in which globalisation affects women's citizenship. Given that Mauritius is an island which was isolated from international feminist networks before the internet revolution, local women's organisations had to cope with stronger odds due to the conservative patriarchal norms governing respectable femininity that were resistant to progressive change in women's rights. Support and exchange of ideas with international feminist networks was of capital help to the dynamic mobilisation of women's organisations in Mauritius. Women's mobilisation in Mauritius has been significantly influenced by recommendations from the international community, especially from the United Nations Decade of Women, the Nairobi Forward-Looking Strategies, CEDAW, the Beijing Platform for Action and more recently, the SADC Declaration on Gender and Development. These recommendations have given international backing to local women's initiatives and as such, have served as a powerful lobbying mechanism employed by women in different national contexts on issues pertaining to women's rights and citizenship. In the Mauritian plural society where governance is influenced by strong religious, ethnic and communal lobbies, issues pertaining to women's rights are often given minimal importance. With globalisation and the international focus on women's rights, the Mauritian government had no choice but to give greater consideration to women's rights. The support of global feminist networks and the UN strengthened the women's movement in Mauritius. However, globalisation has had a mixed impact on women's economic citizenship. While it initially empowered a class of women who had only basic education, the benefits have been temporary due to the global requirements for a flexible labour force in the EPZ. As such, new challenges are facing women's economic citizenship, especially the older generation of women who do not possess marketable skills.

Notes

1. Funding for this research was provided by the American Association of University Women, the University of Cape Town and the A.W. Mellon Foundation.
2. Pateman (1988), Lister (2003).
3. (Pyle 1983; Hein 1986; Ong 1987; Feldman 1992 – cited in Beneria 1999).
4. (Foo and Lim 1987; Lin 1986 – cited in Lim, 1990).
5. Mauritian society is composed of four ethnic groups and four major religions, Ramtohul: Globalisation and the Gender Question, namely, the Franco-Mauritians and Creoles who are Catholic; the Indian community who are Muslim and Hindu; and the small Chinese community, either Buddhist or Catholic.
6. http://hdrstats.undp.org/2008/countries/country_fact_sheets/cty_fs_MUS.html.l (accessed 13 March 2009). UNDP classifies countries with an HDI score of 0.800 and above as being at 'high human development' level whereas those with scores ranging from 0.500 to 0.799 are at 'medium human development' level.
7. The gender empowerment measure (GEM) whether women take an active part in economic and political life. It tracks the share of seats in parliament held by women; the number of senior officials and managers; and of female professional and technical workers; and the gender disparity in earned income, reflecting economic independence (UNDP 2008).
8. http://hdrstats.undp.org/2008/countries/country_fact_sheets/cty_fs_MUS.html (accessed 13 March 2009).
9. According to the 2000 census, the literacy rate of the population aged 12 years and above was 88.7 per cent for men and 81.5 per cent for women (EISA: http://www.eisa.org. za/WEP/mau2.htm - accessed in July 2006).
10. Brautigam (1999a), (1999b); Alladin (1993).
11. The Code Napoléon, backed by the Catholic Church and enacted in 1804, classified married women with children, the insane and criminals as politically incompetent. It restricted women's legal and civil rights, made married women economically and legally subject to their husbands and declared that they belonged to the family, not to public life. This legislation also forbade women from attending political meetings or wearing trousers (Lerner 1993).
12. McCarry (1993: 115).
13. Speech from the Throne, 13 November 1984 (Parliamentary Hansard).
14. Interview with Kokila Deepchand, founder member of the Mauritius Alliance of Women, 25 January 2007.
15. Interview with Kokila Deepchand, 25 January 2007.
16. Statement of Shirin Aumeeruddy Cziffra, cited in Study on the Evolution of Women and Gender Development in Mauritius over Three Generations (MRC 2003: 103).
17. Interview with Shirin Aumeeruddy Cziffra, 31 January 2007.
18. L'Express (13 March 1977) p. 3.

19. Interview with Kokila Deepchand, 25 January 2007.

20. Interview with Sheela Baguant, founder member of the Women's Self-Help Association and the Mauritius Alliance of Women, 25 January 2007.

21. The Muvman Liberasyon Fam is a leftist women's organisation.

22. The four women's organisations that set up the FCOF were: The Muvman Liberasyon Fam, the Ligue Féministe, the women's section of the MMMSP) led by Loga Virahsawmy, and the women's section of the Christian Movement for Socialism led by Jocelyne Minerve.

23. The case is called Shirin Aumeeruddy Cziffra and nineteen Mauritian women against the Government of Mauritius. Available at http://www.law.wits.ac.za/humanrts/undocs/session36/9-35.htm (accessed on 5 August 2008).

24. These are Solidarité Fam and the Mauritius Alliance of Women (MAW).

25. For example: Kokila Deepchand from MAW, Sheela Baguant from the Women's Self-Help Association and MAW, and France Boyer de la Giroday from *Les Ecoles Ménagères*.

26. Interview with Loga Virahsawmy, founder member of Media Watch Organisation-GEMSA – 10 January 2007.

27. Interview with Sheila Bunwaree, 31 January 2007.

28. The press reported that the march had between 150 participants (*Le Mauricien*, 28 March 2005) and 200 participants (L'Express, 29 March 2005), mainly women.

29. These include UNDP, Soroptimist International and Barclays Bank.

References

Ackbarally, N., 2006, 'Foreign workers in Mauritius face torrid time', *Mail and Guardian* 28 November, (http://mg.co.za) 12 October 2007.

Adams, M., 2006, 'Regional Women's Activism: African Women's Networks and the African Union', in Ferree, M. M. and Tripp, A. M., eds., *Global Feminism: Transnational Women's Activism, Organising and Human Rights*. New York and London: New York University Press.

Alladin, I., 1993, *Economic Miracle in the Indian Ocean: Can Mauritius show the way?* Port Louis: Editions de L'Océan Indien.

Basu, A., 1995, 'Introduction' in A. Basu, ed., *The Challenge of Local Feminisms: Women's Movements in Global Perspective*. Boulder: Westview.

Bayes, J. H., Hawkesworth, M. E. and Kelly, R. Mae, 2001, 'Globalisation, Democratisation, and Gender Regimes' in Kelly, R. Mae, Bayes, J. H., Hawkesworth, M. and Young, B., eds., *Gender, Globalisation and Democratisation*, Lanham, Boulder, New York and Oxford: Rowman & Littlefield.

Beneria, L., 1999, 'Global Markets, Gender and the Davos Man', Paper presented at the First Global Forum on Human Development, 29-31 July 1999, New York: United Nations Headquarters.

Brautigam, D., 1999a, 'Mauritius: Rethinking the Miracle', *Current History*, May: 228-231.

Brautigam, D., 1999b, 'The 'Mauritius Miracle': Democracy, Institutions, and Economic Policy', in Joseph, R., ed., State, *Conflict and Democracy in Africa,* Boulder and London: Lynne Rienner.

Burn, N., 1996, 'Mauritius' in Kothari, U. and Nababsing, V., eds., *Gender and Industrialisation: Mauritius, Bangladesh, Sri Lanka.* Port Louis: Editions de l'Océan Indien.

Chinkin, C., 2000, 'Gender and Globalisation', *UN Chronicle*, Vol. 37, No. 2. New York: UN Department of Public Information.

de Haan, E. and G. Phillips, 2002, *Made in Southern Africa* Clean Clothes Campaign. (http://pongrepublic.com/ftp/Africa-report.pdf) 12 October 2007.

Dommen, E. and B. Dommen, 1999, *Mauritius: An Island of Success – A Retrospective Study 1960-1993,* Wellington: Pacific Press; Oxford: James Currey.

Ferree, M. M., 2006, 'Globalisation and Feminism: Opportunities and Obstacles for Activism in the Global Arena', in Ferree, M. M. and Tripp, A. M. eds., *Global Feminism: Transnational Women's Activism, Organising and Human Rights,* New York and London: New York University Press.

Frisen, L. and Johansson, H., 1993, 'Export Processing Zones and Export-led Industrialisation: The Case of Mauritius', Minor Field Study Series No. 44, Department of Economics, Lund: University of Lund.

Frobel. F., Heinrichs, J. and Kreye, O., 1980, *The New International Division of Labour,* Cambridge: Cambridge University Press.

Gouws, A., 2005, 'Introduction', in A. Gouws, ed., *(Un)thinking Citizenship: Feminist Debates in Contemporary South Africa*, Cape Town: UCT Press; Basingstoke: Ashgate.

Hecralall, P and Lau Thi Keng, J.C., 1993, *Impact of Industrialisation on EPZ Women and their Families,* Centre de Documentation, de Recherches, et de Formation Indianocéaniques, CEDREFI: (http://www.cowan.edu.au/library/iorr/text/epz.htm) June 2000.

Hein, C., 1984, 'Jobs for the Girls: Export Manufacturing in Mauritius', *International Labour Review,* Vol. 123, No. 2, pp. 251-265.

Hein, C., 1988, 'Multinational Enterprises and Employment in the Mauritian Export Processing Zone', *Working Paper No. 52,* Multinational Enterprises Programme, Geneva: International Labour Organisation.

Jayawardena, K., 1986, *Feminism and Nationalism in the Third World*, London and New Jersey: Zed Books.

Lerner, G., 1993, *The Creation of Feminist Consciousness: From the Middle Ages to Eighteen-seventy,*, Oxford, New York: Oxford University Press.

Lim, L., 1990, 'Women's Work in Export Factories: The Politics of a Cause', in Tinker, I., ed., *Persistent Inequalities: Women and World Development*, New York, Oxford: Oxford University Press.

Lister, R., 1997, 'Dialectics of Citizenship', *Hypatia*, Vol. 12, No. 4, pp. 6-26.

Lister, R., 2001, 'Citizenship and Gender', Available at (http://www.socsci.aau.dk/cost/gender /Workingpapers/lister.pdf)., 15 August 2008.

Lister, R., 2003, *Citizenship: Feminist Perspectives*, 2nd edn. New York: Palgrave.

Marshall, T.H., 1950, *Citizenship and Social Class*, Cambridge: Cambridge University Press.

Mauritius Alliance of Women and Southern African Research and Documentation Centre, 1997, *Beyond Inequalities: Women in Mauritius*, Mauritius and Harare: MAW and SARDC.

Mauritius Research Council, 2003, *Study on the Evolution of Women and Gender Development over Three Generations in Mauritius*, Rose Hill: MRC.

McCarry, J., 1993, 'Mauritius: Island of Quiet Success', *National Geographic*, Vol. 183, No. 4, pp. 110-132.

McGrew, A., 1992, 'A Global Society', in Hall, S., Held D., and McGrew, T., eds., *Modernity and its Futures*, Cambridge: Polity Press/Open University.

Ministry of Women's Rights, Child Development and Family Welfare, 1995, *White Paper on Women in Development*, Port Louis: MWRCDFW.

Ministry of Women's Rights, Child Development and Family Welfare, 2000, *National Gender Action Plan*, Port Louis: MWRCDFW.

Mitter, S., 1986, *Common Fate, Common Bond: Women in the Global Economy*, London: Pluto Press.

Mukhopadhyay, M., 2004, 'Introduction: Gender, Citizenship and Governance', in *Gender, Citizenship and Governance: A Global Source Book*, Cowley: Oxfam; Amsterdam: Royal Tropical Institute (KIT).

Muvman Liberasyon Fam, 1988, *The Women's Liberation Movement in Mauritius*, Port Louis: Ledikasyon pu Travayer.

Pateman, C., 1988, *The Sexual Contract*, Cambridge: Polity Press.

Patten, P., 2001, *Task Force Report*, Port Louis: Ministry of Women's Rights, Child Development and Family Welfare.

Pearson, R., 2000, 'Moving the goalposts: Gender and globalisation in the twenty-first century', *Gender and Development*, Vol. 8, No. 1, pp. 10-19.

Pettman, J.J., 1999, 'Globalisation and the Gendered Politics of Citizenship', in Davis, N. Y. and Werbner, P., eds., *Women, Citizenship and Difference*, London and New York: Zed Books.

Ramtohul, R., 2000, 'Women's Employment in Free Trade Zones in the Global Economy', MSc dissertation submitted to the University of Bristol (unpublished).

Ramtohul, R., 2007, 'The Gender Dimensions of Slavery in the Indian Ocean Island of Mauritius', Paper presented at the CODESRIA Gender Symposium, 12-14 November, Cairo.

Ramtohul, R., 2008 'Engendering Mauritian History: The Hidden Controversies over Female Suffrage', Paper presented at the CODESRIA conference on African History on 'Re-reading the History and Historiography of Domination and Resistance in Africa', 27-29 October, Kampala.

Ramtohul, R., 2009, 'Women and Politics in a Plural Society: The Case of Mauritius', PhD dissertation submitted to the University of Cape Town (unpublished).

Sachs, A., Tandon B.B. and R. Ahnee, 2002, *Report of the Commission on Constitutional and Electoral Reform*, Port Louis: Prime Minister's Office.

Sen, G., 1997, 'Globalisation in the 21st Century: Challenges for Civil Society', Paper presented at the UvA Development Lecture, University of Amsterdam, 20 June.

United Nations, 1999, *1999 World Survey on the Role of Women in Development: Globalisation, Gender and Work*, New York: UN.

UNDP, 1999, *Human Development Report 1999*, New York and Oxford: Oxford University Press.

UNDP, 2005, *Human Development Report 2005*, New York: Oxford University Press.

Walby, S., 1997, *Gender Transformations*, London and New York: Routledge.

Werbner, P and Yuval-Davis, N., 1999, 'Introduction: Women and the New Discourse of Citizenship', in Yuval-Davis, N. and Werbner, P., eds., *Women, Citizenship and Difference*, London and New York: Zed Books.

Newspapers

L'Express, 13 March 1977, *'Femmes?'* (page 1).

L'Express, 29 March 2005, *'Marche pacifique: FédèrAction n'attire que 200 personnes'*, http://www.lexpress.mu , Accessed on 29 March 2005.

Le Mauricien, 28 March 2005, *'Dans les rues de la capitale à la mi-journée – environ 150 femmes marchent à l'initiative de FédèrAction'*, http://www.lemauricien.com/mauricien.htm, Accessed on 28 March 2005.

12

Rethinking Gender and Citizenship in a Global Age: A South African Perspective on the Intersection between Political, Social and Intimate Citizenship

Sharon Groenmeyer

Introduction

Citizenship as a concept is contested and the dilemmas raised by the term remain largely unresolved and open to different meanings and theoretical positions (Plummer 2003; Meer and Sever 2004; Gouws 2005; Goetz 2007). The classical liberal formulation of citizenship is based on T.H. Marshall's (1950:4) definition as:

> a status bestowed on those who are full members of a community and those who possess this status are equal with respect of the rights and duties with which the status is endowed' (Marshall cited in Plummer 2003:51).

These rights include civil, political and social rights and obligations. Marshall defines social rights as:

> the whole range from the right to a modicum of economic welfare and security to the right to share ... in... social heritage and to live the life of a civilised being according to the standards (of) society' (Sweetman citing Marshall 1950:10).

According to Sweetman, this view of citizenship goes beyond the concerns of politics, national government and legal systems to the interaction of individual's rights with collective groupings at all levels (Sweetman 2003:3). Yuval-Davis (1997:5) agrees that Marshall's definition provides the framework to analytically discuss citizenship as a multi-tiered construct which applies to people's membership in a variety of collectives – local, ethnic, national and transnational. Yuval-Davis (1997) considers this multi-tiered approach important because neo-liberal states have redefined and re-privatised their tasks and obligations thus gendering citizenship to the disadvantage of women. Feminists are concerned with definitions of citizenship because governments often exclude women from citizenship rights because of their work in the private sphere and the problematisation of their inclusion in the public sphere (Gouws 2005:3).

South Africa is an example of a constitutional democracy where women have similar rights to those of their male counterparts. As a liberal democracy, citizens have equal access to rights and opportunities but these are formal rights rather than a measure of substantive equality. For example, without the vote, women are not regarded as citizens; but even when they can vote and be voted for, as citizens, they still have no access to the basic services of water, electricity or housing? (Gouws 2005:3)

This chapter draws on a rights-based framework formulated on the principles of gender justice that underpin the 1979 Convention on the Elimination of all Forms of Discrimination against Women (CEDAW). South Africa is a signatory to CEDAW and to the 1997 Southern African Development Community (SADC) Declaration on Gender and Development. These protocols bind the government to the implementation of rights-based citizenship for women. With the advent of democracy, South Africa realigned its economic policies with the globalising world, with contradictory results for society, especially for women, who provide the bulk of family care. Mirroring global trends, the South African government's welfare provisions became gendered, which resulted in the contradictory approach to implementing the international protocols.

This chapter focuses primarily on different forms of citizenship rights for women and other vulnerable groups such as children and the aged. The gendered nature of citizenship, especially the exclusion of certain categories of women from exercising their rights, is viewed not only as a violation of rights; the lack of legal protection also increases their exposure to institutional and physical violence The recent institutional and physical violence against migrants/refugees and women are viewed with horror by the general public and the outside world but are, in fact, the normal way in which certain sections of South African society interact with minority and vulnerable groups (Fuller

2008:3). To comprehend the disjuncture between formal equality and the reality of the contradictory practices of citizenship, this paper attempts to extend the concept from that of an isolated practice of juridically defined individuals with rights to the recognition by the state of citizen participation within the local community (Gouws 2005).

This chapter concludes with an assessment of the intersectionality between[1] political, social and intimate citizenship and offers alternative ways of rethinking forms of citizenshipin a global age.

Gendered Dimensions of Social, Political and Intimate Citizenship

Feminists have added their voice of discontent to the dilemma of definitions. Meer and Sever (2004) believe that the understanding of citizenship has changed as meanings associated with it have shifted over time. In many countries, notably in Europe, when early definitions of *citizens as warriors* gave way to *citizen voters*, women were able to campaign for inclusion in universal suffrage. Nevertheless, feminists object to the false universalism of citizenship that treats all citizens as ungendered, abstract and disembodied individuals (Lister 1997 – cited in Gouws 2005:4). Women as citizens are acknowledged as members of the nation. However, this notion is often linked to their stereotypical roles as mothers. Meer and Sever (2004) point out that those gender roles continue to be stereotyped because women enter the realms of citizenship within a familial paradigm. This approach raises another conundrum. Feminists question whether the inclusion of women as citizens should be related to their differences from or their similarities to men. Therefore, differences between men and women are often ignored because liberalism constructs a unified/universal subject and in this way makes the concept of citizenship essential.

Post-1994 discourse of rights in South Africa has focussed on human rights and on law reforms that benefit women through personal empowerment in areas such as reproductive rights, the reform of customary unions, addressing violence against women, same sex unions, and women's rights within the workplace (Gouws 2005:8). This liberal rights discourse frames social citizens as individuals engaging with the state. The human rights discourse encouraged the enforcement of collective citizenship rights by the Treatment Action Group when it challenged the government to roll out anti-retroviral medication for people living with HIV & AIDS. Consequently, social movement organisations have combined the individual rights with collective rights for the benefit of their members.

In the sub-Saharan region, the narrow and linear definitions that consider citizenship as the relationship between state and citizen have also been questioned. According to Nyamu-Musembi (2007:236), the rights approach excludes the experience of citizenship mediated by other markers such as relationships between gender inequality, political participation and active social citizenship as key to rethinking the concept within a global age. These definitions s h o w the responsibilities of women within the reproductive sphere by bestowing appropriate social roles and obligations on gender construction. Thus, the gendering of citizenship inhibits individuals, particularly women, from taking on other activities and consequently conceals the multiplicity of roles that any individual may engage in. Therefore, acknowledging the rights of an individual should not be offset against, but rather be part of a continuum of the rights or needs of the family, the community, the nation or territorial state (Goetz 2007). Sadly, too often, the emphasis on whether rights are universal or fixed conceals historical contexts in which particular rights were formulated, and consequently may exclude a large number of people from this process.

Political citizenship defines the roles and relationships inherent in society that dictate who is *inside* and who is *outside;* and which activities are *valued.* Political participation leads to different types and levels of exclusion from the advantages that membership secures. An example of this exclusion is the exemption of personal law from constitutional law in South Africa (SA). In this instance, feminists clashed with traditional chiefs over whether the Bill of Rights should assert the primacy of equal rights for women over the imperative of demonstrating respect for traditional and customary social norms. Consequently, the exemption of personal law from constitutional law in the SA Bill of Rights acknowledged the endurance and intensity of traditional structures. Kabeer (cited in Goetz 2007) identifies this process as the parallel tradition of juxtaposing the moral economy that is founded on norms of reciprocity between socially acknowledged members, with a contract based on agreements with abstract individuals.

As the concept of citizenship has evolved to include the notion of sexual rights, it has become steeped in a history of heterosexist, patriarchal principles and practices (Evans 1993 – cited in Plummer). According to Richardson (2000a; 2000b) cited by van Zyl (2005:224), citizens are normatively constructed as (hetero)sexual subjects and 'excluded citizens' consequently face various forms of discrimination Feminist conceptions of citizenship recognise the public/private dichotomy and how this has gendered social relations between women and men as citizens. Daily experiences of food provision, childcare, income generation, and household duties often limit women's participation outside the private sphere. This divide entrenches women's gender roles and responsibilities within the family, caring and child rearing and the informal workplace; and men's gender roles in decision making, formal politics, economics and the formal workplace. The sexual division of labour is closely linked to certain definitions of citizenship, which traditionally saw men as the holders of citizenship rights on account of their position in the public arena. Women and their concerns were outside the realms of citizenship, and their roles, though contributing to society, were not valued as worthy of membership in terms of decision making and public activity. Therefore, definitions and understandings of gendered roles within citizenship are inevitably partial because the experiences of women and men vary according to their different roles and the nature of power relations within society. Today, the social construction of gender roles enables women to be politicians, soldiers and wage earners, just as men can be peace activists and care workers.

Changes in the global economy have been facilitated by the globalisation of the information and communication networks through which information, like money, flows above and through national boundaries (Lister 2003:55). Globalisation has ushered in market-led technological development coupled with transnational citizenship, but this process tends to impede vulnerable groups from attaining, being granted or reaping the benefits of full citizenship. Consequently, migrants, refugees, asylum seekers, women and children caught in conflict situations such as war do not hold citizenship rights of country of residence. These stateless people are particularly vulnerable to economic or sexual exploitation, especially human trafficking.

Therefore, the discourse on sexual citizenship, especially women's sexuality, includes the problem of rape, gender-based violence, abortion, reproductive rights and debates on assisted conception within intimate relationships. As such, intimate citizenship refers to all areas of life that appear to be personal but are connected to, structured by, or regulated through the public sphere. The intimate relationships or intimate citizenship within the private sphere are deeply embedded in a matrix of power relations played out in the public sphere. Families are structured through laws as well as politics and the intimate sphere is socially produced through a network of passionate human beings engaging with each other, often in highly personal ways (Plummer 2003). Moreover, human beings have rights to sexual pleasure as part of basic health based on the principle of autonomy or personhood. Because human beings have agency, they have a choice to exercise rights to intimate citizenship.

With increasing globalisation, gendered inequality may be relegated to markets or family. Notwithstanding the former, the high incidence of female-headed households[3] and the increasing dependence on a weak social security net makes a market or family solution non-existent. Thus, extending the boundaries of citizenship illustrates the interdependence of the public and private spheres. Because people are members of more than one community at the same time, and can simultaneously experience oppression and privilege, intersectionality as a feminist theory appears to be an appropriate explanation of how identities are constructed, deconstructed and reconstructed. Intersectional analysis aims to reveal multiple identities, exposing the different types of discrimination and disadvantage that occur as a consequence of the combination of identities. It also aims to address the manner in which racism, patriarchy, class oppression and other systems of discrimination create structural inequalities for women. This approach takes account of historical, social and political contexts but also recognises unique individual experiences resulting from the coming together of different types of identity.

Forms of Citizenship in Apartheid South Africa

The apartheid era stripped black South Africans of their citizenship, legally making them citizens of one of ten tribally based and nominally *self-governing bantustans* (tribal homelands), four of which became nominally independent states.[2] The homelands occupied relatively small and mainly economically unproductive areas of the country. Many black South Africans, however, never resided in their identified *bantustans*. The *bantustan* system disenfranchised black people residing in urban, white South Africa by restricting their voting rights to their own identified black homeland. The government segregated education, medical care, and other public services, and provided black people with services greatly inferior to those of whites, and, to a lesser extent, to those of Indians and coloureds. The education system practised in black schools was designed to prepare blacks to live as a labouring class.

When the National Party came into power in 1948, its primary endeavour was to attain a white supremacist Christian National State and implement racial segregation.[3] The state passed two laws that paved the way for grand apartheid, which was centred on separating peoples on a large scale, through spatial divisions; that is, compelling people to live in separate places defined by racial classification. The Population Registration Act 30 of 1950, which necessitated that all citizens be categorised according to race, with the category recorded in their identity documents. Official teams or boards were established to come to an ultimate conclusion on those people whose racial classification was unclear. Much heartache was caused especially for people of 'mixed descent', breaking up their families as members were allocated to different racial groups. The Group Areas Act 21 of 1950 put an end to non-racial group areas and determined where one lived according to racial classification. Each racial grouping was allotted its own area, which was used in later years as a basis for forced removal.

The government justified its plans on the basis that South Africa was made up of different nations, asserting that government policy was, therefore, not a policy of discrimination on the grounds of race or colour, but a policy of differentiation on the grounds of nationhood, of different nations, granting to each self-determination within the borders of their homelands, hence this policy of separate development.[4] The policy of separate development came into being with the accession to power of Dr. H.F. Verwoerd in 1958. He implemented the homeland structure as a cornerstone of separate development.[5] The Tomlinson Commission of 1954 decided that apartheid was justifiable, but stated that additional land ought to be given to the homelands, favouring the development of border industries. In 1958, the Promotion of Black Self-Government Act was passed, and proponents of apartheid began to argue that once apartheid had been implemented, blacks would no longer be considered citizens of South Africa; they would instead become citizens of the *bantustans*.[6] In terms of this model, blacks became migrants who merely worked in South Africa as the holders of temporary work permits.

The apartheid government divided South Africa into a number of separate states by allocating 13 per cent of the land to the black homelands. Four *bantustans* were granted 'independence', although this was never recognised by any other country. Each homeland controlled its own education and health system.[7] Once a *bantustan* was granted its independence, its designated citizens had their South African citizenship revoked, and replaced with citizenship of their *bantustan*. These people were then issued passports instead of passbooks. Citizens of the supposedly autonomous homelands also had their South African citizenship circumscribed; meaning they were no longer legally considered South African.[8] The South African government attempted to equate their view of black citizens of the *bantustans* with the problems that other countries face through the entry of illegal immigrants.

Women were the most affected by the impact of colonialism and apartheid since they suffered both racial and gender discrimination. Oppression of African women was different from discrimination against men. Women had very few or no legal rights, no access to education and no right to own property. Employment was often hard to find and many African women worked as agricultural or domestic workers earning extremely low wages, if any at all.[9] Children in the *bantustans* suffered from diseases caused by malnutrition or lack of clean water because of the lack of basic services. Consequently, child mortality rates were high. The controlled movement of African workers within the country through the Natives Urban Areas Act of 1923 and the pass laws, separated family members from one another as men usually worked in urban centres, while women without the relevant travel or work documentation were forced to stay in rural *bantustans*.

Globalisation and its Impact on Citizenship in Post-apartheid South Africa

In post-apartheid South Africa, communication between state and citizens is an important aspect of the reciprocal relationship between rights and duties. A breakdown in the reciprocal relationship between the duties and rights of the state and its citizens creates communal or inter-personal violence which is exacerbated by the inability of the state to respond effectively to the voices of the citizens. The freedom to voice concerns is an acknowledgement that in an emerging democracy, the people are supposed to give expression to their political rights. In post-apartheid South Africa, socio-economic status still determines whose voice is heard. Consequently, unequal social relations result in some individuals and groups being more able to claim rights than others.

A common understanding of citizenship is the membership of a community and the benefits derived from this affiliation. The South African 'imbizo' system[10] of participatory democracy is a form of citizenship where the South African president meets local communities to discuss community-related issues. Often, angry and disillusioned communities have voiced their opinions regarding the lack of service delivery and access to basic services. Recent campaigns by South African social movement organisations against the rising cost of basic foods, the lack of basic services or the right to medical treatment for people living with HIV demonstrate the indivisibility of rights beyond the dichotomy between first and second generation rights. They also highlight the role of the state as a guarantor of rights. In other words, rights determine access to resources and authority, and in order to claim rights an individual needs to have access to resources, power and knowledge (Meer and Sever 2004).

Ramphele (2008) notes that all South Africans are newcomers to the citizenship of an inclusive democracy. Although sixteen years of formal democracy have created the ethos of equality, this formal democracy is supported by a neo-liberal macro-economic agenda. Citizenship has not guaranteed a life of dignity because such dignity depends on freedom from economic want (Sweetman 2003:6). Nor has citizenship guaranteed a life free from poverty or inequality. This is because citizenship tends to focus on political and civil rights at the expense of economic rights. According to Goetz (2007), political and civil rights tend to be seen as absolute and non-negotiable first-generation rights whereas economic, social and cultural rights, seen as second-generation rights, have tended to be formulated as relative and culturally specific because resource-strapped states cannot provide concrete entitlements. From this perspective, Goetz (2007) interprets the state's role in protecting rights as a *'negative function'* of its duty to protect liberties or to prevent violence.

In the global context, this has meant that developing countries enter the global economy on unfair terms and furthermore, that economic globalisation prevents states from protecting the livelihoods and human rights of their inhabitants. According to Hassim (2005), the core characteristics of this approach to social policy are predicated on the principle of affordability and sustainability and therefore should be 'financially viable, cost efficient and effective'. Therefore, the cost-recovery approach to social policy negates citizens' social rights and citizens' right to autonomy because high unemployment levels alter the state-society relations in favour of those who can afford the service.

While personal autonomy is bestowed on all citizens, the challenges of high levels of unemployment, high food prices and poor service delivery have given rise to violent inter-personal crime. Notwithstanding the fact that the South African Constitution grants women full and equal citizenship rights, deep-seated patriarchal ideologies impose an experience of citizenship that confines women's choices to a limited range of gender roles. Therefore, the achievement of gender equality based on claiming certain second-generation rights is often contradictory, contested and constantly re-negotiated according to circumstances and context. This viewpoint is supported by Hassim (2005) who argues that Section 27 of the Bill of Rights, namely the right to universal social security, is limited to 'available resources by the state' (Hassim 2005: 632). She notes two examples of this approach, the Reconstruction and Development Programme (1994) and the White Paper on Development Social Welfare (1998) that are explicitly concerned with the redistributive role of the state.

In fact, the policy on social welfare recognises that economic growth in itself will neither enhance the well-being of citizens nor lead to equality. The issue of the exercise of socio-economic rights such as the right to basic services made the Grootboom[11] judgement in 2000 a landmark case where a community threatened with eviction took a City Council to the Constitutional Court. This community (an 'informal settlement' of shacks) won the right to on-site provision of services and facilities. The Constitutional Court ruled in the Grootboom judgement that, regarding positive obligations, the right of access to housing requires the state to formulate and to execute housing programmes that are 'reasonable' (Dugard citing Grootboom, note 9, para 41). This judgement did not only define socio-economic rights for South Africans but also became a reference point in constitutional law throughout the world. This historic victory became the first building block in creating jurisprudence in socio-economic rights that accords members of particular communities the right to enjoy other rights of dignity, freedom and equality (Dugard 2008). However, authorities treated the court ruling with disdain and have been lethargic in implementing it. Irene Grootboom, died prematurely at the age of 39, her dream was not realised because she died in abject squalor and her living conditions contributed to her demise.

Socio-economic rights were upheld in the case of Mazibuko[12] & Others v City of Johannesburg & Others involving the City of Johannesburg's alleged infringement of the applicants' constitutionally-guaranteed right of access to water, through forcibly installing pre-payment meters and limiting their free basic water (FBW) allocation to a one-size-fits-all amount of six kilolitres per property per month. In a judgement remarkable for its sensitive understanding of both the law and the plight of poor people, the judge found the City of Johannesburg to have violated the applicants' water rights, and ordered the City to provide 50 litres of free basic water per person per day (roughly double the current allocation in a household of eight people) and the choice of conventional credit meters as provided to other Johannesburg residents to each of the applicants and to all other similarly placed residents of Phiri Township.[13] Ensuring that poor people have access sufficient water to meet basic needs benefits everyone because it reduces the incidence of cholera, diarrhoea and other water-borne diseases, resulting in a decreased strain on the national health system and the public purse (Dugard 2008).

As a signatory to CEDAW, the South African state endorses the elimination of all forms of discrimination, especially against those considered 'different or alien' based on race, class, ethnicity, gender, sexual preference and nationality.

The SA Constitution and Bill of Rights endorse individual rights to equality and create the space for socially excluded groups to claim citizenship rights which release them from relationships of bonded labour, patron-client relationships or ascribed roles in the family. The emphasis on the social relations of citizenship in respect to rights to safety and protection of vulnerable groups, especially women and children, is because citizenship is a contract between an individual and the society in which he or she lives (Sweetman 2003:7). Meer, cited in Meer and Sever (2004) interprets citizenship as a tiered system – both a status (identity) and a practice (process) of relating to the social world through the exercise of rights/protections and fulfilment of obligations.

The exclusion of migrants and refugees (economic or political) from the benefits of membership of nations and communities are some of the negative effects of the tiered system of citizenship. Often, exclusion has served as the basis for citizenship struggles and an indispensable lever for demanding inclusion and a fair share of public resources and social recognition. Examples of such demands can be found in past anti-colonial struggles in Africa to include the colonised as full and equal citizens, and the more recent citizenship struggles to include the right of poor people to basic resources in different parts of South Africa. The difficulties of access to scarce resources and the high levels of unemployment are some of the main factors that gave rise to the recent xenophobic attacks in South Africa. Thus, exclusion and marginalisation from full citizenship is not only about being an outsider in a geographical sense, but also closely linked to the denial of socio-economic rights.

Sexual Rights Within Intimate Relationships as a Form of Citizenship

The democratic transition in South Africa heralded the introduction of gender-sensitive policies and introduced many gains that have contributed to the development of legislation and policy to address violence against women and the termination of pregnancy (Meer 2005). Other programmes geared towards the emancipation of women include the provision of free health services for pregnant women and children under the age of five years. Since the 1994 democratic elections, social policies promoting gender equality have become a cornerstone of policymaking and are enshrined in the South African Constitution (1996), which asserts that 33.3 per cent of all parliamentary seats must be held by women. This target has been achieved and the 50/50 per cent campaign for equal representation of male and female members of parliament is gaining ground. Similarly, through various affirmative action policies, the government promotes greater representation of women in the private and public sectors. However, the shift from struggle to development means that progress on gender equality made during the transition does not automatically translate into gains for women. For example, South Africa has the highest incidence of gender-based violence in the world as well as one of the highest HIV infection rates, both of which are detrimental to women (Gouws 2005:71).

The struggle for equal sexual citizenship rights has been a history of challenging the terms of privacy around sexuality – the gender-based violence movement wanted to expose abusive patriarchal family relationships and conversely, lesbian and gay rights asserted the right to privacy of persons in consenting same-sex relationships (van Zyl 2005:226). Van Zyl further notes that struggles for sexual rights are deeply personalised, with the body and affective relationships regarded as primary signifiers – both of which are deeply imbued with notions of safety, security and belonging.

Sexual violence is well documented in South African research as a means to control and punish women. Rape is used against South African women as a means of controlling or curbing their agency in choosing foreign men and as a punishment for their waywardness. This divide between the public and private can be extended to the sphere of intimate relationships. According to McFadden (2003), for the majority of black women, the connection between power and pleasure is not often recognised, and remains a largely unembraced and undefended heritage. An understanding of this connection is one of the most precious legacies passed on to women by their foremothers. In often obscure ways, this connection lies at the heart of female freedom and power; and when it is harnessed and deployed, it has the capacity to infuse every woman's personal experience of living and being with a liberating political force (McFadden 2003).

The fear of expressing sexual preference and of considering the possibilities such pleasure suggests for imagining oneself differently, is directly linked to the construction of women's sexuality as 'bad', 'filthy' and 'morally corrupting' (Oakley 1996; Hollibaugh 1996 cited in McFadden 2003). These constructions are aggressively invoked whenever women seek to make independent choices, when they become public and visible as aspiring citizens, when they seek social mobility through their educational skills and material resources, and when they transgress cultural and social boundaries that are defended in the name of tradition.

Therefore, rethinking sexual ethics which focus on democratic and egalitarian social exchanges by sidestepping the good/bad normalisation of sex and judging sex acts by the way in which partners treat one another, the level of mutual consideration, the presence or absence of coercion, and the quantity and quality of the pleasures they provide challenges the fear-induced approach to sexual engagement (Rubin cited in van Zyl 2005:228). Society's systematic suppression of women's sexual inclinations in heterosexual, lesbian and transgender relationships has led to the conflation of sexuality and reproduction within a hetero-normative cultural and social matrix. This suppression is maintained through vigilant cultural surveillance, and has led to the muting of what is defined as feminist sexual memory and instinct, which is negotiated between the two people on the basis of equality in the context of that relationship (McFadden 2003).

The fears that these concerns often raise constitute what McFadden refers to as *socio-sexual anxiety*. Expressing one's sexual pleasure as a heterosexual or lesbian woman is considered outside the norm of private intimate relationships. The intensity of this anxiety is generated by the fact that there is an extremely intimate relationship between sexuality and power; a connection which is manifested in a range of circumstances and experiences. Consequently, by dispelling the notion of universal truths and deconstruction of social relations between men and women, one's identity is made and remade through interaction, relationships and political struggle as well as through discourse and representation. The notion of sexual citizenship is about human security and autonomy and intersects the personal and political realm of the body.

The intersection of power and citizenship as exercised by the powerful over the powerless was shown when a young lesbian woman charged Jacob Zuma with rape. In the Zuma trial the fact that the complainant was declared mentally ill, did not prevent her from distinguishing between rape and consensual sex. This tactic of patriarchy to keep women silent and frozen in fear is a necessary condition for the maintenance of male power over women (Motsei 2007:150). The result is a sexual and political cul-de-sac of violation and repression of self and consequently citizen rights because all too often, women find themselves in a dark and dreadful place, windowless and airless, with seemingly no way out (McFadden 2003). Therefore, citizenship rights can be constructed and deconstructed depending on the relationships of power that transcend the public/private domain.

Protection against gender-based violence is an important aspect of exercising sexual rights. Often these rights are contravened by the misogynistic behaviour of men towards women. According to Salo, a feminist anthropologist based in Cape Town, the incidence of domestic violence has possibly increased because society perceives husbands or male spouses as the breadwinners of the family and responsible for the upkeep of the household (Salo cited in Naidoo, 2008). The high level of substance abuse remains the main cause of domestic violence on the Cape Flats in the Western Cape and this is exacerbated by the high cost of living and unemployment in a context where many couples are already faced with high debt and the inability to keep up with payments (Naidoo 2008). Ultimately, children are also affected and their school grades begin to drop.

The economic burden of increasingly high costs of food and other basic services is one of the many reasons why men are becoming more violent or abusive towards their wives, mainly because they feel that their position in the household is under threat. This irrational behaviour has a negative impact on intimate relationships between men and women. Domestic violence is not exclusive to a specific group but occurs across the board and is also involved or implicated in incidents of psychological or emotional abuse. Furthermore, socio-economic hardships are not the only reasons for interpersonal conflict in intimate relationships. Misogyny is also a dominant theme in certain cultural settings where women bear the brunt of men's violent behaviour. Misogynistic behaviour of family members directed toward a daughter or sister-in-law is commonplace in certain traditions or communities. Moreover, women become scapegoats in times of economic hardship or communal conflict and war.

An equally pertinent example of essentialising citizenship can be seen in the recent xenophobic attacks in South Africa that reveal the gender-blind approach of the authorities towards addressing the violent displacement of non-South Africans. Women's and children's needs were subjugated to the wider community in addressing the humanitarian crisis. Two weeks into the attacks, humanitarian calls were made for women-specific needs such as sanitary pads, toiletries and nappies for babies. The humanitarian crisis demonstrated that it is not only migrant and refugee women who were being exposed to the xenophobic violence. South African women married to foreign nationals were also targeted in the conflict between South African and foreign nationals. According to Fuller (2008), black South African men accused foreign nationals of 'taking our women'. This speaks directly to the pervasive ideology of patriarchy in South Africa, which is so entrenched that women are broadly perceived as possessions that can be 'owned' by different groups of men.

Intimate citizenship brings into stark focus the gendered nature of global citizenship. The globalisation of economies creates porous borders in the Southern African Development Community (SADC) because of the vestiges of the migrant labour system and the onslaught of the international financial crisis on African national economies. Increasing numbers of women are migrating in search of work. In this search, they are the focus of pimps or traffickers preying on vulnerable women and children. It is well known that South Africa is a source, transit and destination country for men, women and children trafficked for forced labour and sexual exploitation (Frescura 2006:142). According to Frescura (2006), an internet search will reveal two things: first, South Africa is an internal source for trafficked persons and secondly, it is a major transit country for people being trafficked into prostitution, forced labour and child labour as well.

Conclusion: Rethinking Citizenship Within a Global Context

In South Africa it is common for people to talk about their rights and how the Constitution enables them to claim rights. However, when the implementation of rights or the effectiveness of claiming a right is explored one becomes increasingly aware of the limits of these rights (Gouws 2005:79). Citizenship is multi-layered and operates on several frontiers, from the local to the global, enabling people to express multiple and overlapping loyalties and identities (Lister 2003:57). In enforcing formal rights, citizenship is legally constructed and the boundaries reworked but the outcome of this challenge is directly linked to the power relations between the parties involved in the social contract. The rethinking of citizenship as personal, intimate, sexual, political as well as social has consequences for the shifts in its meanings and definitions. Intimate citizenship incorporates affective egalitarian relationships that recognise the interdependence of the public and private spheres.

Therefore, the concept of inter-sectionality demonstrates how the social, political and economic spheres become the nexus for citizens, especially black women and children to be included or excluded from the community. Post-apartheid South Africa's discourse of rights also combines individual with collective rights, which stretches the definition of citizenship beyond its borders. Consequently, citizenship is situated or context-dependent because the cultural, political or institutional contexts define priorities and limitations to advance gender equality (Goethe 2007). These shifts in meaning uncover different levels of citizenship, where people continue to be included on the basis of some roles/identities and excluded on the basis of others. The challenge remains to create a set of principles that encapsulates rights and responsibilities that shift the concept of citizenship to transcend the local to the global community.

Notes

1. According to Symington (2004), intersectionality is a methodological springboard for social justice action based on the premise that people espouse multiple, layered identities derived from social relations, history and the operation of structures of power.

2. http://en.wikipedia.org/wiki/Apartheid#Institution_of_apartheid accessed 31 March 2009.

3. The key building blocks to enforcement of racial segregation were (i) the arrangement of the population into African, coloured, Indian and white racial groups; (ii) strict racial segregation in the urban areas; (ii) restricted African urbanisation; (iv) a tightly-controlled and more restricted system of migrant labour; (v) a stronger accent on tribalism and orthodoxy in African administration than in the past; and (vi) a drastic strengthening of security legislation and control.

4. 'Mixed descent' refers to children who have one parent classified as white and the other parent classified as coloured, African or Indian.

5. Verwoerd came to believe in the granting of "independence" to these homelands. Border industries and the Bantu Investment Corporation were established to promote economic development and the provision of employment in the homelands (to draw black people away from white South Africa).

6. http://en.wikipedia.org/wiki/Apartheid#Institution_of_apartheid, accessed 31 March 2009.

7. Not all the homelands chose to become self-governing. Those that did choose autonomy were the Transkei (1976), Bophuthatswana (1977), Venda (1979) and the Ciskei (1981)accessed 31 March 2009.

8. http://en.wikipedia.org/wiki/Apartheid#Institution_of_apartheid, accessed 31 March 2009.

9. Imbizo is a forum for enhancing dialogue and interaction between government and people. It provides an opportunity for government to communicate its Programme of Action and the progress being made. It promotes participation of the public in the programmes to improve their lives. Imbizo also highlights people's concerns, grievances and proposals about government's work. Finding that the City of Johannesburg's current free basic water (FBW) allocation was insufficient to meet the needs of the multi-dwelling households in Phiri Township, the judge emphasised an equitable water management approach. Relying on the evidence of international expert Dr Peter Gleick, who considers 50 litres per person per day to be the minimum amount of water required to sustain a healthy and dignified existence, the judge found that the City could, within its available resources, meet this basic need. (http://www.info. gov.za/issues/imbizo/index.html) accessed 31 March 2009.

10. Irene Grootboom lived in a shack settlement in Wallacedene, in the Cape Town suburb of Kraiifontein in the Western Cape Province.

11. Ma Lindiwe Muzibuko, a woman living in Phiri Township died one year before this landmark judgement. Mazibuko slipped while carrying a bucket of water from the tap to her home; she broke her neck and got paralysed.

12. In finding that Johannesburg's current free basic water allocation was insufficient to meet the needs of the multi-dwelling households in Phiri Township, the judge emphasised an equitable water management approach. Relying on the evidence of international expert Dr. Peter Gleick, who considers 50 litres per person per day to be the minimum amount of water required to sustain a healthy and dignified existence, the judge found that Johannesburg could, within its available resources, meet this basic need.

Bibliography

Cole, C.M. et al., 2007, Africa after Gender? Bloomington: Indiana University Press.

Dugard, J. 2008, 'Power to the People? A Rights-Based Analysis of South Africa's Electricity Services', in a forthcoming book, McDonald, David, ed., *Electrical Capitalism: Recolonising Africa on the Power Grid*, Cape Town: Human Sciences Research Council.

Frescura, L., 2006, 'There is no escape from that miserable life', *Agenda*, No. 70, Durban.

Fuller, R., 2008, 'Double Jeopardy: Women Migrants and Refugees in South Africa', in *Perspectives in Political Analysis and Commentary from Southern Africa*, Cape Town: Heinrich Boell Stiftung, Vol. 3: 08.

Goetz, A., 2007, 'Gender Justice, Citizenship and Entitlements' in Mukhopadhyay, M. and Singh, N., eds., 2008, *Gender Justice, Citizenship and Development*, Canada: IDS.

Gouws, A., ed., 2005, (Un)thinking *Citizenship: Feminist Debates in Contemporary South Africa*, Lansdowne: University of Cape Town Press.

Gouws, A., 2005, 'Shaping Women's Citizenship', in Gouws, A., ed., *(Un)thinking Citizenship: Feminist Debates in Contemporary South Africa*, Lansdowne: University of Cape Town Press, pp. 71-90.

Hassim, S., 2005, *Gender, Welfare and the Developmental State in South Africa*, Geneva: United Nations Research Institute for Social Development.

Hill, Collins. P., 2005, Black Sexual Politics: African Americans, *Gender and the New Racism*, New York: Routledge.

Hooks, Bell, 2000, *Feminist Theory from Margin to Centre*, Boston: South End Press Classics.

Lee, C.K., 1998, *Gender and the South China Miracle: Two Worlds of Factory Women*, Berkeley: University of California Press.

Lister, R., 2003, *Citizenship: Feminist Perspectives*, 2nd Edition, New York: New York University Press.

Lovaas, K.E. and Jenkins, M.M., 2007, *Sexualities and Communication in Everyday Life: A Reader*, Thousand Oaks: Sage Publications.

McFadden, P, 2003, 'Sexual *Pleasure as Feminist Choice*, Feminist Africa, Issue 2. (http://agi.ac.za/feminist-africa-issue-2-2003-changing-cultures).

Meer, S. and Sever, C., 2004, *Gender and Citizenship*, Overview Report, Brighton: IDS.

Meer, S., 2005, 'Freedom for Women: Mainstreaming Gender in the South African Liberation Struggle and Beyond', in Porter, F and Sweetman, C., eds., *Mainstreaming Gender in Development: A Critical Review*, Cowley: Oxfam Publications.

Motsei, M., 2007, *The Kanga and the Kangaroo Court: Reflections on the Rape Trial of Jacob Zuma*, Johannesburg: Jacana Media.

Nyamu-Musembi, C., 2007, 'Addressing Formal and Substantive Citizenship: Gender Justice in Sub-Saharan Africa', in. Mukhopadhyay, M. and Singh, N., eds., *Gender Justice, Citizenship and Development*, Canada: IDS.

Plummer, K., 2003, *Intimate Citizenship: Private Decisions and Public Dialogues*, Seattle: University of Washington Press.

Ramphele, M., 2008, *Laying Ghosts to Rest: Dilemmas of the Transformation in South Africa*, Cape Town: Tafelberg.

Sweetman, C., 2003. 'Editorial', *Gender and Development* Vol. ll, No 3.

Symington, A., 2004, '*Intersectionality*: A Tool for Gender and Economic Justice', *Women's Rights and Economic Change*, No. 9, August.

Van Zyl, M., 2005, '*Heteronormative* Bondage: Sexuality in Citizenship', in Gouws, A., ed., *(Un)thinking Citizenship: Feminist Debates in Contemporary South Africa*, Lansdowne: UCT Press.

Yuval-Davis, N., 1997, 'Women, Citizenship and Difference', *Feminist Review*, No. 57, Autumn, pp. 4-27.

Newspaper

Naidoo, Y., 2008, 'Money woes fuel domestic violence', in *The Cape Argus*, 16 June.

Dugard, J., 2008, 'All South Africans should celebrate the Mazibuko water rights judgment', in *Mail & Guardian*, 30 May.

Websites

Department of Provincial and Local Government (DPLG), 1998, White Paper on Local Government, para 2.3., South African Government Information System. (http://wwwfo.gov.za/issues/imbizo/index.html).

Constitution of the Republic of South Africa, Act 108 of 1996. (http://www.info.gov.za/documents/constitution/index.htm).

Committee on the Elimination of Discrimination against Women (CEDAW). (http://www2.ohchr.org/english/bodies/cedaw/index.htm).

History of apartheid South Africa. (http://en.wikipedia.org/wiki/Apartheid#Institution_of_apartheid). 31 March 2009.

www.ingramcontent.com/pod-product-compliance
Lightning Source LLC
Chambersburg PA
CBHW060024030426
42334CB00019B/2176